D1457423

SPORT IN THE AMERICAN WEST
Jorge Iber, series editor

MORE THAN
JUST PELOTEROS

MORE THAN JUST PELOTEROS

Sport and US Latino Communities

Edited by Jorge Iber

Texas Tech University Press

This book is typeset in Minion Pro. The paper used in this book meets the minimum requirements of ANSI/NISO Z39.48-1992 (R1997). ∞

Designed by Kasey McBeath

Library of Congress Cataloging-in-Publication Data
More than just peloteros : sport and US Latino communities / edited by Jorge Iber.
    p. cm. — (Sport in the American west)
    Summary: ""Examines the history of Latino/a athletes in American sports, including baseball, boxing, football, basketball, and horse racing. Also evaluates the role of sports in Spanish-speaking culture in the US." — Provided by publisher.
    Includes bibliographical references and index.
    ISBN 978-0-89672-907-0 (hardback) — ISBN 978-0-89672-908-7 (paperback) — ISBN 978-0-89672-909-4 (e-book) 1. Hispanic American athletes—History. 2. Hispanic American athletes—Social conditions. I. Iber, Jorge, 1961-
    GV583.M68 2015
    796.08968'073—dc23

                                                        2014032163

14 15 16 17 18 19 20 21 22 / 9 8 7 6 5 4 3 2 1

Texas Tech University Press
Box 41037 | Lubbock, Texas 79409-1037 USA
800.832.4042 | ttup@ttu.edu | www.ttupress.org

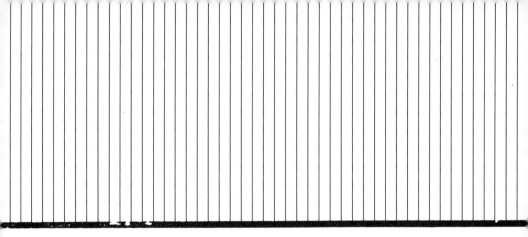

CONTENTS

Contents

Contents

TEN

Major League Soccer Scores an Own Goal in Houston:
How Branding a Team Alienated Hispanic and Latino Fans   256
Ric Jensen and Jason Sosa

EPILOGUE

From "Quarterbacking While Mexican"
to New Horizons in Sports History   281
Jorge Iber

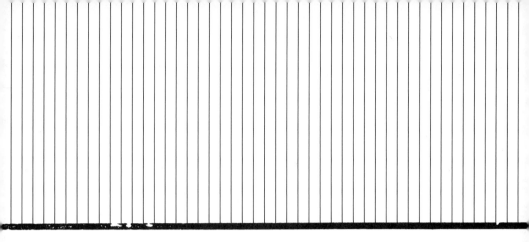

ILLUSTRATIONS

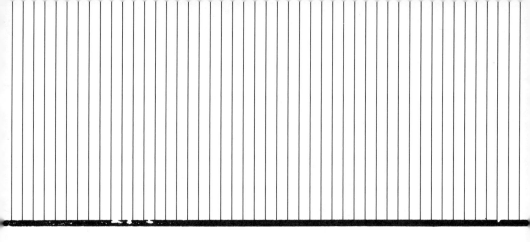

EDITOR'S PREFACE

L ike politics, all history is ultimately local. In regard to sport history, it is, in many ways, a history of community. Locals, no matter where they are, root for their high school, industrial league, and professional teams and invest much of their identity into these squads. Even at the highest levels of play, athletes and coaches always hearken back to their home communities. Notice how even a recent ESPN series visited the hometowns of individuals such as Mike Ditka and Lee Corso to search for the meaning of sports in their—and indeed all our—lives. Until recently, however, notably absent from these anecdotal histories of sport were the experiences of Latinos and Latinas.

I have found it rewarding to share my passion for history with my students through the lens of sports; something that most of my charges care very much about. While many students are unabashed in telling me that "I never liked history," most are willing to give the topic a chance when they discover that one area of focus is sports. Thus, instead of discussing important aspects of the "race, class, and gender" mantra via topics such as Progressivism, business history, and military studies (all important in their own right, most assuredly), a professor can bring students into just as rigorous and meaningful discussions by bringing up topics such as the 1966 Texas Western Miners, the Wayland Baptist University

Flying Queens, and the story of the spread of *beisbol* throughout the Caribbean and Latin America.

This engagement, in a nutshell, is the goal of this collection. Our sincere hope is that our colleagues in other fields (Latino studies, sociology, journalism, and other areas) will benefit from reading and sharing the essays included herein with their students. Sports are an excellent way to entice students into the deeper understanding of American history and daily life. With this grand hope, the collaborators of this project offer it to the academic community as well as to the general public.

As is normally the case with manuscript projects, it has been a long and sometimes difficult road to bring this undertaking to fruition and completion. With great thanks I wish to acknowledge each and every one of the contributors for their fine scholarship and patience as this project slowly made its way through the writing, editing, and rewriting process. All of the men and women involved are to be commended for their scholarship and passion to bring such wonderful stories to print. At Texas Tech University Press, I wish to thank Robert Mandel for having the vision to establish this series and to Judith Keeling for her tireless work in bringing this and the other works in the series to realization. I also wish to thank the two outside reviewers of the manuscript whose comments and suggestions helped make this final version more focused and effective.

The final thanks in this preface are, as usual, the most heartfelt and important of all. To my father, Manuel, who engendered within me love of sport (of baseball, in particular), and who introduced his son to the history of baseball in our native Cuba and to the fantastic athletic ability of the great Roberto Clemente (making me a lifelong Pirates fan). In addition, it was wonderful to learn about *futbol Americano* with Dad during my youth in Little Havana during the early 1970s. While we could never afford to attend a Miami Dolphins game during those years, we lived close enough to the Orange Bowl to feel as if we were there with the great squads of that era. I hope to be able to do as effective a job of passing along the passion and love of sport to my son. This book is also dedicated to the memory of my dear mother, Bertha, who did not live to see me achieve my doctorate, but who instilled in me a love of books and learning that continues to fuel my career and life.

Finally, this book is lovingly dedicated to my wonderful wife, Raquel, and to our son, Matthew. I cannot express sufficient thanks for all of the joys and blessings you have brought to my life. I love you both with all my heart.

MORE THAN JUST PELOTEROS

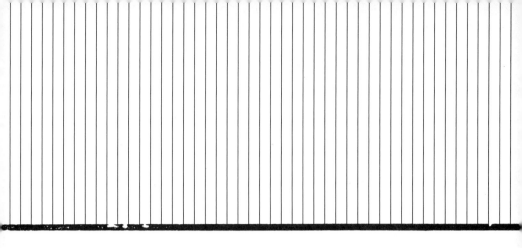

INTRODUCTION

The Perils and Possibilities of "Quarterbacking While Mexican": A Brief Introduction to the Participation of Latino/a Athletes in US Sports History

Jorge Iber
Texas Tech University

I n the annals of collegiate football in the United States, few teams lay claim to a more storied past than the University of Southern California (USC) Trojans. Beginning in football's earliest years in the American West (1888), and through the eras of renowned head coaches such as Howard Jones (1925–1940), John McKay (1960–1975), John Robinson (1976–1982 and 1993–1997) and Pete Carroll (2001–2009), USC has been a dominant gridiron power: winning eleven national championships, boasting seven Heisman Trophy winners, and sending dozens of players to the pinnacle of US professional sport, the National Football League (NFL).[1] In addition to its on-field success, the USC program has often been a catalyst for social change, fielding integrated teams as early as the first decades of the twentieth century, and featuring their first black All-American, Brice Taylor, in 1925.

In addition to breaking down racial barriers on their team, the Trojans also participated in one of the most significant games in the history of the collegiate gridiron against the University of Alabama on September 12,

1970, in the city of Birmingham. In this contest, an integrated Trojan team (which included twenty African Americans) came to the very heart of the recently desegregated Dixie and administered a 42-21 thumping upon one of the last all-white squads in the sport (although Alabama did have at least one African American player on its junior varsity squad by then), the Crimson Tide, coached at the time by the legendary Paul "Bear" Bryant. The principal weapons in USC's offensive arsenal that evening were two African Americans: running backs Clarence Davis and Sam "Bam" Cunningham. After the nationally televised debacle the Crimson Tide, which had harbored national championship aspirations, sputtered to a mediocre record of six wins, five losses, and one tie.

The impact of this crushing defeat made it possible for Bear Bryant to commence a more earnest effort to recruit African American athletes for his program, eventually integrating black men more fully into the heart of the American South's most popular sport. Not surprisingly, when Alabama won the 1979 national championship, its squad was fully integrated. Indeed, during the decade of the 1970s the Crimson Tide featured a host of great African American athletes such as Wilbur Jackson (the first African American on scholarship for the Crimson Tide), Sylvester Croom (recently head coach at Mississippi State University, the first African American head coach in the Southeastern Conference—the SEC. He now serves as the running backs coach for the NFL's Tennessee Titans), Ozzie Newsome, Dwight Stephenson, and Don McNeal—many of whom would have left the region if segregation had continued on the collegiate gridiron.[2]

Given USC's tradition of inclusion, and being located in a city with a substantial Latino[3] population, it is also not surprising to note that Trojan squads have also featured players of this background, including offensive lineman John Aguirre (in the 1940s), linebacker Ron Ayala (during the 1960s), and placekicker Quin Rodriguez (during the late 1980s), among others. Such players contributed to the magnificent legacy of USC, but analysts are nearly unanimous in arguing that the greatest *jugador* (player) ever to don a cardinal and gold jersey was Anthony Munoz, an offensive lineman who played from 1976 until 1979. Munoz competed professionally between 1980 and 1992, became a star for the NFL's Cincinnati

Bengals, was recognized as part of the All-NFL seventy-fifth anniversary team (in 1994), and earned enshrinement to the Hall of Fame in 1998.

For many decades, the Trojans were known among football fans as "Tailback U" and featured great running backs such as Davis, Cunningham, the now disgraced O. J. Simpson, Charles White, Marcus Allen, and many others (particularly during the tenures of McKay and Robinson). Since the arrival of Pete Carroll (who coached USC through the end of the 2009 campaign and who is now the head coach of the NFL's Seattle Seahawks), however, USC's offense has morphed into a modern and highly sophisticated aerial attack. The results have been impressive, with the program garnering two more national championships, an overall record of 76-14 by the start of the 2008 campaign, and three more Heisman winners: quarterbacks Carson Palmer (now playing for the Arizona Cardinals) and Matt Leinart (selected in the first round by the Arizona Cardinals, but cut by the club just prior to the start of the 2010 season, he has since been with the Houston Texans, Oakland Raiders, and most recently was brought in for a tryout with the Buffalo Bills, but did not make the final 2013 roster), and running back Reggie Bush (drafted by the New Orleans Saints, played for the Miami Dolphins, and now with the Detroit Lions). Not surprisingly, and thanks to this revamped offensive philosophy, USC is now referred to as "Quarterback U." Since 2001, then, being the Trojans' starting signal caller has earned that player the benefit (or predicament?) of holding down the "most high-profile spot in college football." In 2007 a fourth-generation Mexican American, Mark Sanchez, began his quest to lay claim to this most visible of all positions in the world of American collegiate football. The opportunity has brought him notoriety, but also controversy.

Sanchez came to USC as a highly touted quarterback from nearby Mission Viejo (Orange County) High School. There he earned numerous accolades playing with the Diablos, winning a state championship and being named to every national, state, and local all-star squad after his senior season in 2004. For most programs such an impressive resume would have catapulted Sanchez to the status of starter after learning the college game during his freshman campaign, but not so with the Trojans. In 2005 Mark Leinart and Reggie Bush led USC to the national championship game against the University of Texas (a contest won by the Longhorns, 41-38). In 2006 John David Booty earned the starting quarterback slot, keeping his team in contention for the national title until an upset loss to its bitter crosstown rival UCLA in the campaign's last weekend.

In 2007, however, Booty missed three contests because of a broken finger, and Sanchez saw his first significant action at the helm of the Trojan offensive juggernaut. He started games against Pacific Coast Conference (the PAC10 then, now the PAC12) opponents the Arizona Wildcats and Oregon Ducks and, most significantly, against USC's greatest nonconference rival, another storied program, the Notre Dame University Fighting Irish. Upon this grand stage an innocent gesture by Sanchez demonstrated the still precarious status of Latino athletes in the perception of some American sport fans.

There are many hallowed football stadiums throughout the United States, but none is held in higher renown and awe than Notre Dame Stadium in South Bend, Indiana. Mark Sanchez and his USC teammates strode into this celebrated coliseum on October 20, 2007, for the Trojans' annual battle against the well-known midwestern Catholic institution. This particular contest was not as highly anticipated as in previous seasons because Notre Dame was having its worst season in decades and prognosticators foresaw an utter rout. They were not disappointed as the final score, 38-0 in favor of USC, was quite atypical in the historic intersectional rivalry. Sanchez performed effectively, dissecting the Irish defense by completing twenty-one of thirty-eight passes for 235 yards, four touchdowns, and no interceptions. Normally, such a convincing triumph would have been cause for celebration among the Trojan faithful, but not all were in a joyous mood regarding their quarterback's stellar performance. Apparently, Sanchez had done something terribly wrong during this game, and many fans criticized him severely. His faux pas was that he had been bold enough to demonstrate pride in his ethnic background shortly after the American body politic had gone through a tumultuous summer debating the pros and cons of immigration by millions of undocumented Mexicans and other Latinos (primarily from Central America).

Sanchez's "crime" was in asking the team dentist to produce a mouthpiece featuring the tri-colors of the Mexican flag: red, white, and green

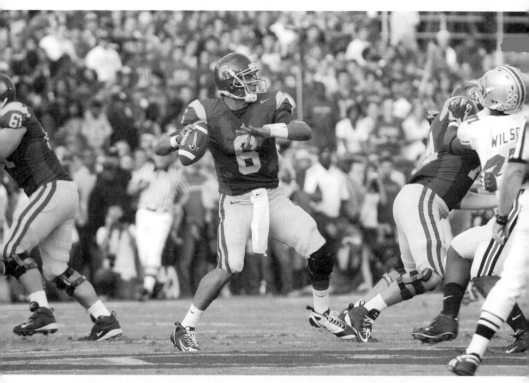

Mark Sanchez in action for the USC Trojans in a contest against the Ohio State
Buckeyes, October 20, 2007. Courtesy of USC Sports Information.

and featuring an eagle and snake (that nation's symbols). While many
teammates similarly personalized this equipment, the fact that an individual of Mexican descent had openly demonstrated pride in his family's
history helped spark a controversy. Instead of commenting on Sanchez's
on-field accomplishments, one fan grumbled that the young man needed
to discard the specialty mouthpiece because many "will think that he is a
Mexican citizen, and it is an insult to this country, where he was born and
raised. Mexico is not giving Sanchez the opportunity that he is getting
right now, so why is he showing his love for Mexico?"[4] Nor was this the
only commentary along these lines. According to the USC football office,
the team "received hate mail, phone calls and emails aimed at Sanchez"
after the Notre Dame contest.[5] One writer for a local alternative newspaper argued that the blowback was the equivalent of "quarterbacking

while Mexican," meaning that for some in the majority population, Sanchez had taken over an important slot on the football field that Latinos had no business occupying.[6]

The majority of opinion regarding the incident, however, was positive; in Los Angeles and throughout the rest of the United States and in the time since this contest, many Spanish-surnamed individuals have expressed pride in Sanchez's accomplishments. Since becoming the starting quarterback (at the beginning of the 2008 campaign), for example, Sanchez was, time and again, the recipient of accolades and often sees "men in Mexican wrestling masks and serapes, flanked by other fans carrying signs . . . [of] 'Viva Sanchez!'"[7] The importance of a Latino quarterback at USC was lucidly articulated by *ESPN the Magazine* reporter Jorge Arrangue, Jr., in a November 2008 story:

> It is at this moment that Sanchez realizes that he is playing not just for himself and his team. Whether he likes it or not, he's playing for people whose names sound like his; for those from south of the border who work thankless jobs for little pay; for those who are reminded daily that they live in a country that does not know what to do with them. These are the fans who once cheered for Valenzuela [a pitcher for the Los Angeles Dodgers in the early 1980s] and Plunkett [a quarterback at Stanford University in the late 1960s and the first Latino to win the Heisman Trophy] and now cheer for Garciaparra [formerly the second baseman for the Dodgers and now a commentator for ESPN] and De La Hoya [Mexican American boxer]. They are his fans, too. On this day, Sanchez has arrived in Los Angeles.[8]

The story of this young man and the significance of his playing quarterback for one of the most powerful collegiate football programs are still to be fully documented and analyzed by academicians, but from an overview of the articles written about him in the popular literature and sports magazines, Sanchez clearly comprehends well the importance of his role to the broader Latino population. Additionally, he also recognizes that he stands upon the shoulders of many Spanish-surnamed men (including his father and brothers, who also played collegiate football) and women who helped break down athletic, social, and racial barriers in previous eras. Individuals such as these, who participated in local and school playgrounds and professional courts and fields and broke down stereotypes, thus helped to open doors of opportunity not only for Mark Sanchez but for players such as Jeff Garcia (quarterback for several NFL teams, including the Buccaneers, 49ers, Raiders, and Eagles, who recently led the offense for the Omaha Nighthawks of the minor-league UFL), Tony Romo (quarterback of the Dallas Cowboys), and many others in the late twentieth and early years of the twenty-first century.

Although the Latino population of the United States has grown exponentially since the 1960s, the scholarly analysis of their role in the history of American sport did not generate much interest until the 1990s. One of the few academicians writing about this topic before then was Mary Lou LeCompte, who published two articles in the *Journal of Sport History* in the mid-1980s.[9] In "The Hispanic Influence on the History of Rodeo, 1823–1922," and (coauthored with William H. Beezley) "Any Sunday in April: The Rise of Sport in San Antonio and the Hispanic Borderlands," LeCompte argued that the Spanish-speaking people of the United States were

> often not afforded much credit for contributions to the development and story of sport in this country (by contemporaries or historians). Particularly, she notes, there has been a historical tendency to either ignore (for example, contributions to the rise of rodeo) or to try to suppress sporting or leisure activities (such as bullfights, fiestas and fandangos) that were significant and unique aspects of this people's cultural landscape.[10]

Some of most important contributions to this area are the works of Samuel O. Regalado. Specifically, his notable 1998 book, *Viva Baseball! Latin Major Leaguers and Their Special Hunger*, increased awareness of the subject matter and demonstrated the potential value of the subfield to both Latino and US sport historians. Throughout his career, Regalado has been at the forefront of expanding efforts to document this story, generating essays on topics such as the social significance of barrio-based baseball leagues, the importance of Spanish-language radio and coverage of sport, and analyzing how the majority population has reacted (often negatively and derisively) to Latino athletes such as the late Pittsburgh Pirate Hall of Famer Roberto Clemente.[11] Regalado's pathbreaking undertakings have inspired a few individuals to follow in his intellectual footsteps. Among these are Adrian Burgos, Richard Santillan, Jose Alamillo, Gregory Rodriguez, Juan Javier Pescador, and Jorge Iber, who have commenced an examination of the nuances of Latino sport history in various locations throughout the United States. One recent key development has been the publication of an edited collection titled *Mexican Americans and Sports: A Reader on Athletics and* Barrio *Life*, which features articles dealing with the role of sports such as baseball, football, soccer, softball, and track and field in *comunidades* (communities) throughout the United States during the twentieth century.[12]

With this particular collection of essays we attempt to build upon this trend and provide readers with an introduction to a burgeoning theme within American sports history. To this end, we offer the following articles, arranged in rough chronological order and covering eras from the early 1700s through the present. The goal is to present a cursory survey and analysis of the role of athletic activities in the lives of Spanish-surnamed people in locales throughout what is now the United States. While the state of Texas is the locus for five of the articles (with one piece spotlighting physical activities in colonial San Antonio, two others concentrating on high school football in the southern region of the Lone Star State known as the Rio Grande Valley, one dealing with masculinity and sport in El Paso, and the final piece dealing with Major League Soccer in Houston), we also offer broader coverage detailing the significance of sport (particularly, competing for the state high school basketball championship) to children of Mexican American miners living in Miami, Arizona, in the post–World War II years, the importance of athletic endeavor to identity maintenance and community pride for Latinos during the years of the Great Depression in Chicago, and a discussion of how one Mexican American challenged the perceptions of privileged whites ensconced in exclusive Southern California tennis clubs during the 1940s and 1950s.

In addition to the items noted above (all of which appeared as a special issue of the *International Journal for the History of Sport* in June 2009 with the exception of the El Paso and Houston essays), this anthology includes four new articles. While, geographically speaking, the subject matter of the first new offering falls outside of the explicit parameters set by the Sport in the American West Series (with the subject matter focused upon New York City), we believed it was critical to add this work because of the importance (and lack of extensive existing research) of the topic addressed. The article centers on the career of Cuban pugilist Eligio Sardinas (more famously known as "Kid Chocolate") and further complicates the story of Latino athletes through a dissection and discussion of the fighter's racial identity. Particularly, the piece sheds light upon efforts to "claim" "Kid Chocolate" by both the Spanish-language and African American press (and populations) of New York City during the 1920s and 1930s. The second addition highlights the significance of sport to the establishment and maintenance of a sense of community, belonging, and virile masculinity among young Mexican American men in the border town of El Paso, Texas, in the years just prior to and after World War II. Next, we feature a piece on the bungled efforts by the ownership group in Houston to rename their newly purchased MLS franchise (formerly the San Jose Earthquakes) with a moniker that proved a bit insensitive toward the feelings of many of the Latino fans they hoped to attract. Finally, the last new item added to this collection discusses with how Minor League Baseball players deal with the growing diversity (including, of course, Latino ballplayers) in the clubhouses of the early twenty-first century. How are players interacting with teammates, and how are players presenting a positive and diversified face to communities throughout the nation?

In summary, our goal for these articles is to

> demonstrate how people of Mexican [and other Latino] descent have used sport in the United States to build community and challenge the majority population's notion of Mexican American intellectual, athletic and cultural weakness; they also wanted to reconstruct a neglected part of . . . history in order to demonstrate the potential for this line of study.[13]

Obviously, given space limitations, the breadth of coverage provided in this collection is by no means exhaustive of this burgeoning area of study. For example, scholars of Puerto Rican studies have not provided much treatment of the impact of sports on their communities spread mostly throughout the northeastern states. A case in point is the excellent study *From Colonia to Community: The History of Puerto Ricans in New York City* by Virginia Sanchez Korrol.[14] While the author makes brief mention of groups dedicated to athletics in neighborhoods (such as the Puerto Rican Athletic Club), she does not detail any of their activities or membership. A superior illustration of the possibilities for this subject matter among Puerto Ricans is presented in a dissertation by Norma Carr that provides a fair amount of discussion regarding the creation and social significance of baseball leagues among the *boricuas* (or *borikis*) of Hawaii.[15]

Another lacuna can be seen through the works of Florida-based authors, such as Gary Mormino and Wes Singletary, who have effectively chronicled aspects of the twentieth-century role of sport in the lives of Cuban/Spanish Americans living in the Ybor City section of Tampa.[16] However, almost nothing in the historical literature regards the role of sport among a larger community, the Cuban Americans living in Miami since the Castro Revolution of 1959.[17] These are but two geographical locations that deserve further study and demonstrate the potential for research in numerous (traditional locations such as the American West and elsewhere) areas of Latino concentration.

A final and highly significant gap is the exclusion in sports history materials of the athletic interests of Spanish-surnamed women. With the exception of authors like Joan L. Duda,[18] Katherine Jaimeson,[19] and the late Julie Laible,[20] little progress has been made in the academic study of individual Latina athletes, or the role of such pursuits in the daily lives of the *mujeres* (women) in such communities over time.

In summary, while the study of the role of sport in the lives of other ethnic and racial groups in the United States, such as African Americans and Jews, is by now well developed, research regarding the history of participation in athletic competition among this nation's largest minority population is still in its infancy. A few important and tentative strides have taken place in the past decade or so, but the amount of material yet to be covered is vast. This collection is but one more stride toward bringing this subject to the attention of the academic community.

Notes

1. Nick Schwartz and Tim McGarry, "The NFL Is the Most Popular Sport in America for the 30th Year Running," *USA Today*, January 26, 2014.

2. Steve Travers, *One Night, Two Teams: Alabama vs. USC and the Game That Changed a Nation* (Lanham, MD: Taylor Trade Publishing, 2007).

3. See Linda Martin Alcoff, "Latino vs. Hispanic: The Politics of Ethnic Names," *Philosophy and Social Criticism* 31, no. 4 (2005): 395–407, for a discussion of the differences and meaning of these collective terms for the Spanish-surnamed population of the United States. In this work, the terms "Latino" and "Hispanic" are used interchangeably.

4. David Davis, "Why Do People Have a Problem with OC-Raised USC Quarterback Mark Sanchez Being Proud of His Mexican Heritage?" *OC Weekly*, August 21, 2008, 1.

5. Jorge Arrangue, Jr., "Viva Sanchez!" July 30, 2008, *ESPN the Magazine*, http://www.sports.espn.go.com/espnmag/story?id=3511275.

6. Davis, "Why Do People Have a Problem," 1.

7. Arrangue, "Viva Sanchez!"

8. Ibid.

9. Mary Lou LeCompte, "The Hispanic Influence on the History of Rodeo, 1823–1922," *Journal of Sport History* 12, no. 1 (1985): 21–38, and Mary Lou LeCompte and William Beezely, "Any Sunday in April: The Rise of Sport in San Antonio and the Hispanic Borderlands," *Journal of Sport History* 13, no. 2 (1986): 128–46.

10. Jorge Iber, "Just How Does One Say 'Woo Pig Sooie' in Spanish?" unpublished article.

11. Samuel O. Regalado, *Viva Baseball!: Latin Major Leaguers and Their Special Hunger* (Urbana: University of Illinois Press, 1998).

12. Jorge Iber and Samuel O. Regalado, *Mexican Americans and Sport: A Reader on Athletics and Barrio Life* (College Station: Texas A&M University Press, 2007).

13. Ibid., 15.

14. Virginia Sanchez Korrol, *From Colonia to Community: The History of Puerto Ricans in New York City* (Berkeley: University of California Press, 1994).

15. Norma Carr, "The Puerto Ricans of Hawaii: 1900–1958" (PhD diss., University of Hawaii, 1989). The term *boriqua* is used for self-reference by

Puerto Ricans both on the island and on the US mainland. The term *borinki* is used for self-reference by Puerto Ricans who live in Hawaii.

16. Gary R. Mormino and George E. Pozzetta, *The Immigrant World of Ybor City: Italians and the Latin Neighbors in Tampa, 1885–1985* (Urbana: University of Illinois Press, 1987), and Wes Singletary, *Al Lopez: The Life of Baseball's El Senor* (Jefferson, NC: McFarlan, 1999).

17. Maria Cristina Garcia, *Havana USA: Cuban Exiles and Cuban Americans in South Florida, 1959–1994* (Berkeley: University of California Press, 1996).

18. Joan L. Duda, "Goals and Achievement Orientations of Anglo and Mexican American Adolescents in Sport and in the Classroom," paper presented at the tenth World Congress of the International Sociological Society, 1982.

19. Katherine M. Jaimeson, "Reading Nancy Lopez: Decoding Representations of Race, Class, and Sexuality," *Sociology of Sport Journal* 15, no. 4 (1998): 343–59.

20. Julie Laible, "The Educating of *Muchachas de La Frontera*: Educational Practices that Promote Success of Mexican American Females in Texas/Mexico Border Schools" (PhD diss., University of Texas at Austin, 1995).

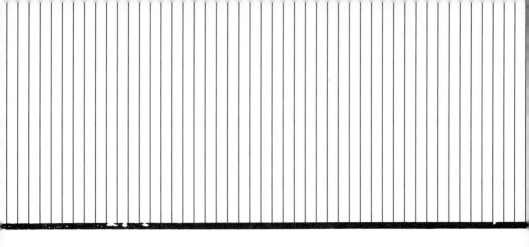

CHAPTER 1

"Buena gana tenía de ir a jugar": The Recreational World
of Early San Antonio, Texas, 1718–1845[1]

Jesús F. de la Teja
Texas State University–San Marcos

San Antonio de Béxar, today's San Antonio, Texas, came into existence in spring 1718 as a way station between New Spain's frontier settlement line hundreds of miles to the south on the Rio Grande and the border with French Louisiana hundreds of miles to the northeast.[2] As the largest and most robust of the settlements occupying the northeastern end of the viceroyalty of New Spain (colonial Mexico), the city's history illustrates many of the characteristics common to Spanish settlements throughout the region. Isolated and lightly populated, San Antonio had few amenities to offer either its own residents or visitors. Nevertheless, Bexareños, as scholars commonly refer to the people of the area, managed to find ways of amusing and entertaining themselves.

Although the record is sparse, enough documentation survives to give some idea of how the people of San Antonio celebrated life even under the most difficult of circumstances, from the first arrival of Mexican frontiersmen in the early eighteenth century until the arrival of Anglo American and European immigrants over a century later. Sports, as we have come to understand the term in the course of the twentieth century—regularly practiced and organized competitions of physical skill and endurance, including both amateur and professional practitioners—were unknown in eighteenth- and early nineteenth-century Texas. Nevertheless, Bexareños did participate in recreational activities calling for physical prowess, some of which, as the reader will see, have contemporary analogues in the sports world—horse racing, bocce, rodeo. Other activities, also very much familiar to us today, such as dancing and gambling, played important roles in filling the leisure time of all classes of people. Bexareños, then, were not just reduced to fighting Indians, surviving natural disasters, and eking out a hand-to-mouth existence on a remote frontier.

To understand what was possible by way of recreation and leisure to Spanish colonial frontiersmen (and not just in Texas but throughout much of the Spanish world), one should understand the role that Bexareños filled within that empire. At the turn of the eighteenth century, Spain, France, and England had become involved in a series of dynastic/colonial wars that led each nation to seek strategic advantage in the interior of North America. Spain, fearful for its silver-producing colony of New Spain, met French penetration into the Gulf of Mexico region by exploring and eventually settling Texas as a buffer to encroachments of its valuable Mexican possessions. In the process, the native peoples of the region became the objects of attention of Spanish missionaries and French traders. In establishing its forward line of defense in the Texas-Louisiana border area, Spaniards had to overcome a five-hundred-mile-wide gap in settlement. Military officials chose the vicinity of present-day San Antonio as the most suitable location for an entrepot between the Spanish outpost of San Juan Bautista del Río Grande (present-day Guerrero, in the Mexican state of Coahuila) and the Spanish Texas capital at Los Adaes (present-day Robeline, Louisiana).

San Antonio started as a mission-presidio complex—that is, a collaborative project between religious and military agents of the Spanish crown. Aside from the regional Indian groups gathered into Mission San Antonio de Valero (the facility better known as the Alamo), the first settlers were a motley collection of mixed-blooded frontier men and women. Within two years of its founding the Franciscans had established a second mission, and a decade later three more dotted the banks of the San Antonio River as it flowed in a southeasterly direction toward the Gulf of Mexico. Also, in 1731 a group of Canary Islander families, totaling fifty-six individuals, received a royal charter to found a town and acquire land in the area. In the century that followed, the descendants of these original Mexican, Canary Islander, and Indian inhabitants were joined by other subjects of His Catholic Majesty, and later by Mexican citizens, Anglo-American frontiersmen, and European immigrants. From an original population of about one hundred, San Antonio grew into a city of about four thousand souls by the time Texas joined the United States in 1845.

From its founding and through the changes in sovereignty until Texas annexation, San Antonio was a military town (in fact, it still is). The presidio, or garrison, was the single largest employer. The vast majority of recruits were locals or men from the two other Texas settlements of La Bahía (today Goliad) and Los Adaes/Nacogdoches, and the neighboring provinces of Nuevo León and Coahuila. The size of the garrison fluctuated, but by the late decades of the eighteenth century it included well over one hundred men. Hundreds more troops came to San Antonio in the early years of the nineteenth century as the Louisiana Purchase gave Spain a dangerous new neighbor, the land-hungry Americans, on Texas's eastern border. At this time the settlement's oldest mission, San Antonio de Valero, found a new role as the headquarters for a cavalry company transferred from San Carlos del Alamo de Parras, a name often shortened to Alamo.

Just about everyone in San Antonio was connected to the presidio in some way. The missionaries relied on soldiers to provide guard and escort duty for them as they went about their tasks of collecting, converting, and "civilizing" the Indians. The missionaries, as well as area civilian farmers and ranchers, also looked to the presidio as a market for some of the surplus agricultural products that the mission Indians grew. Craftsmen and merchants relied on the presidio for work as tailors, cobblers, and carpenters and as a market for goods imported from the interior of Mexico or smuggled in from Louisiana. And, of course, many families were composed of soldiers' kinfolk.

To make the settlement work, Bexareños relied on the river that coursed through or by each community and on the fertile lands the river watered. The site had originally been chosen for its abundant and accessible water supply, its fertile soil, and its plentiful timber resources. In the course of the eighteenth century an intricate water-delivery system of *acequias* (ditches), dams, and aqueducts provided drinking water and irrigation for the agricultural fields of townspeople and mission Indians, and for the orchards and gardens of the town's residents. Farther away from the San Antonio River, other area streams allowed for the watering of the large herds of cattle that made the region the birthplace of the Texas cattle industry.

The agricultural infrastructure that Bexareños put in place supplied the population of the San Antonio River valley to meet its subsistence needs and produced a small surplus for sale in neighboring provinces. By the 1770s, a full century before the great cattle drives of the post–Civil War era (1865–1890), Texas cattlemen drove large herds south into the interior of Mexico and eastward to Louisiana. When crops were abundant enough, mule trains delivered Texas corn and other crop products, sometimes even pecans, to markets in Mexico. This traffic took place over *caminos* (byways) that were little more than deer tracks and Indian trails.

San Antonio was not a wealthy community. Surrounded by vast expanses of Indian-controlled lands, suffering from inadequate communications with other parts of New Spain, and lacking in precious metals or other resources capable of attracting a large population, the settlement remained a simple frontier outpost. The most imposing structures in the area were the missions and the town's church. By the 1770s all five missions were enclosed by stone stockades that also served as the outer walls to Indian apartments, workshops, offices, and storage rooms. The chapels, two of which are handsome structures even in the early twenty-first century, were the product of Indian laborers working under the supervision of stonemasons and other artisans imported from the interior of New Spain. In the town itself, a few stone houses belonging to the most affluent Bexareños neighbored the two plazas, one of which was dominated by the parish church of San Fernando and the other by the buildings that made up the presidio. Most dwellings in the settlement were made of adobe or were *jacales*, a form of thatch-roofed hut of upright poles and mud.

Under such circumstances, opportunities for education or substantial social mobility were limited. Although there is patchy evidence for the presence of teachers throughout the eighteenth and early nineteenth centuries, there is little reason to think that most boys—girls were not thought of as needing formal education—received little more than the basics. A handful did make it out, however, to study for the priesthood or to gain practical experience in the bigger towns and cities of the interior. The presence of books in town is known from a few wills and legal cases for which inventories were made of personal possessions. Nothing suggests, however, that there was much sense of "refined" culture until after Mexican independence, although along with other activities commemorating public holidays, performances of one sort or another and meant to serve the cause of religious edification or respectable entertainment did take place. In the 1820s a group of leading men made an effort to establish a cultural association to stage plays, but the success of that endeavor is unknown. The first documentation of regular "professional" entertainment dates to the Republic of Texas period (1836–1845), when the presence of comedy troupes and mountebanks is mentioned in travelers' journals.[3]

Similarly, there is no evidence for any kind of organized sporting activity in early Texas. That is not to say that organized sports were lacking in New Spain generally, however. By the eighteenth century, Mexico City boasted a number of *pelota* courts, the precursor to modern jai-alai. Immigrants from northern Spain, particularly the Basque country, were very fond of the sport and the merchants among them who could afford it sponsored professional *pelota* players, on whoe performances—as in jai-alai—there was always considerable wagering. Likewise, Mexico City and the other major urban centers of the viceroyalty each had bull rings where young men tested their horsemanship and other athletic skills for the pleasure of large audiences, if not always to the liking of "enlightened" churchmen and nobles. The native Mesoamericans had their own games, particularly variations on ancient ball games that often served religious purposes as well as entertainment. However, nothing in the historical record indicates that any of these competitive activities made it to the northern frontier regions.[4]

To be sure, there were ball games and bullfights in San Antonio, but they played different roles than they did in the metropolises of the interior. Bullfights were held in conjunction with the annual town feasts surrounding the Christmas season, and on other very special occasions, from the mid-eighteenth century until well after Mexican independence in 1821. From early December until the Feast of the Epiphany (January 6), Bexareños held religious and secular feasts that included enclosing one of the town plazas as a makeshift bullring and setting up booths and stalls on the periphery for games and food sales. Although we lack clear descriptions of the bullfights and bullfighters, we can assume that they were much-anticipated opportunities for some of the locals to show off their equestrian skills and personal courage in the manner of the professional events held in Mexico City. There, bulls were fought both from horseback and on foot, in a style that was the direct antecedent to today's elaborate ritual. Aside from providing a special form of entertainment, the bullfights also reaffirmed the population's status as members of the Spanish cultural and religious world—despite official displeasure, both secular and religious—a not unimportant function on a remote and often hostile Indian frontier.[5]

Boys played ball games that could turn quite as dangerous as any encounter with a bull. In summer 1769 Ignacio Flores and Francisco Salinas were playing "a little game of *bolas*" in "the field the children and adolescents play in"[6] when an argument broke out between the two fifteen-year-olds. Flores struck Salinas with the ball, killing him instantly. Although the boys were related and the families argued that the incident was an accident owing to the boys' hotheadedness, the governor sentenced Flores to a year's exile, with the admonition that should he run away the crime would be raised to the level of a capital offense. Given the damage that Flores did, and the description of the accident scene, the game the boys were involved in was probably some variant of bocce, a game widespread throughout Spain's American empire by the mid-eighteenth century. Although subject to wagering, *bolas* appears to have been recognized as a legitimate form of recreation even among adults, and by 1782 the governor had granted a concession for that game and also for bowling to local merchant Juan Manuel Ruiz.[7]

Unfortunately, no identification or descriptions of children's games such as marbles or hide-and-seek have surfaced in the available records. Neither are attitudes toward such games clear from archival documents. When José Francisco de la Mata petitioned for a contract to serve as the town's schoolteacher, he prefaced his request by stating that he had observed the town's children "running around, wasting their time on idle games."[8] Of course he meant boys, since girls were not permitted access to public education. A later set of school regulations makes clear that when schools did operate there was little leisure time and that sports was not part of the curriculum.[9] Given the amount of physical exertion that frontier life demanded of average males, including work on horseback and agricultural chores, the omission of physical education from the school day is not at all surprising.

There is some evidence, however, that horseback riding was not just a utilitarian skill but an accepted recreational activity. In 1781 Governor Domingo Cabello banned the custom of men, women, and youths racing horseback "through the streets of the presidio and villa on the feast days of S. Juan, S. Pedro, Santiago, and Sta. Ana causing much harm." The activity must certainly have been disruptive, for the penalty for youths convicted of this offense was forfeiture of the horse and twenty-five lashes and for adults forfeiture of the animal and one month's labor on reconstruction of the town hall.[10] Cabello's ban proved as ineffective as other efforts to curtail such uses of town streets, for the equestrian custom remained popular in San Antonio well into the nineteenth century. Governor Manuel Salcedo opted for a more measured response to this continued unsavory practice, especially as it was one way in which the sexes might interact in an inappropriate manner. In 1809 and 1810 he issued orders to prevent men and women from riding together on the same horse, galloping through the streets, and most ominously, riding after curfew.[11] As late as 1849 a German visitor to San Antonio noted that on St. Peter's Day, "Young people of both sexes dashed through the streets on horseback and yelled. Mud splashed up to their ears, and the muddier they became the better."[12]

Horseback riding and sporting contests remained popular well into the Anglo-American era. In fact, from that period we have our first depictions of what such events entailed. French immigrant artist Theodore Gentilz painted a "watermelon race" through town streets in the 1840s. The object of the contest was to cross the finish line with an intact watermelon as competing riders tried to take it away by pursuing and jostling the one carrying the fruit. Another similar competition involved snatching a live

21

The Paris-born painter Théodore Gentilz settled in San Antonio in 1849 and devoted his career to capturing Tejano and Indian cultural scenes. His *Corrida de la Sandía* (Watermelon race), records a type of equestrian event going back over a century that combined recreation and the everyday skills of Tejano ranching practices. Courtesy of the Daughters of the Republic of Texas Library, San Antonio.

rooster from the ground or a pole and trying to make it across the finish line as competitors reached for the hapless fowl. John Duvall, a veteran of the Texas War of Independence, recorded a riding match between Tejanos, rangers,[13] and Comanches at about the same time the whole town turned out to witness it.[14]

Equestrian displays were not the only physical exertions through which Bexareños enjoyed their leisure time. Although names and descriptions are lacking for San Antonio itself, mention of games among the Mexican population of the area are available in various records. German immigrant Eduard Ludecus described two games in one of his 1834 letters to his relatives from the Rio Grande country to the southwest of San Antonio. The first consisted of two opponents being bound by the wrists and placed in a crouching position with a stick locking their elbows and knees together.

Episodes of Tejano cultural life that Gentilz painted beginning in the 1840s included street scenes and people at work and at play. Among his most recognized canvases is *Fandango*, named for a popular dance dating back to the Spanish colonial period that became synonymous with balls and parties. Courtesy of the Daughters of the Republic of Texas Library, San Antonio.

Facing each other toe-to-toe, each opponent was given another stick that was to be used in an attempt to knock each other over. The winner of the game, crouching over his helpless opponent, would then poke him in the groin. "The constrained position of the two players produces an extremely comical spectacle, and the laughter does not stop until one of the spectators takes pity on the loser and helps him up again." In the second game a group of people sat in a circle with their feet together, their legs covered by a blanket. Into the center of the circle stepped another person, who was pushed over and twirled around the circle by the prone players. The person who pushed over the standing person would then take his place in the center.[15] Unfortunately, similar descriptions of other physical games have yet to come to light.

In contrast, officials' efforts to regulate one form of recreational exercise—dancing—provide an abundance of documentation on a ubiq-uitous activity. Dancing was considered morally suspect, particularly as practiced among the popular classes. Men and women in too close prox-imity, authorities believed, led to no good.[16] Friar Ilariano da Bergamo, an Italian Capuchin who traveled in New Spain collecting alms for his order's missions in Tibet, commented on this popular entertainment that "ordinarily their songs are quite shameless, but still worse are their dances, which include rather indecent gestures." After noting that there existed three social levels of *fiestas*, he noted that "the third . . . is the so-called *fandango*, which is the most universal one among the common people and where, for the most part, they perform the dances they call the *chuchum-bé*, *bamba*, and *guesito*, which are all quite indecent."[17] The opening stanza of *Chuchumbé* makes clear what Friar Ilariano and Father Fuentes found so objectionable in what went on at fandangos:

> *En la esquina está parado*
> *un fraile de la Merced,*
> *con los ábitos alzados*
> *enceñando el chuchumbé*[18]

> Standing at the corner
> Is a friar of the Merced
> With his habit lifted up
> Showing off his chuchumbé

In San Antonio about a decade later, songs being sung at dances included *fandangos*, *la chinita*, and *seguidillas*, which the singer, who was in trouble with Father Fuentes for singing what the priest considered lascivious lyr-ics, maintained were "harmless *juguetes*," that is, happy and festive tunes.[19]

To men such as Governor Salcedo, who had been educated in the best tradition of the Catholic Enlightenment and whose entire family was composed of government officials, good governance entailed the moral uplifting of the population. His ordinance for good government included the following view of nocturnal entertainments:

> Having come to my attention the disorders committed in the streets
> at night by men and women who in scandalous terms wander the
> streets, as well as in the fandangos which are held with too much fre-

quency, and under which pretense people stay out and commit themselves to all sort of vice . . .

[However,] because I do not seek to take away diversions, but rather to promote wholesome ones, I decree the following:

There will be no fandangos or dances held except in the homes of
trusted owners who will not permit the sale of liquors, *aguardiente*, or
wine, will permit no disorders, and will keep the room well lit.

The dance should not go beyond midnight, unless there is a particular license for it, and there should be no one standing outside the
dance or around the building, since the judges or patrols will arrest
such individuals no matter their class.[20]

Salcedo was sensible to the fact that such fandangos were among the
few recreational activities available to the population in general, and his
action merely restated long-standing governmental practice. As early as
1760 the town council attempted to regulate fandangos and the practice
of nighttime strolls, by prohibiting both activities after 8 p.m., penaliz-
ing lawbreakers with an eight-peso fine and two days in jail. The measure seems to have done little to curtail such activities, however, for in the
following year *Alcalde*[21] Alberto López issued an ordinance prohibiting
fandangos and music after curfew and imposing stiff penalties for both
the hosts and the attendees. At a time when the daily wage of a common
laborer was a quarter peso, fines were set at a steep twelve pesos for the
host and six pesos for those in attendance. The restriction, with a curfew
set at 9 p.m., was repeated in 1776 by *Alcalde* José Salvador Díaz.[22] In 1783
the town council at something of wits' end complained to the governor
because much of the crowd attending or congregating outside fandangos
was composed of "unbridled youths and marked women." They asked that
fandangos should be restricted to certain hours and confined to the inside
of houses, "making the homeowners responsible for the offenses to God
committed through the bad things that are sung, the fights, and disorders
that occur."[23]

Fandangos remained popular and rather rowdy affairs, so the authorities eventually came to terms with them through another means of regulation. By the 1820s regulation took the form of exacting fees, which helped
to fill government coffers and give us some idea of the frequency of the

events. During the mid-1820s, for instance, it cost an individual one-half peso to hold a dance in a private residence, so the fees collected tell us that Bexareños could attend more than one fandango per week, although only on weekends or on holiday eves. In the period immediately after Mexican independence, the regulations were relaxed somewhat, as travelers reported multiple fandangos available on any given evening.[24] The best description of a San Antonio dance comes down to us from this period. August Fretéllièr, an early Alsatian immigrant to Texas, provides a word portrait of a fandango in 1837 that closely matches Theodore Gentilz's painting *Fandango*,[25] created a few years later:

> The sound of the violin drew us to the spot where the *fête* was in full swing. It was in a rather large room of an adobe house, earthen floored, lighted by six tallow candles placed at equal distances from each other. At the back a great chimney in which a fire of dry wood served to reheat the *café*, the *tamales*, and the *enchiladas*: opposite, some planks resting on frames and covered with a cloth, formed a table on which cups and saucers were set out. . . . At the upper end of the room, seated on a chair which had been placed on an empty box, was the musician, which was a violin. . . . The airs, for the most part Mexican, were new to me. The women were seated on benches placed on each side of the room. . . . The dance which I liked best was called the quadrille. It is a waltz in four-time with a step crossed on [e]very slow measure. . . . When the quadrille is finished, the cavalier accompanies his partner to the buffet, where they are served a cup of coffee and cakes. Then he conducts the young lady to her mother or to her chaperon to whom the girl delivers the cakes that she has taken care to reap at the buffet. The mother puts them in her handkerchief, and if the girl is pretty and has not missed a quadrille, the mama carries away an assortment of cakes to last the family more than a week.[26]

An even more common diversion, and an even more problematic one for the authorities, was gambling. The Spanish Bourbon monarchs, concerned as they were with reform of society, looked upon games of chance and wagering in general as contributing to laziness and immorality. Efforts to prohibit gaming were a staple of royal policy throughout the later colonial period, and San Antonio authorities wrestled with prohibition from an early date.[27] As early as 1724 a dispute between the presidio commander and missionaries led to the latter's accusations of Captain Nicolás Flores allowing soldiers to gamble, which the captain strenuously denied. A senior official reviewing the case ridiculed the missionaries' recommendation that soldiers be paid in coin rather than in goods by commenting that "were they to be paid in coin they would soon gamble and whore it away."[28] Even more serious charges were made in 1749 by *Regidor*[29] Antonio Rodríguez Mederos against Governor Pedro del Barrio in a case involving Rodríguez Mederos's rivals on the town council. According to Rodríguez Mederos, since Barrio had arrived in town there had been "perpetual gambling at his house in spite of the royal decree forbidding it."[30]

To the public corruption to which gambling contributed, games of chance, like dancing, also resulted in another moral lapse—the improper mixing of the sexes. In fact, authorities believed that gambling and prostitution were closely related. In 1745 a new arrival in town was considered suspicious not only because he was of mixed blood but also because he had no apparent livelihood, and there were rumors about the woman he lived with not being his wife. Confronted by the authorities, he admitted that he did in fact live from his gambling, although the record did not clarify the state of his "wife."[31] In 1783 the town council sought clarification of civilian officials' authority over the homes of soldiers where "townspeople gather, both men and women, to play prohibited games, commit offenses against God [euphemism for sex], and other things worthy of reform."[32]

Although royal laws against games of chance were well known, if not well respected, by the middle of the century local officials found it necessary to take more direct action. In 1754 *Alcalde* José Curbelo issued an ordinance that made the association between gambling and other social ills explicitly clear. The rule attempted to prohibit loitering, the carrying of concealed weapons, and—because it was the "cause of laziness and disregard for work among many"—gambling.[33] When in 1778 Toribio Farías petitioned for a license to hold cockfights, Governor Barón de Ripperdá recommended to his superior that the request be denied because "the establishment of a cockfight in San Antonio would lead to more gambling than already takes place illegally, since the population is given to drinking and gambling." Subsequent prohibitions of gambling were issued by governors and local officials alike in 1783, 1786, and 1809. In 1825 Governor Rafael González notified the local authorities that he could not approve their request to allow public games of chance, since they were prohibited by state law.[34]

Governor Ripperdá knew of what he spoke. Many Bexareños found themselves drawn too heavily into the addictive qualities of gambling. Francisco de Estrada faced foreclosure on his home, which he had put up as collateral, for what was in part a gambling debt incurred without his wife's knowledge. When parish priest Father Pedro Fuentes placed Juan Agustín Bueno's wife in shackles, had him physically punished, and removed their daughters from their home because of the couple's gambling, Mrs. Bueno exclaimed, according to Fuentes, that "even if the devils took her body and soul, she would not do as he said." What Father Fuentes sought was that the couple stop gambling, which provided their daughters with a very poor example. In the proceedings regarding a murder case, the victim's wife declared that he had been a drunkard, a gambler, and had even attempted to sell her body.[35] In his first full inspection of the garrison, Governor Cabello reported on Lieutenant José Menchaca that although capable as an Indian fighter, he "could not be trusted with financial affairs as he is very fond of gaming and a spendthrift."[36]

The theft of 700 pesos from the home of merchant Santiago Villaseñor in 1774 provides evidence of the widespread nature of gambling in the San Antonio community. According to the documents in the extensive case file, gambling took place in various homes, in nearby woods, and behind corrals, both day and night. One gambler, a tailor, lost five military uniforms worth of work to another player. In fact, the break-in at Villaseñor's house took place while he was gambling. At one of the games was a man whose wife gave birth to their child while he was playing. Pedro Leal, who was arrested but never stood trial, came under suspicion when he left one of the games for two hours then returned to pay off his IOUs. Suspicion mounted when he and his wife began buying bread in larger amounts than normal on succeeding days. Eventually, all but 137 pesos were recovered, and Leal was released from jail having been admonished regarding the perils of gambling.[37]

As the cases above demonstrate, gambling was a recreational activity that brought together people of different socioeconomic status. Cockfights, which eventually became legal once the government decided to turn the activity into a revenue-generating opportunity (and which remained popular until the late nineteenth century), required financial resources on the part of the individual or group responsible for building and running the cockpit, modest resources on the part of breeders and trainers of roosters, and just enough money on the part of anyone else interested in placing a bet.[38] Similarly, other than pickup games, cards required that a few individuals serve as hosts and banks, but the majority of participants only had to show up with betting money or a line of credit. Because San Antonio was a small community, not enough men of substance could keep games socially stratified, so class mixing was inevitable.

Unlike dice, which appear in the records only on the rarest occasion, because of the frequency of official proceedings involving card games, we have the names of some of the games played by Bexareños. One was called *treinta* or *treinta y una*, and like blackjack (twenty-one) consisted of players drawing cards in an effort to get to thirty (or thirty-one) points. In the game *albures*, a game in Spain called *parar*, cards were dealt out to all the players who made bets against the dealer. Subsequently cards were dealt out until there was a match, with the bank losing to the player making the match or winning all the bets if it received the matching card. *Monte* made its appearance in the nineteenth century and should not be confused with three-card monte. The Spanish game involved dealing four cards, two for the dealer and two for the player, and then drawing more cards until a pair was made with one of the four dealt cards. The dealer either lost the amount bet by the other player or won it depending who made the winning pair. At least one parlor card game (although also subject to wagering) also was popular in the late eighteenth century and remains popular in Mexico today—*malilla*. Played by four persons in two teams, it involved dealing all the cards from the deck, with the lead player turning over a trump card. Players won tricks by having a trump or high card in each round. When all the cards had been played the two teams counted the points (cards have different values). The team with the most points won.

One other Spanish parlor game played in San Antonio, which could be played with cards or with other objects, was called *pares y nones* and involved guessing odd or even on whatever object was being hidden. In 1737 Governor Carlos de Franquis Benítez de Lugo ran into accusations that he brought "suspicious women" to his home to play the game at late hours of the night. Because of the possibility of legitimate "recreational" card games, the authorities could not ban the sale and use of playing cards. Indeed, so profitable did the authorities consider the playing card market that by the 1760s the crown decreed a royal monopoly on the sale of playing cards, along with tobacco, gunpowder, and other lucrative products.[39]

Although public gambling remained illegal during the Mexican period, restrictions on this activity were lifted in the post–Texas independence period. Travelers to San Antonio during the 1830s and 1840s commented on the universal popularity of games of chance, but focused on the Bexareño population's particular zeal for the sport. One observed that on the Sabbath, "Many Mexicans leave chapel even before mass was concluded, and repair to the gaming table; where they spent the remainder of the day, and perhaps the whole night." Another visitor to San Antonio commented that "so strong is this passion that even the priests sometimes forget their sacred office and are seen dealing monte, the favorite game of the Mexicans."[40] How disappointed Father Fuentes would have been to learn of some of his successors' weakness for gambling.

Our inventory of recreational activities in early San Antonio would not be complete without a brief comment on alcohol. Already in the 1740s, there is evidence of efforts on the part of town officials to enforce the royal prohibition on contraband liquor, and as early as 1761 *Alcalde* Alberto López's police ordinance reiterated the royal ban on home distillation of sugarcane alcohol, commonly referred to as *aguardiente de caña* or *chinguirito* to distinguish it from regular *aguardiente* (brandy). He then elusively decreed that "because of the grave consequences to this town, no one is allowed to bring *aguardiente* into town except that which is from Castile and brought in for necessary reasons," an amount he estimated at one to two barrels.[41] A few years later Governor Ripperdá carried out the penalty for the production and sale of *aguardiente de caña* and adulterated *aguardiente*—dumping in the plaza tainted liquor belonging to a handful of sellers.[42]

As noted above, drinking accompanied dancing and gambling, which is why it concerned public officials. For instance, during the investigation on the murder of José Antonio Ballejo his wife testified that he was "a drunkard and a gambler." When Governor Ripperdá recommended against permitting Toribio Farías from establishing a cockpit in San Antonio, he specifically mentioned that Bexareños were already too addicted to "drinking and gambling." Governor Salcedo's ordinance regulating fandangos specifically prohibited "the sale of liquors, *aguardiente*, or wine" at the dances.[43]

Among the cases for drunkenness, that of Sub-Lieutenant Manuel de Urrutia stands out for illustrating the range of social ills clergy and officials attempted to fight by regulating the sale and consumption of alcohol. On the night of September 7, 1791, Urrutia attended a fandango held at the home of Corporal José Granados, despite the fact that he was officer of the guard that day. He was drunk on *aguardiente*, "a defect of his that has been his custom for many years." Nothing that Governor Manuel Muñoz did remedied Urrutia, who was in the habit of being drunk on and off duty, and who had developed a severe hatred for the governor. According to *Alcalde* Juan José de la Santa, who made the statement, not only had Urrutia once told him of a plot to kill the governor, it was also notorious that he had an illicit affair with an Indian woman.[44] Hence, alcohol contributed to dereliction of duty, contempt for senior officers, violence, and dissolute behavior.

Our perspective on diversions in early San Antonio is unfortunately skewed by the records upon which we must rely to document recreational and entertainment activities. Except by way of serendipity, missing are the innocent games of children and social leisure activities of adults. The harmless strolls and picnics in neighboring fields during lulls in Indian warfare that allowed for family interaction did not make it into the written record. Storytelling and the arts of painting and sculpture have not been treated in this article, although circumstantial evidence supports the presence of both.[45]

Also, as mentioned earlier, public celebrations sometimes created opportunities for special entertainments. Game booths and food stalls encircled the plaza during the festive season at the end of each year. The bullfights, horse races, and other competitions that took place broke the monotony of everyday existence. Even more special, because of the added entertainments, were extraordinary celebrations like a royal wedding or the birth of an heir to the throne. Fortunately, a report on the celebrations surrounding the ascension of a new king give us a glimpse of just how elaborate such events could become, even in backwaters such as San Antonio de Béxar.[46] After six months of mourning for the departed Philip V, the authorities advised the townspeople to prepare for a celebration and oath to Fernando VI on January 27, 1748. Governor Francisco García Larios requested that residents and soldiers display lights in front of their homes for the three evenings preceding the celebration. On the day of the ceremony, a military escort carried the royal standard to the governor's residence, whence he read the royal decree, which concluded with cries of "Long Live the King" from the citizenry, along with musketry and artillery fire and a speech by García Larios. At three in the afternoon the royal standard-bearer placed the flag to the right of the governor, who—accompanied by the town council and the presidio commander—marched to the parish church. They were preceded in the march by a company of "Moors" with its Grand Turk and officers and a company of "Christians" with its field marshal and officers.[47] After the church blessing, the whole assembly marched to the town plaza where a four-sided castle had been built for the occasion. With the town assembled there, the standard-bearer knocked at the castle door and the "castellan" responded by letting him in so that the royal standard could be hoisted at the topmost part of the structure and the guards set. The governor and town council then retired while the "Moors" made their passes around the castle.

So began the celebrations, which went on for another eight days. On the second day of the festivities, the procession to the church with the royal standard was repeated, and a mass of thanksgiving was sung, after which the "Moors" and "Christians" made processions. The following four days witnessed bullfights, followed by a day of skirmishes between the "Christians" and "Moors" and another day of bullfights. Finally,

> On the morning of 4 February the Moors and Christians held their battle, with all possible luster and with the Moorish prisoners carrying the [image] of the town's patron saint in procession to the church, where mass was sung and St. Ferdinand was left in his church. The promenade then resumed, making a turn about the plaza with the

Moorish prisoners. At three in the afternoon a comedy was presented, which everyone attended, and after which the artillery fired three volleys and the [celebration] concluded with the oath to Our King and Lord, whom God protect.

The festivities surrounding the oath to the new king were neither unique to San Antonio nor exotic.[48] They were, however, the clearest indication of how closely Bexareños culturally identified with the Spanish world. Bullfights, *moros y cristianos*, and processions with Christian religious icons were all parts of a pageant meant to remind the population of its Spanish heritage even as it provided relief from the daily routine. Despite their own chronic warfare with the autonomous tribes that surrounded them, Bexareños never attempted to stage a mock battle between Christians and Indians. And the other forms of entertainment we have reviewed here, while limited to those for which documentation exists, point equally strongly to a Spanish culture that served as a source for popular culture in the Mestizo world of northern New Spain. European-origin ball and card games, music, and liquor, were accompanied by equestrian and religious displays that also drew from Iberian practices.

As Anglo Americans and European immigrants, particularly Germans, overwhelmed the Tejano population of San Antonio in the mid-nineteenth century, the local Bexareño culture began to adopt and adapt cultural practices from those sources, including American baseball and German polkas. Eventually, as Bexareños blended the customs of Mexico with those of the United States, they enriched both their own Hispanic culture and American culture at large. At least one modern organized sport can trace its heritage back to Spanish colonial times. The sport of rodeo owes more than just its name to the early Mexican pioneers who brought the associated ranching skills to the American Southwest. To the degree that the modern "cowboy sport" reflects skills, equipment, and dress that had their origin in Spanish colonial Texas and other parts of what is now the American Southwest, it unwittingly celebrates the way that Tejanos, Nuevomexicanos, and Californianos lived, worked, and entertained themselves.

Notes

1. The phrase in the title means, "I had a strong urge to go play."
2. The following description of San Antonio and its environs is based on Jesús F. de la Teja, *San Antonio de Béxar: A Community on New Spain's Northern Frontier* (Albuquerque: University of New Mexico Press, 1995). For a historical survey of colonial Texas, see Donald E. Chipman, *Spanish Texas, 1519–1821* (Austin: University of Texas Press, 1992).
3. Jesús F. de la Teja, ed., *A Revolution Remembered: The Memoirs and Selected Correspondence of Juan N. Seguín*, 2nd ed. (Austin: Texas State Historical Association, 2002), 16; Jesús F. de la Teja, "Discovering the Tejano Community in 'Early' Texas," *Journal of the Early Republic* vol. 18, no. 1 (Spring 1998): 92–93.
4. Robert Ryal Miller and William J. Orr, eds., *Daily Life in Colonial Mexico: The Journey of Friar Ilariano da Bergamo, 1761-1768*, trans. William J. Orr (Norman: University of Oklahoma Press, 2000), 118–21; Juan Pedro Viqueira Albán, *Propriety and Permissiveness in Bourbon Mexico*, trans. Sonya Lipsett-Rivera and Sergio Rivera Ayala (Wilimngton, DE: Scholarly Resources, 1999), 185–87, 200–201.
5. Activities surrounding the succession of Fernando VI, May 25, 1747, Bexar Archives, Center for American History, University of Texas at Austin (hereafter cited as BA); Petition to Be Exempted from Hauling Stone for the Erection of Public Buildings, February 7, 1771, Nacogdoches Archives Transcripts, Texas State Library, Austin (hereafter cited as NAT); Representation of republicanos and vecinos of Béxar, March 1, 1790, BA; Bandos of Governor Manuel Salcedo continued, January 16, 1809, BA; Cabildo minutes book, January 17, 1821, 125, BA. A good contemporary description of a Mexico City bullfight, complete with moralistic commentary, can be found in Miller and Orr, *Daily Life in Colonial Mexico*, 119–20. A good survey of the evolution of bullfighting in eighteenth-century New Spain is Benjamín Flores Hernández, "Organización de corridas de toros en la Nueva España del siglo xviii y primeros años del xix," *Anuario de Estudios Americanos* vol. 61, no. 2 (2004): 491–515.
6. Sentence against Ignacio Flores, September 15, 1769, BA.
7. Auto of Governor Barón de Ripperdá, August 13, 1770, BA; petition of Juan Manuel Ruiz, July 14, 1782, BA.

8. Petition of José Francisco de la Mata, May 1, 1789, BA.

9. School code, March 13, 1828, BA.

10. Bando of Governor Domingo Cabello, June 24, 1781, BA.

11. Bandos of Governor Salcedo continued.

12. W. Steinert, quoted in De la Teja, "Discovering the Tejano Community in 'Early' Texas," 96.

13. Until the term became synonymous with the post–Civil War law enforcement organization known as the Texas Rangers, rangers were horsemen who acted as a frontier defense force. Composed mostly of Anglo Americans, these early ranger forces also contained Tejanos.

14. Dorothy Steinbomer Kendall, *Gentilz, Artist of the Old Southwest* (Austin: University of Texas Press, 1974), 27, 84–85; de la Teja, "Discovering the Tejano Community in 'Early' Texas," 95–96; Joel Huerta, "Red, Brown, and Blue: A History and Cultural Poetics of High School Football in Mexican America" (PhD diss., University of Texas at Austin, 2005), 35–45.

15. Louis E. Brister, trans. and ed., *John Charles Beales's Rio Grande Colony: Letters by Eduard Ludecus, a German Colonist, to Friends in Germany in 1833–1834, Recounting His Journey, Trials, and Observations in Early Texas* (Austin: Texas State Historical Association, 2008), 146.

16. Viqueira Albán, *Propriety and Permissiveness*, 123–24. An analysis of these dances and songs, based on documentation from the records of the Holy Inquisition, is found in Sergio Rivera Ayala, "Lewd Songs and Dances from the Streets of Eighteenth-Century New Spain," in *Rituals of Rule, Rituals of Resistance: Public Celebrations and Popular Culture in Mexico*, ed. William H. Beezley, Cheryl English Martin, and William E. French (Wilmington, DE: Scholarly Resources, 1994), 27–46.

17. Miller and Orr, *Daily Life in Colonial Mexico*, 116.

18. Rivera Ayala, "Lewd Songs and Dances," 31. I have replaced the original English translation in the article with my own.

19. Francisco García vecino de la villa de S. Antonio de Béxar, contra el Sr. Gobernador de la provincia por haberlo castigado por delitos que se expresan. Año de 1778, Archivo de Gobierno, Saltillo Leg. 5 exp. 314, Spanish Materials from Various Sources, vol. 840, no. 4 (transcript), Center for American History, University of Texas at Austin.

20. Bandos of Governor Salcedo continued.

21. The Spanish office of *alcalde* combined administrative and judicial duties, and can be roughly translated as "magistrate." In modern times, the office has become akin to that of mayor in many parts of the Hispanic world.

22. Bando of Cabildo, October 26, 1760, BA; Bando of Alberto López, January 10, 1761, BA; Bando of José Salvador Díaz, January 21, 1776, BA.

23. Cabildo to Cabello, February 28, 1783, BA.

24. Arnoldo De León, *The Tejano Community, 1836–1900* (Albuquerque: University of New Mexico Press, 1982), 172–73; Jesús F. de la Teja and John Wheat, "Bexar: Profile of a Tejano Community," *Southwestern Historical Quarterly*, vol. 89, no. 1 (July 1985): 23; de la Teja, "Discovering the Tejano Community," 90.

25. Kendall, *Gentilz*, 10, 25, 59.

26. Quoted in de la Teja, "Discovering the Tejano Community," 90.

27. A summary of government efforts to prohibit and control games of chance can be found in Teresa Lozano, "Los juegos de azar. ¿Una pasión novohispana? Legislación sobre juegos de azar en Nueva España. Siglo xviii," *Estudios de Histora Novohispana* vol. 11 (1991): 155–81. See also Teresa Lozano Armendares, "Tablajeros coimes y tahures en la Nueva España ilustrada," *Estudios de Historia Novohispana* vol. 15 (1995): 67–86.

28. Autos sobre diferentes puntos consultados por el gobernador de la Provincia de los Texas muerte de un correo y otras materias. Año de 1724, Archivo General de la Nación de México, ramo Provincias Internas vol. 183 (microfilm), Benson Latin American Collection, University of Texas at Austin.

29. The office of *regidor* is akin to that of alderman, although there were specific administrative tasks assigned to each *regidor*. By royal charter, San Antonio was entitled to six *regidores* on its town council.

30. Autos fhos. a representación de D. Antonio Rodríguez Mederos, regidor decano de la Villa de San Fernando en la Provincia de Texas, sobre que salgan de dha. Villa D. Vicente Travieso, alguacil mayor, y D. Francisco de Arocha escribano de cabildo, por falsos, reboltosos, y pertubadores de la paz pública, July 19, 1749, BA.

31. Proceedings on legitimacy of a marriage, October 4, 1745, BA.

32. Cabildo to Cabello, January 24, 1783, BA.

33. Bando of José Curbelo, January 12, 1754, BA.

34. Petition of Toribio Farías, January 12, 1778, BA; Order of Gov. Cabello, Oc-

tober 7, 1786, BA; Bandos of Governor Salcedo continued; Governor Rafael
González to Jefe Político of Béxar, November 18, 1825, BA.

35. Petition of Juan José Flores, January 26, 1754, BA; Criminal investigation
on the death of José Antonio Ballejo, June 4, 1776, BA; Juan Agustín Bueno,
queja contra el cura de la villa de Sn. Fernando sobre haberle castigado a su
mujer y depositado a sus hijos. Archivo de Gobierno, Saltillo Leg. 5 exp. 314
(transcript), Spanish Material from Various Sources, vol. 840, no. 4, Center
for American History, University of Texas at Austin; Extracto de la revista de
inspección ejecutada por mí el Coronel de Infantería Don Domingo Cabello,
July 1, 1779, Archivo General de Indias, Audiencia de Guadalajara 104-6-20
(transcript), Texas State Archives, Austin.

36. Extracto de la revista.

37. Sumaria del robo hecho a D. Santiago Villaseñor, entrando por una ventana
de su casa la noche del 24 al 25 de Octre. de 1774, de la cantidad de 700p, en
Sn. Antonio de Bexar, October 28, 1774, BA.

38. Petition of Toribio Farias; Vicente Bernabeu to Gov. Manuel Muñoz, December 27, 1790, BA; Intendente Bruno Díaz de Salcedo to Gov. Muñoz, January
4, 1796, BA; De León, *Tejano Community*, 184–85. The history of this activity
in colonial Mexico can be found in María Justina Sarabia Viejo, *El juego de
los gallos en la Nueva España* (Seville: Escuela de Estudios Hispanoamericanos, 1972).

39. Testimonio de las diligencias ejecutadas en la Provincia de Texas en virtud de
superior despacho del Exmo. Sor. Virrey de este Reino, por el gobernador del
Nuevo Reino. de León contra el coronel don Carlos de Franquis Benítez de
Lugo actual gobernador. de la Provincia de los Texas y electo de la de Tlaxcala, April 17, 1737, Archivo General de Indias, Audiencia de Guadalajara 67-
2-27, Spanish Materials from Various Sources, vol. 29, Center for American
History, University of Texas at Austin; Order of Gov. Cabello, Oct. 7, 1786,
BA; Causa criminal formada de oficio por el Governador contra Prudencio
Barrón, Vecino del Preso. de Sn. Anto. de Béxar, y Villa de Sn. Ferndo. sobre
la muerte ridenta de Clemente Xavier Méndez, March 12, 1775, BA; Order
of Gov. Cabello, October 7, 1786, BA; de la Teja, "Discovering the Tejano
Community," 92; Susan Deans-Smith, *Bureaucrats, Planters, and Workers:
The Making of the Tobacco Monopoly in Bourbon Mexico* (Austin: University
of Texas Press, 1992), 7. The names and descriptions of the card games men-

tioned come from various editions of the *Diccionario de la lengua española*,
dating between 1726 and 1899—see "Nuevo Tesoro Lexográfico de la Lengua
Española," http://buscon.rae.es/ntlle/SrvltGUILoginNtlle (accessed July 18,
2008). Additional information on *malilla* was taken from "Malilla," http://
www.pagat.com/manille/malilla.html (accessed July 18, 2008).

40. Quoted in de la Teja, "Discovering the Tejano Community," 92.
41. Quote, Bando of Alberto López, January 10, 1761, BA; Case of Isleños v. Mederos, June 17, 1750, BA.
42. Order of Gov. Ripperdá, March 27, 1775, BA.
43. Criminal investigation on the death of Jose Antonio Ballejo; petition of Toribio Farias; Bandos of Gov. Salcedo continued.
44. Certification of Alférez Manuel de Urrutia's conduct by D. Juan José de la Santa, *regidor* and acting *alcalde* in absence of Francisco Arocha, September 9, 1791, BA.
45. See, for instance, Adina De Zavala, *History and Legends of the Alamo and Other Missions in and around San Antonio*, reprint ed. (Houston: Arte Público Press, 1996); and Gilberto M. Hinojosa and Anne A. Fox, "Indians and Their Culture in San Fernando de Béxar," in *Tejano Origins in Eighteenth-Century San Antonio*, ed. Gerald E. Poyo and Gilberto M. Hinojosa (Austin: University of Texas Press for the Institute of Texan Cultures, 1991), 113–18.
46. Activities surrounding the succession of Fernando VI.
47. On the Reconquista reenactment spectacle known as "Moros y Cristianos," see Mas Harris, *Aztecs, Moors, and Christians: Festivals of Reconquista in Mexico and Spain* (Austin: University of Texas Press, 2000).
48. See, for example, Cheryl English Martin, *Governance and Society in Colonial Mexico: Chihuahua in the Eighteenth Century* (Stanford, CA: Stanford University Press, 1996), 100–105.

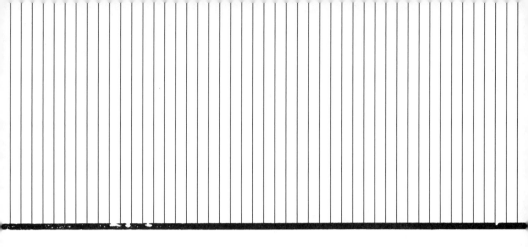

CHAPTER 2

A Variable of Unwavering Significance: Latinos, African Americans, and the Racial Identity of Kid Chocolate

Enver M. Casimir
The Brearley School

In the summer of 1928 a seventeen-year-old Cuban boxer named Eligio Sardiñas came to New York City to pursue his career in the then mecca of boxing, hoping to build on the success he had achieved in his hometown of Havana. The man the world would come to know as Kid Chocolate emerged from humble origins to embark on a career that would make him an international celebrity. Sardiñas was born in Havana in 1910, the youngest of four boys and two girls. His mother, the daughter of slaves, washed clothes for income, and his father worked as a public works laborer until his death, which occurred when Eligio was five years old. After the death of his father, he and his siblings did what they could to contribute to the family income. His sisters worked as domestic servants, and instead of going to school, young Eligio, like many poor youths who lived in Havana, "was forced to find daily sustenance in the streets performing whatever jobs were available." Sardiñas shined shoes and sold newspapers, living and working in the Havana neighborhood of El Cerro where he was born.[1]

Sardiñas entered the boxing world at a very early age. As a young boy he regularly attended fights at the nearby Arena Colón, where his oldest brother often participated. At the arena, Eligio met North American welterweight Young "Chico" Wallace, who reportedly helped the youngster develop his skills as a boxer while Sardiñas carried his bags.[2] Growing up poor, black, and uneducated in Havana left him with few options for earning a living, and the appeal of boxing was almost certainly to a large degree financial.[3] The example of his brother and other neighborhood boys and the ever-pressing need to make money apparently induced Sardiñas to try his hand at boxing, and at the age of eleven in 1922 he entered a tournament for paperboys held by the Havana newspaper *La Noche*.[4] The tournament fights attracted a significant following among local fans, and one such program attracted an estimated two thousand spectators.[5] The exact origins of the Kid Chocolate moniker are unclear, but Sardiñas had begun to use it by the time of his earliest recorded formal competition at the age of eleven. According to one account, his oldest brother, Domingo, had boxed under the name Chocolate, and thus the young Eligio adopted the name for the *La Noche* tournament.[6]

While the exact origin of his stage name may be lost to history, Chocolate attracted fans and established a reputation for himself as a skilled boxer even as a boy.[7] The speed and knack for defensive maneuvers that would become the hallmarks of his professional career were apparent at an early age. As early as July 1922, when he was eleven years old, the newspaper *La Noche* described Chocolate as a champion and emphasized his superior ability. On one Sunday that month he defeated two opponents in one night, forcing the first to quit before the fight was over and giving the second a "pitiful" beating. The reporter's description of the performance by Chocolate ended with a simple but clear declaration: "Chocolate has no equal."[8] By February 1923 he reigned as the defending tournament champion in the seventy-pound weight class.[9]

After repeated success in the annual tournaments staged by *La Noche*, Chocolate went on to fight with irregular frequency in Cuba through 1927, motivated more than anything by the immediate need to generate income.[10] Estimates of the number of fights he fought as a young amateur and semiprofessional vary considerably, and the exact total may never be known with certainty.[11] Yet the words of at least one sports reporter from the period seem to confirm the fame and success that Chocolate had garnered in Cuba as a young boxer:

> Kid Chocolate!!! . . . That marvel of a boy with gloves. First he was amateur champion at seventy pounds, then eighty, then ninety, and lastly at one hundred ten pounds he was able to maintain his glorious undefeated status. Fans saw him grow up inside the ropes of the ring.[12]

With his success as an amateur and semiprofessional within Cuba, Chocolate attracted the attention of Luis "Pincho" Gutiérrez, who would take over as Kid Chocolate's manager in April 1928 and offer him an opportunity to box in the United States.[13] Chocolate left for New York in June.[14]

Within months of his arrival in New York, Chocolate became a phenom with a reputation for delighting fight fans and amazing sportswriters. By the end of the year, *The Ring* magazine, the self-proclaimed "bible of boxing," would call him "the sensation of New York,"[15] and the United Press would summarize his meteoric rise to boxing prominence in 1928 by noting that he had arrived in New York in June "without a penny and unknown," and left in December as "the idol of New York fans."[16] For the next four years Kid Chocolate enjoyed status as one of the most skillful competitors and heralded celebrities in the world of professional boxing. He competed in marquee fights that drew tens of thousands of spectators to prominent venues such as Madison Square Garden, Ebbets Field, and the Polo Grounds. He cemented his status as a top fighter by winning the world junior lightweight championship in July 1931 and the world featherweight championship in October 1932. From 1928 to 1932 his ability to excite fans and draw them to the arena was virtually unmatched. In July 1931 the Associated Press flatly declared, "There is not a boxer in any weight class who brings as many people to the stadium as Kid Chocolate."[17] His abilities also made him a favorite among boxing pundits and sportswriters, who regularly praised him as one of the greatest fighters of his day, if not of all time. One writer observed that Chocolate was "rated highly even by the most critical veterans, who have watched the fistic parade go by for forty years,"[18] and a New York State Athletic Commissioner declared him "the most brilliant fighter of our time,"[19] while

The Ring magazine insisted, "Such fighters as Chocolate are developed but once a decade."[20]

This essay compares the ways in which African Americans and Latinos negotiated the racial and national identities of Kid Chocolate. Through the use of the African American newspaper the *Chicago Defender* and the New York Spanish-language daily *La Prensa* in particular, this study seeks to highlight the similarities as well as the differences between the ways African Americans and Latinos ascribed significance to the racial identity of Kid Chocolate, and drew on those similarities and differences to articulate broader conclusions on the relationship between athletic competition and racial and national hierarchies in the early twentieth century. Given the significance that boxing matches held as a metaphors for competition between racial and national groups in the 1920s and 1930s, the national or racial identity of a boxer was an inextricable component of his public persona. As a Cuban of unmistakably African descent, Kid Chocolate was a relatively rare case in which both his race and status as a foreigner were relevant and regularly mentioned by the American press. In addition, observers attributed varying degrees of significance to the various components of Kid Chocolate's identity. Despite their differences in which aspects of his identity they found to be most significant, both the African American and Latino communities treated Kid Chocolate as a hero and champion of their respective communities, and viewed his career in similar ways.

In an analysis of the career of American football player Franco Harris, historian Nicholas P. Ciotola has documented the ways in which sports spectatorship can emerge as a means of expressing ethnic identity and pride.[21] In noting that "the most profound form of ethnic expression for Pittsburgh's people of Italian descent came through sport," as they reacted to the career of Franco Harris in the early 1970s,[22] Ciotola documents another example of the symbiotic relationship between sport and ethnic identity that characterized the ways in which Latinos and African Americans both reacted to Kid Chocolate in the 1920s and 1930s. Both groups laid claim to, and expressed considerable interest in, the achievements of Kid Chocolate as a means of expressing a sense of ethnic or racial pride and solidarity. As a successful athlete in the highly commercialized world of spectator sport, Kid Chocolate generated a persona that was seized on by two different groups for the purposes of ethnic or racial self-expression.

That two different groups could feasibly lay claim to Kid Chocolate as one of their own also spoke to the contingent and variable nature of his racial and ethnic identity. At times highlighted as Latino and at other times as African American, Kid Chocolate navigated a cultural terrain where the significance of various components of his identity shifted based on the observer. This condition highlighted the degree of ambiguity in the ethnic or racial identity of an individual who could be appropriated by two different ethnic groups. The involvement of two such groups could mean that the celebrity himself might be involved in balancing such competing claims.[23] Thus, an examination of the career of Kid Chocolate can help us to better understand the very contingency of ethnic or racial identity itself.

Race, Nation, and the Stakes of Athletic Competition

By the 1920s and 1930s athletic competition had taken on considerable significance internationally as an indicator of national or racial capacity. The increased attention to sport at a time of the rising influence of eugenics and social Darwinism is not without significance.[24] Social Darwinists who saw life as a struggle among races and nations argued that physical strength was key to the "survival of the fittest" for human societies.[25] In an age where social Darwinism held considerable influence, athletic competition became a metaphor for Darwinian competition. Boxing in particular, given its ritualized format of physical confrontation between two individuals, was especially invested with meaning for those concerned with the Darwinian notion of the "survival of the fittest." In the United States the fact that by the 1880s the heavyweight championship of the world had left the hands of British boxers and remained consistently in the possession of North Americans symbolized the rise of the United States to the status of a world power at the expense of declining British influence. Champions such as John L. Sullivan, Jim Corbett, and Jim Jeffries stood as "shining example[s] of American strength and racial superiority."[26] Because the boxing ring served as a site where one man could exhibit direct physical mastery over another, by the early twentieth century the sport became closely associated with the ideology of social Darwinism. "In every country where boxing was practiced, the relative quality of elite boxers vis-à-vis elite boxers of other nations was held up as emblematic of . . . the general Darwinian struggle for world power."[27] Indeed the doctrine of social Darwinism encouraged the view that boxing was an acceptable form of physical training and entertainment, and boxing would come to be "sustained ideologically by notions of social Darwinism."[28] When Jack Johnson became the first black heavyweight champion of the world in 1915, he elicited pride among African Americans and generated a maelstrom of anxiety and concern among whites in the United States and around the world.[29] Success in the ring, especially if it led to the heavyweight championship of the world, came to symbolize not only individual achievement but also racial or national superiority.[30] Boxing matches became symbolically loaded as metaphors for competition between racial or national groups, and boxers became male heroes whose triumphs and defeats had direct implications for the members of the collective they represented. This ideological symbolism helped to stimulate the popularity of boxing worldwide. By the late 1920s, the appeal of boxing assumed international dimensions. The 1920s and 1930s constituted the "Golden Age" of boxing. By this time, it became "one of the most highly commercialized of all sports,"[31] reaching unprecedented heights in popularity and prestige and enjoying exceptional commercial success.[32]

During this time boxers functioned as symbolic icons and were inextricably linked to their national or racial identities. Far more than an individual seeking to make a living as an athlete, a top-ranked boxer was an ambassador who embodied the aspirations, ambitions, and anxieties of the nation or race he represented. When Argentine Luis Firpo challenged Jack Dempsey for the world heavyweight championship in 1923, two different North American newspapers, the *New York Times* and the *Brooklyn Eagle*, suggested that should Firpo win, North Americans would have to rethink the Monroe Doctrine and its meaning.[33] In the spring of 1929 an article in the New York Spanish-language newspaper *La Prensa* highlighted the fact that the success of a boxer was seen as an issue of national importance. The article, titled "The Foreign Invasion," observed, "The pugilistic supremacy of the United States is seriously threatened," as boxers in Europe, South America, and the Caribbean were consistently improving in quality. *La Prensa* added that *New York Telegram* columnist Harry Grayson was especially fearful of Spaniard Paulino Uzcudun and German Max Schmelling, so much so that Grayson issued a patriotic plea to North American Gene Tunney to come out of retirement.[34]

For high-profile boxers, every victory and defeat carried with it a larger symbolism and commentary regarding national or racial prestige, power, and status. As a result, professional boxers were repeatedly situated within a racial or national grouping that was cast as a central aspect of their identity by the American press. The relative success of different athletes carried larger symbolic significance for the broader capacities of the groups they represented, and in an era of social Darwinist thought, the link between individual athletic achievement and group characteristics was inextricable, not just in the popular press, but in scholarly writing as well.[35] Even native-born white boxers of certain backgrounds were consistently identified by their ethnicity, such as Italian American, Jewish, or Irish American, perhaps because their whiteness needed to be qualified or because even among whites a hierarchy of nationalities or ethnicities needed to be established. These boxers became champions of the collectives they were understood to represent. As a Spanish-speaking individual of unmistakably African descent, Kid Chocolate emerged as a champion for both the African American and Latino communities in the United States.

Kid Chocolate and African Americans

The African American press paid close attention to Chocolate, claiming him as one of their own. The *Chicago Defender* reported on the career of Chocolate beginning with his very first fight in the United States.[36] For the editors at the *Defender*, the racial identity of the new boxer seemed much more significant than his national identity; at one point the paper mistakenly noted that Chocolate was from Panama.[37] The publication was explicit in highlighting an image of Chocolate as a representative of all African-descended peoples, regardless of his national origin. In reporting on one fight the publication observed, "Chocolate had a chance to put the white boy away in the third round, but passed it up."[38] In fact the paper repeatedly used the term "white boy" to describe the opponents

Chocolate faced, thus emphasizing Chocolate's racial identity as African-descended.[39] The *Chicago Defender* repeatedly invoked Chocolate as a representative of African Americans even though he was a foreigner. Like the mainstream media, the *Defender* cast Chocolate as the heir to the legacy of George Dixon, the African American great of the first decade of the twentieth century, calling him "the closest approach to George in the present era of Colored fighters."[40] Two months later it described Chocolate as one of several well-known "race fighters."[41] Reports of an opportunity to compete for the world lightweight championship prompted a headline announcing, "Kid Chocolate May Bring Tenth Title to the Race." The accompanying article noted, "Ethiopians have held every title except the flyweight crown and the synthetic junior welterweight championship."[42] Two months later Chocolate was again cited as an example of the fact that "throughout all time the Race [*sic*] fighter has stood up and held his own with the best of them."[43] Two weeks before his junior lightweight title bout with Benny Bass, the *Pittsburgh Courier* noted that Chocolate would become the first black individual to be champion of that division.[44] The *Defender* repeatedly referred to Chocolate as one "our boys." Kid Chocolate stood as a representative of blacks more generally regardless of national background. Thus African Americans had an investment his success. Their investment indicated that identity and sympathy along racial lines transcended boundaries of nationality in the world of athletic competition.

Chocolate also seemed to be particularly popular among African Americans in general. In Harlem he was "invariably accompanied" by "a horde" of young admirers. On one morning in December 1928 he walked through the neighborhood surrounded by a "swarm of boys of his race" who cheered him on with loud screams. As with all boxers "of his race" who had attained success, Chocolate became a hero and idol among Harlemites, who "greeted him with enthusiasm" whenever he appeared in public in the neighborhood.[45] He also consciously and purposefully engaged the African American community in the United States. While in Chicago for a fight in the summer of 1929, Chocolate attended a Negro League baseball game between the Kansas City Monarchs and the American Giants, and was introduced to the crowd by the game announcer.[46]

During his time in Chicago, Chocolate also visited the *Chicago Defender* printing plant.[47] Thus Chocolate himself seemed to embrace the forging of transnational links based on racial identity.[48]

That Chocolate subscribed to a transnational sense of racial identity can also be seen in the way in which he was said to have developed his technique as a young boxer. Chocolate developed his style in part by observing films as a young boy of Joe Gans and George Dixon, two African American boxers who fought near the turn of the century and won championships.[49] These films were shown at theaters in Havana, and the young Sardiñas attended screenings frequently. One particular film of two fights by Gans held the boy "fascinated, in his seat." The first time he saw the film he reportedly sat through five showings in one day, and returned the following day to view it again. Sardiñas "avidly drank in every detail of Gans' remarkable style and . . . went home and rehearsed before the mirror," attending screenings of the film every day for a week.[50] The purposeful imitation of successful African American boxers informed the development of his own fighting style, and Chocolate consciously sought to imitate African American boxers early in his career. We may never know with certainty why Chocolate chose to imitate Gans and Nelson instead of other fighters, but his decision to imitate these athletes suggests that identification and imitation along racial lines seemed logical, perhaps even natural, even to a young boy.[51]

Kid Chocolate and Latinos

The first mention of Kid Chocolate on the sports pages of the New York Spanish language daily *La Prensa* occurred in mid-September 1928, two months after his first professional fight in the United States.[52] Initially it seems that *La Prensa* was slow to cover the career of Chocolate in detail, but this would rapidly change as his fame in New York boxing circles grew. The paper announced his October 1928 fight with Johnny Erickson with a full-page headline on its sports page.[53] Weeks later, *La Prensa* printed a story giving detailed background on Chocolate's career in Cuba before he came to the United States, presumably satisfying a desire by readers to know more about the latest metropolitan boxing sensation.[54]

The Spanish-speaking community of New York also adopted Kid

Chocolate as a hero and demonstrated particular affection for him. At one outdoor fight, "hundreds of Cubans living in New York" attended despite poor weather and applauded Chocolate "with enthusiasm."[55] Two weeks later a "major crowd in which a large part of the Cuban colony predominated" cheered Chocolate on at another fight and carried him off to his dressing room on their shoulders after his victory.[56] Cuban establishments in New York where Chocolate dined were "full of admirers" anxious to greet him.[57] The community seemed particularly enthusiastic of his defeat of Al Singer in August 1929, holding a banquet in his honor at the Cuba Athletic-Social Club in Harlem.[58] Throughout the late 1920s and early 1930s Spanish Harlem was the site of several events in his honor. Through his success Kid Chocolate became a hero to the Latino and Cuban American community in New York as well as the African American community within and outside New York.

Like the *Chicago Defender*, *La Prensa* provided consistent and dedicated coverage of Chocolate's career that was based on a sense of ethnic or racial solidarity. The publication touted his accomplishments as proof positive that Spaniards and Latinos were as "fit" and capable as any other group. He was cited along with Chilean Estanislao Loayaza and fellow Cuban Armando Santiago as the reason that "Hispanic stocks have experienced a considerable rise in the pugilistic market."[59] The paper repeatedly pointed to the exploits of Chocolate as proof of the "important role that our boxers play . . . in the Mecca of the sport."[60] The implicit corollary to such a statement was that Latinos themselves could make meaningful contributions to civilization outside the world of sport.

Coverage of the career of Kid Chocolate in the pages of *La Prensa* fit into a larger pattern of coverage of Hispanic or Latino athletes more generally. The paper regularly ran a column on the sports page titled "Of Our Sportsmen" that detailed the exploits of Spanish-speaking athletes in New York. It also habitually reported on the accomplishments of promising or successful athletes, such as Cuban baseball teams traveling in the United States. When Cuban chess master José Raúl Capablanca competed at a chess tournament in Bavaria, Germany, *La Prensa* included a report on tournament results.[61] When Spanish heavyweight Paulino Uzcudun predicted he would win his upcoming fight with Max Schmelling by knockout, the story made front-page headlines.[62] Coverage of the career of Kid Chocolate reflected an understanding by the *La Prensa* editors that their readership would identify with Spanish-speaking athletes from throughout the world and would be interested in their accomplishments.

But *La Prensa* also recognized Chocolate as a representative of African-descended peoples as well as Hispanics. The first article on Chocolate to appear in La Prensa described him as the "small Cuban boxer of the negro race," and noted that many observers were hailing him as a second George Dixon, adding "there is a great similarity in the style and constitution of Kid Chocolate and the unforgettable American gladiator of the negro race."[63] The paper frequently referred to him as the "little Cuban of the negro race (*el cubanito de la raza negra*)."[64] Staff writer Julio Garzón observed, "It cannot be forgotten that the white race is not the only one that [participates] in sports. I thus claim for Cuba the credit of producing the best sporting 'material' of the black race."[65] Another way in which *La Prensa* highlighted Kid Chocolate's identity as African-descended was to also cast him as the heir to the legacy of African American boxing greats George Dixon and Joe Gans, calling him the "best boxer of his race to have emerged since the days" of the two boxing legends.[66] Unlike the *Defender*, *La Prensa* recognized Kid Chocolate as both Latino or Hispanic and African American. In contrast, the *Defender* highlighted Kid Chocolate's identity as African-descended and tended to ignore his identity as Cuban.

In all likelihood, Chocolate's very physical appearance likely made it impossible to ignore his racial status as an individual of African descent. Chocolate's appearance likely encouraged sportswriters to categorize him as at least African-descended, if not African American. Correspondents regularly used poetic language to highlight his physical features and thus convey his racial identity without explicitly mentioning it. At times they used culinary metaphors, as when the *Evening Graphic* dubbed him a "long, lean Cuban stick of licorice,"[67] a practice undoubtedly encouraged by his own moniker. In other instances, references to his complexion sufficed, as when the *New York Times* observed that his "wide ivory smile [worked] overtime in a face as black as polished marble."[68] The writers of *La Prensa* were similar to white North American sports journalists in their use of poetic and evocative language to describe Chocolate's appear-

Kid Chocolate, from Folder 10 (126 Pounds), Box 62, Series 5 (Fighters by Weight Class), Part of Sub-Group I. The Hank Kaplan Boxing Archive, Brooklyn College Archives and Special Collections. Brooklyn College Library.

ance and, by extension, his racial identity, referring to him, for example, as "the little Cuban gladiator who looks like an ebony statue with porcelain teeth."[69] The periodical repeatedly described him as the "little ebony soldier,"[70] or "small ebony warrior,"[71] emphasizing his skin color. Though he was a foreigner, his appearance and unmistakable phenotype encouraged writers to engage his racial identity as African-descended. Indeed, it may have been impossible for them to do otherwise.

Reporting on Kid Chocolate and considerations of his racial identity in *La Prensa* at times revealed the ambiguous and nebulous quality of the very concept of race itself. While *La Prensa* might on one occasion describe Chocolate as belonging to the Negro race (*la raza negra*), on another occasions the paper would describe him alongside Argentine Luis Angel Firpo and Spaniard Paulino Uzcudun as boxers of the Hispanic race ("*gladiadores de la raza*").[72] The fact that boxers who were as different in physical appearance as Chocolate and Firpo or Uzcudun could be said to belong to the same "race" served as an indicator of the malleable nature of the term. Moreover, the reporting of *La Prensa* indicated the ways in which different aspects of the identity of Kid Chocolate would be highlighted at different times, even within the same group of observers.

Variations in the characterization of Chocolate as black or Latino occurred even for one individual observer. In November 1931 *La Prensa* staff writer Julio Garzón wrote a column titled "From Joe Gans to Kid Chocolate" that placed Chocolate squarely in the line of great African American boxers of the early twentieth century. Garzón went on to note that the considerable popularity that Chocolate enjoyed was significant given the general aversion to African American boxers that he felt persisted in the United States.[73] The column was striking in light of the fact that about a month earlier on Columbus Day, Garzón had written a piece titled "The Generous Contribution by Our Race to the World of Sport," which discussed Chocolate in the context of Spanish-speaking athletes who had made a name for themselves and thus followed in the steps of Columbus in bringing prestige to Spanish speakers around the world. The earlier piece noted that Spanish-speaking athletes were blessed with the "initiative, nobility and courage" of the Spanish conquistadors who had colonized the Americas in the sixteenth century. As a tribute to these athletes, who were

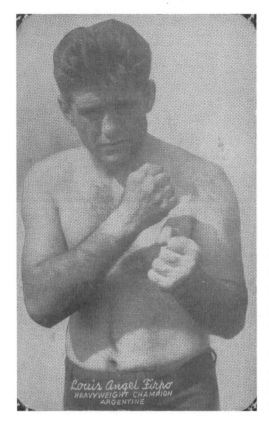

Luis Angel Firpo, from Folder 6 (Early 20th Century), Box 65, Series 6 (Subject Files), Part of Sub-Group I. The Hank Kaplan Boxing Archive, Brooklyn College Archives and Special Collections. Brooklyn College Library.

described as "champions of the race," *La Prensa* ran a special section on Columbus Day documenting their accomplishments.[74]

That Kid Chocolate, the descendant of African slaves, could be said to belong to the same "race" as the Spanish conquistadors when race was the very concept used to distinguish his ancestors from those conquistadors underscores the historical contingency of the term. Used during the colonial project to divide members of Spanish colonial societies into discrete castes, by the 1930s the term "race" was being used in the United States to refer to the entire collective of people who constituted those societies. By the early twentieth century a new quasi-racial category had emerged that overlapped the categories of white and black, and united Spanish speakers throughout Spain and the Americas.[75] This identity undoubtedly assumed even greater salience for those individuals who had moved to the United

Paulino Uzcudun, from Folder 3 (Paulino Uzcundún), Box 51, Series 1 (Champions and Contenders), Part of Sub-Group VII. The Hank Kaplan Boxing Archive, Brooklyn College Archives and Special Collections. Brooklyn College Library.

States and regularly interacted with non–Spanish speakers. The meaning of race thus evolved to accommodate new social developments. As historical circumstances shifted and brought different groups of individuals into contact, historical actors recalibrated the concept to help them make sense of these shifts. In this context the Hispanic or Latino category served as a supranational or supplemental category based on a hybridization of race and nation that indicated the fluidity of race beyond the more conventional categories of white or black.

Competition as Metaphor and the Fairness Principle

Whether observers highlighted his identity as black, Cuban, or Latino, all would have felt an impulse to ascribe some sort of collective identity to Kid Chocolate. Chocolate's achievements had significance for whichever racial, national, or supranational group he was seen to represent. Soon after arriving in New York at the tender age of seventeen and becoming a professional boxer, Chocolate entered a world where racial and national identities shifted in importance and might even collapse on each other, but their significance never waned. The racial or national identity of a competitor was of utmost importance because his achievement carried significance for the group he represented. It was because of this symbolic significance that both *La Prensa* and African American publications were particularly vocal in criticizing what they felt were unfair decisions against Kid Chocolate during his career. Awareness of the stakes of championship fights in particular led to accusations that boxing officials would do anything in their power to prevent the conquest of a title by an African-descended or foreign fighter. In April 1929 Chocolate fought Bushy Graham in front of a crowd of over eighteen thousand at the New York Coliseum in the Bronx. Despite the fact that the New York State Athletic Commission at the time recognized Graham as the world bantamweight champion, the commission refused to recognize the fight as a title match. The *Chicago Defender* accused the commission of racist motivations for not designating it a title contest, insisting,

> The boxing commission booted a good chance to clear up the muddled situation that prevails in [the bantamweight] class, besides giving the impression that it draws the color line. . . . It is the general opinion that they fear the Race [*sic*] lad [Chocolate] may win the crown.[76]

On the other hand, Hype Igoe, writing for the *New York World*, expressed disbelief that such motivation existed, declaring, "The commissioners . . . couldn't be that unfair. They wouldn't be that unsportsmanlike. They wouldn't make boxing look that cheap!" Igoe was confident that racial prejudice played no part in the decision, though he did not offer an alternative explanation. He invoked a notion of fair play in competition that he was confident would overcome any sense of racial bias, though he conceded that several promoters did exhibit a tendency to shun the scheduling of inter-racial bouts.[77] Commentary on the Graham fight indicated a degree of controversy and disagreement as to whether racist motivations subverted the ideals of merit and equal opportunity that were supposed to govern sport.

Similarly, when Chocolate lost by decision to Christopher "Battling" Battalino in his first bid for the featherweight championship in December 1930, *La Prensa* denounced the decision as indefensible and was explicit in attributing it to racial and national bias: "to believe that two local judges and a referee would find in favor of a black foreigner and give him a world championship is, simply put, to be guilty of naiveté." The daily criticized officials for letting racial bias cloud their sense of fairness and sportsmanship, taking the decision as an indictment of American hypocrisy:

> Before we came to live in the United States, we had the impression that this was a country where general honesty was emphasized in the field of sports. We believed that the word "sportsmanship" was a sacred one for the good Yankees. But it is clear that since then boxing has fallen to the point where it currently finds itself in the hands of utter "crooks" who have converted a sport that was once steeped in etiquette into something nauseating that now disgusts us.

The paper noted that even one reporter from Battalino's home state of Connecticut who sat ringside confessed that Chocolate had given Battalino "the beating of his life."[78] *La Prensa* articulated the position that fairness and objectivity were inviolable ideals in the world of sport, but racial or national affinities often undermined these ideals. The paper insinuated that because a championship was at stake, the arbiters of the contest were reticent to decide in favor of a black foreigner. Instead the desire to preserve a sense of white and American superiority clouded their judgment and led to an unjust decision. The commentary revealed the ways in which the racial and national symbolism of athletic competition might undermine the character of sport as an objective measure of ability.

When Chocolate failed in his attempt to take the lightweight title from Tony Canzoneri in a highly controversial split decision in November 1931, *La Prensa* again argued that the decision was unjust and that Chocolate should have at least obtained a draw. The paper cast the decision as further proof that foreign boxers who came to New York to fight against local boxers for championships should give up all hopes of "equity and justice."[79] Days later *La Prensa* attributed the victory by Canzoneri to "pure anti-hispanism," comparing the bout to what it considered to be a similarly unfair decision in a recent fight between Paulino Uzcudun and

Tommy Loughran.[80] The staff of the publication saw what it deemed the injustice of the decision in purely racial or nationalist terms. In their view, there was no other possible explanation for the result.

The *Chicago Defender* joined *La Prensa* in its assessment of the reasons behind the outcome of the Canzoneri fight. The African American newspaper went on at length about the unlikelihood that a boxer of color could ever win a championship via decision. The paper insisted that the loss should come as no surprise, advising its readers "there is little chance for one of your boys to gain a title on the decision of three men." The paper pointed out that the crowd attending the fight was overwhelmingly white, a fact it suggested influenced the decision of the judges:

> Nineteen thousand fans saw this fight, the greatest in 20 years. Of that total less than 200 were you and me, if you get what I mean. Now how can you expect anything else but a win for the champion where no knockout is present? We may be wrong, but asking Nordic judges and referees to decide against a majority like that is stretching the point. Only a knockout can map a clean path for the officials who would dare say to a gathering where we were greatly outnumbered like that, "I hated to give the fight to the Cuban, but he was the better man."[81]

Like *La Prensa*, the *Defender* was quite pessimistic that fair play could consistently overcome racial bias, and indeed indicated that it was naive to think that this would ever happen. At the same time, it used a notion of fairness that was understood to be a central tenet of sport to conduct a critique of what it deemed to be racist behavior. Closely contested and controversial decisions were, and are, far from uncommon in boxing, and it would be difficult to definitively determine if prejudice played a part in the decisions against Chocolate. But the fact that both the *Chicago Defender* and *La Prensa* unequivocally saw race or nationality as the dominant underlying theme indicated the degree to which the sport was imbued with considerable implications for debates regarding racial and national hierarchies. The *Defender* and *La Prensa* may have differed in what aspects of Kid Chocolate's identity they sought to emphasize, but their responses to what they saw as biased decisions against Kid Chocolate during his boxing career were remarkably similar.

Conclusion

In July 1931, several days before a fight in Philadelphia, Kid Chocolate attended a Negro League baseball game on the outskirts of the city. The *Chicago Defender* and the *Pittsburgh Courier*, another African American newspaper, both documented his presence,[82] and his attending this particular game could be interpreted as simply another example of Chocolate's conscious embrace of the African American community in the United States, if not for one significant detail. Chocolate was likely drawn to the game by the fact that fellow Cuban Martín Dihigo played for one of the teams.[83] That Chocolate could attend a racially defined event in the form of a segregated baseball game to watch another Afro-Cuban athlete pursuing his career in the United States was testimony to the ways in which racially defined social practices and codes of behavior and the significance of one's status as African-descended crossed national borders.[84] But it was also an indicator of the fact that categories such as black or Cuban or Latino by themselves only captured part of the lives of individuals like Chocolate and Dihigo as lived by these individuals. While certainly at times these athletes were defined by their racial identities, at other moments their national identities were of greater relevance, and still at other moments neither category was fully adequate in describing their lived experience. Athletes such as Dihigo and Chocolate navigated a cultural terrain where the relative importance of racial and national identity ebbed and flowed in relation to each other, contingent upon specific circumstances.

Writing on the career of Kid Chocolate in the press indicated the significance that both racial and national identity carried with respect to athletic competition in the 1920s and 1930s. Chocolate was seen in the United States as both a racial and supranational hero, fulfilling both roles in different degrees depending on the orientation and perspective of his fans. The elision between the categories of race and nation that were evident in the sports pages of dailies that discussed boxing obviated any contradiction between being a racial or national hero, for the similarities between the two categories made it quite easy for Chocolate to be both. Chocolate could be, and was, cited as proof that both African-descended peoples and Hispanics were just as fit and capable as other racial or national groups. African Americans and Latinos in the United States both laid claim to Kid

Chocolate as one of their own in ways that sometimes revealed considerable elasticity in contemporary notions of what constituted a nation or a race.

Reactions to Kid Chocolate's career in *La Prensa* and the *Defender* also show the ways in which sport gave people a sense that objective rules and "fairness" should structure life chances. Such logic could also be used to challenge notions of racial or national hierarchies as archaic and contrary to notions of objective measure and fair play.[85] Commentaries in all sectors of the North American press also highlighted a notion of fair play and justice that was supposed to form a core component of athletic competition. This notion indicated a sense of sport as an arena where merit was of primary importance, and the superior competitor was supposed to win regardless of any biases or considerations on the part of judges, referees, or administrators. As historian Allen Guttmann has observed, "The relationship between equality and the achievement principal is a vital one."[86] The idea that sport provided an objective and fair means of comparison between individuals was central to its cachet as a metaphor for Darwinist competition between racial and national groups. Of course, whether the actual world of boxing always matched this ideal of fairness and the supremacy of merit is debatable at best. Indeed, the African American and Latino press in the United States often used this very critique to highlight the injustice of racial bias in the sporting world. Thus notions of fairness in athletic competition opened up discursive space where critics could deride racial bias as backward and archaic. If participation in sport and success in athletic competition did in fact exemplify modernity and development, writers in the African American and Latino press used the sporting ideal to imply that racial bias was decidedly unmodern. For some, sport was a cultural site where ideas about the supposed superiority of certain groups could be sustained. But through the success and fame of boxers like Kid Chocolate, it also became a site where such ideas could be challenged or inverted in ways that were intelligible to and accepted by individuals throughout the world. While they may have differed in which aspects of Chocolate's racial or national identities they emphasized, both the African American and Latino press seized on this notion of fair play to call for fair treatment of a competitor they considered to be their champion.

Notes

1. Elio Menéndez and Víctor Joaquín Ortega, *Kid Chocolate: El boxeo soy yo* (Havana: Editorial Obre, 1980), 11; Jorge Alfonso, "Campeón de campeones: Kid Chocolate," *Bohemia* 66 (August 9, 1974): 43.

2. Alfonso, "Campeón de campeones," 43; Menéndez and Ortega, *Kid Chocolate*, 12.

3. Biographers Menéndez and Ortega state flatly that "hunger was the primary impulse" into boxing for Chocolate (Menéndez and Ortega, *Kid Chocolate*, 13). Observing that "an impoverished society . . . is fertile ground for a flourishing boxing industry," Michael Messner has pointedly summarized the reasons why the poor and disadvantaged seemed to be overrepresented in the ranks of boxers. "Even though nobody forces young boxers to enter the ring, it would be foolish to suggest that most of them freely choose boxing from a number of attractive alternatives. . . . In any society which restricts the opportunities of certain groups of people, one will be able to find a signifi-cant number of those people . . . willing to pursue very dangerous careers for the slim chance of 'making it big' " (Michael A. Messner, "Why Rocky III?" in *Sex, Violence and Power in Sports: Rethinking Masculinity*, ed. Michael A. Messner and Donald F. Sabo [Freedom, CA: Crossing Press, 1994], 78).

4. Menéndez and Ortega, *Kid Chocolate*, 13.

5. *La Noche*, July 10, 1922, 12.

6. Menéndez and Ortega, *Kid Chocolate*, 15. Enrique Encinosa notes that Eligio's older brother competed under the name "Knockout Chocolate," and while the elder brother was apparently mediocre in the ring, the younger brother would adopt his name. See Enrique Encinosa, *Azúcar y chocolate: Historia del boxeo cubano* (Miami: Ediciones Universal, 2004), 53.

7. Menéndez and Ortega report that Chocolate debuted in 1922 by beating a fifteen-year-old when he was only eleven. Cuban boxing historian Jorge Alfonso indicates that Chocolate went undefeated in the 1922 tournament as well as in the one held the following year, winning sixteen bouts in all. See Menéndez and Ortega, 15, and Jorge Alfonso, *Puños dorados: Apuntes para la historia del boxeo en Cuba* (Santiago de Cuba: Editorial Oriente, 1988), 52–53. The earliest mention of Kid Chocolate in the collection of *La Noche* available at the Instituto de Historia in Havana occurs in July 1922, and at that point the publication was already referring to him as a champion. See *La Noche*, July 3, 1922, 18.

8. *La Noche*, July 3, 1922, 18.

9. *El Imparcial*, February 15, 1923, 11.

10. Menéndez and Ortega, *Kid Chocolate*, 16–17.

11. According to *The Ring Record Book and Boxing Encyclopedia*, Kid Chocolate fought in over one hundred bouts as an amateur, winning all of them. Nat Loubet and John Ort, *The Ring Boxing Encyclopedia and Record Book* (New York: *The Ring* Book Shop, 1978), 53. On the other hand, Cuban boxing historian Jorge Alfonso states that only the victories of the *La Noche* tournament are verifiable. He contends that the record of one hundred wins as an amateur was instead a fiction created by manager Luis "Pincho" Gutiérrez to make Chocolate a more appealing prospect to New York promoters during their first trip in 1928. Alfonso asserts that in actuality Chocolate fought rarely, if ever, between his stint as a child boxer in the *La Noche* tournaments and his reappearance in the Havana boxing scene in late 1927. See Alfonso, "Campeón de campeones," 43–44, and Alfonso, *Puños dorados*, 54. Menéndez and Ortega state that Chocolate would occasionally fight in small prize fights to stay in shape (see Menéndez and Ortega, 17). Reports appearing in the *El Imparcial* newspaper indicate that Chocolate did fight in at least two fights in the fall of 1926, but missing issues make it impossible to fully reconstruct his record during this part of his life. See *El Imparcial*, October 15, 1926, 6, and November 27, 1926, 6.

12. *El Mundo*, October 19, 1927, 27. The paper also reported a record of sixty-four amateur victories for Chocolate, suggesting that while the record of over one hundred wins as an amateur published in *The Ring Record Book* may be an embellishment, it is not far off the mark.

13. Menéndez and Ortega, *Kid Chocolate*, 22; *Diario de la Marina*, April 4, 1928, 16.

14. *Diario de la Marina*, June 22, 1928, 19.

15. Milton Baron, "Boxing in Cuba," *The Ring*, December 1928, 33.

16. *Diario de la Marina*, December 22, 1928, 19.

17. Associated Press article printed in *Diario de la Marina*, July 7, 1931, 14.

18. Wilbur Wood, "Negro Boxers Revive Glories of Dixon Heyday," *The Ring*, July 1930, 20.

19. *La Prensa*, December 10, 1929, 5.

20. Nat Fleischer, "Marvelous Body Balance by Kid," *The Ring*, February 1930, 25.

21. See Nicholas Ciotola, "Spignesi, Sinatra, and the Pittsburgh Steelers: Franco's Italian Army as an Expression of Ethnic Identity, 1972–1977," *Journal of Sport History* 27, no. 2 (Summer 2000): 271–89.

22. Ibid., 28.

23. While Kid Chocolate seemed to successfully negotiate a sense of belonging among Latinos as well as African Americans in the 1920s without any overt conflict between the two groups, Ciotola notes that Franco Harris was not as fortunate, and that his embrace of Italian American fans resulted in alienation from African American fans. Ciotola's work suggests that this alienation was in part due to tensions between African Americans and Italian Americans in Pittsburgh during the 1960s and 1970s. Thus, historical circumstances also seem to dictate how successful a celebrity athlete can be in navigating the significance ascribed to different components of his identity (see Citoala, "Spignesi," 281–83).

24. For a discussion of the rise of social Darwinism as an influential ideology, see Mike Hawkins, *Social Darwinism in European and American Thought, 1860–1945: Nature as Model and Nature as Threat* (Cambridge: Cambridge University Press, 1997).

25. Barbara Keys, *Globalizing Sport: National Rivalry and International Community in the 1930s* (Cambridge: Harvard University Press, 2006), 20.

26. Jeffrey T. Sammons, *Beyond the Ring: The Role of Boxing in American Society* (Urbana: University of Illinois Press, 1988), 30–33.

27. Patrick F. McDevitt, *May the Best Man Win: Sport, Masculinity, and Nationalism in Great Britain and the Empire, 1880–1935* (New York: Palgrave McMillan, 2004), 61.

28. John Sugden, *Boxing and Society: An International Analysis* (Manchester: Manchester University Press, 1996), 29–33.

29. For detailed discussions of the career of Jack Johnson and its effect on American society in the early twentieth century, see Geoffrey C. Ward, *Unforgivable Blackness: The Rise and Fall of Jack Johnson* (New York: Vintage, 2006); Randy Roberts, *Papa Jack: Jack Johnson and the Era of White Hopes* (New York: Free Press, 1983); Kasia Boddy, *Boxing: A Cultural History* (London: Reaction Books, 2008), 181–208; Al-Tony Gilmore, *Bad Nigger! The National Impact of Jack Johnson* (Port Washington, NY: Kennikat Press, 1975); Graeme Kent, *The Great White Hopes: The Quest to Defeat Jack Johnson* (Gloucestershire,

UK: Sutton Publishing, 2005); and Thomas Hietala, *The Fight of the Century: Jack Johnson, Joe Louis, and the Struggle for Racial Equality* (Armonk, NY: M. E. Sharpe, 2002).

30. Sugden, *Boxing and Society*, 33.

31. Biddy Bishop, "Mental Equipment of Boxers," *The Ring*, June 1927, 12.

32. Sammons, *Beyond the Ring*, xvii; Sugden, *Boxing and Society*, 35.

33. Cited in Daniel Fridman and David Sheinin, "Wild Bulls, Discarded Foreigners, and Brash Champions: U.S. Empire and the Cultural Construction of Argentine Boxers," *Left History* 12 (spring/summer 2007): 57. Firpo would lose the fight via a second-round knockout, but not before knocking Dempsey clear out of the ring in the first round.

34. *La Prensa*, April 4, 1929, 5.

35. For an example of how this link manifested itself even in scholarly writing of the period, see Jorge Iber, Samuel O. Regalado, Jose Alamillo, and Anroldo de Leon, *Latinos in U.S. Sport: A History of Isolation, Cultural Identity, and Acceptance* (Champaign, IL: Human Kinetics, 2011), 73–75.

36. *Chicago Defender*, July 21, 1928, 8.

37. *Chicago Defender*, November 10, 1928, 8.

38. *Chicago Defender*, December 8, 1928, 9.

39. For another example, see *Chicago Defender*, June 6, 1931, 9.

40. *Chicago Defender*, May 4, 1929, 9.

41. *Chicago Defender*, June 8, 1929, 9.

42. *Chicago Defender*, August 8, 1931, 8.

43. *Chicago Defender*, September 26, 1931, 9.

44. *Pittsburgh Courier*, June 27, 1931, section 2, 4.

45. *Diario de la Marina*, December 20, 1928, 17.

46. *Chicago Defender*, August 3, 1929, 9.

47. Ibid., 1. A photo documenting his visit appeared in the newspaper.

48. In his recent monograph, Frank Andre Guridy convincingly argues that African Americans and Afro-Cubans both consciously sought to establish ongoing transnational connections based on a sense of identity as African-descended, thus "forging" diaspora. Chocolate's decision to imitate African American boxers may not have reflected a conscious attempt to forge diaspora as Guridy defines it, but nonetheless reflects a tendency to identify along racial lines, even across national boundaries. See Frank Andre Guridy,

Forging Diaspora: Afro-Cubans and African Americans in a World of Empire and Jim Crow (Chapel Hill: University of North Carolina Press, 2010).

49. *New York World,* September 16, 1928, 4S. Joe Gans boxed from 1891 to 1909, winning the world lightweight title in 1902 (Loubet and Ort, *Ring Boxing Encyclopedia,* 57). George Dixon boxed professionally from 1886 to 1906. Nicknamed "Little Chocolate, he won the world bantamweight title in 1890 and the featherweight title in 1892. He held the featherweight title for ten years and is described by *The Ring Boxing Encyclopedia and Record Book* as "one of the greatest fighters of all time" (Loubet and Ort, *Ring Boxing Encyclopedia,* 55). Gans and Dixon were contemporaries and had a close personal friendship. For a detailed account of their lives and careers, see Nat Fleischer, *The Three Colored Aces: Story of George Dixon, Joe Gans and Joe Walcott and Several Contemporaries,* vol. 3, *Black Dynamite: The Story of the Negro in the Prize Ring from 1782 to 1938* (New York: Ring Athletic Library, 1938), 6–195.

50. *New York Daily Mirror,* December 4, 1928, 29.

51. In her introduction to *Between Race and Empire,* Lisa Brock posits the existence of an African aesthetic that permeated the cultural expressions and athletic endeavors of African Americans and Afro-Cubans. Brock argues that this aesthetic affinity points to the existence of a "cultural memory" that harkened back to West African origins. The fact that Chocolate consciously chose to imitate Gans and Dixon suggests that similarities in style between African-descended peoples in different countries in the Americas may have been due as much, if not more, to self-conscious identification and imitation along racial lines as to any atavistic tendencies. See Lisa Brock, introduction to *Between Race and Empire: African Americans and Cubans before the Cuban Revolution,* ed. Lisa Brock and Digna Castañeda Fuertes (Philadelphia: Temple University Press, 1998), 18–29.

52. *La Prensa,* September 17, 1928, 5.

53. *La Prensa,* October 1, 1928, 5.

54. *La Prensa,* October 27, 1928, 5.

55. *United Press* article in *Diario de la Marina,* September 1, 1928, 19.

56. *United Press* article in *Diario de la Marina,* September 18, 1928, 17.

57. *Diario de la Marina,* December 20, 1928, 17.

58. *La Prensa,* September 3, 1929, 5; *La Prensa,* September 5, 1929, 5.

59. *La Prensa,* December 19, 1928, 5.

60. *La Prensa*, April 12, 1929, 5.

61. *La Prensa*, August 16, 1928, 5.

62. *La Prensa*, June 28, 1929, 1.

63. *La Prensa*, September 17, 1928, 5.

64. See, for example, *La Prensa*, April 13, 1929, 5.

65. *La Prensa*, October 27, 1928, 5.

66. *La Prensa*, August 29, 1929, 5.

67. Cited in *New York Times*, August 22, 1971, S5.

68. *New York Times*, January 4, 1929, 24.

69. *La Prensa*, October 8, 1928, 5.

70. *La Prensa*, August 27, 1929, 5.

71. *La Prensa*, August 29, 1929, 5.

72. *La Prensa*, November 2, 1929, 5.

73. *La Prensa*, November 19, 1931, 5.

74. *La Prensa*, October 12, 1931, section 2, 2.

75. In a discussion of the potential that language has to provide the basis for what he calls fictive ethnicity, Etienne Balibar provides an explanation for the emergence and persistence of a pan-Hispanic identity, as is clearly seen in the pages of the New York publication *La Prensa*: "The language community . . . connects individuals up with an origin which may at any moment be actualized and which has as its content the common act of their own exchanges, of their discursive communication. . . . Even if it were the case that individuals whose social conditions were very distant from one another were never in direct communication, they would be bound together by an uninterrupted chain of intermediate discourses. They are not isolated—either de jure or de facto." Balibar also notes that language can serve to root historical populations "in a fact of 'nature,'" and give meaning to "their continued existence." See Etienne Balibar, "The Nation Form: History and Ideology," in *Race, Nation, Class: Ambiguous Identities*, ed. Etienne Balibar and Immanuel Wallerstein, (London: Verso, 1991), 96–97.

76. *Chicago Defender*, April 13, 1929, 9.

77. *New York World*, April 9, 1929, 10.

78. *La Prensa*, December 16, 1930, 5.

79. *La Prensa*, November 21, 1931, 5.

80. *La Prensa*, November 23, 1931, 5.

81. *Chicago Defender*, November 28, 1931, 8.

82. *Pittsburgh Courier*, July 11, 1931, section 2, 5; *Chicago Defender*, July 11, 1931, 9.

83. *Pittsburgh Courier*, July 11, 1931, section 2, 5. Described by one author as "the best Cuban baseball player of all time," Dihigo played for twelve years in the American Negro Leagues, but also played and managed in Cuba and Mexico. He starred as a pitcher but could play every position, and he is enshrined in the American, Mexican, and Cuban baseball halls of fame. See Roberto González Echevarría, *The Pride of Havana: A History of Cuban Baseball* (New York: Oxford University Press, 1999), 26, 180–82.

84. As in the United States, baseball in Cuba was at times segregated along racial lines. Roberto González Echevarría has observed, "Early Cuban baseball practiced an apartheid that would be perpetuated by Cuban amateur baseball during the years of the Republic." While professional and semiprofessional teams and teams associated with sugar mills became open to Afro-Cubans after the Spanish-American War, amateur baseball "systematically excluded" players of African descent until 1959. See González Echevarría, 102–3, 115, and 189–91.

85. Historian Allen Guttmann has argued that equality is a central distinguishing characteristic of modern sport. By definition, modern sport "requires, at least in theory, that no one be excluded from participation on the basis of ascriptive traits (such as race or ethnicity) and that the rules of the game be the same for all participants." See Allen Guttmann, *Games and Empires: Modern Sports and Cultural Imperialism* (New York: Columbia University Press, 1994), 2–3. For a more involved discussion of the concept of equality as it relates to modern sport, including the disjuncture between ideals and practice, see Allen Guttmann, *From Ritual to Record: The Nature of Modern Sports* (New York: Columbia University Press, 1978), 26–36.

86. Guttmann, *From Ritual to Record*, 26. Similarly, Barbara Keys notes that by the 1930s, "The notion that sport was inherently democratic . . . became a staple of public discourse." See Keys, *Globalizing Sport*, 80.

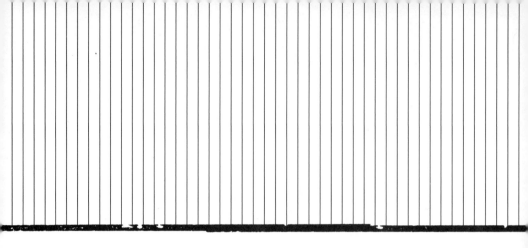

CHAPTER 3

Beyond the Baseball Diamond and Basketball Court: Organized
Leisure in Interwar Mexican South Chicago

Michael Innis-Jiménez
University of Alabama

I n a 1980 conversation with a Mexican South Chicago community
leader, Gilbert Martínez recalled being a young man in 1930s South
Chicago. He recalled getting on a streetcar to go play baseball in
Washington Park: "So what we used to do is put on the uniform, with
spikes and everything and go over there and get the number 5 streetcar
on Sundays. We used to take out bats and balls—a couple of new balls—
and go to Washington Park." Before long, Martínez and his teammates
were "tangling up, playing ball with the Irish." Getting on the streetcar
and heading over to Washington Park is significant because most other
contact between Mexican youth and other ethnic groups within their own
neighborhood of South Chicago usually led to confrontation. In order to
gain regular access to baseball fields and avoid confrontation, many *Mexicanos* felt that they had to leave their regular stomping grounds and go
where anti-Mexican tensions were less pronounced.[1]

For Mexicans in South Chicago during the Great Depression, baseball
was much more than a way to cope while waiting for a job or relief. Gilbert Martínez, Serafin Garcia, Pete Martínez, and Angel Soto may have

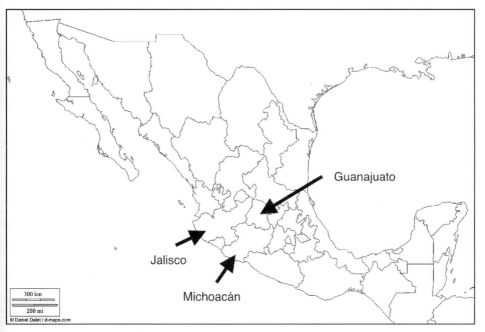

The vast majority of Mexican immigrants to Chicago
before World War II were from three states.

been struggling to survive financially, but when they put on a uniform
and competed against non-Mexican teams or Mexican teams from outside
of South Chicago, they contributed to their community by representing
them and providing a welcome distraction from the realities of daily life.
In addition to the physical activity and sense of community built by the
participants and spectators of teams like the Yaquis, the Mayas, the Excelsiors, and the Atlas, organized sports also provided them the opportunity to become familiar with other neighborhoods and ethnic groups.
This article traces the development of these teams and their leaders from
organizers of recreational activities to organizations that helped coalesce a
Mexican South Chicago identity and provided a means of interaction with
other communities in and around Chicago.[2]

In 1914, a four-year-old Gilbert Martínez and his family left Torreón,
Mexico. His father had been working at a plant when "the revolution,
fighting, came through there." Martinez offered a succinct summary of
the effects of the Mexican Revolution: "Everything stopped and hardship."

Noon Hour, Illinois Steel Company, South Chicago, Ill.

Postcard of Noon Hour at Illinois Steel, c. 1910.

His extended family, which included two of his uncles and their families, traveled to Ciudad Juarez in freight cars. They crossed into El Paso, where the women and children stayed while the men shipped out for seasonal work on railroad crews throughout the American Southwest. Three years after leaving Torreon, the men contracted with an *enganchista*, or labor agent, for railroad work in the Midwest. Gilbert Martinez and his immediate family ended up in Galesburg, Illinois. Nine years later, the Martinez clan moved to South Chicago.[3]

In the twelve years of their journey from Torreón to South Chicago, Martinez and his family experienced several facets common to those who left Mexico and found themselves in the American Midwest. Economic difficulties created by the upheaval of the Mexican Revolution prompted tens of thousands to leave for the United States where they hoped to find work. Mexican men's entry into the United States industrial labor force was overwhelmingly through positions on railroad maintenance crews

Postcard of Steel Mills at Night, South Chicago, c. 1915.

as *traqueros*. Men contracted with *enganchistas* for guaranteed work at and transportation for themselves and their families to railroad company worksites throughout the Midwest.[4]

Mexicanos entering South Chicago saw steel mills and foundries dotting the landscape. For those coming from the Mexican countryside or the sugar beet fields of the Midwest, the incessant smoke from the stacks framed by a gray, polluted sky, the large mill buildings, the stench, the rundown houses, and the soot that covered everything must have been daunting and disorienting. Those entering at night saw smoke rising through the illumination provided by the glare from the furnaces. Also, the slag dumped by the mill onto the banks of Lake Michigan created new "land," adding to the smell of the crowded, working-class neighborhood, which featured, not surprisingly, poor sanitation and wide unpaved streets and alleyways. The steel mills occupied much of the land of the neighborhood and controlled most lakefront property and the area's economy.[5]

Back-of-the-Yards, Near West Side, and South Chicago were the three main Mexican neighborhoods before World War II.

South Chicago Mexicans used recreation, primarily organized sports, not only to persist and persevere, but as a vehicle to create organizations to improve their everyday lives. Important to the survival of the community during the Great Depression, organized leisure time activities and the organizations originally formed to support teams became important catalysts in the formation of community among *Mexicanos* in South Chicago and its leaders during and after the Great Depression. People created a sense of community and pride for their barrio by participating in organized recreational activities. Leaders who emerged from these organizations often advocated for and aided their fellow Mexicans in arenas off the ball field and basketball court.

Those who came to South Chicago during the 1920s and 1930s created a community in order to defend against social, political, and economic harassment and discrimination. Until recently, the assumption of most scholarship on Mexicans in this area was that weak, fractured communities existed within the three major concentrations of Mexicans in Chicago and that no citywide community existed because they tended to stay, work, and play within their neighborhood. However, the community in South Chicago created and maintained ties to area Mexican communities.

In forming communities that were in part shaped by the demands on its members, *Mexicanos* in the other areas of Mexican concentration— Back-of-the-Yards, the Near West Side, and two towns in Indiana, East Chicago and Gary—developed differently than that of South Chicago. Many who settled in South Chicago lived near the gates of the steel mills. Mexicans who chose Back-of-the-Yards did so because of its proximity to work available at the slaughterhouses and the railroads. And others, the majority of those not working in the mills or the slaughterhouses, chose to live in the city's Near West Side neighborhood because of its proximity to industry and downtown service jobs as well as the assistance and amenities available to them at Jane Addams's Hull House. A few of the northwest Indiana cities had sizeable Mexican populations and, unlike the Chicago neighborhoods described above, shared, with South Chicago, the steel industry as the primary employer. Because of the common industry and proximity between South Chicago and these Indiana cities, South Chicago Mexicans frequently interacted with their counterparts in East Chicago and Gary, Indiana. Located on the southern tip of Lake Michigan, East Chicago was only a few miles east of South Chicago, just west of Gary. Mexicans entered both Gary and East Chicago at roughly the same time and rate as they entered South Chicago.[6]

Individuals in South Chicago, including grocery store owner and Yaquis sports club founder Eduardo Peralta, newspaperman and newsstand owner Eustebio Torres, and steelworker Jack Garcia became community leaders and activists through their involvement in organizations that were originally created to support baseball teams. Contemporary scholars who dealt with Mexicans in Chicago during the interwar period assumed that such leadership did not exist—or need to exist—because of a strong consular and settlement-house worker presence. Although settlement-house workers played an important role in the Near West Side and Back-of-the-Yards Mexican communities, the lack of a large, secular settlement house in South Chicago placed a larger burden on community members to lead from within. This need for Mexican leadership became most significant in times of economic crisis, when the dominant society often blamed them for taking jobs from "Americans" and lowered wages by their perceived presence in the workplace.

Historians have defined leisure activities, which include sports and recreation, as those providing personal satisfaction and pleasure, rather than those done for use.[7] Such a simple dichotomy fails to account for the range of responsibilities among Mexicans and thus their varied choices about time away from the workplace, particularly during periods of un-employment. The separation between work and leisure for women, both mothers and older female children who often assisted in the care of siblings, was not as transparent as it was for men. Although many women who worked outside the home lost their jobs during periods of high unemployment during the 1930s, their household duties remained the same or increased as men lost work. These gendered responsibilities, along with cultural mores that circumscribed adolescent girls' and unmarried women's movements to limit unsupervised contact with unrelated boys and men, restricted women's opportunities to participate in organized leisure activities.

The examination of recreation, like other forms of leisure activities, is a useful window into the everyday lives of working-class immigrants and how participants—both active and bystanders—contributed to a sense of community. In the case of Mexican South Chicago, the analysis of these activities provides insight into how immigrant and US-born adults and children reacted to pressures brought by groups both hostile and friendly to force them to assimilate, or "Americanize." Employers and city leaders attempted to control and contain *Mexicanos* to specific fields of employment and geographic areas of the city while trying to Americanize them. In so doing, members of the larger, white community sought to control this group by keeping them within certain community, workplace, and recreational boundaries.[8]

In South Chicago, park staff, community center staff, and volunteers who came from outside of the barrio primarily organized youth sports. Leaders from within the Chicago-area Mexican community—such as Eustebio Torres and Eduardo Peralta—organized the men's athletic teams and leagues, rarely working in concert with the outside agencies that promoted youth activities. Under local leadership, men's organizations that began as baseball or basketball teams quickly grew into multifaceted associations with influence and importance far beyond the playing fields and courts. These organizations had a significant direct and indirect influence on the welfare of the community. In investigating interwar leisure time activities such as organized sports and social gatherings, several things become clear. First, Chicago-area Mexicans, including those in northwest Indiana, were not isolated from each other. Second, leaders emerged from within barrios to create organizations that improved quality of life and advocated for their constituents' needs and concerns. Third, despite the rigors and drudgery of workplace and home labor, leisure time activities played a central role in *Mexicano* life.[9]

Chicago's extensive public park system was fundamental in providing Mexicans with amenities, such as shower facilities, recreation, and recreational space for adults and families, including organized, supervised activities for the community's youth. A considerable amount of time passed before other ethnic groups—and in some cases park staff—allowed *Mexicanos* free and unrestricted access to area parks. The all-too-common ethnic turf wars throughout South Chicago and the racial and ethnic discrimination that existed within the park system limited Mexican access to parks and recreational facilities through the early 1930s.[10]

The lack of park access was a significant impediment for young Mexicans. In a 1928 study on Chicago's park system, Marian Osborn asserted that play and recreation were critical for adults as well as children. She argued that parks were not only a character-building necessity for children but also an important outlet for adults. Children's play was more than just "natural and necessary," she maintained; skillfully supervised and directed play was "one of the most powerful agencies in character building." Access to parks and recreational activities was also important for adults who needed diversion from the "drudgery and drabness" of the industrial workplace.[11]

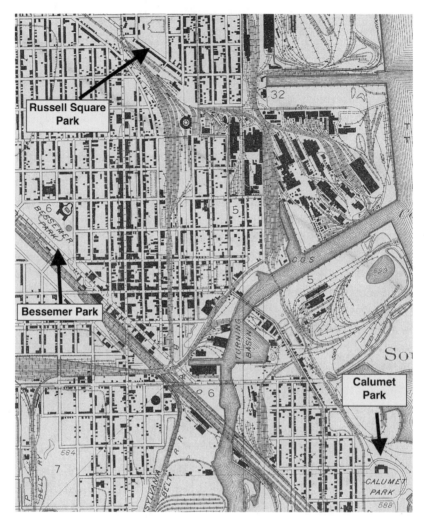

South Chicago Neighborhood Parks. Map courtesy of the University of Chicago Library's Map Collection, home of the original 7.5-minute series (topographic): Chicago and vicinity. Washington, DC: Geological Survey; Urbana, IL: Geological Survey Division, 1928–1929.

Although public parks are best known for open fields and play equipment, many Mexicans found Bessemer Park through necessity. While
growing up in a family of six children in South Chicago during the 1920s,
Anthony Romo, along with his family, utilized the park's shower facilities
as a practical necessity. The time and difficulty of having to warm up bath-
water for six children on a kitchen stove made the Park shower facilities
an indispensable amenity. By the late 1920s, Mexicans, primarily adults,
were using Bessemer Park shower facilities at a rate of seventy-five per
day in the summer and fifteen per day in the winter. By 1927—despite
interethnic hostility—Chicago-area Mexicans were using Bessemer Park
for organized Mexican Independence Day celebrations and for the staging
of Spanish-language plays in the fieldhouse auditorium. Yet records show
that only two Mexican children participated in organized park activities in
1927. The park director reasoned that the lack of youth in park activities
was because the facility was too far from their homes. However, the primary reason that young Mexicans avoided Bessemer Park in the 1920s was
intimidation by youth of other ethnic groups. Gilbert Martínez recalled
he and his friends would frequently "get beat up by the guys that would
hang around there, the *Polackos* I guess, I don't know who the hell they
were." These youth, Martínez explained, came from "around from where
the police station" was and controlled the park. As with Bessemer, Spanish
speakers were not welcome at Calumet Park throughout the 1920s.[12]

During the Great Depression, parks became an escape from the economic crisis for unemployed adults and their families, thus increasing the
Mexican community's determination to use the parks despite hostile attitudes by park officials and others who frequented the parks. For many,
access to the parks, whether for team sports, family outings, or simply an
evening stroll, was important for the physical and psychological survival.
Of the South Chicago parks, Mexicans used Bessemer Park more than
any other during the height of the Great Depression. Bessemer's facilities
included a field house, gymnasium, auditorium, outdoor swimming pool,
wading pool, playground and athletic field, branch library, tennis courts,
and a toy lending service. Other area parks frequented by Mexicans included Russell Square Park, Calumet Park, and several facilities in northwest Indiana.[13]

South Chicago's community centers did not have the human, social, and financial resources of the Near West Side's Hull House or the Back-of-the-Yards' University of Chicago Settlement House. In a 1928 study, Anita Edgar Jones argued that, unlike the two other major Mexican communities in Chicago, those living in South Chicago were left to their "own organization" when it came to recreation. The religious affiliations of South Chicago's community centers were also important factors in distinguishing the resources available between the various Mexican neighborhoods. Though not entirely left to their own devices, as Jones suggests they were, members of South Chicago's Mexican community played a more active role in organizing and promoting recreational activities than did members of the other barrios due to the inequality of resources.[14]

The South Chicago Community Center, also referred to as Bird Memorial, located at Ninety-First Street and Brandon Avenue, was established in 1923 and was financially supported by the Chicago Congregational Union, a fact that eventually led the Catholic Church to ban the faithful from utilizing the center's gymnasium and activity rooms. Another important institution that was also off-limits was the Baptist-funded South Chicago Neighborhood House, at Eighty-Fourth Street and Mackinaw Avenue. Priests and nuns told *Mexicano* youths that using the facilities or participating in organized activities at the above institutions and the Y.M.C.A. was sinful because of the institutions' Protestant affiliation.[15]

South Chicagoan José Cruz Díaz recalled being confronted by Father James F. Tort, the parish priest at Our Lady of Guadalupe Church, for using the recreational facilities at Bird Memorial, "Father Tort said that it would be a mortal sin if we went to the Congregational church." Tort defined going to the Bird Memorial not only as a sin, but also as a major one that put an individual's soul at risk. Cruz Díaz continued to go to Bird Memorial to play organized basketball for teams such as the Elks and the Mayas because of the facilities and because he felt he was treated, "awful nice . . . in fact we had the run of the place." With the ethnic tension and discrimination at public parks and other area facilities, the fact that Mexican teens "had the run" of the recreational facilities at Bird Memorial was indeed significant. Cruz Díaz understood that Father Tort and church officials were trying to keep them away from Bird because "hanging around the Protestants was a sin . . ." Cruz Diaz did not see the logic in such a policy because he and his friends had little, if any, contact with the pastor and believed that Bird Memorial's motive was simply to keep them off the street. Despite the fact that many Mexican youth and families adhered to the Catholic Church's order, many—Catholic as well as Protestant—frequented Bird Memorial because of its resources, the staff's outreach into the barrio, the comfortable, nondiscriminatory atmosphere of the center, and a lack of comparable Catholic-run facilities in the neighborhood.[16]

In contrast, the director of Common Ground, Rev. Raymond Sanford, was able to establish and maintain a cooperative relationship with the Catholic Church despite Congregational Church sponsorship. Unlike the city's public parks, Bird Memorial, and the South Chicago Neighborhood House, Common Ground was an organization run out of a small office at 3029 East Ninety-First Street. Sanford, general director of cultural activities of the local Congregational churches, was given $250,000 by the Chicago Congregational Union "to erect buildings to start and carry on this constructive cultural work" within South Chicago. Instead, Sanford developed a sort of "welfare clearinghouse" for members of the community. Common Ground worked among the various racial and ethnic groups in the neighborhood.[17]

Sanford's organized recreational activities for neighborhood youth included field trips to local museums, libraries, stock shows, automobile shows, the Adler Planetarium, the Chicago Historical Society, and other "events of importance [that] occurred during the year, including ball games." Sanford gained access to seven Catholic churches as well as most Protestant facilities to use their recreational halls in order to accomplish its primary mission: human-welfare work. Common Ground used whatever was available for recreation. This included "old buildings, woodsheds, garages, etc.," and on rainy days "some of the activities [were] carried on under the sidewalks which are very much in the nature of tunnels."[18]

With the Works Progress Administration (WPA) financing much of the equipment and personnel needed for recreational activities, Common Ground organized many youth activities, including basketball, baseball, football, soccer, chess, checkers, photography, and crafts. WPA workers and University of Chicago students played a significant role within the preexisting organizations in planning and supervising youth activities throughout South Chicago.[19]

Women and girls faced many obstacles and hardships when it came to leisure time activities. Socials hosted by girls' clubs at Bird Memorial, although supervised by staff members, provided a venue for adolescent boys and girls to meet without parents or other family members being present—something frowned upon within the more traditional *Mexicano* circles. The cultural expectations within the community facilitated limitations that husbands and parents put on the behavior and the types of work women and girls participated in. They also placed limits on the social behavior of women and girls. Many husbands and parents restricted the freedoms of wives and girls in much the same way that nineteenth-century American reformers attempted to control the behavior of the flood of women entering the industrial workplace. They believed that Mexican women and girls needed protection from a more Americanized ethnic population that perpetuated evils of society such as promiscuity and the breakdown of the patriarchal household.[20]

The perceived need to protect young women and girls from the "evils of society" was not limited to the Mexican community of South Chicago. Mary Odem, for example, argues that campaigns to protect the morals of young women in the United States had been around since urbanization and industrialization. Although these earlier campaigns focused on the moral protection of middle-class, white, American young women who worked outside of the home, advocates set up missions in working-class neighborhood in order to provide an evangelical Protestant–inspired ministry. Although these campaigns were national, they reflect what was going on in the Chicago area, and eventually in the area's Mexican communities. Even as many of the morality-based restrictions placed on Mexican women and girls came from within the community, South Chicago Protestant missions played a role through their neighborhood-based recreation and Americanization programs.[21]

Historian George J. Sánchez points out that Mexican women in Los Angeles were targeted for early twentieth-century cultural assimilation programs. Just as American men had backed the education of nineteenth-century American women because of their role as mothers and caretakers of future citizens in their sons, assimilationists used the ideals of republican motherhood to target Mexican immigrant women for integration into society because of their prominent role in the domestic sphere, including housework and raising children. Those wanting to Americanize Mexicans believed that Mexican immigrant women had the greatest ability to either "advance [their] family into the modern, industrial order of the United States" or to "inhibit them from becoming productive American citizens." Simultaneously, many male and female immigrants within the Mexican community believed that women had the primary responsibility of maintaining cultural traditions. Despite the fact that Sánchez's focus is on the Mexican community of Los Angeles, these Americanization and cultural concepts were not foreign to Chicago-area Mexicans and assimilationists.[22]

In Mexican Chicago, like elsewhere, husbands and parents were anxious about the "Americanization" of their wives and daughters because of increased independence that, they believed, would lead to a greater opportunity for social and sexual autonomy. Participation in social and leisure time activities undermined familial control by creating a youth culture where daughters explored romantic relationships away from the watchful eye of parents and relatives. Parents attempted to control coeducational interaction in schools and during leisure activities. Socorro Zaragoza, an elementary school student in nearby Gary, Indiana, complained that her father would not let her do anything because "he is afraid I will be like Americans." She protested that although—or perhaps because—her father had been in the Chicago area for sixteen years, he did not want her hanging around American girls because they "go out alone, talk back to their parents and don't help their mothers." She then reasoned that her father was right because he had seen how "American girls treat their mothers." Furthermore, Zaragoza's father excused her from gymnasium class because he believed it was immoral and only let her attend movies or social gatherings two or three times a year when he came along as chaperone.[23]

Parents expected adolescent girls to be accompanied by either a parent or older brother to social events involving adolescent boys or men. "I like to belong to the club because we get a chance to meet other girls and we have a lot of fun when we have our socials," stated a girl interviewed at

Bird Memorial in the mid-1930s. She mentioned they invited boys but emphasized that it was not open to the public, only to boys who were members of a club that met at Bird. "On these occasions no parents are invited," she continued, "That's why we girls have so much fun. We don't have anybody watching us." These girls also resisted demands from parents that younger sisters participate in club meetings and parties. As with the issue of women working outside of the home, more traditional parents "viewed with alarm" the fact that other neighborhood residents allowed the attendance of unchaperoned women and girls at social events.[24]

Generational differences existed between the older Mexican immigrants and their offspring, whether the children were born in Mexico or the United States. While many men assimilated only to the extent necessary to get and keep a job, the children were less worried about negotiating the cultural obstacles between being Mexican and being "American." When not using the facilities at a park or a community center, boys and girls organized their own recreational activities to emulate "what other American kids did." These activities included using cardboard or barrel sheaves to sled in the winter and broomsticks and smashed cans to play street hockey in the summer. Playing games with tops and marbles were also popular activities. Other activities for the boys included going to "Eggers Grove," a recreational and picnic area on the east side of the neighborhood that had wooded areas. Anthony Romo recalled doing "whatever boys did in a field of strictly woods. Play around, Tarzan or Daniel Boone, or whatever. Then [we would] come home late at night." Swimming and fishing in Calumet Park or in a small lake behind US Steel, going on bicycle trips, and making visits to a nearby dump to hunt for things of value were also common summer activities. The fact that first- and second-generation kids played previously unheard of games such as street hockey, Tarzan, and Daniel Boone underscores the generational rifts between children and parents in their attitudes toward acculturation into American society.[25]

Men and boys had many more opportunities to participate in team sports than did women and girls. The Chicago Park System, Bird Memorial, Common Ground, and the Catholic Youth Organization (CYO) at Our Lady of Guadalupe were the primary institutional organizers of youth baseball and basketball teams in South Chicago. Many youth first discovered Bird Memorial and Common Ground because of their baseball programs. Staff and volunteers at these organizations coached, officiated, and organized tournaments where participants took home trophies and reserved playing courts and fields for games. South Chicago's Mexican boys and girls also traveled to the Back-of-the-Yards and the Near West Side neighborhoods to participate in settlement house–sponsored activities, team sports, and tournaments. The settlement houses serving these neighborhoods, the University of Chicago Settlement House for the former and Hull House the latter, provided the large Mexican communities in their neighborhoods with group activities and leagues that in many cases were exclusively Mexican. Older boys who participated in baseball leagues also coached junior baseball teams. These teams, rarely lasting more than a single season, provided further interaction within the community as the junior teams played local and area teams, Mexican and non-Mexican. In addition to baseball leagues organized by social service organizations and settlement houses, Mexican boys in South Chicago organized their own pickup baseball games and softball leagues with teams named after the streets they lived on, such as the Baltimore Aces and the Buffalo Braves.[26]

Although little information exists about organized sports leagues for girls, 1934 Spanish-language newspaper articles mention the presence of Mexican girls' basketball teams. One article stated that "the year of 1934 has unusually awakened the youth from both sexes to the basketball attraction" with the girls' teams "both being of first magnitude" and playing a "clean cut game" with a final score of 18-8. Although played at the University of Chicago Settlement House in the Back-of-the-Yards neighborhood, the teams consisted entirely of *Mexicanas*, some of whom undoubtedly lived in South Chicago.[27]

Aside from the physical activity and sense of community built by the participants and spectators of the games, organized sporting activities provided the opportunity for barrio residents to become familiar with other neighborhoods and ethnic groups. Although Mexicans in South Chicago were not isolated from communities around them, local youth traveling to sporting events visited ethnic communities that they would otherwise avoid. One of the first Mexican boys' basketball teams, organized by a group of five friends and sponsored by Bird Memorial, was the Southern

Arrows. Pete Martínez, an original member of the team, remembers "traveling everywhere." From Bird Memorial, Martínez was exposed to a range of communities: "Oak Park, Villa Park, wherever they would tell us to go play, we would go play." José Cruz Díaz, another member of the team, remembers traveling all over Chicago playing basketball: "If we couldn't go [or] get somebody to take us, we used to take the streetcar to all these places." He added, "We went to some places that had never seen Mexicans at all whatsoever, and they used to ask us, 'Are you Mexican?' We said, 'Yeah.' We were like an exhibit."[28]

The idea of being treated like an exhibit highlighted the perception that Mexicans were outsiders and unequal to members of the white and ethnic European communities of Chicago. Martínez, nevertheless, credits the basketball team with making players aware "that there were other neighborhoods, other people, other groups." For many Mexican youth, their street had been their "whole world." Paralleling the experiences of other ethnic youth who grew up in Chicago, the fact that Mexican teams sometimes traveled out of the neighborhood to compete against other ethnic teams undermined the potential isolation of *Mexicano* youth.[29]

The Catholic Church's ban on the use of Bird Memorial forced the Southern Arrows to disassociate themselves with their home court. Father Catalina, who at the time was a priest at St. Francis of Assisi, the Mexican Catholic Church in the city's Near West Side neighborhood, confronted team leaders Pete Martínez and Angel Soto. In attempting to get members of the South Chicago community to use a Catholic facility that Catalina established on the Near West Side, the good father reminded the boys that Bird Memorial was not a Catholic church. In response, they decided to cut the club's ties to Bird Memorial: "Instead of going against him, we'll just break up and do it on our own on the outside. Which we did." After the separation, Martínez regretted the decision, and the team disbanded a short time later. South Chicago community organizations continued to create youth baseball and basketball teams with the height of their popularity coming during the pinnacle of the Depression.[30]

Meanwhile, leaders of South Chicago's Mexican community created, advocated for, and managed community-based organizations originally formed to support men's baseball and basketball teams. Baseball was the most popular team activity and spectator sport, peaking in popularity and participation during the Depression and as a result of high unemployment and sporadic work. Because Mexican baseball teams were unable to use Bessemer Park until the late 1920s, earlier squads practiced and played in nearby open prairies. Not until 1929, with a flood of immigration to the area, did the group make inroads regarding park access. It took the Great Depression and the large number of unemployed adults to open Bessemer Park completely to all *Mexicanos*. By the turn of that decade, baseball games in Bessemer Park involving local teams regularly drew upward of one thousand people. Access to the other South Chicago public parks, Calumet and Russell Square, followed a similar timeline.[31]

Unable to find work and not wanting to remain at home, men in the community, like Jack García, created and joined baseball teams. García remembered having a full life even when unemployed, playing baseball in the summer and basketball in winter. Manuel Bravo, an out-of-work steelworker, concisely summed up his experience during the Depression: "There was nothing, no work, no nothing. The only recreation was playing baseball and more baseball, basketball and more basketball. So we turned out a lot of great baseball players and basketball players." Organized sports were clearly a central part of the everyday lives for unemployed Mexican men.[32]

The Depression did not significantly improve recreational and leisure time for women. Although they participated by supporting the male athletes of the community through attendance at games and added domestic responsibilities, the vast majority of women did not have the recreational opportunities or the leisure time despite the popularity of the athletic clubs.

Leaders of South Chicago's Mexican community were responsible for organizing baseball and basketball teams that grew into larger, multidimensional organizations and eventually became critical cogs in the well-being of the community. Owner of one of the first grocery stores to serve the South Chicago Mexican community, Eduardo Peralta not only organized and managed a baseball team, but also recruited others to start their own teams. He founded the Club Deportivo Yaquis in 1932. According to one participant, the name was chosen after they "found out most of the players were from Sonora," a home of the Yaqui Indians. As chair of the Club Deportivo Yaquis, Peralta characterized his club in a 1936 WPA interview as having thirty-five members, meeting once a month during the winter and meeting often during the summer. The organization eventually expanded to include a basketball, football, and "indoor-ball" team. Aside from the transparent benefits to the community of having a locally run team that brought people together for games, the importance of the organization to the community became more pronounced after the Yaquis sponsored fund-raising dances several times a year to raise money to buy uniforms and equipment.[33]

The Yaquis provided "no educational training, except that which is connected with our line of work." Although team members had been working at the steel mills before being laid off, the type of training mentioned by Peralta is open to speculation. Despite that fact that the Yaquis did not serve as a mutual aid society by collecting dues and providing guaranteed benefits in case of death or injury, team members helped other members when they were ill or were injured while playing for the team. Claiming that the organization's aim was "to do right in every way possible to the community, and to procure the welfare of our members at the same time," Peralta mentioned that the Yaquis had ties to the Club Deportivo Monterrey of South Chicago, also founded in 1932, and the Sociedad Pro-Mexico, an organization dedicated to promoting Mexican culture and patriotic holidays. The Yaquis were also members of the South Chicago Chamber of Commerce. Peralta significantly underestimated the overall significance of the club and its activities to the community by only emphasizing the benefits of their being free entertainment and an economic boost by purchasing team equipment within the barrio.[34]

By the mid-1930s, multipurpose clubs were more common. Although the Club Deportivo Monterrey remained a one-sport club (baseball), by 1936 it consisted of thirty members and held "social festivals" four times a year. Unlike the Yaquis, Club Deportivo Monterrey did serve as a mutual aid society. Members of Club Deportivo Monterrey paid ten cents a week to enroll in a disability plan that paid members two dollars and fifty cents a week for up to four weeks if unable to work because of sickness or accident.[35]

Like the Yaquis, the Pirates baseball team was an organization originally formed by members of the community, without help from non-Mexican
groups. Started around 1927 by a group that included Gilbert Martínez
and Angel Soto, the Pirates experienced firsthand the discrimination of
other ethnic groups and park officials that limited their access to Bessemer
Park.[36] These groups and officials forced the team to practice and play on
sandlots and open prairies until team members discovered the baseball
fields at Washington Park.[37]

Baseball became more popular with local Mexicans as the Depression
deepened. Members of the community were no longer working twelve- to
fourteen-hour shifts, six days a week. As the number of people playing
and watching baseball games grew, the Pirates merged with another team.
Eustebio Torres, owner of a local newsstand and publisher of the short-
lived *Anunciador* newspaper, named the new team the Excelsiors, after
the major Mexico City newspaper that could be found on his newsstand.
Team members speculated that Torres's motivation for choosing the name
was a hope that the *Excelsior* newspaper would cover his team and pay
more attention to the *Mexicanos* of Chicago. As the larger organization
that revolved around the baseball team took shape, the Excelsiors created
a board of directors, president, vice president, and other officers, including nonplaying members whose duties were to contribute "to the welfare
of the team." Like the Yaquis and the Monterrey sports clubs, the Excelsior
club held regular dances to raise funds. The organization eventually expanded to include an acting club that put on a production at J. N. Thorpe
School, a local public school. The drama drew the attention, attendance,
and support of members of the Board of Education as well as the Mexican
Consul. The Atlas and the Mayas, like the Excelsiors and the Yaquis, are
teams with lasting legacies that remain part of barrio lore to this day.[38]

In "The Playing Fields of St. Louis," historian Gary Ross Mormino
highlights the importance of sports (primarily soccer, football, baseball,
and basketball), and organizations that contributed to the success of the
teams, in the development and preservation of an Italian culture in St.
Louis. Mormino, while focusing on the years between 1925 and US entry
into World War II, argued that "sport encouraged not only the preservation of an ethnic subculture, but the preservation of the community

itself."[39] Sports played a significant role in unifying a historically divided Italian immigrant community. In addition, he argues, the neighborhood athletic federation that emerged from the community's interest in sports became a "powerful signal of ethnic group identity."[40] A significant difference between Italians in St. Louis and Mexicans in South Chicago was the level of racial discrimination experienced by both groups. Although working-class Italians did face discrimination in St. Louis, they had reached a level of whiteness that remained elusive to Mexican immigrants.

In *Making Lemonade out of Lemons*, historian José M. Alamillo argues that Mexicans in Corona, California, were able to use community baseball and sports clubs for a variety of purposes, including community formation. Unlike in South Chicago, the earliest Mexican teams and leagues in Corona were organized by large employers with the expressed goal of Americanizing and instilling discipline in Mexican workers. Within short order, *Mexicano* "sports clubs, mutual aid organizations, churches and small businesses" were creating teams and forming leagues. The most significant difference between these two communities is in the evolution of these teams and organizations. In Corona, dynamic preexisting organizations created baseball teams while Chicago support organizations were created either simultaneously or after the creation of the baseball team.[41]

According to historian Douglas Monroy, *Mexicano* baseball in Los Angeles started as a "high society" sport as early as 1916. "Because of the high level of competition and the number of teams, a cross-section of Mexican social classes undoubtedly took to the field together" in Los Angeles.[42] The first of these developments did not happen in Chicago possibly because of the minuscule number educated and "high society" Mexicans in the Second City and newness of the Mexican migration to Chicago, especially in comparison to cities, like Los Angeles, that had once been part of Mexico. As for Monroy's second point, a "cross-section of Mexican social classes" in Chicago was involved in baseball, but no evidence exists that members outside of the working class "took the field." Keep in mind that Chicago's cross-section was much more of a bottom-heavy triangle than in Los Angeles. One other interesting difference in Monroy's Los Angeles from Chicago or Corona is the role of businesses. Unlike employer-initiated teams and leagues in Corona, teams in Los Angeles were organized and sponsored by local business. Although South Chicago Mexican business owners were involved in organizing teams and leagues, teams were supported primarily by the organizations created by team members and boosters, and by local businesses to a lesser extent. Additionally, team names were not predominantly named after businesses while some neighborhood businesses were named after popular teams.[43]

Once community leaders created more teams throughout Chicago's three major Mexican communities, as well as in Northwest Indiana, they formed leagues. The teams used at least one enclosed park, in Indiana Harbor, where minimal entry fees could be charged to raise funds for the teams. Game attendance by community members was impressive. Cruz Díaz, a member of the Mayas, boasted about being a member of "one of the best baseball teams in South Chicago." During the height of the depression, the boys baseball team would draw upward of one thousand spectators in Bessemer Park as they played almost daily. "We had nothing else to do," he recalled. He reasoned that because of lack of jobs and "work was very slow," members of the community traveled throughout Chicago and Northwest Indiana by truck or by foot to watch the team play. According to a newspaper report, over twenty-five hundred spectators witnessed the Club Deportivo Monterrey defeat the Drexel Square Athletic Club in Washington Park in September 1933. Because of the popularity and quality of the Excelsior and Atlas baseball teams, they traveled "over the middle west as semi-professional teams." Mexican-owned small businesses in South Chicago and the other area barrios named their businesses after popular local teams to capitalize on the teams' success and the high level of community pride.[44]

Cruz Díaz credits the Great Depression for strengthening the community through sports. Others felt that the sports teams and the organizations that sprang up to support teams and leagues did more than just boost morale and foster a sense of unity among Mexicans throughout Chicago and Northwest Indiana. They believed that the quality of the basketball and baseball teams in South Chicago earned them respect among some anti-Mexican elements in the Polish community. Sidney Levin, a classmate and friend of several of the Mexican athletes during this period, agreed that there was more respect for the ballplayers. Speaking of "Polish roughnecks," Levin explained that these roughnecks, who "used to be out to get one or two lonely guys that used to walk to the game, stopped it completely." Levin argues that this was not "due to the respect or the fear of the numbers of the people who came to the game" but because of the quality of the games that were being played.[45]

Although the influence and respect that these organizations fostered because of the quality of the teams' athletic performances, the influence of organizations such as the Yaquis, the Excelsiors, the Atlas, and the Monterrey extended far beyond the diamond and the court. The most visible nonsports activity sponsored by these organizations were the dances and concerts that organization leaders held to raise funds for expenses related to team equipment and activities. These dances and concerts widened the influence and importance of these organizations by providing venues for recreation and facilitated social gatherings that allowed community members, as well as some people from outside the community, to expand social networks, including interethnic relationships. Although the organizations were not the only groups holding dances and concerts, they were usually the most widely anticipated and attended because of the popularity of the teams and their athletes' status in the community. Several venues existed for these dances. In the South Chicago area these included the basement of the Steel City Bank, Croatian Hall, the Masonic Temple, Columbus Hall, Lillian Hall, Eagles Hall, and Lincoln Hall, not to mention "wherever they figured they could make the most money, or the place was available." South Chicago Mexicans also attended dances at Hull House's Bowen Hall. Organizers put on dances as part of festivals that included basketball tournaments involving teams from different Mexican communities. The first two musical groups that played at these dances were the Cubanos and the Royal Castilians, both all-Mexican bands. As the organizations sponsored an increasing number of dances, the number of youth and adult bands quickly grew.[46]

Clearly, the sports-centered organizations served several functions within the South Chicago barrio. These groups facilitated social activities for adults and youth and provided the opportunity for better communication and fellowship within and between the Mexican clusters of the Chicago area. Because of the respected status of the teams and athletes in the community, these organizations quickly—and successfully—expanded to provide other services and diversions for the community during time of crisis.

As a result of their need to expand the space available to them for leisure activities during the interwar years, Mexicans in South Chicago rallied around organized sports. As team activities occupied a growing amount of leisure time, the organizations grew in importance and influence despite the fact that ethnic prejudice, gender inequalities, and lack of resources created physical, economic, and psychological boundaries. Leaders emerged and used their sports teams and organizations as vehicles to push beyond their externally imposed boundaries and claim their rights as residents of this country. Organizations like the South Chicago Community Center and Common Ground were important organizers, but members of the community took the initiative to push the externally imposed boundaries and establish teams. The teams evolved into multifunctional organizations that proved to be anchors for many *Mexicanos* who struggled financially and psychologically to remain and persist during the Great Depression and the repatriation movement. Consequently, these clubs, their organizers, and the participants improved their community's quality of life during and long after the Great Depression.

Notes

1. Gilbert Martínez, interview by Jesse Escalante, March 17, 1980, tape recording, Jesse Escalante Oral Histories (JEOH), Global Communities Collection, Chicago Historical Society, Chicago. Labels, as always, are problematic. Throughout the essay I use "Mexican" or "*Mexicano*" to identify Mexican immigrants and Americans of Mexican descent who preferred to identify as Mexican; these were the most common terms among the community's mostly working-class population. The term "white" describe non-Mexican, white residents of the United States. Southern and Eastern European immigrants are sometimes included as part of a "white" category when the context emphasized Mexicans against all non-Mexicans. I use "barrio" and "Mexican neighborhood" to identify areas with a cluster of Mexicans. My definition of "community" is much more specific. When people share a culture, resources,

and the use of physical spaces in a single geographical location, they form community not only when they interact with one another but when they consider themselves part of the group; they must also believe that they share a common bond and concern for one another.

2. For a discussion on the importance of *Mexicanos* in the Los Angeles area, see Douglas Monroy, *Rebirth: Mexican Los Angeles from the Great Migration to the Great Depression* (Berkeley: University of California Press, 1999), 46–48.

3. Martínez, interview.

4. Jeffrey Marcos Garcilazo, "'Traqueros': Mexican Railroad Workers in the United States, 1870–1930" (PhD diss., University of California, Santa Barbara, 1995), 68; Mark Reisler, *By the Sweat of Their Brow: Mexican Immigrant Labor in the United States, 1900–1940* (Westport, CT: Greenwood Press, 1976), 14–17; Vicki L. Ruiz, *From out of the Shadows: Mexican Women in Twentieth-Century America* (Oxford: Oxford University Press, 1998), 7. Garcilazo argues that railroad companies used Mexican Americans in New Mexico as early as 1871. Railroad company use of Mexican immigrant and Mexican American labor in the Southwest was common by the 1880s (74–75). For more on the use of Mexicans by railroad companies, see Zaragosa Vargas, *Proletarians of the North: A History of Mexican Industrial Workers in Detroit and the Midwest, 1917–1933* (Berkeley: University of California Press, 1993), 34–41.

5. James R. Grossman, *Land of Hope: Chicago, Black Southerners, and the Great Migration* (Chicago: University of Chicago Press, 1989), 113.

6. Gabriela F. Arredondo, *Mexican Chicago: Race, Identity and Nation, 1916–1939* (Champaign: University of Illinois Press, 2008).

7. Jeffrey Hill, *Sport, Leisure, and Culture in Twentieth-Century Britain* (New York: Palgrave, 2002), 6.

8. See Allen Guttmann, "Sport, Politics, and the Engaged Historian," *Journal of Contemporary History* 38, no. 3 (July 2003): 363–75; for a helpful discussion of politics, sports, and the role of historians in linking the two.

9. For more on the interconnectedness of Chicago's Mexican neighborhoods, see Louise Año Nuevo Kerr, "The Chicano Experience in Chicago: 1920–1970" (PhD diss., University of Illinois at Chicago Circle, 1976); Arredondo, *Mexican Chicago*; Michael Innis-Jiménez, "Persisting in the Shadow of Steel: Community Formation and Survival in Mexican South Chicago, 1919–1939" (PhD diss., University of Iowa, 2006).

10. Max Guzman, interview by Jesse Escalante, February 7, 1980, JEOH; Anthony Romo, interview by Jesse Escalante, December 28, 1981, tape recording, JEOH; Anita Edgar Jones, "Conditions Surrounding Mexicans in Chicago" (master's thesis, University of Chicago, 1928), 72–73; Jesse John Escalante, "History of the Mexican Community in South Chicago" (master's thesis, Northeastern Illinois University, 1982), 23; Sidney Levin, interview by Jesse Escalante, May 29, 1980, JEOH; Martínez, interview.

11. Marian Lorena Osborn, "The Development of Recreation in the South Park System of Chicago" (master's thesis, University of Chicago, 1928), 1–2.

12. Romo, interview; Levin, interview; Jones, "Conditions Surrounding Mexicans," 72–73; Escalante, "Mexican South Chicago," 23; Martínez, interview. Chicago-area Mexican youth frequently referred to working-class European immigrants (other than the Irish and Italian) as "Polish," regardless of their national origin.

13. Guzman, interview; *Leisure Time Directory* (Chicago: n.p., 1940), 133–34. The city of Chicago listed Russell Square Park and Rocky Ledge Park as the other two public parks within the South Chicago neighborhood.

14. Jones, "Conditions Surrounding Mexicans," 72.

15. Levin, interview; Martínez, interview; *Leisure Time Directory*; Arthur J. Todd, William F. Byron, and Howard L. Vierow, *The Chicago Recreation Survey: Private Recreation*, 5 vols. (Chicago: Chicago Recreation Commission and Northwestern University, 1937), 3:27. Henry Seymour Brown et al., "Report of the Committee on Findings Set Up by the Comity Commission of the Chicago Federation of Churches on the Survey of South Chicago by the Department of Research and Survey under the Direction of Professor Holt" (1928), Comity Committee Folder, box 9 (new), Chicago Church Federation Papers, Chicago Historical Society, 3.

16. Jose Cruz Díaz, interview by Jesse Escalante, October 12, 1979, JEOH; Levin, interview. For more on the struggle between the Roman Catholic Church and Protestant churches over the "hearts and minds" of Mexican Chicagoans, see Anne M. Martínez, "Bordering on the Sacred: Religion, Nation, and U.S.-Mexican Relations, 1910–1929" (PhD diss., University of Minnesota, 2003), and Malachy Richard McCarthy, "Which Christ Came to Chicago: Catholic and Protestant Programs to Evangelize, Socialize, and Americanize the Mexican Immigrant, 1900–1940" (PhD diss., Loyola University, 2002).

17. Raymond Sanford, interview by Victor Chavez, December 8, 1936, Box 40,

Foreign Language Press Survey, University of Chicago Special Collections, Chicago; Todd et al., *Chicago Recreation Survey*, 3:158. The Recreational Survey states that Common Ground served twenty-six nationalities, with members of the Polish community predominating.

18. Sanford, interview; Todd et al., *Chicago Recreation Survey*, 3:158.

19. Cruz Díaz, interview; Sanford, interview.

20. Francisco Huerta, in Paul S. Taylor Papers, Bancroft Library, University of California, box 11, file 32, June 1928; Vargas, *Proletarians*, 133–34. On Mexican perceptions of the dangers of the dominant US culture, see Ruiz, *From Out of the Shadows*, chap. 2. Arredondo, *Mexican Chicago*, chap. 4, explores these dynamics for Mexicans in Chicago as a whole.

21. Mary E. Odem, *Delinquent Daughters: Protecting and Policing Adolescent Female Sexuality in the United States, 1885–1920* (Chapel Hill: University of North Carolina Press, 1995), 1. For the experiences of ethnic European women immigrants in Chicago, see Joanne J. Meyerowitz, *Women Adrift: Independent Wage Earners in Chicago, 1880–1930* (Chicago: University of Chicago Press, 1988). Directories of general social services and recreational facilities list several Protestant-run programs and sites; Catholic programs specifically for Mexicans did not appear in South Chicago until the late 1930s. Kerr, "Chicano Experience," 57–58; Brown et al., "Comity Report"; *Leisure Time Directory*; Todd et al., *Chicago Recreation Survey*.

22. George J. Sánchez, " 'Go After the Women': Americanization and the Mexican Immigrant Woman, 1915–1929," in *Unequal Sisters: A Multicultural Reader in U.S. Women's History*, ed. Vicki L. Ruiz and Ellen Carol Dubois (New York: Routledge, 1994), 284; Arredondo, *Mexican Chicago*, 88–90. Linda Kerber first named this concept "republican motherhood" in relation to white women's roles in the early Republic. More recent scholarship has expanded the idea of republican motherhood to one of republican womanhood to include other women's roles. For more on this, see Catherine Allgor, *Parlor Politics: In Which the Ladies of Washington Help Build a City and a Government* (Charlottesville: University Press of Virginia, 2000).

23. Socorro Zaragoza, interview by Paul S. Taylor, box 11, file 32, Paul S. Taylor Papers. Arredondo, *Mexican Chicago*, 119–25; Vicki Ruiz, " 'Star Struck': Acculturation, Adolescence, and the Mexican American Woman, 1920–1950," in *Building with Our Hands: New Directions in Chicana Studies*, ed. Adela

de la Torre and Beatriz Pesquera (Berkeley: University of California Press, 1993).

24. Edward Jackson Baur, "Delinquency among Mexican Boys in South Chicago" (master's thesis, University of Chicago, 1938), 55, 98; Levin, interview; Ruiz, *From out of the Shadows*. Ruiz provides a thorough examination of the conflicts between Mexican parents and their daughters in the Southwest caused by the girls' "Americanization," particularly in social activities.

25. Cruz Díaz, interview; Romo, interview; Escalante, "Mexican South Chicago," 28; Baur, "Delinquency," 171.

26. Escalante, "Mexican South Chicago," 28; Romo, interview; Baur, "Delinquency," 132, 134.

27. "Youth Basketball," *El Nacional* (Chicago), February 17, 1934.

28. Baur, "Delinquency," 152; Martínez, interview; Cruz Díaz, interview.

29. Romo, interview.

30. Martínez, interview; Baur, "Delinquency," 152.

31. Cruz Díaz, interview; Levin, interview; Pete Martínez, interview by Jesse Escalante, January 19, 1980, JEOH.

32. García, interview; Manuel Bravo, interview by Jesse Escalante, June 19, 1980, JEOH.

33. De Avila, interview; Levin, interview; Eduardo Peralta, interview by Nicolas M. Hernandez in Chicago, December 11, 1936, box 40, Foreign Language Press Survey, University of Chicago Special Collections, Chicago. Justino Cordero, interview by Jesse Escalante, October 22, 1979, JEOH.

34. Peralta, interview.

35. Alberto Cuellar, interview by Nicolas M. Hernandez, in box 40, Foreign Language Press Survey, University of Chicago Special Collections, Chicago, 1936.

36. Martínez, interview.

37. Escalante, "Mexican South Chicago," 24.

38. Ibid.; García, interview; Baur, "Delinquency," 132; Cruz Díaz, interview; Martínez, interview.

39. Gary Ross Mormino, "The Playing Fields of St. Louis: Italian Immigrants and Sports, 1925–1941," *Journal of Sports History* 9, no. 2 (Summer 1982): 5.

40. Ibid.

41. José M. Alamillo, *Making Lemonade out of Lemons* (Urbana: University of Illinois Press, 2006), 107.

42. Monroy, *Rebirth*, 46.

43. See Steven A. Riess, ed., *Sports and the American Jew* (Syracuse, NY: Syracuse University Press, 1998), for a collection of essays.

44. Martínez, interview; Cruz Díaz, interview; "Monterrey Baseball Team Defeats Drexel Square A.C.," *El Nacional* (Chicago), September 2, 1933; Baur, "Delinquency," 152.

45. Levin, interview.

46. Bravo, interview; García, interview; Levin, interview; Martínez, interview; "Cuauhtemoc Club Festival," *El Nacional* (Chicago), January 6, 1934.

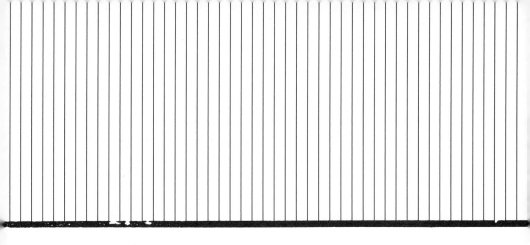

CHAPTER 4

Los Heroes del Barrio: Mexican Americans, Race, and
Masculinity in Sports in El Paso, Texas, 1940–1950

Eduardo García
Central New Mexico College

T he 1949 baseball season was the most productive and successful for the Bowie High School Bears from South El Paso, Texas. With only one loss during the regular season, they qualified for the regional playoffs and had a shot at the state championship. This quest led them to traverse Texas in a bus. The road was not easy as regional qualifiers were against Odessa High School and Lubbock High School, and the team faced much racism and hostility at every turn, including signs in restaurants that warned, "No Dogs or Mexicans." A group of Mexican Americans in Odessa attended the game in support of the Bears but watched from outside behind a fence. The perplexed Bowie players approached the group and invited them in. They shook their heads, fixed their gazes on the ground, and responded that whites did not permit them to even stand in the ballpark. For the Bowie *peloteros*, the racial slurs and hostility never ceased. Some of the rants coming from opposing fans included "Dirty Mexicans," "hot tamales," "greasers," and "Mexican jumping beans." In Odessa, it was so intolerably denigrating and infuriating that a Bowie player took the scissors from the first-aid kit and dared the hostile crowd to come and repeat those words to his face.

Bowie defeated Odessa High School and Lubbock High School and advanced to the state tournament in Austin, where hotels in the capital refused the team accommodations. In desperation, they turned to the University of Texas where the players slept on cots underneath Memorial Stadium. During their stay, the young athletes walked across the field to use restrooms and showers. Before bedtime, they would line up their cots and used them as hurdles in races to pass the time. Sports journalists could not fathom that a team of "Mexican jumping beans" had made it to state. The press went as far as ranking Bowie tenth out of eight teams competing. Bowie's first opponent was Stephenville, and the Bears recorded an easy 5-1 win. The second game against Waco was the toughest and longest, ending in a 4-3 victory in twelve innings, as Bowie advanced to the final. Austin High School, the home team, played Bowie for the championship. In the seventh inning, the locals were at bat with two outs. With players on first and second, the batter hit a sharp grounder to third. Bowie's Galarza quickly picked up the bounce and threw it to first ending the game with a final score of 3-2 in the Bears' favor. Bowie had won the state championship, and the boys in the dugout rushed to the field and the entire team jumped and ran around the diamond. Bowie's coach, Nemo Herrera, did not escape his cheerful team and was knocked down in the fervor of celebration. Their happiness for winning the championship was overpowering. They were also, they recalled, very, very happy to get out of Austin and leave all of the racial aggressions far behind them.[1]

The story of the 1949 Bowie baseball champions reveals important factors involved in sports and daily life. During the 1940s, El Paso's local sports scene was bustling, but few outside of the area knew of this. El Paso newspapers described a complex and vivid community very much involved in sports as both athletes and spectators. The cultural and social meanings of sports can allow for a deeper historic analysis, and athletic competition reveals more than just the factual summaries in sports pages. Athletics, race, class, and gender are all intricately intertwined. Sporting events have many meanings and fulfill many functions in society. Sports carry importance for the societies and the individuals who play a part in such events. The Second World War had devastating effects around the world, but in El Paso it opened some doors for Mexican and African Americans in the military, sports, and society.

Traditionally, Jim Crow had been in place in El Paso, and athletics were not exempt. In this system, blacks were completely segregated, and Mexicans experienced limited inclusion. Still, African Americans and Mexican-origin El Pasoans did use sports to resist cultural domination, especially concerning notions of manhood. Masculinity construction and cultural hegemony were all active factors involved in sports. Participation, skill, and success in sports reaffirmed masculinity among minorities. Blacks and Mexicans promoted leadership, athletic development, and masculinity within segregated athletic environments. Sports allowed marginalized groups to establish a sense of community and belonging. Athletic events involved the entire community even though men were the principal actors. Lastly, newspaper journalists used language that merged sports with World War II. The press conflated patriotism and sports in their rhetoric. Athletic ability translated to proficiency on the front lines. In this essay I identify and trace these issues over the ten-year period from 1940 to 1950 in the border town of El Paso, Texas. I uncover a few unknown episodes in local history here, and it is not hard to imagine similar scenarios around the United States where other Mexican-origin and Hispanic communities congregated.

There is a great need of a serious study of sports in El Paso and other border cities, one that goes beyond naming stars and reciting endless statistics. Despite recent efforts by various historians and scholars, there is still a gaping hole in this historiography. There is much to be done to recover the rich history of the region. Local sports history has been largely neglected except for a few initial attempts. The *El Paso Herald-Post's* longtime, and retired, sports columnists Bob Ingram and Ray Sánchez authored *The Miners: The History of Sports at the University of Texas at El Paso*. The authors emphasized, "We think you'll enjoy learning the history of the Miners."[2] This book is packed with information but is not a history book. At most, it remains a choppy account of the local university's athletic program. After all, they are professional journalists and only provide a long string of facts. The book is arranged chronologically, but lacks analysis and narrative. The authors leave out much information, including the politics of race, class, and gender that accompanies sports. However, they do a good a job in tracing the trajectory of the program between 1914 and the 1990s. *El Paso's Greatest Sports Heroes I Have Known* and *The Good, the Bad, and the Funny of El Paso Sports History*, by newspaper sports writer Ray Sánchez, is another effort to document local sports history.[3] This biographical work dedicates a few pages to notable local sports figures. The book's main strength is that it includes male and female athletes from diverse ethnic backgrounds. Bob Ingram is the author of *Baseball from Browns to Diablos*, which is a great abridged account of the local baseball team in the minors.[4] However, these works have limited value for public or academic history at large. They lack organization, analysis, and narrative. Not being historians, Sánchez and Ingram do not interpret or make sense of the information they present, although they have wonderful facts and statistics and we must commend them for these initial efforts. Therefore, my modest essay here attempts to begin an important discussion regarding sports history, particularly in El Paso.

Efforts are under way to document a more inclusive history of sport in the United States. *Mexican Americans and Sports*, edited by Jorge Iber and Samuel O. Regalado, looks at this understudied topic.[5] This collection of essays surveys diverse case studies around the United States but ignores El Paso and other places with high concentrations of Mexican-origin populations. It also focuses on Mexican Americans in traditionally non-Mexican areas like the Midwest and the US-Canadian border. The book offers valued and resourceful analysis and a serious approach to sports history. Currently, other scholars are presently making positive strides to close the gaps within the various fields of the history of Latinos in the United States. But why focus research efforts on sports? Sports mirror society and are important to understand cultural and societal practices. They offer congruent values and standards of the societies that develop them. Historian Juan Javier Pescador questions why few scholars concentrate on the social significance of organized sports in Hispanic communities in the United States. Pescador critiques present Chicano historiography because it has not incorporated sports and recreational culture in its approach and debate. Sports history has just recently begun to investigate the intricate connection between race, class, gender, immigration, nation, and sports in urban settings.[6]

Sports were more than mere recreational competition. Western sports were also a tool for imperialistic and hegemonic purposes. Anglo-American colonization of the US Southwest, including El Paso, occurred slowly and steadily after the United States' war with Mexico. Railroads accelerated this process in the early 1880s. Paseños and blacks composed the majority of the working and marginalized class in El Paso in the decades thereafter. The Anglo population saw a need to integrate this Mexican-origin population at the most basic level, and Americanization projects often included sports. In this work, the term *Paseños* designates Mexican-origin local residents, and El Pasoans refers to all the population regardless of ethnic background. Popular American sports such as boxing, baseball, American football, and basketball helped assimilate and establish cultural Anglo dominance over the large Mexican-origin population. Scholars from different disciplines have established the relationship between colonization, hegemony, and sports. An editorial from Wesleyan University, in Middletown, Connecticut, for example, argued that sports "play their part in making sturdy citizens, and training men in the invaluable qualities of loyalty, self-sacrifice, obedience, and temperance."[7] Sports thus were fused and inseparable from patriotic, Protestant, Anglo-American values also shared by the white dominant class in El Paso. Historian Colin D. Howell asserts that sports spread out from developed nations to the rest of the world and entered host cultures at the elite level before descending through the social order to the working class and urban poor in what is called the diffusion model.[8] Sport facilitated colonialism in its various forms and helped establish dominance over subjugated peoples. Noted sociologist Michael Messner writes in *Power at Play* that as in Britain, organized sports in the United States emerged in the nineteenth century mostly with upper- and middle-class whites who were concerned with "building character." Blue-collar workers and minorities were largely denied access to major sporting institutions; however, by the turn of the century "recreation of the masses" was seen by the elites as a means of integrating immigrants and the growing industrial working class.[9] To increase worker productivity and foster company loyalty, US business-es often subsidized sports teams along the US-México border including places like El Paso.[10] Company sports offered an alternative to "immoral" and "subversive" leisure activities, such as gambling, drinking, and cock-fighting.[11] In essence, any annoying or inferior traits of the mongrel Mexican and Mexican American culture could, many believed, be cured with a good dose of American sports. Moreover, spectator sports facilitated an accommodation to industrial capitalism as a leisure time diversion for the urban lower-middle and working classes. In an effort to curve "immoral and unproductive" behaviors, ball parks and arenas were located in the city and admission fees were relatively low and at times completely non-existent, thereby encouraging attendance.[12] Sports were structured so that boys learned to be men in a competitive, capitalist society where produc-tivity was valued, and in a political context in which a strong military was believed to be a requirement for national security and economic expan-sion.[13]

According to these beliefs, Paseños and blacks on the border could surely benefit from organized sports. Progressives believed that participa-tion provided young men with the opportunity to develop physical skills and improve fitness, learn social and emotional skills, and develop mor-al values. In addition, a good dose of sports could increase competence, self-esteem, and self-confidence.[14] These traits were surely welcomed in the newly devilioping industries in the El Paso borderland. For pro-gressives, the social meaning and importance of sports could attract and mobilize a large cross-section of the population to solve America's social, political, and moral problems.[15] Paseños and blacks stood at the center of these American problems and Progressives hoped that sports could be-gin alleviating such problems in El Paso. Athletics in many ways reflect-ed American social order as well as that of the work place. In a Marxist approach, sociologist Eric Dunning argues that sport reproduced bour-geois social relations such as selection and hierarchy, subservience, obe-dience, and organizational ideology involving competition and records.[16] The regulating body of officials and organizers symbolized politicians, the upper class, and job supervisors and managers. Those who remained at the bottom of the hierarchy had no choice but to "play by the rules of the game" and accept their condition. Thus, sports were an instrument used to reinforce hegemony and social control and conditioned men to accept and function within the established social hierarchy and in the workplace. As in the sports arena, contesting rules could be unfavorable to athletes, in life contesting social or labor conditions could also prove detrimental.

Sports functioned as an important tool for cultural hegemony and colonization. Organized sports, especially baseball, came to symbolize modernity, progress, and civility. The most powerful Western nations often used derogatory and racist connotations to describe what they called "barbaric" or "primitive" in non-Western societies they conquered, colonized, or subjected to domination.[17] In the United States, the "civilizing mission" meant Americanization. Ample evidence of this trend comes from the pages of the *El Paso Times*. For example, a headline announced, "Minor Leagues Offer Help Down Under." The paper reported that American baseball was "to expand its helping hand to the West Indies and the Latin Americas." Robert L. Finch, publicity chief of the National Association of Professional Baseball Leagues (the minors), traveled from New York to the "Down Under" to bring organized baseball. Finch went to "Havana for a conference with members of the Cuban Winter League then to San Juan with the president of the Puerto Rico League." He also visited the Dominican Republic, the Panama League, and the Canal Zone Circuit.[18] Both Finch and the journalist failed to recognize that each of those distinct Latin American nations already had organized and successful baseball leagues, and that these places would export many talented and successful players to the US major and minor leagues. In this instance, Americanization meant the exportation of products, symbols, ideologies, and organizational practices of the United States. This produced a prepackaged Americo-centric view of how the world should be, including the ways people should act. It was a corporate and social phenomenon that involved American influence over other nations.[19]

On the other hand, sports were a platform to resist and contest social control, hegemony, repression, and colonialism. The structure and values of sport emerged and changed historically, largely as a result of struggles for power between groups of people, much like institutions such as the economy, politics, and the family. Marginalized El Pasoans frequently used sports to resist cultural domination and to negotiate equality. Sports, like all other social institutions, were largely shaped by, and in the interests of, those who held power. Nonetheless, the control and domination of the ruling groups was never absolute.[20] Sports went beyond athletic competition and recreation and entailed so much more and became a highly politicized space. Historian Juan Javier Pescador reveals that the football (soccer) pitch became a border space that further accentuated differences between players and sponsors, Mexican laborer migrants and middle-class Mexican Americans, the city government and the oppressed barrio, the state and the Mexican community, male players and female nonplayers, urban segregation and recreational sports. Paradoxically, it was in these spaces that men in particular contested domination yet sought to establish their dominance over other men.

Sports were important to minorities because they could prove their managerial and organizational skills by coaching winning teams and creating and running sports leagues. Additionally, they could easily disprove racist notions of the superiority of the white race. Some of these racialized notions of the mind and body operated within sports to the point where various positions were defined almost exclusively by "race," otherwise defined as racial stacking. It involved moving players of color from "intelligent" to "physical" positions.[21] Paseños and blacks proved that they, too, endured the rigors and discipline required to succeed in sports and in the process demonstrated their intellectual and physical abilities. Furthermore, these athletes showed that they were worthy opponents or teammates to whites. On the field, they proved to be indeed equals; however, socially, economically, and politically they still played with a handicap. Within the world of sports, subordinated groups of men resisted racist, colonial, and class domination. Their resistance most often took the form of claims to manhood.[22]

Masculinity is a central issue in sports studies and to this work, yet it is not an easy concept to define. Regardless, an effort should be made to further understand it within this context. Discussions of masculinity treat it as if it is measurable and some men have more of it while others less. Masculinity did not exist in isolation from femininity. Men were commonly described as aggressive, assertive, independent, competitive, and insensitive. Another popular image of masculinity was that of man the hero, the bread winner/hunter, the competitor, the conqueror.[23] Masculinity, manliness, or manhood was also understood as lack of compassion, weakness, fear, or the appearance of vulnerability, because these were all traits associated with women.[24] The connection between sports and masculinity becomes apparent since these are traits often desired in top athletes. Some social scientists have agued that without historic rites of passage modern men were confused about what it meant to be a man. Competitive sports helped fill that void. Others view sports as a mechanism that socialized boys with the socio-positive psychological characteristics necessary in an industrial culture. Sports allowed governments and the media to transmit dominant and political values. Also, athletics elevated the male body as superior to that of women and weaker men (effeminate, unmanly, etc.) through displays of strength and violence. Sports embedded elements of competition and hierarchy among men. This was made clear with collisions and intentional fouls in contact sports.[25] Stronger and more skillful men immediately outranked and dominated the weaker or less talented. Scholars call this hegemonic masculinity, a form of masculinity, which is characterized by aggression, competition, physical prowess, and heterosexuality.[26] Aside from competitive displays of manliness, sports provided an exclusive homosocial space and conduit for masculinity. Historian José M. Alamillo writes that in addition to helping weld social networks and alliances, baseball games also provided masculinized forms of sociability. Apart from the game's competitive *machismo*, postgame drinking parties became a popular activity among the athletes.[27] Within these spaces, men bonded and interacted. Manly interactions did not always have to be strictly confined to the field. Drinking was an acceptable way to celebrate a victory or help drown the sorrow of defeat.

Sports presented Paseños with the prospect to break away from poverty and life in marginalized barrios. The Mexican-origin population encountered limited economic opportunities and racially restricted environments. In this context, sport clubs provided counterpoints to grim material realities encountered at work and the community. Athletes could potentially attain social status, respect, and dignity while realizing their own "field dreams."[28] For a few, it was not hard to dream and accomplish.

For example, Manuel Ortíz picked peas in California for seventy-five cents a day and was a regular spectator at amateur boxing fights. One day he accepted a boxing challenge, and within a month, he became a Golden Gloves champion. Shortly thereafter, he was a contender for the world bantamweight championship as a professional prizefighter. With his winnings, Ortíz bought a brand-new zoot suit, and that made him very proud. His new outfit had such heavily padded shoulders that his wife would not dare to go out with him in public. She soon changed her mind after she found many fans swooning over her spouse. Ortíz aimed high and confessed that he wanted the boxing world crown to go with his new suit.[29] By the middle of the nineteenth century, urban poverty, racial and ethnic discrimination, and relative deprivation had been established as the common denominators of prize fighting and professional boxing.[30] The case of Manuel Ortíz provides an example of this. He found financial success impossible to attain on the starvation wages that the farm fields offered. Ortíz served as an example to other young aspirants in the barrios and boxing arenas. They, too, could box and maybe one day make it big. For Paseños, the poor quality of their schools, the attitudes of their teachers, as well as the antieducation atmosphere, made it extremely unlikely that they would succeed as students. Sports consequently became the ground on which they attempted to thrive, and claim equality and manliness.[31]

Sports were important to Paseños as they helped establish a sense of community and belonging. Apart from watching their favorite team or athlete, these spaces offered families with an opportunity to reunite with extended relatives and friends.[32] Historian Samuel O. Regalado claims that sports increased notoriety and bridged important gaps between people of Mexican origin and whites. Sports also played an instrumental role in shaping the identities of people living in rural colonias and urban barrios.[33] José M. Alamillo argues that under economic exploitation, racial discrimination, and resilient nativist attacks, Mexican Americans used baseball to proclaim their equality and "Americanness" through athletic competition to demonstrate community unity and strength.[34] Sports such as baseball took on a particular importance. More than simple games for boys or girls, the teams and contests involved many in the community. Games often had political and cultural objectives, like the fiestas celebrating Cinco de Mayo and Mexican Independence Day. Sports were, in this way, a thread that united the community.[35] This reaffirmed Mexican identity and cultural attachments, which whites tried to strip from Paseños. Free time before and after games provided plenty of opportunity to visit with friends and family. Moreover, the community could engage in significant social and cultural rituals. This was precious time to gossip or organize festivities or other community events. Children played with other children and learned from their parents their place in society. Women were segregated to their own sphere as spectators and maybe packed snacks and drinks for the team and family. Sports blended with other important society and community practices. Enrique Fernández, an El Paso Texans baseball star, married Inés García in a ceremony right before an official game at Dudley Field. Pancho López, the star pitcher of the Ciudad Juárez Indios baseball club, gave the bride away before spectators. The fans pooled funds and presented the newlyweds with $212.50.[36] The baseball players felt part of a vibrant community and celebrated this joyous occasion before their fans. In addition, the athletes gained status and acceptance in the eyes of their peers and the community.

However, Paseños did not have equal access to all sports. Some required special, consistent, and expensive training and equipment, while others entailed regular expenditures. Therefore, economic status restricted many from recreational activities like tennis, golf, and bowling. Private sports clubs had absolute control to turn down prospective members based on class, race, or any other reason they saw fit. Participation in professional sports, much like today, was off limits to most people. Therefore, working-class El Pasoans developed their own leagues where they found recreation, exhilarating competition, and community life. As a result, some sports were more popular than others. Some equipment was easier to come as it could be borrowed, bought used, passed down, or team members could pitch in to buy it. Public parks or perhaps even empty lots around the city served as the training and playing spaces. Regardless of economic hardship, marginalized residents found ways to carve niches within the local scene. This is clearly evident during the years of World War II.

Even before US entry into the conflict, El Pasoans were well aware of international circumstances. Some of the local newspapers announced in big, bold headlines, "Neutrals Fear Nazi Invasion; Call Reserves," "Russians Bomb South Finland," and "Nazis Destroy Three British Submarines" among others.[37] Among such headlines the sports life of El Paso was revealed, and it showed a fully engaged community. One particularly eye-catching vignette was the widely advertised and controversial boxing match between Sebastian González and Jimmy Fletcher, scheduled for February 9, 1940. The newspaper headline announced, "Fletcher Believes He'll Beat Gonzales in Rematch." They had previously boxed in a match that ended without a clear winner and the judges decided on a draw. Unhappy with the call, Jimmy Fletcher confessed, "I was the aggressor throughout. I know how to fight González better this week." He expressed his masculinity and superiority by adding, "I'm going to paste him with uppercuts until I jar him out of it."[38]

The following day, the *Herald-Post* announced González's arrival in El Paso and reported that "he captured the imagination of his countrymen" more than any other fighter. English-language papers immediately transformed the Mexican boxer into the "Other," but nonetheless he became a favorite of fans in Liberty Hall (a local boxing and wrestling arena). In the sports pages, not only was he distinguished by his windmill swings but also by his dark skin.[39] The underlying factor of the fight was to learn if a dark-skinned Mexican could match a white fighter. Given the amount of racial tensions then extant, it is possible that many Paseños were excited about González and hopeful that he could beat a "*gringo*." Clearly, the editors constructed a match beyond the two men to include two entire nations and charge the emotions of El Paso boxing fans.

El Continental and the *El Paso Herald-Post* both reported that González was "*rechoncho*" or pudgy. The English-language newspaper went on to announce that the Mexican boxer felt confident about a victory over Fletcher. González believed the second fight would not end in a draw because he was going to use his kidney punch.[40] One day prior, the paper declared that Fletcher's camp would protest González's kidney punches since they were illegal under Texas boxing regulations. The papers had described González as an unorthodox, prohibitive, fat, dark-skinned, cheating Mexican, which only antagonized him, and which in many ways was parallel to the popular perception of Mexicans across the United States. On the other hand, Fletcher was none of those things, and the papers described him as a handsome man. After the press characterized González as pudgy, the sport pages reported that Fletcher had a weight advantage of five pounds over his foe.[41] Fletcher was interviewed at least three times whereas González only once. Instead of allowing the Mexican to voice his thoughts and opinions, the Anglo media merely constructed a negative impression of him. Fletcher was able to address the newspaper readers and thus became more familiar to local sports fans, which allowed him to prop up his image as the white hero.

On fight day, the *Herald-Post* confidently announced "Fletcher-Gonzalez Fight May End in Knockout," and the paper predicted that González would knock out Fletcher. After declaring that González was an El Paso favorite, the press stated that fans were closely divided between the combatants. Somehow, the much-antagonized Sebastian González convinced the local press of his superiority during the training sessions. The sub-headline announced, "Mexico Boy Is Favored In Main Go." It ran a picture of the fighters in their trunks, gloves, and boots. They both looked fierce and exuded masculinity in their technical boxing stance and the visible muscles from their naked arms and torsos.[42] Their bodies were living proof of rigorous training and discipline. If readers ignored the text, they could recognize both men as equals in the photograph. The expectation that had been building over the last weeks finally came to an end the night of February 9, 1940, at Liberty Hall. González and Fletcher stepped into the ring and exchanged blows as both personal and national honor were at stake. After the ring of the fourth-round bell, González did not get up to continue the fight. He said there was a "ball" in his ankle and he could not move about without pain. After a brief inspection, the attending medic did not find a sprain or fracture on González. With no other choice, the referee called a technical knockout and declared Fletcher the winner.[43] Journalists had overrated the brawl, and in the end the spectacle did not amount to much of a match and its culmination was anticlimactic.

The various papers revealed the details over the following days. Journalists, the boxing commission, and the public were unforgiving. Three physicians examined González's foot and found no discolorations or swelling. His pay was withheld as punishment for breach of contract.[44] He did not comment after the fight, and the reasons for his decision to forfeit remain unknown. Sebastian González renounced to his own masculinity by easily surrendering to another man. Grueling physical punishment made him incapable of continuing the fight, and he chose to quit. The *El Paso Herald-Post*'s headline was "Gonzales' [*sic*] Acts Show Appalling Stupidity." Noted local sports columnist Bob Ingram wrote about González, "If he was half smart, could have done a better job of faking and probably could have gotten by with it. If he wanted to get out of there, he could have feigned being knocked out. . . . In the middle of it [González] lost his heart. It looks like he doesn't like to stick it out when the going gets rough." Ingram dismissed González as a "complete idiot" and no more than a coward. Ingram suggested that González could have faked a knockout from the first round and walked away with a full paycheck.[45] Perhaps in some way this particular incident fit the larger narrative that Mexicans were inferior physically and intellectually, and lesser men in all other aspects.

Boxing surely captured the attention of El Pasoans, and a new competition debuted in January 1942. This was the Golden Gloves Tournament, which very quickly became a fan favorite. It was an amateur boxing contest, which has opened some doors for a number of Paseño athletes. Over one hundred fighters enrolled in the first tournament, and the event was so important and momentous that the *El Paso Times* covered the event in its front and sports pages. During the tournament, the spectators cheered and had a good time, and in attendance "were many El Paso women in the crowd, there were prominent citizens of El Paso[,] . . . there were the inevitable sports fans who never miss any event." Other spectators included, "soldiers and even [the] occasional sailor. There were high school youths who had come to see their schoolmates fight. . . . But most of all there were the people of El Paso shouting and laughing and enjoying themselves."[46] Indeed this event brought together a large cross-section of denizens who felt part of the community due to this type of mass-spectator event. The press provided language that permitted violence in certain contexts such as sports. This kind of rhetoric glorified boxing and other sports as purely violent displays of masculinity. Boxing fans at the third annual Golden Gloves tournament "[was] composed of mainly violent partisan groups,

[who] yelled excitedly across the hall during most of the bouts."[47] Within the permitted violent parameters of sport, spectators cheered for the fighters to kill and finish each other. One of the attractions of contact sports was the promise of brutality and cruelty. Young fighters literally attempted to annihilate their opponent, as this was an opportunity for success. Moreover, boxing was a sport where men of color could in fact prove their masculinity and physical equality to whites via physical force and pugilistic skill. Beginning in 1944, Bowie High School held an annual boxing tournament similar to the Golden Gloves, as did other local entities, such as the Catholic Community Center.[48] Some of the competing fighters also boxed in the Golden Gloves.[49] Young men continued their formation as athletes in arenas that the community provided. These contests provided spaces for training and networking. High schools and churches had traditionally represented community pride and identity and were important meeting places for athletes, children, parents, families, and other community members.

During the 1940s, El Paso was home to popular boxing heroes who rose through the ranks of the local scene and as a consequence rose through the social ranks. Mexican American professional fighters secured a modicum of financial stability and notoriety in the community. The most prominent figures of the 1940s included Santos Quijano, Adolfo "Dolph" Quijano, Lotario Ramírez, and Eddie Quiroga. Santos Quijano during his stint as an amateur fighter supplemented his income as a car-parts salesman.[50] He later joined the army, where he rose to sergeant. In the military, he became a proficient and noted pugilist. Santos Quijano became a mentor to other fighters, including his brother, Adolfo Quijano. Under his brother's guidance, Adolfo became a champion and local hero as well. The press wrote about these individuals with a tone of respect and admiration, unlike the case of Sebastian González. One writer noted, "[Adolpho] Quijano possesses a murderous left which slows his opponents down . . . [and] the crowd loves." Dolph Quijano defeated Bob Sikes in the first state heavyweight championship fight held in El Paso. With this win, the Paseño held the light-heavyweight and heavyweight titles. In 1948 Quijano fought as many as four bouts.[51]

Paseño Lotario Ramírez was a professional boxer who also climbed to fame. He debuted against Phil Romano in Liberty Hall on January 21, 1944. Ramírez won his first bout with a knockout and instantly became a favorite of El Paso boxing fans.[52] Journalists and the public alike respected him. Another successful barrio hero was Eddie Quiroga. The press singled him out only because he was of Chinese and Mexican background. The papers never failed to mention this detail. In pictures, however, Quiroga did not look particularly of Asian descent, but the press exaggerated this fact in order to exoticize him.[53] Journalists were fascinated with the fact that a Chinese Mexican could be such a successful fighter. Eugenics and scientific racism invented the Chinese as one of the most effete and degenerate races. Such xenophobic ideas remained in the American subconscious and were commonly reflected in the papers—hence the fascination with men like Eddie Quiroga. Boxing was such a prominent sport that promoters brought high-profile fights to El Paso. One such example was the bantamweight championship match between Héctor Márquez and Tony Olivera.[54] Entertainment options were fewer than today, and during that time, fights were held throughout the week and not exclusively on the weekends. Sports satisfied appetites that television, radio, moving pictures, or theater could not, and thus their popularity.

Next to boxing, baseball was the favorite local sports pastime, and baseball leagues allowed Paseños many opportunities. Defending baseball titleholders Union Shoe Shop Cobblers signed Beto Méndez for the 1943 Commercial Baseball League season. Méndez was already a veteran pitcher of the area's amateur leagues and dean of El Paso's baseball players. In the previous season, Méndez had played with the Coca-Cola team in the International Baseball League. Beto Méndez, N. Rodríguez, and F. Madrid were the local star pitchers for the Cobblers; the team signed all three in hopes of retaining the championship title.[55] Beto Méndez was an intriguing figure and a prominent local star. He played in amateur and semiprofessional leagues, and local teams sought after him for his talent. Journalists praised him well above professional baseball players, including the local professional team, the Texans. Men like Méndez were able to engage in friendly yet demanding competition that allowed them to assert claims to manliness on the field. After retiring from the local leagues, he was still connected to the game and the community. Chuck Whitlock, a sports columnist for the *El Paso Times*, referred to Méndez as "the local baseball czar." The baseball veteran eventually became the president of both the Lower Valley and Río Grande Leagues. Méndez secured five fields around the city for the Commercial, International, City-Valley, Río Grande, and Border Leagues to use. By mid-1949 he was president of all the amateur baseball leagues in El Paso.[56] Méndez became a respected member of El Paso, including the athletic community, because of his skill and talent. In addition, he was able to manage two leagues simultaneously. His managerial skills put him in a category often reserved for whites exclusively. Since baseball was a much more accessible and popular sport for Paseños, baseball leagues were the most numerous in the city. Most leagues did not require players to pay a membership, admission, or equipment fees like in golf or bowling clubs. Equipment was more readily available and at lower cost in comparison to other sports, not to mention the convenience and access of borrowing gear from teammates. Popular rec leagues such as the Commercial and International Baseball Leagues allowed greater participation of working-class El Pasoans since costs were low or nonexistent and the camaraderie drew in athletes.

In contrast, the local professional team, the Texans, sought most of its talent from outside the city's environs.[57] *El Paso Herald-Post*'s Bob Ingram often wrote and rated the newly acquired talent in his column, "As I Was Saying." When the Boston Red Sox acquired the Texans for their farm system in 1945, the franchise immediately reinforced its roster with Anglo players. However, the team did make a few concessions and imported talented athletes of color from Latin America. Manager Andy Cohen secured Cuban Roberto Cabal, a left-handed "hard-hitting outfielder and pitcher." Antonio "Loco" Ruiz from Chihuahua City, México, also signed a contract with the club. Later, Manager Syd Cohen assured the El Paso press that Enrique "Bacotete" Fernández accepted remaining in El Paso with an increase in salary and the prospect of moving up the line of the Red Sox system.[58] His talent put him in a position where he could negotiate to his advantage before Anglo managers and team executives. This is why local baseball leagues were important for Paseños. These were spaces where Paseños found recreational activities and acceptance. The baseball teams for Colón and La Unión theaters held the opening game of the

City-Valley League, but no scores were given. On the other hand, scores and tables were always given for the different Fort Bliss leagues (softball, volleyball, and bowling).[59] Journalists did not think that the different amateur leagues controlled by Paseños were as worthy as leagues for whites.

Basketball was the third-most-popular sport in El Paso after baseball and boxing. Mexicans were not segregated under the Texas Jim Crow legal system, but they still faced de facto exclusion. In a meeting, officials announced eight men to function as referees for a city-district basketball tournament at Austin High School. Among the men were Syd Cohen, Bob Carson, Mike Devlyn, Luther Harding, John Keefe, William Reed, Dick Steward, and Tom Chávez.[60] Only one Paseño served in an authoritative capacity for the tournament. In college basketball, Santos "Kayo" Pérez was a three-year letterman and senior for the Miners. He was the team captain and also played American football. According to the newspaper, he was the shortest man in the entire Border Conference.[61] Short stature was a common physical description for Mexicans. In spite of this "handicap," Pérez performed on par and better than taller white athletes despite his height disadvantage. Under the direction of Coach Nemo Herrera, the Bowie Bears basketball team were serious contenders for the state AA championship in 1948. They won the 4-AA and 3-AA championships, allowing them a chance to compete for the state title. Ten Bowie boys departed in a Continental Airlines flight from the El Paso Municipal Airport to Austin. There was a big farewell for the players, and they even practiced at the College of Mines before leaving. The young Paseños appear in a photograph in two-piece business suits and look calm, confident, and proud. In the team were Rubén Huerta, Joe Galarza, Jesús López, Jimmy Ochoa, Carlos Gardea, Miguel Reyes, Rogelio Chávez, Luis López, Ricardo Jacquez, and Javier Montez, the only Bwie player with previous flight experience.[62] The team finished fourth in the state competition. Young athletes saw Paseño coaches like Nemo Herrera lead winning teams and hold respectable positions. This inspired pupils to succeed since they had tangible and immediate examples to emulate.

American football was a sport that did not quite match the popularity of other athletic competitions in El Paso and was dominated by Anglos. The press handpicked the All-Southwest Conference Team. It was composed entirely of white players. The American football team included

Walker, Berry, Watson, Rote, Burk, Williams, Kilmen, McFadin, Mouse, Murphy, and Ison, who were all college seniors. The press presented these white athletes as heroes. Blacks and Paseños did not fit into the heroic and admired world of American college and high school football, and legal segregation and tuition costs were major roadblocks to higher education. In contrast, the *El Paso Times* All-District team was slightly more diverse. From Bowie High School came Andy Morales, Rogelio Chávez, and Rocky Galarza. Jim Angelos, Royal Gorman, Jim Webber, Billy Walsh, and Fred Edens were from Austin High School. Gene Odell and Gene Gills, from Ysleta, completed the team. This all-star team did not include African Americans.

Language in the papers changed when Austin and Bowie High Schools met. The press automatically labeled the Bowie Bears as the "Southsiders" and magnified class and racial differences. South El Paso was commonly portrayed as ugly, dirty, and disease- and crime-ridden, traits also used to identify the Mexican families that inhabited this neighborhood. Furthermore, the school system had not appropriated funds to provide outdoor athletic facilities for Austin or Bowie until September 1948 when Austin opened its outdoor sporting facilities before Bowie. Bowie High School was an older school, but preference was given to the more affluent Eastside community. Austin served primarily Anglo El Pasoans and upper-class Paseños. This forced Bowie to travel to Austin High School, other schools, Dudley Field (home of the Texans), or Kidd Field (College of Mines) for "home" games.[63] The school lacked a baseball diamond and an American football field; a pretty serious omission of athletic space for Southside Mexican-origin students.

Sporting events also celebrated national holidays, which united the community. Bowie High School attended a track meet in Ciudad Juárez, Mexico, to celebrate Cinco de Mayo. The meet was at the Juárez horse track, and the Juárez crowd was happy to see Bowie athletes compete against their students. Both communities were enthusiastic about these sorts of competitions and hoped to see more in the future.[64] The Spanish language newspaper, *El Continental,* depicted a fluid Juárez–El Paso border. It represented one united Paseño-Juarense community while the *Herald-Post* and *Times* tended to portray two very separate and different communities. Celebration of Mexican holidays reaffirmed Paseños cultural awareness and renewed their sense of a binational community in El Paso barrios.

Paseños celebrated American holidays with the same fervor as the Mexican ones. The El Paso Texans played for a crowd of three thousand at Dudley Field for a July Fourth celebration against the Saltillo (Mexico) Parrots. The Texans took the win, 13-7. Laureano Camacho hit the only home run. Local star Bacatete Fernández was a key player in the Texans' victory.[65] The International Baseball League also promoted community events that celebrated American national holidays. The *El Paso Times* announced, "Local League Lists Two Sunday Games to Celebrate 4th of July." One of the games was at Dudley Field in El Paso between recreation league teams Gantt Jewelers and La Norteña. The Reception Center met the Coca-Cola team at the Borunda Park in Juárez as part of the doubleheader.[66] Paseños embraced and celebrated American holidays in part thanks to the Americanization projects in schools and other social institutions, but also because of long-standing ties already established in the US Southwest. They identified themselves as citizens of two nations. This duality of Mexican Americans was one key factor in their decision to join the US armed forces during World War II. Paseños thus freely and joyously celebrated national holidays like Independence Day and Cinco de Mayo. These holidays also came with time off from work, adding to the appeal of such leisure activities.

US intervention in the Second World War affected every aspect of daily American life, and sports were no exception. Activity in Fort Bliss increased, which not only brought new spectators but also athletes to El Paso. Paseños served proudly in the US armed forces during World War II. While in service, they attested their masculinity in two ways. One way was by proving their patriotic and manly duties in military service as outstanding citizens. The other was by still engaging and succeeding in sports. This was the case of boxing manager Tony Herrera and his student Manny "Pete" Ortega. Tony Herrera was a retired and nationally recognized lightweight. He enlisted in the air force and was stationed at Biggs Air Field, where he trained new, young Mexican American talent. Herrera was "one of the greatest boxers ever turned out in El Paso," according to the Biggs Field Public Relations Office. Pete Ortega started boxing in 1941 and was one of the winners of the first Golden Gloves Tournament in 1942. That same year, Ortega advanced to the state semifinals and joined the army.[67] Another successful Paseño in the army was Sergeant Bob Chapa. Chapa was a catcher for the Old Biggs softball team and helped the team win thirty-eight out of forty games. Sergeant Chapa had an impressive eight home runs and a batting average of .340. The paper honored Chapa with a caricature in recognition of his accomplishment. He was portrayed proud in his baseball uniform, and his brown skin was handsomely accentuated.[68] Sports imitated military life in other ways. Local high school athletes were honored with banquets, picnics, and award ceremonies. Those events resembled award ceremonies for war heroes. They included speeches and special guests. The Latin American Progressive Union, the Bowie Ex-Alumnae, the Veterans and Citizens Unity Club, and the Bowie Parent Teacher Association sponsored a picnic in honor of Bowie student athletes. Approximately 350 people attended the event, including 175 athletes.[69] These athletes were commended for their heroic feats, much like military heroes. This type of ceremony further encouraged students to continue to do well in sports and perhaps encouraged others to also take up sports, as parents and relatives rejoiced from this type of recognition and positive reinforcement. Their peers might see these young athletes as heroes, too.

Historian Pamela Grundy asserts that athletic competition has proved so enthralling to Americans because it engages so much of human potential. This is because playing sports demands and displays physical agility, mental skill, individual achievement, collective effort, and moral fortitude, all of which appeal to the masses. The parallels between organized team competition, the conflicts of politics, and the developing structures of industrial capitalism transformed sports into a multifaceted metaphor for American society, its strengths, and its failings.[70] Sports facilitate additional understanding of the intricate connections between race, class, and gender. They are a complex cultural and social experience that can help us navigate and understand the past. Although sports were part of Americanization projects and used to homogenize, assimilate, and control minorities, Paseños and African Americans used sports to resist subjugation and social control. Paradoxically, these men fostered leadership, athletic development, and masculinity in sports. They have left a significant imprint on sports in the United States. Their accomplishments on the field allowed them the opportunity to strive for social justice and equality off the field. Success in the athletic arena did not necessarily result in instantaneous rewards off the court. This was merely a stepping-stone for the slow and overdue change to come for minorities. Those athletes refused to accept the status quo and sought to prove their equality and masculinity, and sports provided that conduit.[71]

US intervention in World War II had important impacts on the El Paso sports scene. Sports played a crucial role in the home front. Athletic events celebrated national holidays like July Fourth baseball games in El Paso's Dudley Field and Juárez's Borunda Park. This created a homogenized American mind-set in which sports promoted patriotism among all the citizenry. Furthermore, sports proved to be essential to uplift the morale of military personnel and civilians alike. In addition, newspaper journalists merged the language used in sports and in World War II. The two activities almost became direct synonyms. This idea revolved around masculinity, duty, and citizenship construction. Sports and war were the ultimate masculine expressions, and violence and dexterity needed in sports transplanted to war applications. Wherever sports failed to turn boys into men, war exceedingly filled that role.

In sports, Paseños extended their sense of community and belonging. Sports created a space where men could socialize with other men and engage in healthy competition. On game day, families could mingle with friends, relatives, neighbors, and other community members. In this manner, neighborhood networks continuously revitalized as community relationships became stronger. Both Mexican and American holidays and celebrations brought the community together. Sports offered attractive incentives to the working class. A few Mexican American athletes found the ticket to fame and fortune in athletics. Successful athletic careers provided a pathway out of the marginalized and poverty-stricken barrios. This success came with the respect and recognition from the entire community—as it did for pugilists like Lotario Ramírez and Adolfo Quijano, who found distinction and success. They proved that South El Paso and other poor neighborhoods were not breeding grounds for crime, disease, and idleness as the dominant society presumed.

Social histories reveal much, and sports history largely remains undocumented and unchallenged. I have offered a few episodes that open a window into El Paso; similar efforts in other locales would likely also be fruitful. Newspapers are the primary sources that guide this research, which reflect how journalists during the 1940s perceived local sports figures and events, and in turn how they communicated that information to El Pasoans. Nonetheless, newspapers do not tell the complete story. There were many pickup games on El Paso streets, empty lots, schoolyards, and parks that were not recorded and went by unnoticed. Those games were just as meaningful to the community. They are proof of both Americanization and resistance. Paseños accepted American sports but were able to modify them to barrio rules.

Notes

1. *El Paso Herald-Post,* June 3, 9, 11, 1949; *El Paso Times,* June 3, 1949; Elpasotimes.corm/ci_11587757 and Elpasotimes.com/Socorro/ci_12574649 (accessed April 5, 2010).

2. Bob Ingram and Ray Sánchez, *The Miners: The History of Sports at the University of Texas at El Paso* (El Paso, TX: Mesa Publishing Corporation, 1997).

3. Ray Sánchez, *El Paso's Greatest Sports Heroes I Have Known* (El Paso, TX: Sunturians Press, 1989). Sánchez followed with *The Good, the Bad, and the Funny of El Paso Sports History* (El Paso, TX: Mesa Publishing Corporation, 2013).

4. Bob Ingram, *Baseball from Browns to Diablos* (El Paso, TX: Paul Brothers Publishing, 1991).

5. Jorge Iber and Samuel O. Regalado, eds., *Mexican Americans and Sports: A Reader on Athletics and Barrio Life* (College Station: Texas A&M University Press, 2007).

6. Juan Javier Pescador, "*Los Heroes del Domingo*: Soccer, Borders, and Social Spaces in Great Lakes Michigan," in Iber and Regalado, *Mexican Americans and Sports,* 74.

7. Michael A. Messner, *Power at Play: Sports and the Problem of Masculinity* (Boston: Beacon Press, 1992), 7.

8. Colin D. Howell, "Baseball and Borders: The Diffusion of Baseball into Mexican and Canadian-American Borderland Regions, 1885–1911," *NINE: A Journal of Baseball History and Culture* 11, no. 2 (spring 2003): 16.

9. Messner, *Power at Play,* 11.

10. José M. Alamillo, "Peloteros in Paradise: Mexican American Baseball and Oppositional Politics in Southern California, 1930–1950," in Iber and Regalado, *Mexican Americans and Sports*, 52.

11. José M. Alamillo, "Mexican American Baseball: Masculinity, Racial Struggle, and Labor Politics in Southern California, 1930–1950," in *Sports Matters: Race, Recreation, and Culture*, ed. John Bloom and Michael Nevin Willard (New York: New York University Press, 2002), 90.

12. Michael S. Kimmel, "Baseball and the Reconstruction of American Masculinity, 1880–1920," in *Sport, Men, and the Gender Order: Critical Feminist Perspectives*, ed. Michael A. Messner and Donald F. Sabo (Champaign, IL: Human Kinetic Books, 1990), 62.

13. Jay Cackley, "Organized Sports for a Twentieth-Century Invention," in *Learning Culture through Sports: Explaining the Role of Sports in Society*, ed. Sandra Spickard Prettyman and Brian Lampman (Lanham, MD: Rowman and Littlefield Education, 2006), 5.

14. Peggy McCann and Martha Ewing, "Motivation and Outcomes of Youth Participation in Sport," in Prettyman and Lampman, *Learning Culture through Sports*, 35.

15. William J. Morgan, *Why Sports Socially Matter* (New York: Routledge, 2006), 136.

16. Eric Dunning, *Sports Matters: Sociological Studies of Sport, Violence, and Civilization* (London: Routledge, 1999), 107.

17. Ibid., 42.

18. *El Paso Times*, March 25, 1948.

19. Toby Miller et al., *Globalization and Sport: Playing the World* (London: Sage Publications, 2001), 130, 15.

20. Alamillo, "Mexican American Baseball," 8, 12.

21. Gamal Abbel-Shehid, *Who Da Man? Black Masculinities and Sporting Cultures* (Toronto: Canadian Scholars' Press, 2005), 119.

22. Messner, *Power at Play*, 19.

23. Arthur Brittan, *Masculinity and Power* (New York: Basil Blackwell, 1989), 1–3, 77.

24. Morgan, *Why Sports Socially Matter*, 34.

25. Ibid., 23, 29, 48.

26. Sandra Spickard Prettyman, "Coaches, Language, and Power," in Prettyman and Lampman, *Learning Culture Through Sports*, 76.

27. Alamillo, "Peloteros in Paradise," 57.

28. Alamillo, "Mexican American Baseball," 86.

29. *El Paso Herald-Post*, July 7, 1942.

30. Kath Woodward, *Boxing, Masculinity, and Identity: The "I" of the Tiger* (London: Routledge, 2007), 10.

31. Michael A. Messner, "Masculinities and Athletic Careers: Bonding and Status Differences," in Messner and Sabo, *Sport, Men, and the Gender Order*, 108.

32. Alamillo, "Peloteros in Paradise," 58.

33. Samuel O. Regalado, "Invisible Identity: Mexican American Sport and Chicano Historiography," in Iber and Regalado, *Mexican Americans and Sports*, 234.

34. Alamillo, "Peloteros in Paradise," 50.

35. Richard Santillán, "Mexican Baseball Teams in the Midwest, 1916–1965: The Politics of Cultural Survival and Civil Rights," in *Sports and the Racial Divide: African American and Latino Experience in an Era of Change,* ed. Michael E. Lomax (Jackson: University Press of Mississippi, 2008), 146.

36. *El Paso Times*, August 30, 1948.

37. *El Paso Herald-Post*, January 14–16, 1940.

38. *El Paso Herald-Post*, February 5, 1940.

39. *El Paso Herald-Post*, February 6, 1940.

40. Ibid., and *El Continental*, February 7, 1940.

41. *El Paso Herald-Post*, February 8–9, 1940.

42. *El Paso Herald-Post*, February 9, 1940.

43. *El Continental*, February 10, 1940.

44. *El Paso Herald-Post*, February 12, 1940.

45. Ibid. After this scandal, Sebastian González disappeared from the local boxing scene until he made an inconsequential comeback a few years later.

46. *El Paso Herald-Post*, January 22, 1942.

47. *El Paso Herald-Post*, January 13, 1944.

48. *El Paso Herald-Post*, May 7, 1947.

49. *El Paso Herald-Post*, December 11, 1949.

50. *El Paso Times*, February 3, 1944.

51. *El Paso Times*, March 5–6, 1948; April 10, 1948; August 25, 1948; September 9, 1948; December 1, 1948.

52. *El Paso Times*, January 22, 1944.

53. *El Paso Times*, December 29, 1943; January 13, 1944.

54. *El Paso Times*, May 5, 1947.

55. *El Paso Times*, March 10, 1943. These tournaments were part of the different amateur leagues that flourished around El Paso.

56. *El Paso Times*, January 21, 1949; August 11, 1949; *El Continental*, June 14, 1949.

57. The Texans were later called the Sun Kings (1960s), El Paso Dodgers (1972), and the Diablos after 1974. Sánchez, *El Paso's Greatest Sports Heroes I Have Known*, 202. The Tiguas or Ysleta del Sur with Matt LaBranche bought 59% share of the AA franchise in 2011 and leased the team's home, Cohen Stadium, until 2016 (built in 1990 with a $6 million bond). The Diablos played their last home game August 25, 2013 and the team was forced to move to Joplin, Missouri with the arrival of the new AAA team, the El Paso Chihuahuas who debuted for the 2014 season. In 2013, the city of El Paso made national news when it demolished its own newly upgraded city hall and science museum to make way for the new AAA stadium with a $62 million taxpayer bond. The city now rents office space from the El Paso Chihuahuas owners' renovated historic Mills Building next door to the new Stadium. http://www.elpasotimes.com/ci_23936674/diablos-baseball-final-homestand and http://grantland.com/features/el-paso-chihuahuas-triple-a-minor-league-baseball-mlb-san-diego-padres-stadium-public-funding/ accessed 08/17/2014.58. *El Paso Times*, July 22, 1945; May 17, 1947; March 28, 1948.

59. *El Paso Times*, April 14, 1947.

60. *El Paso Times*, January 8, 1949.

61. *El Paso Times*, December 8, 1949.

62. *El Paso Times*, March 3–4, 1948.

63. *El Paso Times*, April 9, 1948; September 5, 1948.

64. *El Continental*, May 7, 1941.

65. *El Paso Times*, July 5, 1946.

66. *El Paso Times*, July 4, 1943.

67. *El Paso Herald-Post*, January 12, 1943.

68. *El Paso Times*, July 15, 1945.

69. *El Paso Times*, May 17, 1947.

70. Pamela Grundy, *Learning to Win: Sports. Education, and Social Change in Twentieth-Century North Carolina* (Chapel Hill: The University of North Carolina Press, 2001).

71. Lomax, *Sports and the Racial Divide*, xxxii.

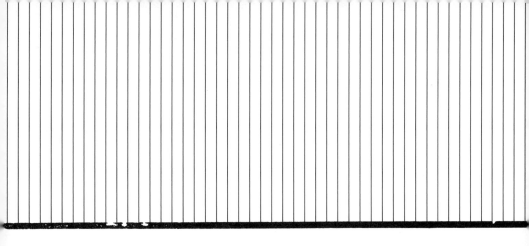

CHAPTER 5

"Bad Boy" of Tennis: Richard 'Pancho' González, Racialized
Masculinity, and the Print Media in Postwar America

José M. Alamillo
California State University Channel Islands

I've always fought, because I've always been pushed around.

Richard "Pancho" González, quoted in Marshall Smith,
"This Old Oro Is Just Too Mean to Quit," *Life*, September 12, 1969, 77.

When people consider the image of the "bad boy" of tennis, they typically recall John McEnroe and his infamous confrontations with umpires and racquet-throwing temper tantrums. Today, however, few remember Richard "Pancho" González. During the 1940s González was considered an earlier tennis bad boy who hailed from the "other side of the tracks" and stunned the tennis world with two national championships in 1948 and 1949. As a Mexican American growing up during World War II in Los Angeles, his bad-boy image in the English-language print media took on both racialized and gendered dimensions. In *Man with a Racket*, González told his story to Cy Rice, who wrote his autobiography. González commented about the English-language media,

> I read the write-ups. Every guy does, no matter how earnestly some
> might tell you that they don't. But ever since the time of my suspen-
> sion for playing hooky, when some writers branded me as anything
> from a "juvenile delinquent" to "Public Enemy No. 1," I stopped be-
> lieving everything I read in the papers.[1]

In contrast, the Spanish-language media portrayed him as a national
hero and role model for Mexican Americans. By the early 1950s González's
image changed as he became a professional tennis player, a married man
with three kids, and a US Davis Cup team member. During the height of
the Cold War, the English print media portrayed González as a model
"American" family man and a weapon of Cold War democracy whose success could help defuse criticism of racial inequality in the United States.
González was very media savvy, often criticizing reporters for their negative portrayals and mischaracterizations. Even after his retirement he
continued to fight for more accurate representation of himself and for
Mexican Americans to gain respect from the sports media and broader
US society.

In this essay I examine the print media's coverage of Richard "Pancho"
González from his amateur years in the 1940s to his professional tennis
career in the 1950s. After providing a brief biography, I analyze González's
image in English- and Spanish-language newspapers, tennis magazines,
sports journals, tennis publications, and mainstream magazines. I show
that the English-language print media constructed González as the bad
boy of tennis within the wartime context of the zoot suit and "Pachuco"
menace that provoked anti–Mexican American hostility in Los Angeles
and throughout the nation. Then I examine the Spanish-language media's
praise of González's athletic achievements and his position as a positive
role model for Mexican American youth. Another topic of analysis is the
coverage of the "Operation Gonzalez" story, which reveals the interplay
between sports, nationalism, and politics. Finally, I show how the print
media during the Cold War constructed Richard González's athletic successes into a "Horatio Alger" narrative as evidence of a color-blind and
democratic America. Despite attempts to represent González as a symbol
of Cold War integration, he still faced racial prejudice and discrimination.
González's responses must be viewed through a gendered lens of mascu-

linity to illuminate how he negotiated his public image with his private life. Ultimately, I argue that racial and gender ideologies communicated through media sources played an important role in the representation of Richard "Pancho" González and the contributions of Latino athletes in US sports.

Ricardo Alonzo González was born on May 9, 1928, and raised in a working-class neighborhood of South Central Los Angeles. Richard's parents were immigrants from Chihuahua, Mexico, who worked long days to help support their seven children. To keep the restless young boy off the streets and out of trouble, his mother bought Richard a fifty-one-cent wooden tennis racket at a local drugstore. At the age of twelve, Richard taught himself to play tennis at a nearby public park. "Exposition Park was where I learned my tennis," González wrote.

> It wasn't as swanky as the Los Angeles Tennis Club—not quite. It was a public playground with eight hard-surfaced courts, standing in the shadow of the Los Angeles Coliseum. Many Mexicans and Negroes learned the game there. Most of us at Exposition Park had two things in common—very little money and a love of tennis.

In contrast to the multiethnic composition of Exposition Park, the Los Angeles Tennis Club (LATC) was the exclusive domain of a wealthy white tennis establishment, which consciously barred African Americans and Mexican Americans from club membership. After winning several public courts tournaments, González was invited to play at the LATC by tennis promoter Perry Jones, who allowed him to borrow a locker. Not surprisingly, González experienced a sense of isolation at the exclusive country club. He recalled, "I found not a familiar face as I started for the locker room. No one smiled at me. No one even talked to me."[2]

He also felt isolated at Manual Arts High School, which contributed to his poor academic performance and high truancy record. Once González dropped out of school in 1945 he was banned from LATC tournaments. Soon thereafter González enlisted in the US Navy until he was dishonorably discharged in 1947 for lack of discipline. Upon returning to the tennis circuit, the nineteen-year-old Mexican American became a star amateur player but was soon suspended for breaking tournament rules. When he finally reconciled with Perry Jones he was allowed to play against Herbie Flam for the Southern California Tennis Championship. After defeating Flam, González traveled to Forest Hills, New York, to play in the national championship. At twenty years old González stunned the tennis world by winning the 1948 national championship. The *New York Times* referred to him as "the rankest outsider of modern times [to sit] on the tennis throne."[3] The following year he proved his "American" patriotism by helping the United States capture the Davis Cup, and a year later he won the US national singles title again. After appearing on the cover of *American Lawn Tennis* with his new wife, Henrietta, he decided to turn professional and join the world tennis circuit.

González signed a contract for sixty thousand dollars to play matches against Jack Kramer in a world-wide professional tennis tour. During the first year he lost ninety-seven matches and won only twenty-seven. To spend more time with family, González put down his tennis racket and did not return the following year. Between 1951 and 1953 González played tennis sporadically, trying new hobbies like bowling, golf, poker, and hot-rod racing. Three years later he was invited by Jack Kramer to rejoin the pro tour.

Now more self-assured, González dominated the tour, winning ninety-one singles titles and earning the world's number-one ranking from 1954 to 1962. Despite his ascendancy in the tennis world, he had a series of contract squabbles with Kramer and often experienced racism on and off the court. For instance, he was denied a visa to play tennis in South Africa during the 1950s.[4] Even though González was a US citizen and identified as a "Mexican American," South African officials identified him racially as a "Mexican." In addition, González's profile in the front cover of a tennis program was "whitened," depicting him as a white, blond-haired tennis player. The English print media depicted González as uncooperative, hot-tempered, angry, and always picking fights with tennis officials and fans. He once told a reporter, "I don't think I ever had a chip on my shoulder, but people said that about me. I think when a fella feels pushed around, it may appear he has a chip on his shoulder because he is defending himself."[5]

The origins of Richard's nickname and the spelling of his surname revealed his attempt to gain recognition and respect from the sports media. Chuck Pate, a former high school tennis coach, gave Richard the nickname of "Pancho." This nickname is typically reserved for the name Francisco or Francis and was offensive to both Richard and his mother. During the postwar period, the name "Pancho" was often used in a derogatory manner toward Mexican males. They were considered rebellious and combative, like the legendary Mexican Revolution general, Pancho Villa, who fought against corrupt government officials. One sportswriter observed that "[Richard] took note of every slight, such as Anglos' habit of calling every Mexican Pancho."[6] Despite his early objections to the nickname, he reluctantly tolerated it for promotional and publicity purposes. When Richard's father immigrated to the United States, US officials changed his last name from "Gonzalez" to "Gonzales," thus passing it down to his children.[7] Official tennis publications and sportswriters continued using the incorrect English spelling. "People Americanized my name," complained Richard, so in the 1970s he was inspired by the Chicano movement to change his surname to its original Spanish spelling with a "z" at the end.[8]

His defensive shield affected his family life and relationship with women. In 1947, seventeen-year-old Richard first met Henrietta Pedrin at his sister's party, and within a year they eloped to Arizona. The newlyweds moved into an apartment and lived off the prize-money González earned as an amateur player, which was not nearly enough; when Richard turned professional it meant being on the road and away from his wife and kids. González later admitted that his absence caused much strain in his family life. Subsequently he divorced and later married five times. In 1962 he coached the US Davis Cup team to a successful victory. He had many retirements that did not last—returning to play in several tournaments during the Open Era (the period after 1968 when professionals were allowed to compete in Grand Slam tournaments)—and in 1968 he was finally inducted into the International Tennis Hall of Fame. At the end of his contract with Jack Kramer he retired in 1961 and took a job as a tennis coach at a Bahamas tourist resort and later built an eight-acre tennis ranch in Malibu with his second wife, Madelyn Darrow (a former beauty queen, model, and Hollywood actress). Not until the mid-1970s did González finally retire; he worked as a professional tennis coach at Caesar's Palace in

Las Vegas, where he met the Agassi family. On March 31, 1984, Gonzalez married Rita Agassi, the twenty-three-year-old sister of tennis champion Andre Agassi. He died in Las Vegas on July 3, 1995, of stomach cancer.

"Bad Boy" of Tennis in Wartime Los Angeles

During the 1940s, newspaper and magazine sportswriters repeatedly emphasized González's ethnic and racial identity as opposed to Euro-American competitors who were considered normative "white" tennis players.[9] They referred to him as a "dark Mexican American youngster"[10] or a "husky 20-year-old Mexican American"[11] or a "tall colorful Mexican American."[12] They even linked his fighting spirit on the court to Mexican revolutionary heroes. For example, a *Los Angeles Times* sports columnist remarked that because of "the way he murders that tennis ball . . . his real name is Pancho Villa, not Gonzales."[13] Another *Los Angeles Times* article compared him to a Mexican gunslinger: "National Champion Richard (Pancho) Gonzales unlimbers his big guns and opens fire today in the 31st annual Los Angeles Metropolitan tennis championships at Griffith Park."[14] Even though he was born and raised in the United States, these descriptions functioned to mark González as a perpetual Mexican foreigner and cultural "other."[15]

González's bad-boy image was partially attributed to his early teenage years when he "played hooky" from school and was sent to reform school for stealing. But the scar on his face and his ethnic identity were given greater importance within the racially charged atmosphere of wartime Los Angeles.[16] The public image of González was influenced by sensationalist newspaper headlines about juvenile crime supposedly perpetuated by Mexican American youth subculture known as "Pachucos" and "zoot suiters."[17] The large scar on the left side of his face due to a childhood car accident contributed to his "Pachuco" image.

While playing for the 1947 Southern California Tennis Championship at the Los Angeles Tennis Club, González overheard a remark from a spectator in the front row: "Look at that scar on his face. It must be a knife wound."[18] Angered by the remark, he later wrote, "Thousands of tennis spectators believe it to be true, because they think a knife scar and Mexican American youth go hand in hand."[19] One sportswriter attributed his 1949 national championship victory against Ted Schroeder to his face scar. "They said you could always tell when Pancho Gonzales was mad. The scar on his cheek—the mark left by an accident in his youth—caught fire. It sent an angry flame across his face."[20] His face scar contributed to a common stereotype of hot-tempered Latino men.[21]

One commentator called him a "hot-headed Latin" whose "blood boiled" and the "flame on his cheek burn[ed] hotter" when he heard discouraging remarks.[22] "The scar affected my mother more than me," recalled González:

> She had always prided herself on her appearance, as well as her family's appearance. All of her children had smooth, olive skin, and my scar was very visible. Worse, there was a Mexican song popular at that time called *Juan Charrasqueado* (John the Scarface) about a man who was the lowest of the low. Concerned that this scar might give me an unjust reputation, she rubbed cocoa butter cream on my face every day. I walked around smelling like chocolate.[23]

Gonzalez's family was even upset when the print media attached the "Pachuco" label to his aggressive behavior on and off the court. Los Angeles newspapers popularized the term to refer to maladjusted Mexican male youths involved in gangs and juvenile delinquency. For this reason, according to a *Life* magazine reporter, "The entire González clan resents the legend that he grew up as a zoot-suiter *pachuco*." Richard's mother insisted that her son "was a 'good boy.' The only crime he ever did was not go to school."[24]

González's bad-boy image was also attributed to his penchant for Mexican food. A *Time* magazine reporter described his preference for beer and beans:

> As the game's brightest young star, Pancho is now eligible for becks & nods from the social set that patronizes big time tennis. But, he says, "I don't drink cocktails—just beer." Besides, the food at fancy parties does not appeal to Pancho's cast-iron stomach, which thrives on beans (with or without chili and cheese) and tortillas.[25]

When González scored two major upsets at the 1947 Pacific Southwest

Tennis Tournament, the *Los Angeles Times* credited his victory as "Muy Caliente and hotter than a piping bowl of chili."[26] In addition, *American Lawn Tennis* recounted how González was "leaping around like a Mexican jumping bean [and] seems to be as hot as a bowl of chili on the center court."[27] The same tennis magazine attributed González's victory at the Southampton Tennis Championship to his Mexican food diet. "You don't have to have chili sauce in your veins or jumping beans in the tennis balls to win at Southampton but it helps. Next time we will inspect the Meadows Club Invitation tournament silverware. We're going to look closer for engraved *tamale*."[28]

Another common perception was that González was a natural athlete whose on-court playing style resembled a "jungle cat" and a "toro" (bull) in the middle of a bullfight. In a close quarterfinal match against top-seeded Frank Parker at Forest Hills, González was described as having "fought back like a tiger and pulled out of the set" to win the match and tournament. Parker often described his matches against González like "bullfights" because of his cannonball serves that landed like bullets and his "incessant volleying attack."[29] Because of his low-crouching playing style in anticipation of his opponents' serves and attacking the net, he was often compared to a "tiger" that "snarled at opponents, drilled balls at judges' heads, and . . . rushed into the stands to strong-arm a heckler."[30] When González turned professional and joined the pro tennis world tour in the 1950s, he was asked by tour organizer Jack Kramer to "ease up a little" against his opponents. But according to Kramer, "That was like asking an angry jungle cat to claw gently." Kramer added, "Pancho gets 50 points on his serve and 50 points on terror."[31] The use of animal metaphors to describe González resembled the racist perception of African American athletes as naturally athletic, compared to white athletes who are more technical and mentally tough.[32]

"Maestro de la Raqueta" and the Spanish-Language Press

In analyzing the press coverage of González in the Spanish-language newspaper *La Opinión,* the bad-boy image so prevalent in the English language media was largely absent. There were repeated accounts of this Mexican American athlete who became "El Maestro de la Raqueta" (master of the tennis racquet) in a predominantly white sport.[33] *La Opinion* protested the Los Angeles sportswriters' frequent use of the nickname "Pancho" and instead preferred to call him by his given name of "Ricardo." "It is those sports editors and tennis officials that call him 'Pancho' but to us he is Ricardo Gonzalez."[34] *La Opinión* sportswriters celebrated his athletic achievements and anointed him as a "role model" for Mexican American youth. This Los Angeles–based newspaper also followed his whereabouts at the Pan-American Tournament in Mexico City and local tennis tournaments organized by a Mexican American tennis club.

When González was banned from playing tennis at the Los Angeles Tennis Club, he headed for the public tennis courts at Exposition Park, Griffith Park, and Evergreen Playground. González participated in several tennis tournaments at Evergreen Playground. A Mexican American Tennis Club was formed at Evergreen Playground in the late 1930s and, with the financial sponsorship of the Mexican Athletic Union (UAM), organized several tournaments with visiting tennis players from Mexico.[35] One of González's main rivals and close friends was Fernando Isais, the founding secretary of the Mexican Tennis Club, who later became national horseshoe pitching champion. Isais boasted about never losing a tennis match to his close friend. "Ricardo González has yet to beat Fernando Isais," asserted *La Opinión*. "The UAM has much to be proud of when its champion Isais competes against González who was named the future champion of the world by the white tennis establishment."[36]

La Opinión's sports columnists routinely referred to tennis at the Los Angeles Tennis Club as "el deporte blanco" (the white sport) for its association with exclusive country clubs, the predominance of white players, and barring African Americans from professional tennis from the beginning.[37] Visiting tennis players from Mexico complained to *La Opinión* about "discourtesies" they received at an LATC tournament in which they were denied tennis balls for practice and were ejected from their seats while watching the tournament.[38] Even though Richard González was allowed to play at the LATC, he did not always feel welcome. *La Opinión* sports columnists were surprised that Gonzalez, a "dark-skinned young man" nicknamed "el muchacho travieso" (troublemaker boy), was allowed into the "white tennis world, despite the long history of racism in the sport."[39]

Inclusion, however, did not always lead to equal treatment. Nevertheless, *La Opinión* celebrated González's accomplishments in the realm of tennis. "The triumph of González was one of the biggest and amazing successes in the annals of white tennis," declared *La Opinión* sports columnist Rodolfo Garcia, reminding readers that "González is Mexican—because he is a son of Mexican parents. He is Mexican because it does not matter where he is born—achieved an amazing career in just twenty years of age in the history of white tennis."[40] After winning the 1948 national title, González received the Best Athlete Award from the Helms Athletic Foundation. Garcia reflected on the meaning of this prestigious award for Mexican American youth.

> This award represents something important for all Mexicans that were born in this country and those that reside here, who struggle daily against [racial] prejudices. He shows that perhaps these prejudices may disappear in the near future. . . . The Mexican population that resides in southern California should be ready to deliver a tribute to Gonzalez for what he has achieved, triumph that he has reached by his own effort, spirit of initiative, and stoicism that allowed him to confront barriers that always interfere against those that are not born with a silver spoon in their mouth. The case of Gonzales is an example for our Mexican youth, who at 20 years old has already obtained financial security with a perseverance and talent, and reached a place where he can determine his own successful future. He is the example for youngsters of Mexican origin.[41]

La Opinión boasted about González's athletic achievements to instruct Mexican American youth to follow a similar path. Like their English-language counterparts, these sportswriters also emphasized his Mexican national identity and promoted a middle-class ideology of "racial uplift" by instructing youth that through moral refinement and hard work they could advance socially and economically.[42]

After González won his second national title, *La Opinión*'s Rodolfo Garcia again reminded readers that González was in fact the champion of the world, similar to a prizefighter who—winning a championship title—earns the right to declare himself "champion of the world." Garcia added that it should be, "Equally, in tennis . . . The one who wins the national championship is really the champion of the world, since the United States produces the best tennis players in the world."[43] Years later, when González was losing matches against Jack Kramer, *La Opinion* sportswriters encouraged readers to attend his matches in Los Angeles because "by having Mexican fans maybe his luck will change."[44] Even González believed things would be different upon returning to his hometown. In front of six thousand spectators, including many Latinos, at the Pan Pacific Auditorium in Los Angeles, González soundly beat Kramer in a three-set match.[45]

In 1951 González played in ten all-expense-paid tournaments that violated the amateur rule of only eight tournaments per year. As a result he was suspended by the United States Lawn Tennis Association (USLTA). While González waited for a decision on his appeal from USLTA, the English and Spanish print media reported that Mexican government officials offered González to trade his US citizenship for a Mexico citizenship. In addition, the Bank of Mexico offered González to pay for his college education and a job at Mexico's consulate office in Los Angeles.[46]

This story became known as "Operation Gonzalez" in the English-language press, and it revealed how sports and politics play an important role in power struggles between nations. The story began in October 1947 when González played in his first Pan American Tennis Tournament in Mexico City. Eduardo Aguilar, president of the Bank of Mexico, founded the tournament in 1942 to develop tennis in Mexico, increase tourism to Mexico City, and promote "goodwill relations" with its northern neighbor.[47] This tournament was part of President Franklin Roosevelt's Good Neighbor Policy program that sought to promote inter-American cooperation between the United States and Latin America.[48] During the 1947 tournament, González "caught the fancy of local tennis patrons," including Aguilar, considered "the man behind the tennis movement south of the border," who invited him to play in Mexico.[49] González accepted Aguilar's invitation and attracted the sports media, which penned glowing accounts about his athletic performance.[50] When González defeated Mexico's national champion, Armando Vega, *El Excelsior* wrote that "we were left with the consolation that at least he was a player of Mexican blood."[51] *American Lawn Tennis* magazine billed it as a "real Mexican blood match."[52] Even though González did not win the championship, the *Los Angeles Times* claimed that since then "[González] has been pondering over the problem . . . of whether or not to don the cloak of Mexican citizenship."[53]

Once the story broke, Los Angeles newspapers updated readers on González's final decision and blamed the "tennis tycoons," mainly Perry Jones and the USLTA, for their "attempted sale of the nation's most promising young player to Mexico."[54] Ned Cronin of the *Los Angeles Daily News* reminded readers that after González beat local talent at the 1947 Pacific Southwest Championship, "Jones & Co. had launched a campaign to sell Gonzales to the Mexicans." Cronin claimed,

> Word got around that it would be a wonderful thing for Gonzales to go to Mexico where he could be among his own people and get the breaks he so richly deserves. As an American citizen he must have felt out of place way up here in the United States—a former G.I. lost and bewildered with nobody to turn to except his own countrymen.[55]

Cronin berated the "tennis moguls" for their "stony silence" on Mexico's offer. "One might wonder why Jones and the United States Lawn Tennis Association didn't kick up a horrific fuss over Mexico trying to put the hustle on our tennis talent." He then compared this situation to the "baseball war" between the United States and Mexico when Jorge Pasquel, head of the Mexican Baseball League, lured "the big leaguers south of the border," and "baseball fathers" fought back.[56] Cronin argued that this was "the same music with different words . . . might have been expected from the tennis set . . . But the brass in the net ranks kept its collective lip well buttoned."[57] Paul Zimmerman, *Los Angeles Times* sports columnist, blamed González for his lack of education in violating USLTA rules:

> Tennis had been his life. He had not cared at all for grammar school but instead spent long hours on the public courts perfecting his net game. When the Mexican offer came it appeared that his hopes of stardom had been brooked by rules he never had bothered to understand.[58]

Being acutely aware of his public image in the press, González manipulated the story to his own advantage in order to avoid suspension and gain a spot on the US Davis Cup team. He told the *Los Angeles Times*, "It's a hard decision, and I haven't been able to make up my mind yet. . . . I must give my answer, but there are so many things to consider that right now I don't know which way to turn."[59] Ultimately, González decided to keep his US citizenship, citing his military service in the US Navy and desire to represent the United States in the international arena. When asked why he rejected Mexico's offer, González responded, "I prize my [US] citizenship above all these benefits [offered by Mexico]. After discussing the problem with my parents I made up my mind to stay right here."[60] The *Los Angeles Times* praised his decision: "Pancho Gonzales, the new sensation on the Southern California tennis horizon, has been described as an irresponsible young man. We prefer to think that he proved the contrary when he decided against giving up his citizenship just to become a tennis bum in Mexico."[61] The newspaper concluded that "his faith in the American way will continue to pay dividends."[62] *Newsweek* magazine reported on González's desire to join the US Davis Cup team. "A friend finally made up his mind for him by asking if would rather play for the American Davis Cup team or the Mexican. Pancho's response was the American [team]."[63] Ultimately, the USLTA rewarded González for keeping his US citizenship by giving him a shorter suspension of six months, thus allowing him to participate in the larger tournaments.

Only *La Opinion* newspaper raised doubts about the Mexican government's job offer to González. "The job offer was not very credible. . . . Most likely this was a forged story created to give publicity to the boy." The story generated widespread publicity, allowing González to leverage Mexico's offer against the US tennis officials. The newspaper did confirm, however, that González was given a proposal to play under the Mexican flag, but the offer was given by the Mexican Tennis Association, not the Mexican government. This distinction was important, since the sports association could not hire employees for the Mexico consulate office. *La Opinion* also observed that "the [Mexican] government is not very interested in sports, especially in tennis. The idea that he will become Mexican again does not ring credible south of the Rio Bravo."[64] Although tennis was overshadowed by baseball and soccer, the Mexican government did attempt to develop the sport by sponsoring a Davis Cup team (beginning in 1924) and create the Mexico Tennis Association to develop junior tennis players at the city's premiere tennis club, Centro Deportivo Chapultepec.[65]

Cold War Warrior on and off the Court

After González won his first national title, a *Los Angeles Times* reader penned an editorial titled "No Hyphen Needed" and criticized the newspaper for references to the "the tall, colorful Mexican-American."[66] The reader argued that González's ethnicity "can add nothing to his prestige as a great tennis champion and American champion," and since Euro-American tennis players are not hyphenated, "Why then make reference to him as a Mexican-American any more than to some of our other fine tennis players." The reader concluded, "He is an American and will, undoubtedly, play as an American in foreign competition in the future." The reader expressed the prevailing view during the early days of the Cold War that the United States was a democratic society with equal opportunities for racial minority athletes in sports. Jackie Robinson's debut with the Brooklyn Dodgers in 1947 not only signaled the successful integration of professional baseball and other sports but also symbolized Cold War integration. As Damion Thomas has suggested, "Robinson's success helped characterize integrated sports as proof that a world with the United States as the 'leader of the free world' held forth a realistic change that all people of the world would experience progress and be able to live 'the good life.' "[67] In fact, African American athletes, including Althea Gibson—the first black female to compete in integrated tennis tournaments—were recruited by the US State Department to participate in goodwill tours around the world as part of the government's effort to promote "American democracy" abroad.[68] Although González did not participate in state-sponsored goodwill tours, his athletic achievements in a predominantly white sport were used by the sports and mainstream media to dispel the notion that the United States was undemocratic and discriminatory toward racial minorities.[69]

After winning two national championships and helping the United States win the Davis Cup in 1949, González's image shifted from the bad boy of tennis to an all-American athlete who achieved the benefits of American democracy. For example, when González won his second national title in 1949, his victory took on a new meaning as Cold War hysteria reached new levels in the United States. After mainland China established a communist regime there was concern that Soviet Russia was installing communist regimes around the world. But as Mary L. Dudziak has convincingly argued, the image of American democracy was also at stake when Communist countries criticized the United States' poor record on race relations.[70] So when prominent African American activist Paul Robeson made a speech before the World Peace Congress criticizing American racism and claiming that African Americans would not fight on behalf of the United States, his remarks were not well received by the American press.[71] A *Los Angeles Times* sportswriter used González's athletic success to counter Paul Robeson's remarks. He wrote,

> While Paul Robeson was raising accusations that discrimination is destroying the hope of American youth, the complete reply was being played out on the tennis courts of Forest Hills, just 40 miles away. Gonzales is 21, the son of a Mexican American family similar to so many in this community. He had no advantages above those granted any other youngster in this region, but he made the most of what was available. Gonzales scored a great victory, and in so doing marked a victory as well for the American way of life.[72]

Robeson was also criticized by Jackie Robinson and made national headlines when he testified against communists at House Un-American Activities Committee hearings.[73]

In an attempt to manipulate foreign perceptions of American race relations, the sports media applied the Horatio Alger myth to the life story of Richard González. *American Lawn Tennis* magazine used the Horatio Alger narrative to explain González's individual achievement in the sport as evidence of the superiority of America's capitalist system. "When national champion Richard Gonzales battered the defending champion into submission in the Los Angeles Metropolitan tennis championship," wrote Bion Abbott, "he wrote the final chapter in a success story which reads like a volume straight from Horatio Alger."[74] When tennis writers discussed his trajectory, they began with his family's working-class roots followed by his transformation into a tennis champion, winning prize money and exclusive endorsement contracts. As Paul Zimmerman of the *Los Angeles Times* put it, "Pancho definitely is an 'across the tracks' athlete. Yet, like most of them, he has poise, modesty, charm, gracious court mannerisms, and sparkling color."[75] Several years the later the same newspaper emphasized his high earnings. "Big Pancho Gonzalez may have spurned a formal education during his tempestuous youth, but he picked up a rudimentary knowledge of mathematics along the way. . . . Pancho's favorite indoor sport is adding up the dollars that roll in from his professional tennis endeavors."[76]

For González, earnings from the tour and endorsements were important, but he also wanted to help win the Davis Cup for the United States. In 1949 González was selected to the Davis Cup team by the USLTA and helped to win the international tennis trophy against Australia. Although he did not rejoin the Davis Cup team when he became a contracted professional player in the 1950s, he continued to support the team by training with them. As one Davis Cup coach asserted, "The US Lawn Tennis Association has not instructed us to hire Gonzales, but [he] will help us, out of patriotism. If [he] can work out with us they will not only test our games to the utmost but will give a terrific boost to our morale."[77] In 1962 Gonzalez became a coach for the US Davis Cup team and quickly earned a reputation for "drilling" his players and "losing his temper" with players who did not try harder to win for their country.[78] "Most people regard Wimbledon as the most important tourney on the world circuit, but not Pancho," wrote one sports columnist. "He rates Davis Cup play as No. 1 because you're representing your country." He was quoted as stating that "I think an American would rather win his own title than Wimbledon. . . . I don't think I'd ever trade my national championship over Ted Schroeder for anything I ever won."[79]

Another prevailing image of González during the Cold War era was the "male breadwinner" and "father" who spent quality time with his wife, Henrietta, and three children when not playing tennis. As Elaine Tyler May has argued, the traditional family was portrayed as the defense of democratic capitalism and against external threats such as nuclear bombs and communist subversion.[80] A *Los Angeles Times* article titled "Pancho

Rests by Helping at Home" described his "vacation from the tennis wars" by spending time with wife and three sons. The picture shows González tinkering with hot-rod cars with his three sons while his wife watches. González stated, "This is my first summer at home with my family in six years. . . . Now all I have to do is help my wife Henrietta, feed the kids, fix up the house, clean out the garage, trim the shrubbery, get the kids from school, bring in groceries." Even though he was spending time with family, he was restless and always finding new hobbies. The article described his new hobby of racing hot-rod cars on the weekends. Henrietta complained, "When he warmed up the car outside our garage last week, neighbors came flying out of their homes like an atom bomb had gone off."[81]

The home life of the Gonzalez family was not, however, as romantic as depicted by the print media. When he returned home from the pro tour he had a difficult time readjusting to home life, and he admitted that it was hardest on Henrietta and his three young sons. "When I was on the tennis tour, I didn't spend as much time with them as I should have. So, while I wasn't rough on them like my father was with us, I wasn't as good a father as I should have been."[82] After separating for three years and reconciling, the couple divorced in December 1958. Henrietta testified in court, "Last June, my husband called me from New York and told me he had not been happy at home and would not return to me when his tour ended."[83] In the final divorce settlement, Henrietta received the family home, a monthly alimony for the children, and an insurance policy, while Richard retained his bank accounts, tennis and advertising contracts, and property investments. One court official sarcastically blurted out, "This is the most important match he has ever lost."[84] This was only the beginning of his many divorces, which eventually totaled six, and he had eight children with four different wives. Richard later admitted, "I just can't hold still long enough to be a model husband. I can't relax. I've got too much energy. I can't come home at night, put on my house slippers, and lead a domestic, by-the-fireside existence."[85]

Despite the image of González as a symbol of Cold War democracy and integration, his inclusion in the tennis world did not mean he was free of racial discrimination. During his pro tour in Texas, González described a racist incident in Central Texas in which he, his brother Manuel, and

Pancho Segura were denied service in a restaurant with a "No Mexicans Served Here" sign. Even though they protested that Segura was not Mexican but Ecuadorian, and that González was a world tennis champion, the owner said it did not matter; they were refused service because "those Mexs are all alike." When an Anglo customer called González a "wetback spic," he turned around and punched him. According to Segura, "We had to keep him from fighting. He had no fear. He'd challenge anybody."[86]

Upon returning to Los Angeles he discussed the incident with his lawyer, who told him that he had escaped many overt forms of racial discrimination because of his celebrity status, but it had finally caught up to him. The lawyer advised González to pay more attention to his social responsibility to "your people—the Mexican Americans. Their roots grow in shallow soil here. They need help. Especially the kids. They need understanding."[87] Richard heeded his lawyer's advice and began to meet with local leaders like Ignacio Lopez, publisher of El Espectador, and Ed Roybal (the first Mexican American city council member of Los Angeles) to gain a better understanding of the problems confronting Mexican Americans.[88]

González attributed many of the problems confronting Mexican American youth to racism. He wrote, "Unlike European immigrants, Mexicans can be fourth generation, but if their skin is dark and if they have a Spanish name, they are never accepted—they're always known as Mexicans."[89] In researching the "gang" problem, González concluded,

> They [Mexican Americans] cry for recognition, a life without restrictions, equal rights, to find employment with chances for advancement. When they can't find a place in the American way of life, they are forced to resort to their own groups, their own behavior patterns which are neither American nor Mexican. And they become a clique widely separated from the majority of their countrymen.

González sympathized with Mexican American youth because they had "two strikes against them the day they enter the world," which leads to bewilderment and isolation. González empathized with alienated Mexican American youth because he was once lost and in need of some guidance while trying to gain inclusion into the white tennis establishment. He "resolved to do something to help" by holding tennis clinics in his Malibu home for Mexican American kids from East Los Angeles.[90]

The image of González was "whitened" for the front cover of the 1959 program of Jack Kramer Presents World Championship Tennis. The image featured the body of Richard González but with blond hair, lighter skin, a smaller nose, and smaller lips. There is no mention of the player's identity on the front cover, but compared to another image inside the 1957 program, it closely resembles González. "The way he was treated during his prime is summed up in a Kramer tour program featuring Pancho Gonzalez on the cover," noted Richard's younger brother Ralph Gonzales in an article he cowrote for a Latino magazine. "This Pancho, however, was altered to make him more acceptable to country club crowds. This Pancho, through the miracle of printing, was given a blond head of hair and light skin."[91] González later admitted that his feud with Kramer was about money. "I didn't always see eye-to-eye with Jack when we were playing for money. It changes the nature of the game, and I suppose I did become temperamental. But we played in some awful conditions, and I think [Kramer] sometimes paid more attention to money than conditions."[92] One newspaper article reported, "The rivalry between the two was a natural social and ethnic one; and since both men were loud and outspoken, the rivalry was set ablaze later by their angry quarreling."[93] According to his first wife, Henrietta, Richard resented Tony Trabert's frequent slights in correcting his English.[94] The only person he preferred to spend time with during the tour was Pancho Segura, originally from Ecuador; Segura was recruited by the University of Miami to play college tennis and then joined the pro tour in 1954. According to Australian player Lew Hoad, both "Panchos" were "close pals" because they were "born on the wrong side of the tracks," and "Their rich friendship has bloomed in their own vernacular Spanish."[95] Pancho Segura admitted that they developed a close friendship because "we were both Latin-American."[96]

It was not only tennis players that González had difficulty befriending; the umpires and fans were often a thorn in his side. For example, during an Australian match against Ken Rosewall, fans "erupted in a storm of hisses, boos, and foot pounding" against González. The fans continued to taunt "the Los Angeles star by shouting excerpts from a newspaper dispatch in which Gonzales said Rosewall didn't have a chance against him."[97] At another Australian match against Lew Hoad, the majority of fans booed González. In response, "Gonzales slammed the ball angrily into the stands."[98] One spectator kept yelling at González until he stopped the game and threatened the spectator to "come onto the court and we'll have it out."[99] Some hecklers called him a "poor sport" and a "crybaby," especially when González threw or broke his racket. In another incident, González walked to the first row of the stands and asked the heckler to come forward. The heckler came forward, and before a fight broke out, the tennis umpire intervened.[100]

Racialized Masculinity

The postwar tennis world had many advantages for male tennis players compared to their female counterparts; higher prize money, more sports media attention, more endorsement offers, and more coaching resources.[101] Richard's relationship to female players, referees, and fans was largely determined by his masculine behavior. Pancho Segura once told a reporter about how Richard related to women: "You know, the nicest thing [Pancho] ever says to his wives is 'Shut up.'"[102] González's relationship with women and notions of masculinity stemmed from his relationship with his strict father.[103] At thirteen years old, Richard recalled an incident when his father broke his tennis rackets because he considered tennis "a sissy sport," claiming that "Mexicans were proud people who worked hard for a living."[104] Initially Richard himself regarded tennis as a "sissy" sport compared to team sports like basketball and football, but gradually changed his mind when he started playing competitively and winning "alone [with] no help from anybody."[105]

The dominant cultural stereotype of *machismo* cannot fully explain Richard's masculine behavior. Monolithic generalizations about Latino masculinity have been criticized by scholars for ignoring changing regional and social contexts as well as race, sexuality, and class factors.[106] Latino masculinity is more complicated, contradictory, and situated within a racial hierarchy of manliness in which some forms of masculinity are more dominant while others are subordinated or marginalized.[107] Richard's responses to, and relationships with, women and men should be interpreted through the gendered lens of "racialized masculinity."[108] His attempt to succeed in the white tennis world was as much about establishing and defending his manhood on and off the court.

At a 1972 Queen's Club tournament in London, González was disqualified by a female referee during a semifinal match when he argued a close line call and then yelled at her, "Don't come too close to me, lady, or I might lose my temper."[109] The lady referee stood up to González until he walked away toward the locker room as he shouted, "I don't need preaching from any referee—any lady referee."[110] González defended his antagonistic behavior toward fans and umpires. He wrote,

> A tennis player is entitled to temperament. Nobody criticizes an actor or actress for temperamental outbursts. Is tennis so unrelated to the stage? On a court in an important match a player performs before thousands. . . . He's crowd conscious; perhaps not of individual faces, but of the throng which includes the swelling tide of voices, the thunder of applause, the groans of sorrow. He becomes part athlete with a generous slice of ham thrown in.[111]

González attributed his on-court power and prowess to an attempt to defend his manhood on the court. As he explained to a newspaper reporter after losing at the 1969 US Open, "I'm not what I used to be. Preparation used to bring me to a point where I could play at 100 percent of my capacity about 85 percent of the match. And I could always call on my best when I had to. I have to take one match at a time. . . . I used to feel less of a man when I lost. But now I've satisfied myself that I'm a winner, so now I can accept defeat."[112] His aggressiveness and boisterousness on the court, combined with the frequent traveling and racial micro-aggressions, also made him into a loner. He was frequently labeled a "lone wolf" by his tennis opponents because he was reclusive at times, and during the 1958 pro tour he "live[d] like a monk."[113]

Although González's aggressive playing and unflagging ferocity on the court boosted his tough male image, the English-language press also constructed him as an exotic male "other." Throughout the 1950s, magazine and newspaper stories frequently mentioned his sex appeal to white female fans. A *Los Angeles Examiner* article noted his appeal for women: "The movies haven't a more virile specimen of masculinity. He causes the feminine heartstrings to make like soft chimes."[114] *Life* magazine observed, "Women find him fascinating when he steps on the court . . .

gaunt and sinister, and begins stalking his prey. Men are intrigued by his hoodlum appeal, his angry and sullen manner."[115] Pancho Segura admitted that when they both went out together in the evenings, González was "always the Tesoro, the target of all the females"; "the dark-eyed, dark-skinned, six-foot-three tennis god, with mysterious scar and the sensuous panther-like body, was a magnet to the opposite sex."[116] One white suburban lady described González, "Why, he's like a bronze Greek god, of course. He's so beautiful. I just flip over him, I tell you. Just flip. I could stare at him for hours. There's such an aura of masculinity about him, and isn't that rare among American men now?"[117] For this white woman, González represented a refreshing image to the dominant images of white middle-class men represented as feminized and emasculated by the suburban lifestyle and crass consumerism of the 1950s.[118] He possessed an "exotic" masculinity not unlike Mexican American actor Anthony Quinn, whose imposing physical presence and racial ambiguity made him a favorite Hollywood celebrity.[119]

Conclusion

Richard constantly felt under scrutiny from the sports media and public eye in part because of his racial and ethnic identity. González once wrote, "I've got the feeling that the interest in 'Pancho' Gonzales was not based on what I could do with my racket, but rather on what I had achieved off the court—as a non-conformist. I was a curiosity number."[120] He told one sports editor, "I've always fought, because I've always been pushed around."[121] These statements reveal how deeply aware González was of his image in the sports media.

This defensive posture began early in life as a rebellious teenager who defied his parents, truant officers, tennis elite, umpires, fans, and the press. During his amateur years in the 1940s he was depicted as the "bad boy" of tennis who threatened to revoke his US citizenship and play tennis for Mexico. However, after he won two national titles and helped the United States win the Davis Cup, his image began to change. During the Cold War years, González was hailed as a symbol of American democracy and a Horatio Alger figure as well as a family man. His all-American-boy image was touted as a model of racial progress and American nationalism.

In contrast, the Spanish-language press portrayed González in a positive way, touting his athletic achievements and upholding him as a role model for Mexican American youth. Even though he entered the professional ranks and toured around the world earning prize money, he still faced racial discrimination inside and outside the tennis world. His responses to racism in the tennis world, however, were also gendered. Using the concept of "racialized masculinity" to interpret Gonzalez's behavior, we gain a more complicated understanding of Latino masculinity.

His experience made him conscious of the civil rights struggles of African Americans and Mexican Americans in the United States. When African American tennis great Arthur Ashe enrolled at the University of California, Los Angeles, González offered advice and coaching tips. Ashe wrote, "Three stars shone brighter than all the others in my sky. One of them was Pancho Gonzalez, who was not only the best player in the world but also an outsider, like me, because he was Mexican American."[122] González also closely identified with Althea Gibson, considered the "Jackie Robinson of tennis," who overcame racial and gender barriers in the white tennis world to win eleven major championships but still faced "cool treatment" from spectators in many cities.[123] During one of her "goodwill tours" sponsored by the US State Department, she lost her temper with a photographer and a sportswriter. He defended her reaction since she was "constantly in the public eye. If she stubs her toe, it has news value. Due to racial barriers, she is a test case."[124] The burden of being a "race pioneer" combined with lower prize money for female athletes in the pre-open era of tennis made it financially difficult to continue in the sport of tennis. Unlike Gibson, González had more opportunities to play because of his male privilege.

Notes

1. Pancho Gonzales and Cy Rice, *Man with a Racket: The Autobiography of Pancho Gonzales* (New York: A. S. Barnes and Company, 1959), 53.

2. Ibid., 24–25.

3. *New York Times*, December 19, 1948.

4. *Los Angeles Sentinel*, March 5, 1970.

5. *Los Angeles Times*, February 18, 1975.

6. S. L. Price, "The Lone Wolf," *Sports Illustrated*, June 24, 2002, 71.

7. Doreen Gonzales, *Richard "Pancho" Gonzalez: Tennis Champion* (Springfield, NJ: Enslow Publishers, 1998), 9–10.

8. *Los Angeles Times*, July 5, 1995.

9. *Los Angeles Times*, September 17, 1948.

10. *Los Angeles Times*, September 18, 1948.

11. *Los Angeles Times*, September 19, 1948.

12. *Los Angeles Times*, September 20, 1948.

13. Gonzales and Rice, *Man with a Racket*, 129.

14. *Los Angeles Times*, January 16, 1949.

15. On Mexican American stereotypes in the print media, see Luis Reyes, "Behind the Mask of Zorro: Mexican American Images and Stereotypes in Western Films and Television," in *Mask of Zorro: Mexican Americans and Popular Media* (Los Angeles: Gene Autry Western Heritage Museum, 1994), 20–46.

16. On the racial climate in Los Angeles during World War II, see Kevin Leonard, *The Battle for Los Angeles: Racial Ideology during World War II* (Albuquerque: University of New Mexico Press, 2006).

17. Eduardo Obregón Pagán, *Murder at the Sleepy Lagoon: Zoot Suits, Race, and Riots in Wartime L.A.* (Chapel Hill: University of North Carolina Press, 2003).

18. Gonzales and Rice, *Man with a Racket*, 26.

19. Ibid., 61.

20. Will Grimsley, "Pancho's Greatest Hour at Forest Hills," in Grimsley, *Tennis: Its History, People, and Events* (Englewod Cliffs, NJ: Prentice Hall, 1971), 299.

21. Donald Frio and Marc Onigman, "'Good Field, No Hit': The Image of the Latin American Baseball Players in the American Press, 1871–1946," *Revista/Review Interamericana* 9 (Summer 1979): 199–208.

22. Will Grimsley, "Pancho Gonzales—Latin Fire and Fury," in Grimsley, *Tennis*, 96.

23. Rita Agassi Gonzalez, "The Power and the Fury," *World Tennis*, September 1987, 75.

24. Gene Farmer, "Pancho Gonzales: Amateur Tennis' No. 1 Bad Boy Is Also Its No. 1 Star," *Life*, June 6, 1949, 77.

25. "Indoors and Out," *Time,* April 4, 1949, 77.

26. *Los Angeles Times,* September 26, 1947.

27. Bion Abbott, "Pancho Gonzales Stars as Real Giant Killer," *American Lawn Tennis,* November 1, 1947, 34.

28. Jeane Hoffman, "Conquistador Gonzales Reigns at Southampton," *American Lawn Tennis,* September 15, 1948, 87.

29. "Life a Bullfight," *Time,* September 27, 1948, 64.

30. "Pancho at 41," *Time,* February 16, 1970, 57.

31. Ibid.

32. Sundiata Djata, *Blacks at the Net: Black Achievement in the History of Tennis* (Syracuse, NY: Syracuse University Press, 2006), 183–91.

33. *La Opinion,* September 19, 1949

34. *La Opinion,* January 9, 1950.

35. *La Opinión,* November 5, 1939; *La Opinión,* August 25, 1946.

36. *La Opinión,* May 11, 1947.

37. Djata, *Blacks at the Net,* chap. 8.

38. *La Opinión,* December 5, 1941.

39. *La Opinión,* September 27, 1947; *La Opinión,* September 19, 1948.

40. *La Opinión,* September 20, 1948; *La Opinión,* September 21, 1948.

41. *La Opinión,* November 17, 1948.

42. On "racial uplift" ideology, see Kevin Gaines, *Uplifting the Race: Black Leadership, Politics, and Culture in the Twentieth Century* (Chapel Hill: University of North Carolina Press, 1996).

43. *La Opinion,* September 7, 1949.

44. *La Opinion* January 8, 1950.

45. *Los Angeles Times,* January 11, 1950.

46. "Lazy, but Wonderful," *Newsweek,* August 2, 1948, 70.

47. *History of Tennis in México* (México City: Talleres Gráficos de la Nación, 1988), 1–3.

48. Amy Spellacy, "Mapping the Metaphor of the Good Neighbor: Geography, Globalism, and Pan-Americanism during the 1940s," *American Studies* 47, no. 2 (summer 2006): 39–66.

49. *Los Angeles Times,* February 7, 1948.

50. "Ricardo Gonzalez, the Mexican tennis player from Los Angeles who was

made famous winning against Frank Parker in the last Pacific Southwest tournament will play with the colors of Mexico in the Pan American Tennis Tournament" (*El Excelsior*, October 9, 1947).

51. *El Excelsior*, October 17, 1947.
52. Mary Hardwick, "Drobny Grits Teeth, Wins Pan-American," *American Lawn Tennis*, October 1947, 6.
53. *Los Angeles Times*, February 7, 1948. According to Mexican citizenship law, those born outside of Mexico but whose parents were born in Mexico could reclaim their Mexican citizenship before their twenty-first birthday.
54. *Los Angeles Daily News*, February 24, 1948.
55. Ibid.
56. "Jorge Pasquel and the Evolution of the Mexican League," *National Pastime* 12 (Washington, DC: Society for American Baseball Research, 1992): 9–13.
57. Ibid.
58. *Los Angeles Times*, September 8, 1948.
59. *Los Angeles Times*, February 8, 1949.
60. Ibid.
61. *Los Angeles Times*, September 13, 1948.
62. *Los Angeles Times*, September 8, 1948.
63. *Newsweek*, August 2, 1948, 70. Although González was not chosen for the 1948 team, he did join the team in 1949 and helped the United States capture the Davis Cup by winning both matches against Australia.
64. *La Opinión*, June 12, 1949.
65. Edward Potter, "Mexico's Smoldering Fires," *Racquet*, April 1952, 14. See also Keith Brewster, "Patriotic Pastimes: The Role of Sport in Post-Revolutionary Mexico," *International Journal of the History of Sport* 22, no. 2 (2005): 139–57.
66. *Los Angeles Times*, October 3, 1948.
67. Damion Thomas, "Playing the 'Race Card': U.S. Foreign Policy and the Integration of Sports," in *East Plays West: Sport and the Cold War*, ed. Stephen Wagg and David Andrews (New York: Routledge, 2007), 215.
68. Melinda Schwenk, "Negro Stars and the USIA's Portrait of Democracy," *Race, Gender, and Class* 8, no. 4 (2001): 116–26.
69. On the sports media spreading Cold War propaganda, see John Massaro, "Press Box Propaganda? The Cold War and *Sports Illustrated*, 1956," *Journal of American Culture* 26, no. 3 (September 2003): 361–70.

70. Mary L. Dudziak, *Cold War Civil Rights: Race and the Image of American Democracy* (Princeton, NJ: Princeton University Press, 2000).

71. Mary E. Cygan, "A Man of His Times: Paul Robeson and the Press, 1924–1976," in *Paul Robeson: Essays on His Life and Legacy,* ed. Joseph Dorinson and William Pencak (Jefferson, NC: McFarland and Company, 2004); John Vernon, "Paul Robeson, the Cold War, and the Question of African American Loyalties," *Negro History Bulletin* 62 (April-September 1999): 47–52.

72. *Los Angeles Times,* September 14, 1949.

73. Ronald Smith, "The Paul Robeson—Jackie Robinson Saga and a Political Collision," *Journal of Sport History* 6, no. 2 (summer 1979): 5–27.

74. Bion Abbott, "Pancho Shows Home Folks How He Did It," *American Lawn Tennis,* April 1949, 12.

75. *Los Angeles Times,* September 22, 1948.

76. *Los Angeles Times,* January 28, 1953.

77. *Los Angeles Times,* November 25, 1954.

78. *Los Angeles Times,* June 10, 1962; December 22, 1963.

79. *Los Angeles Times,* March 18, 1965.

80. Elaine Tyler May, *Homeward Bound: American Families in the Cold War Era* (New York: Basic Books, 1988), passim.

81. *Los Angeles Times,* June 18, 1957.

82. *The Tribune,* December 12, 1987.

83. *Los Angeles Times,* December 23, 1948.

84. Ibid.

85. Gonzales, *Man with a Racket,* 213

86. Caroline Seebohm, *Little Pancho: The Life of Tennis Legend Pancho Segura* (Lincoln: University of Nebraska Press, 2009), 80–81.

87. Ibid.

88. On Ignacio Lopez and his muckraking Spanish-language newspaper *El Espectador* from Pomona, California, see Matt Garcia, *A World of Its Own: Race, Labor, and Citrus in the Making of Greater Los Angeles, 1900–1970* (Chapel Hill: University of North Carolina Press, 2001).

89. Gonzales, *Man with a Racket,* 214.

90. Ibid., *Man with a Racket,* 134–39.

91. Paul Teetor and Ralph Gonzales, "¡Viva Pancho!" *Oye Magazine* 2 (September 1994): 27.

92. *Los Angeles Times*, December 12, 1987.

93. *Chicago Sun-Times*, July 5, 1985.

94. Ibid., 73.

95. Lew Hoad with Jack Pollard, *The Lew Hoad Story* (Englewood Cliffs, NJ: Prentice-Hall, 1958), 134.

96. Seebohm, *Little Pancho*, 82.

97. *Los Angeles Times*, February 5, 1957.

98. *Los Angeles Times*, January 11, 1958.

99. *Los Angeles Times*, February 13, 1959.

100. *Los Angeles Times*, April 27, 1969.

101. Althea Gibson started an all-female tour in 1959 but did not garner the same amount of publicity, fans, and prize money. The tour's failure left her in debt for years (*Los Angeles Times*, September 9, 1959); Mary Jo Festle, "Jackie Robinson without the Charm: The Challenges of Being Althea Gibson," in *Out of the Shadows: A Biographical History of African American Athletes*, ed. David Wiggins (Fayetteville: University of Arkansas Press, 2008), 203.

102. Seebohm, *Little Pancho*, 88.

103. "The Power and Fury: The Childhood That Produced the Great Pancho Gonzalez," *World Tennis*, September 1987.

104. *The Tribune*, December 12, 1987.

105. Gonzales, *Man with a Racket*, 40.

106. For more critical interpretations of Latino masculinity, see Maxine Baca Zinn, "Chicano Men and Masculinity," *Journal of Ethnic Studies* 10, no. 2 (1982): 29–44; Pierrette Hondagneu-Sotelo, *Gendered Transitions: Mexican Experiences of Immigration* (Berkeley: University of California Press, 1994); Matthew Guttman, *The Meanings of Macho: Being a Man in Mexico City* (Berkeley: University of California Press, 1996).

107. Robert Connell, *Gender* (Cambridge: Polity Press, 2000).

108. Michael Uebel, "Men in Color: Introducing Race and the Subject of Masculinities," in *Race and the Subject of Masculinities*, ed. H. Stecopoulos and M. Uebel (Durham, NC: Duke University Press, 1997), 1–14.

109. *The Telegraph*, February 1, 2011.

110. *Los Angeles Times*, June 24, 1972.

111. Gonzales, *Man with a Racket*, 152–53.

112. *Chicago Sun Times*, July 5, 1985.

113. *Los Angeles Times*, March 28, 1959. See also S. L. Price, "The Lone Wolf," *Sports Illustrated*, June 24, 2002.

114. Mike Agassi, *The Agassi Story* (Toronto: ECW Press, 2004), 98–99.

, 115. Marshall Smith, "This Old Pro Is Just Too Mean to Quit," *Life,* September 12, 1969, 45.

116. Seebohm, *Little Pancho*, 87.

117. *Los Angeles Times*, May 23, 1956. When someone commented about Pancho's tantrums as being "immature" on the court, a female spectator defended them as "appealing" and full of "passion" (*New York Times*, July 3, 1987).

118. James Gilbert, *Men in the Middle: Searching for Masculinity in the 1950s* (Chicago: University of Chicago Press, 2005), passim.

119. Jaime Cardenas, Jr., "Brusque and Exotic: Anthony Quinn, National Identity, and Masculinity, 1951–1966," *Southern Quarterly* 39, no. 4 (summer 2001): 175–88.

120. Gonzales, *Man with a Racket*, 23.

121. Smith, "This Old Oro Is Just Too Mean to Quit," 77.

122. Arthur Ashe and Arnold Ramersad, *Days of Grace: A Memoir* (New York: Ballantine Books, 1993), 5.

123. Festle, "Jackie Robinson without the Charm," 187–205.

124. Gonzales, *Man with a Racket*, 153.

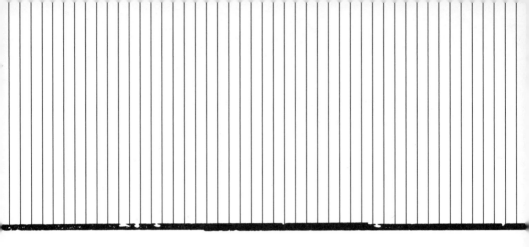

CHAPTER 6

Courting Success and Realizing the American Dream:
Arizona's Mighty Miami High School Championship Basketball
Team, 1951

Christine Marin
Arizona State University

Historians have described the second generation of Mexican Americans as the "G.I. generation," born and raised in the United States. They experienced American phenomena such as the Great Depression and World War II and became political and community leaders in the postwar periods. Historian Mario García has suggested that their politics reflected the twin objectives of ethnic and cultural retention together with integration within the broader Euro-American society.[1] Albert Camarillo used the term "G.I. generation" to refer to those Mexican American leaders who became exposed to community and political consciousness as they grew up, and through the examples provided by their neighbors and families.[2] While García and Camarillo have studied the second generation, they have not expanded their work to include the history and experience of the third generation, the children of the Mexican American, or G.I. generation.

This article is designed, in part, to breach that gap in Mexican American history and use achievement in sports as a symbol of the American

Dream.[3] This essay focuses on athletic endeavor in the period from 1947 to 1951 to explain how third-generation Mexican Americans and their hard-driving high school basketball coach in Miami, Arizona, promoted Americanization, achieved success, and won the 1951 state basketball championship. They revitalized a hometown's pride and team spirit and united a community that had a checkered history of racism and discrimination. Their success reflected the dreams of their second-generation parents who came to Miami in the 1920s and 1930s to improve their economic livelihood for the future of their families. The link between success on the basketball court and educational achievement is explored to explain how the team epitomized the possibilities of the American Dream. Third-generation Mexican Americans came of age in the years after World War II. They attended a segregated elementary school and experienced integration at the high school. As teammates with Euro-Americans and victors on the basketball court, they established cordial friendships and facilitated better ethnic relations in their school and in their copper mining–based community. Many attended college and escaped a working-class environment and achieved upward mobility. In the end, the third generation of Mexican Americans fulfilled their parents' American dreams of success and equality.

In recent years, several scholars in the field of Mexican American studies have begun to include research on sports in their academic work. Texas-based historian Jorge Iber examined the dual themes of sports and education in his 2002 essay, "Mexican Americans of South Texas Football: The Athletic and Coaching Careers of E. C. Lerma and Bobby Cavazos, 1932–1965."[4] He argued that football, when mixed with victories and success, brought about better race and ethnic relations among Texans with a history beset with tension and racism. For example, Iber explained how Everardo Carlos Lerma (also known as E. C.) at age eighteen, earned a starting position on the H. M. King High School's Brahma roster in Kingsville, Texas, in 1933 despite ethnic insults meant to discourage him from participating on the football team.

Richard Santillán made similar arguments about race relationships in his 2001 study of Mexican baseball teams, "Mexican Baseball Teams in the Midwest, 1916–1965: The Politics of Cultural Survival and Civil Rights."[5]

Santillán, however, used sports as a metaphor for ethnic pride, one that reflected accomplishment on the baseball diamond. In two additional examples, Samuel O. Regalado and Tim Wendel examined the sport of baseball and Major League Latino athletes.[6] The authors suggested that sports became the avenue out of obscurity and poverty for hard-hitting and fast-pitching Latino baseball players in the Major Leagues. Regalado explained how they cultivated a "special hunger" for success, a "drive needed to propel them through the pitfalls [of racism] that they inevitably encountered as they pursued their [American] dream."[7] Regalado argued the "Pan-Americanism"[8] of players and connected their athleticism with baseball. He also challenged historians to study the growing relationship between America's favorite pastime and Latino culture in order to gain a better understanding of the "spirit of the Latin."[9] Wendel also examined the Pan-American influence in professional baseball in the United States. His series of minibiographies and photographs of talented and popular Latin baseball stars provides numerous examples that show how they are gradually replacing baseball's All-American white faces with various hues of brown and black faces. Regalado and Wendel challenge us to consider to what extent Pan-American players are Latinizing the All-American sport of baseball.

The recent scholarship of José M. Alamillo and Gabriela Arredondo showed that baseball did not promote Americanization among the second generation of *Mexicanos* in Corona, California, and Chicago, Illinois.[10] In attempts to shield themselves from cultural insensitivities and mistreatment at the hands of Euro-Americans, Alamillo examined how Mexican American baseball players, or *peloteros,* in Corona used their own sports clubs to escape the racism and discrimination that impacted their community. Their leagues also became tools for promoting ethnic or cultural awareness and identity.[11] On the other hand, Gabriela Arredondo maintained that *Mexicanos* turned inward to re-create a "fragile *Mexicanidad*" . . . a "feeling of common peoplehood" based on their memories of a Mexican homeland in order to shield themselves from vestiges of discrimination.[12] In some cases, they formed sports clubs and gave them Aztec names to commemorate their Native American heritage.[13]

This study adds to the literature of scholars whose works link Mexican

American history to sports history. It is important to know the hard-luck story of Mexican American high school students from the copper mining community of Miami, Arizona, and their contributions to the game of basketball. On its way to the state championship, Arizona's only unbeaten prep basketball team from the copper mining town of Miami shattered national high school single-game scoring records in 1951. Through their play, competitive spirit, and success, they gained the admiration of their community and improved ethnic relations in the copper town that set them apart because of their ethnicity.

In this essay on the history of Miami High School basketball, I show that two *Mexicanos*, Larry Franco and Paulino Martínez, shared victories for the first time in 1924 with their Euro-American teammates. By 1928 Charles Herrera and Regino "Salty" Rivera contributed to the team's success and helped gain numerous victories.[14] High school basketball brought Mexican Americans and Euro-Americans together as teammates with a common purpose: to be victorious and bring recognition to the school.

National attention from the sports media and basketball aficionados came in 1928 for the Miami Vandals. In the spring, basketball coach Laurence H. Purdy accepted an invitation from Ames Alonzo Stagg, athletic director at the University of Chicago, to compete in the Tenth Annual National Inter-Scholastic Basketball Tournament. An all-around athlete from the University of Wisconsin, Purdy came to Miami High School in 1922 as the head coach of the boys' basketball and football teams. State divisions in Arizona were represented by regions: west, north, south, and central. The eastern region included basketball teams from Miami, Globe, Safford, Clifton, Morenci, Duncan, Thatcher, Ft. Thomas, and Pima.[15] By the 1940s the Arizona Interscholastic Association (AIA) assigned class designations based on student population to divisional schools, and the eastern divisional schools became known as Class B schools and teams competed within their class designations. In 1922 Purdy coached the girls' basketball team to its first Eastern division championship. They competed in the state championship games in Tucson and placed two players on the All-State team.[16]

In his eight-year tenure at Miami High School, from 1922 to 1929, Purdy's Vandals won the Eastern Conference championships in 1926,

1927, and 1929, and played highly touted teams from Globe, Morenci, Florence, Superior, Safford, and Hayden. Mexican-born and Mexican American players such as Larry Franco, "Tiff" Martínez, Charles Herrera, Paulino Martínez, Regino "Salty" Rivera, Manuel Ramos, Anselmo "Sam" Muñoz, and the Puente brothers, Manuel and Keenus, figured prominently for the Miami Vandals in those years.[17]

In 1928 Miami finished second to Phoenix Union High School in the state basketball tournament at the University of Arizona in Tucson. Phoenix Union also received Stagg's invitation to participate in the Inter-Scholastic Basketball Tournament, but declined. At least thirty-nine high school basketball teams with winning records from throughout the nation competed in Chicago's national tournament in late March and early April. Thirty-four of those teams became state or regional champions.[18]

The Miami Vandals carried their own reputation into the national tournament as champions, having won their regional conference titles in two consecutive years.[19] In the first round of the tournament the Vandals drew the formidable team from Bristol, Connecticut. Bristol had previously won the University of Pennsylvania's Atlantic Seaboard Tournament, in which fifty-two of the finest teams in that region competed. In its game against Bristol, Miami quickly commanded a consistent lead throughout the game. Smooth ball handling and aggressive rebounding gave the Vandals an edge over Bristol and Miami led at the half, 16-7. In the end, Bristol won the game by three points, 27-24.[20]

During the Depression, the teams of coaches Bryant C. "Bud" Doolen and R. V. Zegers captured the Eastern Conference championships in 1930, 1935, and 1938. Doolen, born in Kinmundy, Illinois, came from the University of Illinois in 1929 to take over Purdy's head coaching position, only to be replaced by Zegers in 1936.[21] Faustino "Laca" Encizo's accurate shooting and Martín López's strong defensive play in the season of 1932 took the Vandals to the state finals at the University of Arizona in Tucson that year. The write-up in the high school yearbook, *The Concentrator*, acknowledges their basketball skills and fine play and calls attention to their skills.[22] Miami easily defeated their opponents in the semifinals. In the championship game, however, Doolen's squad met a strong adversary in the Douglas Bulldogs. The teams exchanged leads throughout the game, and they appeared to be equally matched, man for man. López's fine dribbling and ball control, along with his smooth passing to Ascención Vasquez, almost clinched a Vandal victory on the Tucson court that night. The Douglas Bulldogs beat the Vandals by one point, 22-21.[23]

In 1941 the Vandals won their first state basketball championship when they defeated Peoria by the score of 44-40. Coached by Earl McCullar, the Vandals began their winning 1940–1941 season with victories against St. John's, Pima, Morenci, and Clifton.[24] Vicente Cisterna, a sophomore forward and the tallest player on the varsity team at six-foot-two, established himself as a key player in the Vandals' 23-2 record. "Long John," as he was called by his Euro-American teammates, used his height to help Miami win their games through his ability to tip in missed baskets that bounced off the backboard.[25] The Vandals won their second state championship in 1951. That victory came from the leadership and coaching of Ernest Kivisto, the American-born son of working-class Finnish immigrant parents from Ironwood, Michigan. Before he arrived in Miami in 1947, Kivisto became an all-around athlete at Marquette University and played basketball and participated in track and field and intramural softball. He graduated from Marquette in the summer of 1946 with a bachelor of arts degree in philosophy.[26]

In that same year, Kivisto coached the football and basketball teams at St. Ambrose Catholic High School in Ironwood, Michigan, and led them to "an undefeated nine-game season—St. Ambrose's first perfect grid record."[27] His basketball squad "won 25 and lost one."[28] The teams did not see another season with Ernest, however. An arthritic right knee that bothered him whenever colder temperatures arrived prevented him from staying in Ironwood. Kivisto and his wife, Jane Ann, moved to Miami, Arizona, to improve his health and because he had a new job as head coach of the high school's basketball team and junior varsity coach of its football team.[29]

Basketball was important to Miami. Mexican American boys became introduced to the game at young ages, usually by YMCA youth leagues that pitted Mexican American teams from the Mexican Y against the YMCA's Euro-American teams. In 1910 the Miami Copper Company formed an alliance with the YMCA to provide recreational and social activities for its Euro-American employees. The company built a new three-story YMCA building close to the center of the town in 1915. Four years later, YMCA leaders established a "Mexican 'Y'" for Mexican-born and Mexican American laborers at a small, one-room wood-frame building owned by Miami Copper. The Mexican "Y" remained segregated until 1947, twenty-eight years after it opened in 1919.[30] The use of the word "Mexican" to differentiate between the two "Y"s became common in the local newspaper, the *Arizona Silver Belt*. A hint of racism can be seen in the headlines the newspaper ran in its announcements of games between the two leagues: "Mexican League Contests Held," and "Mexican Court League Starts."[31] Alejandro Trujillo, director of the Mexican "Y" from 1925 to 1935, organized basketball games and boxing matches for the organization.[32] Mexican American youths from the segregated Bullion Plaza Elementary School competed against Euro-American students from the George Washington Elementary school or the Inspiration Addition School.[33] By the time they reached seventh or eighth grades, the better players competed against the high school's junior varsity team. Tony Gutiérrez, born in Miami in 1930, recalled his Bullion Plaza Elementary School experience in 1945 at the age of fourteen:

> Ray Cordes was Miami's JV basketball coach. He invited our Bullion Plaza Ramblers to play his JV team and we beat them. Mexican kids like me didn't have uniforms or basketball shoes and we had to borrow each other's clothes and shoes to play basketball. We were better than the *gringos*. We proved it.[34]

As a Bullion Plaza Rambler, Gutiérrez tasted victory and he liked winning basketball games. His self-confidence, and perhaps that of Mexican American youths like him at the Bullion Plaza Elementary School, reflected the toughness of their mining town. Their fathers' mining culture, full of dangers and deaths due to mine accidents, taught them to endure hardships and not be afraid to compete with Euro-Americans. After all, their G.I.-generation fathers' support of the International Union of Mine, Mill and Smelter Workers, Local 586, in the early 1940s provided them with examples of leadership and how to deal with competition.

That same competitive spirit was embodied by Tony Regalado, Gutiérrez's classmate at the Bullion Plaza Elementary School. He and his parents, Estevan and Luz Regalado, lived in a simple wood-frame house in "Mexican Canyon" near the Inspiration Consolidated Copper Company.[35] At school, the Gutiérrez and Regalado boys became good friends, as Gutiérrez stated:

> We both liked basketball and liked competition and felt at ease with it. We were tough kids that grew up tough. At Bullion Plaza, the older guys put up a fight just to see what would happen. Times were tough, too. Everyone was poor. Besides, *Mexicanos* had to be tough to be able to put up with what the *gringos* did to them.[36]

Gutiérrez's toughness, however, did not prepare him for the sting of verbal insults and nonacceptance by Euro-Americans when he arrived at the integrated Miami High School in his freshman year in 1946:

> I had never gone to school with Anglo kids. It wasn't a very easy thing to do. They dressed better than I did and they acted like the school was just for them. There wasn't outright discrimination there, but they made us Mexican kids feel like outsiders because they thought we weren't better than them.[37]

Despite Gutiérrez's uneasiness among Euro-Americans his freshman year, he soon discovered that his love of basketball helped him overcome any negative experiences. Basketball made him feel like a winner among his white peers. And he liked that: "We were better than them as athletes, and that's when they started to like us. They wanted to win. And they needed us *Mexicanos* to win," he said.[38] Believing Mexican Americans possessed athletic skills gave Gutierrez a sense of pride and accomplishment and may have soothed the stings of racism he experienced in his freshman year.

Gutiérrez's penchant for winning endeared him to his new basketball coach in 1947, Ernest Kivisto. When his responsibilities as the junior varsity football coach ended in late November, Kivisto placed a call for boys to report for tryouts for the varsity basketball team. Tony Gutiérrez and Benny Salcines stepped forward. The two Mexican Americans, along with five other Euro-Americans, remained from the original 1946–1947 squad

Miami High School
basketball coach Ernest
Kivisto, c. 1950. Courtesy
of Miami High School,
Miami, Arizona.

of fourteen who played under former basketball coach Ben Cole. Only
seven boys had varsity experience, and Kivisto knew he had to rely on the
junior varsity leaguers from the 1946–1947 teams to make up the squad
he needed.[39]

The junior varsity team played for Coach Ray Cordes and came away
with an exceptional season, winning sixteen and losing only one game.[40]
Tony Regalado, Manuel Delgadillo, and Paul Mireles stood out from that
junior varsity group.[41] Kivisto added them to his varsity team. Up-and-
coming players like Lupe Acevedo, Joe Gutiérrez (Tony's brother), and Albert Sierra made up the rest of Kivisto's 1947–1948 twelve-member varsity
squad, eight of whom were Mexican Americans.[42] Kivisto tested the agility
and the determination of his new team, and the boys endured his grueling

practices daily. They learned his fast-break style of play, the one he learned at Marquette under noted coach Bill Chandler: fast break on offense and the full court press on defense. Elias Delgadillo explained the method:

> One of the keys to the fast break is the pass. The object here is to get the ball down court as quickly as possible. To accomplish this, the passes had to be quick, crisp and accurate. [Kivisto's fast-break style] was quite different from the standard style of the time of setting up for a shot in play.[43]

The fast break, an exciting method of play, may explain the enthusiasm the players had for the game. Manuel Delgadillo believed that Ernest Kivisto may well have been the first basketball coach in Arizona to initiate the weave, or figure 8, exercise, an innovative play in 1947.

Kivisto taught his team the floor routines he learned at Marquette. He reinforced the fundamentals of basketball, with passing and pivoting exercises and shooting drills in their practices. Players took shots at the hoops from every angle and distance on the court. For conditioning exercises, he made the boys run laps around the gym and run sprints up and down the court. "We would run forwards, then sideways and then backwards with our arms extended in a guarding position," Elias Delgadillo emphasized.[44] Kivisto taught them the importance of teamwork in competitive sports and that sports belonged to everyone, a point made clear in Wilfrid Sheed's article, "Why Sports Matter." Sheed linked the importance of sports and teamwork in a community like Miami: "Sports teach . . . teamwork. . . . Schools . . . also teach something by their very nature, which is that [teams play] for a whole community . . . and . . . if you win, the community will join you in experiencing a kind of crazy collective joy. . . ."[45]

The team's resolve and determination to be good at the game became evident early in the practices. It caught Coach Kivisto off guard, as Tony Gutiérrez recalled:

> When I first met Coach Kivisto, I noticed that he had a slight limp and a funny little accent that I never heard before. He was all basketball. He thought that we didn't know anything about basketball, that we were from this little town and knew nothing. I remember when his wife came with him to one of our early practices. He thought he could

dribble the ball and wanted to show us a few things. But he found out differently. He called out to his wife, "Hey, honey! I can't dribble the ball past these guys! They won't let me get by! Isn't that something?" From that point on, he knew we were serious about the game.[46]

In preparation for his first season, Kivisto convinced school administrators to approve the purchase of two complete sets of new uniforms for his players in the school's colors, green and white. New warm-up jackets completed their attire.[47] Tony Gutierrez remembers the surprising contrast between the old and the new uniforms:

> Before Coach Kivisto came along, we wore those ivy-league shirts that players long before us were wearing. They were loose, all worn out, and used again and again. But Kivisto fought for his team and insisted on new uniforms, new outfits, new shoes for his boys. The uniforms were white, like satin, silky-like, with long white or green warm-up pants. Our white jackets had a long square collar in the back that lay flat across the back of our shoulders. We were the first high school basketball team in the state to play in white tennis shoes, high-tops. Every team at that time wore black low-cut tennis shoes. We dazzled them. For some of us Mexican boys, it was the first time we had brand-new shoes that we could call our own, and not some hand-me-downs from the *gringos*.[48]

A new sense of ownership made Gutiérrez feel important. It gave Mexican American boys like him opportunities to become equal, at least on the court, with the Euro-Americans, whose parents may have been able to afford to buy them new shoes. Gutiérrez took pride in the way the team looked in their new uniforms and white high-top tennis shoes. "I tried to keep my high-tops clean," he said. "It was important for us to represent our school and our team by looking good."[49]

According to Gutiérrez, Coach Kivisto set a new trend in the style and color of the tennis shoes Arizona's high school players began to wear in the late 1940s and early 1950s. Jesús F. Romero, student manager of the basketball team in the 1950–1951 season, said that Kivisto used his Marquette University contacts to strike an arrangement with the Converse shoe company to provide Miami High School's basketball team with their white high-top tennis shoes. He also said that Kivisto let the players keep their shoes at the end of the season, a practice he kept in the years he coached the Vandals.[50]

Kivisto's first season in 1947–1948 progressed, and his fast-break style of play and his team's persistence drove them to victory after victory. The Vandals averaged "61.5 points per game [as] scored in 14 games."[51] Kivisto claimed this average as a national interscholastic record, and Arch Ward, sports editor for the *Chicago Tribune,* backed that claim and cited the average of 49 points per game held by the Champaign, Illinois, high school team as the existing record in 1947.[52] This 61.5 point average gave Kivisto's team "the best record of all, the High School National scoring average [record]. No quintet in Arizona [ever received] that honor before. . . ."[53]

Kivisto relied on the "two Tonys," as the sportswriter for the local newspaper called Tony Gutiérrez and Tony Regalado, "for most of their scoring punch" in the team's 1947–1948 seasons of play.[54] Both played the forward positions and their excellent plays on offense became reasons that the Vandals dominated the boards and made high scores against opponents.

The Vandals captured the Eastern Division Conference championship in mid-February in their encounter with the Duncan Wildkats, with the winning score of 57-49. They prepared for the state finals at the University of Arizona in Tucson but lost in the semifinals.[55]

The two Tonys accumulated 667 points between them in 1947–1948 and emerged as the Eastern Division's heroes in Kivisto's first season with the Vandals. His team scored 1,485 points in the 1947–1948 season "for an average of 59.4 points in 25 games played. No team in [Arizona] accomplished such a feat. Miami wound up fifth in the nation in total points scored in one season, a state record of all time."[56]

Kivisto's first season as the new coach of the successful Miami High School Vandals merely hinted at the promise of another good year in 1948–1949 and his continued pursuit of the state championship. Teamwork became the hallmark of the Miami Vandals, and it proved to be their key to success. Tony Gutiérrez linked teamwork to Kivisto's success and suggested that teamwork on the court parlayed itself off the court in smoothing over ethnic tensions between *Mexicanos* and the Euro-Americans in the community:

Yeah, he talked a lot about teamwork. We learned to put away our prejudices about each other and work together for the sake of the team and the school and maybe the town, too. On the court, we were equals, and the courts became our battlefield and we had to count on each other to make plays. Coach Kivisto didn't like prejudice. I kind of got the impression that he knew what the Mexicans had experienced in our town.[57]

Gutiérrez may have been correct in his assessment of the coach. After all, Kivisto came from a similar mining town background and from a town with Finnish immigrants like his father, a miner. Kivisito understood mining town life. Kivisto may have felt an affinity with the Mexican American boys on his team and may have admired them for their tenacity and fire for enduring cultural and ethnic prejudice in their town. Kivisto's distaste for racism became evident when the team traveled to Morenci to play their opponent on their home court on January 2, 1948:

When we went to Morenci, we went to a restaurant that wouldn't let us in. There was a sign on the window that said, "No Mexicans Allowed." Kivisto got mad. . . . He was hurt, too. And he said he was going to do something about it. He went inside and talked to the waitress. He came out and said that she'd get fired if she served us. When Coach asked for the owner, she told him that he was at work, at the mine. That was the first time I witnessed anything about the coach like that. We didn't eat there. He said that we were a team and that if we couldn't eat together, then no one would eat.[58]

This example did not go unnoticed among his Mexican American players, as Gutiérrez explained:

We talked about it, and he became a hero in our eyes. There were other *gringos* who felt the same way that he did. We wanted to win games for him. So did the *gringos* on the team. That [experience] brought the school and maybe [the town] together because soon everybody knew what the coach had done. It became the talk of the town. They really got behind us.[59]

The Miami Boosters, a local, mostly white merchants and civic group that performed activities similar to that of a chamber of commerce, certainly took notice of the basketball team. They honored the team with a steak dinner and banquet held at the high school gym on April 12.[60] C. B. Hostetler, Miami School Board member, served as the master of ceremonies for the evening. His brother, Miami school superintendent Ivan P. Hostetler, and the high school principal, E. E. McClain, made speeches at the event and praised Kivisto and his team for their success. The attention paid to a predominantly Mexican American basketball team at a time when Miami maintained a segregated "Mexican school" is indeed ironic. Glen Wilson, town merchant, recalled the event:

> It had been awhile since we had a winning basketball team, and we wanted to get the town to support them. We [Miami Boosters] sold tickets and we had a good turnout. The [Boosters] donated the food and we made a nice handy profit. The money went back to the school. People from Globe, Superior, Phoenix, and Tucson came out for the dinner.[61]

The "mothers of [the] team's members [prepared] the steak dinner," and members from the high school's Girls' Athletic Association (GAA) club served the dinner guests at their tables.[62] It is possible that this setting presented opportunities for Mexican American women to share pride in their sons' athletic achievements with Euro-American mothers and participate in conversations that might have bridged cultural or ethnic divisions among them. Despite Miami's practice of ethnic and racial separation in the elementary schools, the local Presbyterian church, the Catholic church, and the local YMCAs, it is possible that Mexican American and Euro-American women made attempts to forge new friendships. Their sons' examples of teamwork and their winning performances on the basketball court, when added to their community's pride in their success, illustrates that a culturally mixed group of athletes can bring a community together.

Kivisto's fast-break style of play and aggressive action on the courts brought the team and the town into the spotlight in continuing seasons. The Vandals won the Eastern Conference title but lost in semifinal play

Miami High School Vandals in competition, c. 1950. Courtesy of Miami High School, Miami Arizona.

for the state championship. Kivisto's favorite forward, Tony Gutiérrez, in his last season of play in 1949, set "a three-year varsity record of 818 points," the most points scored by a player in Miami High School's basketball history.[63] After graduation, Gutiérrez accepted an athletic scholarship from Eastern Arizona Junior College in Thatcher, approximately sixty-five miles east of Miami. His friend, Tony Regalado, joined the navy at the end of his sophomore year in 1948 to help meet family responsibilities.[64]

At the end of the 1949–1950 season, the Vandals' record was twenty-four wins and only two losses, while averaging 84.7 points per game. In March 1950 they won their third successive Eastern Conference championship. The local newspaper called attention to the Vandals' Eastern Conference championship that put the copper town "on the map" and bragged about the team's accomplishments.[65] Kivisto and his team prepared themselves for the competition ahead, and they hoped to win the Class B state crown. Miami's chances of winning looked promising.

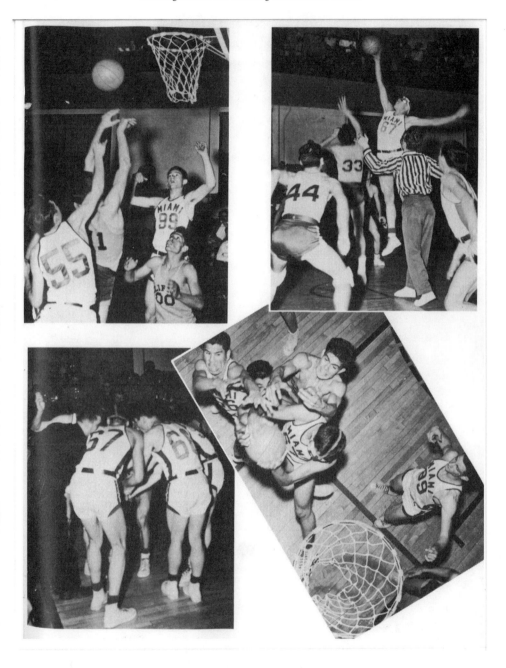

Miami High School Vandals in competition, c. 1950. Courtesy of Miami High School, Miami Arizona.

Miami drew the Florence Gophers as their opponent in the first round of the Class B state semifinals held at the Arizona State College gymnasium in Tempe in early March 1950. Florence fell to Miami by the score of 71-46 in a "racehorse contest."[66] As the Vandals prepared for the second semifinal round of play, Kivisto received numerous good-luck telegrams from a legion of hometown fans and supporters. Booster club member Glenn Wilson recalled the telegrams:

> [The Booster club] sent Kivisto over a dozen telegrams wishing the boys good luck in the tournament, all signed by teachers, kids, townfolk, everybody. The town wanted the state championship, too, just as much as he and the boys did. We had a damned good team and we had been after that championship for three years! We supported the team, and a lot of people went down to Tempe for the games, me included.[67]

On a Saturday morning, the Vandals met a stronger adversary in the Nogales Apaches in the semifinals. They surprised Miami with their sharp shooting and display of boundless energy in "the best game of the tournament" and defeated the Vandals 43-35 and knocked them out of the state competition.[68] In the end, the 1950 Class B State championship went to Coolidge, their "first in the history of Coolidge High School," when they defeated Nogales by only three points, 47-44.[69] After the games, Kivisto and his team "expressed gratitude for the support given them by Miami" and thanked the town for the telegrams, the pages of signatures and good wishes.[70] "We were disappointed, too," said Glenn Wilson, "but Kivisto put Miami on the map, and we were the winners all around. We were proud of him and all the boys."[71]

Miami did not win the 1950 state basketball championship, and Kivisto entered his last season as head coach of the Vandals in 1950–1951. Led by the seniors Lupe Acevedo, Rudy Moreno, Hector Mario Jacott, Alfred Lobato, Elias Delgadillo, and Adolph "Fito" Trujillo, the high-scoring and victorious Vandals, predominantly a Mexican American team, became the All-American sports heroes whose victories remain embedded in Miami's sports history sixty-plus years later.

The portraits that emerge of Lupe Acevedo, Elias Delgadillo, Hector

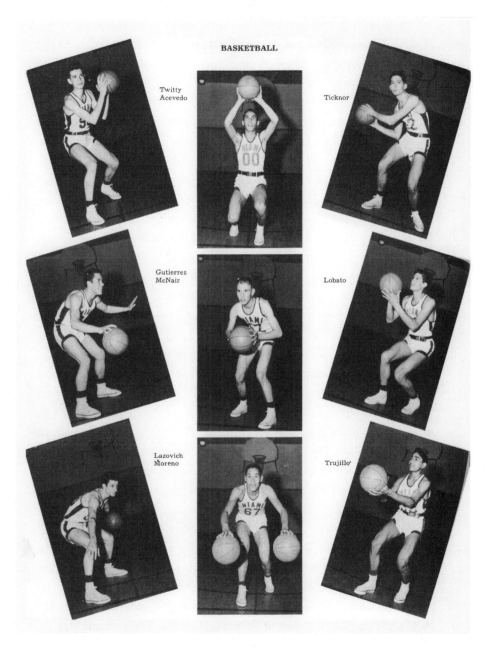

Miami High School Vandals in competition, c. 1950. Courtesy of Miami High School, Miami Arizona.

Mario Jacott, Alfred Lobato, Rudy Moreno, and Fito Trujillo bear similarities. Their families immigrated to Miami from New Mexico; Texas; Sonora, Mexico; and Morenci, Arizona, in the mid-1920s and early 1930s. Their fathers labored in the local copper mines. The youths came from working-class and impoverished backgrounds; they attended the segregated Bullion Plaza Elementary School, and all were reared under difficult economic circumstances. Single parents reared three of them: Lupe Acevedo, Rudy Moreno, and Adolph "Fito" Trujillo. Loretta Apodaca Acevedo died in 1944 from tuberculosis when Lupe was twelve years of age.[72] Francisco Moreno and Refugio Trujillo died of silicosis in 1944 and in 1948 when their sons, Rudy and Fito, reached the ages of twelve and sixteen, respectively.[73] The Acevedo and Moreno families, among other Mexican and Mexican American families, lived on West Live Oak Street. When the Miami Trust Company plotted the West Live Oak Addition in 1947 and redeveloped its properties for the sake of tourist dollars, the company evicted and relocated the Acevedo and Moreno families to the company's properties elsewhere in Miami.[74]

Despite their harsh beginnings, these young Mexican Americans possessed a talent for basketball that changed their lives. Their coach, Ernest Kivisto, recognized that talent and helped them become champions, and their town reveled in their glory and supported their efforts. Their victories on the basketball court enabled them to benefit from the rewards of winning: education and success. Their championship season of 1950–1951 is indeed worthy of a thorough review. The season opener in Vandal territory began on December 9 and pitted Miami against the St. Johns Redskins, "the team that kept [Kivisto] from an undefeated season" in 1949–1950 by only one point, 40-39, according to an article in the *Arizona Silver Belt*.[75] Kivisto's first-team players—Lupe Acevedo, Hector Mario Jacott, Rudy Moreno, and Eli Lazovich—already possessed three years' experience in executing the fast break on offense and utilizing the full-court press on defense. Fito Trujillo came in from the reserves squad and proved to be an invaluable addition to Kivisto's first team. He "recovered 24 rebounds from the backboard" and scored twenty points.[76] Fito Trujillo's accomplishments became noted in the local *Arizona Silver Belt*, where he was labeled an "ace player," an expert in basketball: some recognition for a

Mexican American youth who attended a segregated elementary school![77] Miami handily outmatched St. Johns, 78-41.

That the Vandals possessed some advantages over their opponents in that championship season became clearer as the season progressed. For example, five of Kivisto's ten-member team averaged heights that ranged from six foot to six-foot-four and maintained weights from 170 to 190 pounds. Accurate shooting by Eli Lazovich, Fito Trujillo, and Lupe Acevedo and good board control by Hector Mario Jacott and Rudy Moreno, along with the squad's smooth and efficient passing, enabled the Vandals to become victorious in all seven games played throughout December 1950. In their match against Safford in early January, which Miami won, 94-50, Fito Trujillo scored forty-five points and established a new Arizona high school scoring record for one game. The Vandals also "topped the scoring overall with 172 points" in the Eastern Conference, setting a new state scoring record in the region.[78] When Trujillo fouled out of the game, "The crowd spontaneously rose to their feet and gave [him] one of the loudest ovations ever to echo from the Miami's gym rafters."[79]

Trujillo's forty-five-point individual state scoring record set in the Safford game, however, did not last very long. A week later, Eli Lazovich broke Trujillo's record by scoring fifty points against Clifton. Yet two weeks later, Lupe Acevedo surpassed the records of Trujillo and Lazovich by scoring fifty-six points against Duncan. Remarkably, in one month's time, the state individual scoring record was tested and broken three times—by three players from the same team: the Miami Vandals.[80]

The "scourge of Arizona courts," as one sportswriter described the Vandals, continued on their road to the state championship.[81] High scores against opponents characterized Miami's relentless drive for that prize. They scored over 100 points against five competitors in their 1950–1951 seasons. The high scores delighted Miami fans. Opposing teams, however, criticized Kivisto and his squad for showing "little mercy on its weaker opponents."[82]

When the Vandals' 122-58 score against Clifton proved humiliating for the Trojans and their fans, Coach Gene Taylor chided Ernie Kivisto for purposely running up Miami's score in order to satisfy his own ego, establish his school's records, and enhance his reputation. The controversy over Miami's high scores became weekly fodder for Arizona's sportswriters from Phoenix, Clifton, Globe, and Miami, who debated the matter in the press. The writer for the *Copper Era*, representing the eastern regions of Clifton, Morenci, and Duncan, suggested that all "Eastern Conference schools should boycott [Miami] and forfeit each game" in order to throw a wrench in Miami's scoring average.[83] The ire of Clifton's sports fans reached a fever pitch when Coach Kivisto received anonymous letters containing death threats against Miami's scoring aces Lupe Acevedo and Fito Trujillo. The letters warned him to "expect physical violence during and after the [next Clifton] game."[84] The threats proved fruitless, and sportswriters who wrote about the Clifton-Miami game did not report that racial motives were behind the threats. But a "special detachment of sheriff's deputies accompanied the [Miami] team while they were in Clifton, but no incidents occurred."[85] Clyde A. Eckman, editor of Globe's *Arizona Record*, took a matter-of-fact position in his defense of Coach Kivisto and his players for their competitiveness and athleticism for playing hard and clean basketball—the kind that attracted attention from college basketball recruiters and coaches:

> Most members of the rampaging Vandal squad come from families definitely not in the upper income brackets. It's hardly a secret that colleges offer basketball scholarships to outstanding material. And if a scintillating prep record can mean a college education to a few kids who otherwise might not have been so fortunate, what's wrong with that?[86]

Eckman's comments hit Miami's high-scoring controversy directly on its head, and the issue in the press drew to a close. The Vandals and Coach Kivisto displayed their usual brand of teamwork and broke the all-time national high school single-game scoring record against the Morenci Wildcats by the score of 130-43. Associated Press sports editor Jim Cordy telephoned Coach Kivisto from New York to inform him that the Vandals' score topped the previous scoring mark of 125 points held in 1946 by Muncie (Indiana) High School.[87] Miami clinched its fourth consecutive Eastern Conference championship by defeating the Pima Rough Riders by the score of 57-42 and ran away with the distinction of being Arizona's only undefeated team in the 1950–1951 season.[88] Ahead were the semi-finals, and the state championship games were at the University of Arizona's Bear Down Gym in Tucson. The Vandals and Kivisto remained confident and breezed through the first and second rounds of play, defeating Holbrook, 96-70, and Scottsdale, 104-51. They outscored Clifton in the semifinals by the score of 72-58.[89] To win the state championship, the Vandals had to defeat Carver High School, a segregated African American school in Phoenix. It is unexpected, yet extraordinary, that all-minority players on two basketball teams, all of whom attended segregated schools, the Bullion Plaza Elementary School, and Carver High School, competed against each other in a state basketball championship. At least twenty-five hundred spectators filled Bear Down Gym to watch the action when the two teams met. Miami "proved it had everything, including height, ability and fight" and topped the Monarchs at the end of the game. Miami won the Class B State Basketball Championship by the score of 58-50.[90] Afterward, Kivisto said that he "will never have another bunch of boys like [his Miami Vandals]. They are the 'dream team,' the team every coach hopes and plans for, but never quite gets."[91]

Kivisto's exuberance over the Vandals' victory equaled that of their hometown crowd. "There must have been hundreds of us [Miamians] in the gym at that game," said businessman Glenn Wilson. "We went crazy when we won, jumping up and down and whoopin' it up for our boys. We loved Kivisto that night and we loved our team. They got the championship! How 'bout that?" he exclaimed.[92]

Pride in the Vandals extended beyond the copper town when national and local sources touted their success. For example, a newspaper in Helsinki, Finland, praised the accomplishments of Ernest Kivisto, "a coach of Finnish extraction."[93] A writer suggested that Kivisto's ancestry accounted for his success and linked his cultural heritage to basketball, "a leading sport" in Finland.[94] Publicity about the Vandals appeared in *Memo*, the trade magazine of the Wilson Sports Equipment Company. A photograph of the winning team and a description of their "undefeated season" appeared in a mid-March 1951 issue.[95] In his article, "Champs of the Hardwood," Tom Harmon, former Heisman Trophy winner and football hero at the University of Michigan, and sports editor for *Spark* magazine, said that he did not "know of any high school in history . . . that could seriously challenge Miami's performance . . . [because] Miami's record [remained] by far the best."[96] And a Tucson sports writer called the Vandals "the best team in Arizona's history."[97]

More accolades for Kivisto and the team came from the Vandals' hometown fans, town merchants, and school. The Knights of Columbus (K of C) from Our Lady of the Blessed Sacrament Catholic Church held a banquet at its Amaranth Hall on March 30 and honored Kivisto and his team.[98] The Reverend James T. Weber, state chaplain of the K of C, acted as master of ceremonies and joined in thanking the Vandals for bringing the state championship back to Miami after a long wait of ten years.[99] Edwin "Scotty" McDonald, the basketball coach at Loyola University in Los Angeles, served as the main speaker at the event that evening. The presence of the dean of men from Loyola, Rev. John Dodu, added to the importance of the event. He offered liberal arts scholarships to Fito Trujillo, Lupe Acevedo, Rudy Moreno, Hector Mario Jacott, and Elias Delgadillo.[100] None of the five players accepted the scholarships, however, citing the long distance from Miami, lack of resources, and lack of financial support from their families as reasons for their decisions not to attend Loyola.[101]

The team and their families became honored guests at a testimonial dinner on April 18. Sponsored by the Miami Chamber of Commerce, the event became billed as "Vandal Night."[102] The chamber sold over two hundred tickets to the dinner, and Coach Kivisto and his team received the "tribute of an admiring community."[103] University of Arizona's head basketball coach, Fred Enke, and J. F. "Pop" McKale, athletic director, expressed their admiration for the coach and his team, but offered only one athletic scholarship. Eli Lazovich accepted their offer and played basketball at the University of Arizona after his graduation from Miami High School in 1951.[104] One of the town's most prominent merchants, Abe Bernstein, owner of the United Jewelry Company, presented basketball trophies to Coach Kivisto and each member of his team in celebration of their conference and state victories.[105] "Those boys were really something," remarked longtime resident Glenn Wilson. "They made us all proud to be from Miami. We all came together to support them, and we were really proud of what they did in winning the state championship," he said.[106]

At a special assembly at Miami High School, a proud Coach Kivisto stood on the auditorium's stage and held his state and Eastern Conference basketball trophies in his hands for the wild and cheering crowd to see as he posed for photographs for the school's yearbook.[107] One of the students at the assembly, eighteen-year-old senior Betty Beneteau, recalled the excitement and electricity in the air when Kivisto and his team came onto the stage to stand alongside the high school principal and his staff:

> [I thought] this once-in-a-lifetime team could have beaten just about any team in the nation. . . . Up to that time, nothing had ever happened to our little town of Miami quite like this great basketball team. This was really special.[108]

It is logical for eighteen-year-old Betty Beneteau Rayes not to recall the 1941 state championship team. It is possible that an eight-year-old child might not remember the excitement that followed that 1941 victory. After the post–state championship dinners and celebrations ended, Ernest Kivisto announced his decision to leave Miami High School to accept a head coaching position at East Moline High School in Moline, Illinois. His new duties included overseeing five basketball coaches for grades 9–12 at the high school and serving as a basketball coordinator for grammar schools in the East Moline suburban area. Kivisto also became the assistant football coach at East Moline High School.[109]

Kivisto's record of ninety-five wins against eight losses in his four years at Miami High School made his record the best in the state of Arizona in the years 1947 to 1951. The Vandals earned the honors of winning four consecutive conference championships.[110]

With Kivisto's departure to Illinois, Miami lost more than its high school basketball coach. At the end of the 1950–1951 seasons, the Vandals also lost Kivisto's first-string players and his best reserve guard to graduation—Lupe Acevedo, Adolph "Fito" Trujillo, Rudy Moreno, Hector Mario Jacott, and Elias Delgadillo—all the important reasons that the Vandals won the state championship.[111]

Because of that championship, athletic scholarships and higher education came their way, and the young men chose to pursue them. Herbert Gregg, head basketball coach for Arizona State College in Flagstaff, offered four-year athletic scholarships to Lupe Acevedo and Fito Trujillo, a two-year athletic scholarship to Hector Mario Jacott, and one-year athletic scholarships to Rudy Moreno and Elias Delgadillo.[112] Each of the men accepted the scholarships and played for the Lumberjacks at Arizona State College in Flagstaff, now known as Northern Arizona University.[113]

Lupe Acevedo played as a starting guard on the varsity basketball team from 1951 to 1955 and graduated with a bachelor of arts degree in education in 1955. He was ASC's high point man in 1954 and served in the US Army from 1955 to 1957. He returned to the Pinetop, Arizona, area after military service and became a physical education teacher and basketball official in northern Arizona for over thirty years before his retirement. Acevedo was inducted into the Northern Arizona University's Sports Hall of Fame.[114]

Adolph "Fito" Trujillo's name was added to the list of the Lumberjacks' leading scorers during his four years on the team, and he gained "Most Valuable Player" honors in his senior year and was selected as an All-American player by the National Association of Intercollegiate Athletics (NAIA). After his graduation from Arizona State College with a bachelor of science degree in business in 1955, Trujillo served in the US Army and played basketball for the Thirty-Second Regiment and the Seventh Division in Korea and in Japan. Upon his release from the military, he returned to Miami and earned a living as a bookkeeper for Globe Builders Supply Company and bought the company in 1976.[115]

Hector Mario Jacott played basketball at Arizona State College in Flagstaff for two years before he was drafted into the US Army. He served in the Korean War and returned to Miami, Arizona, and became a cabinetmaker and owner of Jacott Memorials, a headstone company.[116]

Rudy Moreno played on the varsity squad at Arizona State College in Flagstaff from 1951 to 1953 and left school to serve in the US Army. Upon his discharge in 1955 he returned to Miami and worked for the Pinto Valley Mining Company and retired in 1993.[117]

Elias Delgadillo played a year of basketball for the Lumberjacks at Arizona State College before he was drafted into the US Army in 1953. Upon his release from military service, he returned to Flagstaff to attend college and received a bachelor of science degree in 1958. He attended Arizona

State University in Tempe and graduated with a master of arts degree in Spanish in 1963. He became a Spanish teacher in Holtville, California, and retired in 1999.[118]

Tony Gutierrez and his cohorts—Tony Regalado, Lupe Acevedo, Adolph "Fito" Trujillo, Rudy Moreno, Hector Mario Jacott, and Elias Delgadillo—are representatives of their third generation. They had dreams: the chance to own and wear new tennis shoes, the chance to win the basketball championship, and the chance to earn a college degree. Their success epitomized the possibilities of their parents' American Dream and reflected the dreams of their second-generation parents who came to Miami in the 1920s and 1930s to improve their economic livelihood for the future of their families. Perhaps Elias Delgadillo recognized what shaped their winning character:

> First and foremost were our parents. Although [we] came from families of mediocre means, we were never lacking in love, caring, and guidance. In their own quiet way, our parents set the example and assured us that we would grow into decent and responsible adults.[119]

The Mexican American basketball players and their Finnish American basketball coach were not only champions but also winners. They smoothed over ethnic difficulties through their excellent play and brought national recognition to the Arizona copper town that reveled in their victories and success. This third generation of Mexican Americans attended college and became successful. Some worked in their copper mining town as professionals and made contributions to their community. Their rise through sports and education enabled families to realize their American dreams of equality for their children. And what's more traditional than that? The post–World War II period and throughout the 1950s represent an era when high school basketball had unparalleled success as a spectator sport, especially in southwestern mining towns and rural areas where sports dominated the cultural landscape. Basketball afforded higher educational opportunities for Mexican Americans who would use athletic scholarships to escape the working-class lives of their parents. High school basketball teams and players in post–World War II Arizona are collectively an important and overlooked chapter in local and regional history of the saga of prep sports. Scholars in disciplines such as sports history, American culture, and Mexican American and Latino/a studies need to investigate further the history of high school basketball in this period, especially the history of Arizona champions like the mighty Miami Vandals, who won their title by beating an all–African American team from segregated Carver High School in Phoenix, Arizona, in 1951, and in the United States' era of school segregation.

Notes

1. Mario García explains that the term "Mexican American generation" was used by sociologist Rodolfo Alvarez in 1973 to refer more to a "biological generation than to a political generation" (see Mario T. García, *Mexican Americans: Leadership, Ideology, and Identity, 1930–1960* [New Haven, CT: Yale University Press, 1989], 308n1). Richard A. Garcia, David Montejano, and Guadalupe San Miguel, Jr., also discuss this same generation in their works. See Richard A. García, "The Mexican American Mind: A Product of the 1930s," in *History, Culture, and Society: Chicano Studies in the 1980s*, ed. Mario T. Garcia and Francisco Lomeli (Ypsilanti, MI: Bilingual Press, 1983); David Montejano, *Anglos and Mexicans in the Making of Texas, 1836–1986* (Austin: University of Texas Press, 1987); Guadalupe San Miguel, Jr., "The Struggle against Separate and Unequal Schools: Middle-Class Mexican Americans, and the Desegregation Campaign in Texas," *History of Education Quarterly* 23, no. 3 (fall 1983): 343–59.

2. Alberto M. Camarillo, "Research Note on Chicano Community Leaders: The G.I. Generation," *Aztlán* 2 (fall 1971): 145–50.

3. Historian James T. Adams coined the phrase "American Dream" in his 1931 publication *The Epic of America* (Boston: Little and Brown, 1931). The phrase refers to the belief in the freedom that allows Americans an equal opportunity to receive an education and achieve goals in life through hard work and perseverance. For Mexican Americans and Mexican immigrants in Miami, Arizona, who encountered racism, equality and education were the American Dreams for their third-generation children. See Wikipedia.org/wike/ American_Dream (accessed December 5, 2008).

4. Jorge Iber, "Mexican Americans of South Texas Football: The Athletic and Coaching Careers of E. C. Lerma and Bobby Cavazos, 1932–1965," *Southwestern Historical Quarterly* 105, no. 4 (April 2002): 616–33.

5. Richard Santillán, "Mexican Baseball Teams in the Midwest, 1916–1965: The Politics of Cultural Survival and Civil Rights," *Perspectives in Mexican American Studies* 7 (Spring 2001): 131–51.

6. Samuel O. Regalado, *Viva Baseball!: Latin Major Leaguers and Their Special Hunger* (Urbana: University of Illinois Press, 1998); Tim Wendel, *The New Face of Baseball: The One-Hundred-Years Rise and Triumph of Latinos in America's Favorite Sport* (New York: Rayo, 2003).

7. Regalado, *Viva Baseball!*, xiv.

8. Through their excellent play and competitiveness, Latino baseball players from South and Central America and Mexico captured the attention of baseball fans. Baseball forged positive international relationships among Pan-American nations.

9. Regalado, *Viva Baseball!*, xiv.

10. José M. Alamillo, "*Peloteros* in Paradise: Mexican American Baseball and Oppositional Politics in Southern California, 1930–1950," *Western Historical Quarterly* 34, no. 2 (summer 2003): 191–211; Gabriela Arredondo, "What! The Mexicans, Americans? Race and Ethnicity, Mexicans in Chicago, 1916–1939" (PhD diss., University of Chicago, 1999).

11. Alamillo, "*Peloteros* in Paradise," 196.

12. Arredondo, "What!," xi.

13. Ibid., 220.

14. *Honor the Past, Mold the Future* (Globe, AZ: Gila Centennials, 1976), 49–57.

15. Established by 1920 the Arizona Interscholastic Association (AIA) became the state's athletic governing body that sanctioned the establishment of conference divisions that linked schools' programs to interscholastic competition. See http://www.aiaonline.org.

16. *Honor the Past*, 50.

17. Ibid., 49–51; Hyman Robert Weisberg, "A History of the Miami High School, Miami, Arizona" (master's thesis, Arizona State College at Tempe, 1951), 32–33.

18. "Miami Hoopsters Leave Tonight for Big Tourney," *Arizona Republican*, March 29, 1928; "Miami Cagers Leave for National Meet," *Arizona Republi-*

can, March 30, 1928.

19. *Honor the Past*, 50–51; Weisberg, "History of the Miami High School," 32, 44; "Entire State as Well as Local Fans Backing Crack Quintent," *Arizona Silver Belt*, March 29, 1928.

20. "Miami Basketball Five Eliminated from Chicago Tourney," *Arizona Republican*, April 4, 1928; "Miami Cagers Are Eliminated from Consolation Tournament," *Arizona Republican*, April 5, 1928.

21. *Honor the Past*, 51; Weisberg, "History of the Miami High School," 39, 44.

22. Miami High School, *The Concentrator*, 1932, 25.

23. Ibid.

24. *Honor the Past*, 52.

25. "Miami High School Vandals Win 1941 State Championship," *Arizona Silver Belt*, March 24, 1941.

26. Matt Blessing, head of Special Collections and University Archives, Marquette University Libraries, to Sonny Peña, Tempe, Arizona, February 25, 2004 (copy in author's files).

27. "Ernest Kivisto," *Arizona Republic*, January 3, 1951.

28. Ibid.

29. "Vandals Start Football Practice," *Arizona Silver Belt*, August 28, 1947; Tony Gutierrez, interview with the author, January 12, 2005, Tempe, Arizona; "Miami Mentor Considered for Marquette Post," *Arizona Record*, April 5, 1951.

30. Christine Marin, "Always a Struggle: Mexican Americans in Miami, Arizona, 1909–1951" (PhD diss., Arizona State University, 2005) 49–54.

31. "Mexican League Contests Held," *Arizona Silver Belt*, January 8, 1932; "Mexican Court League Starts," *Arizona Silver Belt*, December 15, 1930.

32. "Y's Guys Team Beat Mexican Y," *Arizona Silver Belt*, December 18, 1931; "Mexican League Contests Held," *Arizona Silver Belt*, January 8, 1932.

33. Gutiérrez interview.

34. In conversations, the word "gringo" is sometimes used disparagingly or scornfully by Mexican Americans to ridicule or insult Anglo Americans.

35. *Miami City Directory, 1926* (Long Beach, CA: Western Directory Co., 1926), 101.

36. Gutierrez interview.

37. Gutiérrez interview. Gutiérrez's recollection of his painful interaction with Euro-Americans in 1946 echoes that of E. C. Lerma's high school experience thirteen years earlier in 1933 in Kingsville, Texas: "I cry because I went

through a lot just to play [football]. . . . It was hard to take the insults and abuse. The Anglo kids . . . would discourage me from coming out for the team [and] it was very hard to take." See David Flores, "'30s Gridder Recalls Pain of Prejudice," *Nuestro* 6, no. 8 (October 1982): 25.

38. Gutiérrez interview.

39. "Vandals Win Open Basketball Season on December 12," *Arizona Silver Belt*, December 4, 1947.

40. Miami High School, *The Concentrator*, 1947, basketball section.

41. Ibid.

42. Ibid.

43. Elias Delgadillo, *Miami High School Class B State Basketball Champions, 1951, Questionnaire*, November 7, 2003 (copy in author's files; hereafter cited as *1951 MHS Basketball Questionnaire*). My thanks to Sonny Peña for sharing with me his questionnaire, notes, photographs, newspaper clippings, scrapbooks, and vast knowledge of the 1951 MHS championship team. His love of basketball and his admiration for the 1951 Vandals sparked many discussions. Elias Delgadillo played for Ernest Kivisto from 1949 to 1951. His older brother, Manuel, played for Kivisto for two seasons, 1947–1948 and 1948–1949.

44. Ibid.

45. Wilfrid Sheed, "Why Sports Matter," *Wilson Historical Quarterly* 19 (winter 1995): 16.

46. Gutiérrez interview.

47. "Vandals Will Open Basketball Season on December 12," *Arizona Silver Belt*, December 4, 1947.

48. Gutiérrez interview.

49. Ibid.

50. Jesus F. Romero, *1951 MHS Basketball Questionnaire*, October 1, 2003 (copy in author's files).

51. "Vandal Cagers Claim National Record," *Arizona Silver Belt*, January 29, 1948.

52. Ibid.

53. *Frank Ballesteros Scrapbook, 1947–48, Miami High School Basketball* (hereafter cited as *Frank Ballesteros Scrapbook*). Ballesteros served as Kivisto's basketball manager in 1947–1948.

54. "Safford Meets Miami Saturday," *Arizona Republic*, February 23, 1948; "Van-

dals Take Tourney Title," *Arizona Republic*, February 23, 1948.

55. "Unheralded Fives District Champs; State Battle on Thursday at Tucson," *Phoenix Gazette*, February 23, 1948.

56. *Frank Ballesteros Scrapbook.*

57. Gutiérrez interview.

58. Ibid.

59. Ibid.

60. "Miami Boosters to Honor Basketball Team with Banquet," *Arizona Silver Belt*, n.d.; *Frank Ballesteros Scrapbook.*

61. Glenn Wilson, interview with the author, Tempe, Arizona, September 22, 1998.

62. "Miami Boosters to Honor Basketball Team with Banquet," *Arizona Silver Belt*, n.d.; *Frank Ballesteros Scrapbook.*

63. Miami High School, *The Concentrator*, 1949, basketball section.

64. Gutiérrez interview.

65. "Vandals Put MHS on the Map with Title Season in 1951," *Arizona Silver Belt*, February 14, 2001.

66. "Miami 71, Florence 46," *Arizona Republic*, March 2, 1950.

67. Wilson interview.

68. "Vandals Lose to Nogales Apaches in Semifinals of State Tournament," *Phoenix Gazette*, March 9, 1950.

69. Ibid.

70. Ibid.

71. Wilson interview.

72. "Loretta Apodaca Acevedo," standard certificate of death, January 25, 1944, Division of Vital Statistics, Arizona State Board of Health.

73. "Francisco M. Moreno," standard certificate of death, November 2, 1944, Bureau of Vital Statistics, Arizona State Department of Health; "Refugio Trujillo," standard certificate of death, March 31, 1948, Bureau of Vital Statistics, Arizona State Department of Health.

74. Jenny Acevedo Olds, interview with the author, Mesa, Arizona, September 30, 2005.

75. "Vandal Cagers Meet St. Johns Redskins in Season Opener," *Arizona Silver Belt*, November 7, 1950.

76. "Basketball Ace Achieves Success the Hard Way," *Arizona Silver Belt*, December 14, 1950; "Vandals Whip St. Johns and Thatcher," *Arizona Silver Belt*,

December 20, 1950.

77. "Basketball Ace Achieves Success the Hard Way."

78. "Miami High Builds Up 81-Point Average While Galloping to Nine Consecutive Cage Triumphs," *Arizona Republic*, January 8, 1951; "Trujillo Sets Scoring Mark," *Arizona Republic*, January 8, 1951.

79. "Miami Cage Star Sets State Scoring Record," *Arizona Silver Belt*, January 11, 1951.

80. "Trujillo Sets Scoring Mark," *Arizona Republic*, January 8, 1951; "Vandals Smash More Records in Walloping Clifton 122-58," *Arizona Silver Belt*, January 18, 1951; "Vandal Cager Scores 56 Points to Break State Record—Again," *Arizona Silver Belt*, February 1, 1951.

81. "Miami High Builds Up 81-Point Average While Galloping to Nine Consecutive Cage Triumphs."

82. "Vandals Host Duncan, Safford and Crush Flagstaff Eagles 101-28," *Arizona Silver Belt*, January 4, 1951.

83. "Miami Vandals Knock Clifton Down and Trample Them into Helplessness," *The Copper Era*, January 19, 1951. For articles about the high-scoring controversy, see "Vandals Smash More Records in Walloping Clifton 122-58"; "Torrid Vandal Quintet Arouses State's Biggest Prep Tempest," *Arizona Record*, February 1, 1951; "Vandal Cager Scores 56 Points to Break State Record—Again"; "Basketball Champs Hit the Road for Two Easy Games," *Arizona Silver Belt*, February 1, 1951; "Vandal Cagers Smash National Record," *Arizona Silver Belt*, February 15, 1951; "Dunkin' with Duncan, by Arnott Duncan," *Arizona Republic*, n.d. See also several newspaper clippings in *Hector Jacott Scrapbook, Circa 1949–1951* (copies in author's files).

84. "Torrid Vandals Quintet Arouses State's Biggest Prep Tempest"; "Vandal Cager Scores 56 Points to Break State Record—Again."

85. "Vandal Cager Scores 56 Points To Break State Record—Again."

86. "Torrid Vandals Quintet Arouses State's Biggest Prep Tempest."

87. Ibid.; "Miami Hits for 130 Points in Morenci Clash," *Arizona Record*, February 15, 1951.

88. "Vandals Win Eastern Conference Tournament; Vie for State Championship at Cage Playoffs in Tucson," *Arizona Silver Belt*, March 1, 1951; "Miami Wins Eastern Tourney Crown, 57-42," *Arizona Republic*, February 25, 1951.

89. "Miami Steals Show as Holbrook Bows," *Arizona Republic*, March 2, 1951;

"Miami Sets All-Time Tourney Records by Crushing Scottsdale Quint, 104-51," *Arizona Republic*, March 3, 1951; "Miami, Carver Win: Favorites Gain Finals in Class B," *Arizona Republic*, March 4, 1951.

90. "Miami Steals Show As Holbrook Bows," *Arizona Republic*. March 2, 1951; Miami Wins, 58-50; Vandals Top Monarchs in B Meet," *Arizona Republic*, March 4, 1951.
91. "Vandals Sweep Tournament to Become State Champions; Climax Perfect Season by Edging Carver 58-50," *Arizona Silver Belt*, March 8, 1951.
92. Wilson interview.
93. "Vandals Sweep Tournament to Become State Champions."
94. Ibid.
95. Ibid.
96. Tom Harmon, "Champs of the Hardwood," *Spark, the Bi-Weekly News Magazine*, April 23, 1951, 19–20.
97. Ibid.
98. "Vandals Sweep Tournament to Become State Champions."
99. The Knights of Columbus, a Catholic order known as "the strong right arm of the Church" and recognized as a fraternal society of Catholic men, was founded in New Haven, Connecticut, on February 2, 1882. See http://www.newadvent.org.
100. "K of C to Fete Miami Champs," *Arizona Republic*, March 21, 1951; Miami High School, *The Concentrator*, 1951, basketball section; "Chamber to Honor Basketball Champs," *Arizona Silver Belt*, March 8, 1951.
101. "Secret of Vandal Cage Success Revealed," *Arizona Silver Belt*, February 22, 1951.
102. "Adolfo 'Fito' Trujillo," *1951 MHS Basketball Questionnaire*, September 16, 2003; "Rudy Moreno," *1951 MHS Basketball Questionnaire*, November 11, 2004 (copies in author's files).
103. "Testimonial Dinner to Honor Cagers," *Arizona Silver Belt*, March 15, 1951.
104. Ibid.
105. Sonny Peña, interview with the author, Tempe, Arizona, September 26, 2005. Just five days prior to the dinner, the Helms Foundation announced Enke's selection to its College Basketball Hall of Fame.
106. "200 Tickets Set for Vandal Feed," *Arizona Republic*, April 13, 1951.
107. Wilson interview.

108. Miami High School, *The Concentrator*, 1951, basketball section.

109. "Remembrances of Coach Ernest Kivisto from the Summer of 1947 to the Summer of 1951, compiled by Betty Beneteau Rayes, 21 November 2003" (copy in author's files). My thanks to Sonny Peña for sharing this information.

110. "Kivisto to Head Coaching Staff at East Moline," *Arizona Record*, June 28, 1951.

111. "Complete Record of the 1950–1951 Miami High School Basketball Team, Eastern Conference–Eastern District and State Champions, compiled by Ernest Kivisto," n.d. (copy in author's files). My thanks to Sonny Peña for sharing this information.

112. Ibid.

113. Jenny Acevedo Olds, interview with the author, Mesa, Arizona, September 30, 2005. Jenny Acevedo Olds is Lupe Acevedo's older sister. She helped her father raise Lupe after the death of their mother when Lupe was twelve years old.

114. Ibid.; "Trujillo, Acevedo Complete Brilliant State Cage Careers," *Arizona Republic*, March 6, 1955; "Obituaries: Acevedo," *Arizona Silver Belt*, March 23, 1993.

115. "Trujillo, Acevedo Complete Brilliant State Cage Careers"; "Fito Trujillo, essay by Sonny Peña," June 30, 2005 (copy in author's files).

116. "Obituaries: Jacott," *Arizona Silver Belt*, August 23, 2000; "Hector Mario Jacott, essay by Sonny Peña," June 30, 2005 (copy in author's files).

117. "Rudolpho Moreno, essay by Sonny Peña," June 30, 2005 (copy in author's files).

118. "Elias Delgadillo," *1951 MHS Basketball Questionnaire*, November 2003.

119. Ibid.

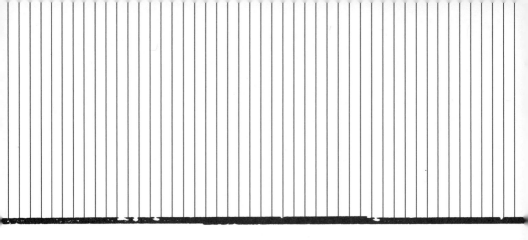

CHAPTER 7

Mexican Americans of South Texas Football: The Athletic and
Coaching Careers of E. C. Lerma and Bobby Cavazos, 1932–1965

Jorge Iber
Texas Tech University

Sports teach, it is in their nature. . . . Schools and colleges also teach something by their
very natures, which is that you are now playing for the whole community and not just
yourself, and that if you win, the community will join you in experiencing a kind of crazy
collective joy that used to more than make up for not getting paid.

Wilfrid Sheed

During the past thirty years the breadth of Mexican American
history has expanded dramatically as researchers explored the
development of various *comunidades* (communities) through-
out the United States as well as spotlighting class, religious, and political
diversity within this group. While much has been learned, some facets of
Mexican American life are still relatively unexplored; athletic endeavor
is one such area. Over the past decade, the works of Samuel O. Regalado
introduced the story of Hispanic baseball players to an academic audience
as he focused his research on athletic achievement as well as on how sport

affected American society's perceptions of Spanish speakers. Additionally, Regalado detailed the importance of baseball *ligas* (leagues) to barrio (neighborhood) life, and the social significance of the Los Angeles Dodgers' Spanish-language broadcasts. These studies clearly provide a foundation for a Hispanic role in baseball history, but recent research reveals that the participation of Spanish-surnamed people in US sporting life extends beyond the diamond. In this essay I expand upon this developing trend and discuss Texans' perceptions of Chicano athletic and intellectual ability as well as summarize preliminary research on the role of two Mexican Americans in the history of Texas high school football.[1]

An increased Latino presence in a variety of professional and athletic activities (with Scott Gomez's contribution to the New Jersey Devils' Stanley Cup run and the emergence of Tony Gonzalez as a Pro Bowl tight end being prime examples) attest to the inaccuracy of stereotyping Spanish-surnamed athletes solely as *peloteros* (baseball players). Yet the history of US team sport, at all levels, is still framed almost exclusively in terms of white/black interactions. Jeffrey T. Sammons's 1994 essay " 'Race' and Sport: A Critical, Historical Examination" is an example of this inclination. Justifiably, Sammons notes Regalado's contributions, but his work provides only passing mention of US Spanish speakers. Only at the end of a seventy-five-page article does he briefly discuss the value of an examination of the Latino role in US sports history. In the case of states or locations with large Mexican American populations, such as southern Texas and the border region, this omission leaves a gap in historical understanding of sport and its impact on social relations. This lacuna calls for the examination of the career of individuals who, as both athletes and coaches, have broken down stereotypes of Mexican American intellectual deficiencies and physical limitations.[2]

Given many Texans' infatuation with high school football, the impact of their success on the gridiron (as both coaches and athletes) can influence how the broader society views individuals of Mexican descent in towns throughout Texas. Historians of Asian Americans, Jewish Americans, Italian Americans, and Native Americans have made similar arguments. In *Crossing Sidelines, Crossing Cultures: Sport and Asian Pacific American Cultural Citizenship*, Joel S. Franks argues that sports (under certain circumstances) encourage Americans of different classes and ethnicities to cheer for athletes of varied backgrounds and that minorities have often used athletic endeavor to represent their communities before the broader public.[3] Steven A. Riess makes a similar statement about Jews in the United States when he states that (particularly boxers) "used sport to help them become acculturated and achieve structural assimilation, gain self-esteem, public recognition, fight stereotypes, and escape the poverty of the ghetto."[4] Gary Ross Mormino reached similar conclusions about Italian immigrant children, such as Yogi Berra and Joe Garagiola. In "The Playing Fields of St. Louis: Italian Immigrants and Sports, 1925–1941," Mormino asserts that sports crystallized a feeling of pride for Italian Americans and created "a public forum from which . . . Americans (could) judge the (Italian) neighborhood from a different perspective, other than busted stills and ethnic caricatures."[5] Anthony Y. Yoseloff arrives at a similar conclusion in "From Ethnic Hero to National Icon: The Americanization of Joe DiMaggio," by contrasting newspaper and magazine characterizations and descriptions of the "Yankee Clipper" before and after his fifty-six-game hitting streak in 1941.[6]

Two recent articles on the history of the Carlisle Indians' football program furnish similar perspectives. In David Wallace Adams's "More Than a Game: The Carlisle Indians Take to the Gridiron, 1893–1917," the author notes that success on the field often led newspaper writers to issue "journalistic pronouncements that stereotypes were outdated," and that Native Americans should be given greater opportunities in American life.[7] In "The Construction, Negotiation, and Transformation of Racial Identity in American Football: A Study of Native Americans and African Americans," Gerald R. Gems notes both the potential benefits and limitations of sport as a vehicle with which to change the majority population's perception of people categorized as "others" or "outsiders": "The minorities' athletic feats and success destabilized norms, expectations, and stereotyping ascribed by whites, but socially they remained members of alternate cultures, marginalized with dual identities, and limited in inclusion, particularly off the field."[8] Considering the amount of work that has been done on other minority groups, it is surprising that so little work has focused on sports' role in the lives of Mexican Americans as well as the impact of athletic competition/success on the perception of Mexican Americans in Texas. The stories of individuals such as coaching legend E. C. Lerma (Benavides High School and Rio Grande City High School) and the high school and college career of Kingsville High School halfback Bobby Cavazos provide historians with entry into a potentially profitable, and largely untapped, vein of history.

The narrative of Mexican American athletic involvement in the Lone Star State has received limited attention. One of the few works dedicated specifically to this topic is the essay "Any Sunday in April: The Rise of Sport in San Antonio and the Hispanic Borderlands," by Mary Lou LeCompte and William H. Beezley.[9] Here the authors detail the development of amusements and sport among a heterogeneous population comprising (by the end of the nineteenth century) Spanish-speaking Tejanos, German immigrants, and white Americans. Among the diversions of this population LeCompte and Beezley noted the practice of bullfighting, rodeo, horse racing, polo, boxing, and baseball. One of these forms of entertainment, the *corrida de toros*, caused tensions among the different groups, and by the 1870s city leaders moved to quell what many whites considered a "barbaric" sport. The Texas legislatures finally prohibited bullfighting in the state in 1891. The outlawing of what had been a traditional Tejano/Mexican diversion reflected the changing nature of economic and political power in Texas. In the decades following the Lone Star State's annexation, this population's social position steadily deteriorated until, by the early decades of the twentieth century, the mass of Mexican Americans toiled for low wages, had little control over their children's education, and were relegated to second-class social status.[10]

The Mexican Americans' precipitous decline in social standing manifested itself in a variety of ways. Historian Arnoldo De Leon notes some of these trends in his monumental 1983 work, *They Called Them Greasers: Anglo Attitudes toward Mexicans in Texas, 1836–1900*. Among the stereotypes accepted by many whites was the belief that Spanish speakers were lethargic and slow-witted as well as compulsively given to debauchery. Some Texans even claimed that Mexican flesh was so corrupt that neither worms nor wild animals would consume their bodies after death.[11]

By the early decades of the 1900s, negative perceptions of Mexican

American intellectual capabilities were rampant in the academic literature of educators. The noted scholar of Mexican American educational history in Texas, Guadalupe San Miguel, noted some of these perceptions in his important work, *"Let Them All Take Heed": Mexican Americans and the Campaign for Educational Equality in Texas, 1910–1981*. He summarized such trends by stating,

> Wherever there were significant numbers of Mexican children in school, local officials tried to place them in facilities separate from the other white children. There were two basic sets of reasons given for separating Mexicans from Anglos: those asserting that association was undesirable from the Anglos' point of view and those asserting that separation was to the advantage of the Mexicans. Anglos usually emphasized the fact that the standard of cleanliness among Mexican children was lower than that among Anglos. . . . Finally, public school officials separated Mexicans on the basis of curricular concerns, irregular attendance, or language ability. Educators argued that because of the language "deficiency" and the lack of school attendance, Mexican children could not effectively participate in schools or classes with their English-speaking peers.[12]

Even more information on such perceptions can be gleaned from studies conducted from the late 1920s through the 1950s by doctoral- and master's-level students in the Department of Education at the University of Texas and other public institutions of higher learning. At best, Mexican American children were considered culturally deprived and intellectually slow; at worst, they were genetic inferiors meant solely for work in the cotton and vegetable fields of Texas. To their credit, many of the writers of this era called for equal educational opportunities and acknowledged the impact of economic deprivation on Mexican American educational progress. However, a brief examination of some studies reveals how certain educators felt about Texas's Spanish-surnamed *estudiantes*.

In his 1927 research on poor, Spanish-surnamed children on the West Side of San Antonio, James Kilbourne Harris listed a litany of complaints about *Chicanitos* that would be oft repeated for several decades. These pupils, he claimed, showed limited intelligence, had few ambitions, and "their brains do not seem to work as rapidly as do the brains of English speaking pupils."[13] Another University of Texas researcher, Genevieve King, asserted that such youngsters were almost devoid of ambition and showed an overall lack "of pride in regard to schoolwork."[14] Several authors placed most of the blame for the lack of progress upon the Mexican Americans themselves, for they supposedly did not emphasize the value of education for their children.[15]

Ambivalent commentary is found in the research dealing with athletic ability. Some writers claimed that Chicanos were physically inferior and showed little interest in participating in sports while others asserted that *estudiantes* loved athletics, but other problems, such as their innate character flaws, often ruined the enjoyment of such events. In her 1936 study, Genevieve King postulated that the Mexican Americans she studied in San Antonio had little interest in exercise.[16] Albert Folsom Cobb argued similarly in 1952 when he stated that Spanish-surnamed pupils were "not as interested or eager to participate in physical education program(s), particularly in inter-school competition, as are Anglo-American boys."[17] Conversely, San Miguel noted that some administrators—such as Katherine Groutt, principal of the Aoy Elementary School in El Paso—held the opposite view. In 1920 she noted that all "Mexicans were particularly gifted in art, music, and athletics." "They make good athletes because they like to play," she stated.[18]

In two studies comparing the physical development of white and Mexican American children, Texas A&I University researchers found substantial differences in lung capacity, height, weight, and other physical traits; in both cases, the majority-population students were judged superior. One researcher noted that the flawed character of Spanish-surnamed pupils made them problematic participants in athletic competition. "The Mexican children are fond of all sports, especially athletic contests. They excel in these but they mar the [games] . . . by being poor losers."[19]

Conversely, University of Texas graduate student Bruce Walsh Shaw argued that his research results countered the notion of Anglo physical superiority. He also claimed that athletic ability did have a slightly positive impact on how Anglo children perceived their Mexican American counterparts.[20] Finally, a 1942 examination of this topic conducted by Merrell

E. Thompson and Claude C. Dove stated that when "equated according to age, health, and weight, the Spanish American boys were *somewhat superior* in all events tested and significantly superior in all but the shot-put." The reasons for this, these authors noted, were based on economic circumstances, lifestyle, and racial characteristics. Because most of these children came from poorer families, the "Spanish-American children seem to lead a more vigorous physical life than do the Anglos. This consideration would seem to produce a more healthy physical development and thereby superiority in the events . . . tested."[21]

Although Mexican Americans' participation on the gridiron was largely ignored, a few writers commented upon and examined some aspects of Mexican American participation in high school football during the first half of the 1900s. Francis Edward Meyer performed a systematic study of this topic in his master's program at the University of Texas. His research provides some insights regarding football coaches' perceptions of the ability and shortcomings of Mexican American football players. "Even though a great number of boys leave the football program after graduating from junior high school, it is held that the boys with the greatest potential of becoming good ball players stay with the program until the completion of their high school careers."[22] Against such perceptions of intellectual inadequacy and the ambivalent recognition of athletic capabilities, E. C. Lerma and Bobby Cavazos battled as they took to the gridirons and sidelines of southern Texas in the 1930s and 1940s.

Over the past four decades, writers such as Harold Ratliff,[23] Bill McMurray,[24] and Carlton Stowers[25] have chronicled Texas's love affair with high school football. In their efforts these authors worked to "record and preserve the sport's high-water marks" and regaled "readers with riveting vignettes of greatness on the high school gridiron."[26] In recent years, a number of works, most notably H. G. Bissinger's controversial *Friday Night Lights: A Town, a Team, and a Dream*, have painted a much darker picture of the rituals and rites surrounding the state's obsession with gridiron battles.[27] Regardless of the authors' analyses of the benefits or shortcomings of the sport, Mexican American contributions to the history of Texas high school football have received limited attention. Stowers's primary focus on Mexican Americans in his *Friday Night Heroes* examines the story of the Asherton Trojans and the forty-game losing steak they endured during the 1960s. A more positive examination of Chicano grid-iron performance is presented in Ratcliff's *Autumn's Mightiest Legions* in a chapter titled, "The Latins Show Them." Here Ratliff praises Donna High School's march to the Class AA championship in 1961. Although there is some praise for players such as quarterback Luz Pedraza, the main impetus of the championship comes from the abilities of the Redskins' coach, Earl Scott. The final paragraph in the chapter leaves the reader with the impression that without Anglo leadership, the "Latins" of Donna High would not have been able to succeed. The championship "paid for all of the hard work the boys had done in showing that the Mexican boy can play football as well as anyone if he has the coach to tell him he can do it and show him how to prepare himself for the task at hand."[28]

In Ty Cashion's 1997 work, *Pigskin Pulpit: A Social History of Texas High School Football Coaches*, the author's informants do little to clear up this ambivalence. Ralph Martin (brother of Robert Martin, a man who was part Mexican American and who coached the legendary Tom Landry at Mission High School) claimed that isolation and poverty in the border area of South Texas kept schools from picking up the sport in the early decades of the 1900s. Additionally, he believed that "the Hispanic culture was reluctant to let football interfere with the more popular pastime of baseball." E. C. Lerma, however, advised Cashion that "racial prejudice was at least as responsible as culture for limiting Hispanic participation." One incident that supports Lerma's contention occurred in a 1930s game involving Diamond Hill High School:

> When the team travelled to Grandview, south of Fort Worth, they found a crowd that grew hostile when they saw "a Mexican boy" [Fred Torres] take the field for pre-game warm-ups. "They had only one set of bleachers, and the rest of them were walking the sidelines. . . . When [Torres] wasn't in there, they'd crowd in and push on him." Before long, he had to stand right next to Varley [the head coach] whenever he came out. When Diamond Hill won, the Grandview fans blocked their exit. "We didn't even make it to the locker room. They were trying to get at Torres, and so the players circled around him and

took off their cleats and started swinging them at the crowd." More than anything, expressed Varley, poor Torres was greatly embarrassed by bringing the incident on his team-mates.[29]

Although they faced discrimination, Mexican Americans never endured the systematic racial segregation foisted upon Texas's African Americans during the first seven decades of the twentieth century, and this situation provided some opportunities that, Cashion argues, "further levelled the social playing field" between Mexican Americans and the majority population. The stories of E. C. Lerma and Bobby Cavazos shed some light upon this assertion.[30]

Everardo Carlos Lerma (E. C.) Lerma was born in the small South Texas town of Bishop in 1915, son of Mauro Lerma and his wife, Carlota Gonzalez-Lerma both from Mier, Tamaulipas, Mexico. The son of migrant workers, E. C. faced difficult circumstances on his path to gridiron and coaching glory. His family moved to Kingsville in 1918, and by the time he turned eight both parents had died. Although he grew up poor and attended segregated schools, E. C. was captivated by gridiron battles and dreamed of becoming one of the first Mexican American football players in the history of Kingsville High School.[31]

For this Mexican American, the achievement of donning a Brahma varsity jersey necessitated more than speed, strength, and knowledge of the game; it required the tenacity of a true pioneer. When Lerma took the field for practice in the early 1930s, he was the only Spanish-surnamed player, and many of his Anglo teammates were less than enthusiastic in their welcoming. One response was to toss the "greaser" into a swimming pool. In a 1997 interview Coach Lerma recalled, "I couldn't even swim."[32]

Through persistence and athletic ability, E. C. won over some of his teammates and capped his high school football career being named all-district offensive end in 1933, the only Brahma player to garner such accolades that season. His athletic ability attracted the attention of Southwest Conference heavyweight Texas Christian University, which offered him a scholarship to play at the Fort Worth–based institution. Lerma, however, decided he did not want to leave his hometown and accepted an offer to play for his local school and team, the Texas A&I University Javelinas (the school is now renamed Texas A&I University–Kingsville) starting in 1934.[33]

Circumstances were little different at this higher level of competition, and the racism and discrimination E. C. faced in high school continued on the freshman squad at A&I. One man on that unit, L. E. Ramey, recounted the first few days of practice in a 1989 speech. One concern that some incoming freshmen had was that a "brown-skinned Mexican" might "be given" a scholarship that should be given to a "real" American.

> This was the middle of the Great Depression and many of these young men would have to go home if they did not earn a scholarship. Understandingly, competition was . . . fierce for there was a limited number of scholarships for freshmen.[34]

Lerma's persistence earned him a certain amount of admiration from his freshmen mates. Still, some varsity players wanted him gone. In order to accomplish this task, the lettermen pressured Lerma's classmates through hazing. Once again, Dr. Ramey's recollections are instructive:

> At the end of daily practice, we would go to the boarding house for our evening meal. Some of the varsity players would be there and inquire, "Is Lerma still out?" We would answer "yes" and they would command, "Freshmen, grab your ankles!" and would proceed to give us twenty licks. After four or five days, my rear end was black and blue and my enthusiasm for A&I football was diminishing. I told the varsity players that they could beat us forever because Lerma was not going to quit, and that we were scheduled to scrimmage them on Monday, and that they could run him off at that time. By this time the freshmen had developed a respect and admiration for E. C. We knew he was a hard-nosed football player that would not be intimidated. Consequently, when we scrimmaged the varsity, we did all we could to see that E. C. got a fair shake. It only took two or three scrimmages for the varsity to realize that Lerma was here to stay, and they also developed respect.[35]

Eventually, E. C. Lerma lettered for the Javelinas from 1935 to 1937 and became an integral part of the A&I team. His cohorts even protected him on the field from disparaging remarks and physical attacks by athletes from the University of Texas, Baylor, Hardin-Simmons, and other schools. The Javelinas' coach, Bud McCallum, contributed greatly to this atmosphere. Ramey recalled that McCallum was "a fair, tough, honest football coach that demanded 100 percent effort at all times. He cared not what the color of your skin was."[36]

Upon graduation in 1938, E. C. began a long and distinguished teaching, coaching, and administrative career at Benavides High School. Lerma served as assistant for two seasons and then applied for the school's head coaching position when it came open in 1940. The reaction of many in town was as expected. Did a "Mexican" have the intellectual capacity it took to guide one of the town's flagship institutions? As Ty Cashion notes, during the 1940s the head football coach position in many Texas communities carried a great deal of weight. "Their success at times united citizens . . . while failures too often erupted into quarrels that tore towns apart. In many cases the harvest reaped from the football field even determined the self-perception of entire communities as well as how outsiders viewed those places." E. C. had a great deal of difficulty in getting the job because "people just couldn't believe that a Mexican American could do as good a job as an Anglo. Well, I think I proved them wrong."[37]

Administrators of the Benavides school district were well rewarded for making Lerma one of the first Mexican American head coaches in the state of Texas. Between 1940 and 1955, the Eagles compiled an impressive run (even by Texas standards) of football glory. The 1942, 1947, 1950, and 1952 teams won district championships. The 1948, 1949, and 1951 squads earned bidistrict titles, and the 1943 and 1949 teams finished with undefeated seasons and claimed regional crowns. After Lerma left for Rio Grande City in 1955, the Benavides Eagles did not make the state playoffs again until 1984. Lerma accomplished this remarkable feat in an area of the state that many in the coaching profession regarded as a "cemetery," precisely because of the large Mexican American population. In addition, E. C. coached all other sports and won district titles in track and baseball, and a regional championship in basketball.[38]

The supervisors of Rio Grande City School District brought Lerma in to work his magic on what had become a moribund program. Prior to his arrival, the Rattlers had won only five games between 1952 and 1954. Within two seasons, E. C. made the team respectable and posted a combined 14-5 record during the 1957 and 1958 seasons. By 1965 this

The stands of E. C. Lerma Stadium at Benavides High School, Duval County, Texas. Courtesy of the author.

now-legendary football field general retired from coaching with an overall record of 154 wins, 98 losses, and 13 outright or shared championships.[39]

Subsequently, Lerma worked as coordinator of physical education at the McAllen school district as well as director of migrant education and supervisor of adult basic education. He also served as principal of elementary schools in McAllen (1969–1973) and Dallas (1973–1974), principal of Robstown High School (1974–1975), and superintendent of schools at Benavides (1975–1976). E. C. Lerma retired after 1980, having broken down barriers to Mexican American participation and leadership in education, administration, and sports. A final honor for this pioneering individual occurred on October 18, 1991, when the Benavides Independent School District named its football stadium in his honor. The com-

The scoreboard at E. C. Lerma Stadium in Benavides, Texas.
Courtesy of the author.

munity that in 1940 doubted whether a Mexican American had sufficient
intelligence and leadership skills to pilot a football program bestowed its
greatest tribute on this son of humble Mexican immigrants. After retiring,
Coach Lerma lived quietly in McAllen until succumbing to complications
from cancer in April 1998 at the age of eighty-three.[40]

The athletic (and later coaching) career of E. C. Lerma presented a dilemma for Texans who believed in the athletic and intellectual inferiority
of Mexican Americans. Clearly, here was an individual who did not fit the
perception of a typical "greaser." If a Spanish-surnamed individual helped
the local team win, perhaps he could be accepted as an equal, at least on
the football field. Lerma's pioneering efforts opened the door for Mexican
American players at Kingsville High (and elsewhere), and during the mid-
1940s Bobby Cavazos ran right through this opening. In the process, he
became a multisport star and, later, a second-team All American at Texas
Tech University.

Bobby Cavazos was born at the world-famous King Ranch in 1931, the fourth child (of five) of Lauro Cavazos, Sr., and Thomasa Quintanilla. The Cavazos clan traces its roots in southern Texas all the way back to 1781, when, in a settlement for a land dispute, the Spanish crown granted an ancestor, Jose Narciso Cavazo, an enormous land grant known as the San Juan de Carracitos grant. This property, estimated at between 350,000 and 600,000 acres, passed down the family tree until its sale to King interests between 1873 and 1889. As with many Spanish speakers in southern Texas with limited or no access to land, Lauro, Sr., eventually put his vaquero skills (beginning in 1912 and continuing until his death in 1958) at the disposal of one of the area's cattle ranches. During a storied career, he participated in skirmishes with Mexican bandits, helped develop the first American cattle breed, and in 1926 became the King Ranch's first foreman of Mexican descent (heading the Santa Gertrudis Division).[41]

Although he had little formal education, his experiences at the ranch gave Lauro, Sr., a sense of better possibilities for the next generation. One way to achieve this was through schooling. Lauro Cavazos, Jr., who became president of Texas Tech University in 1980, recalls that his father's advice to his children was to "educate yourself. . . . It's the one thing that nobody can ever take from you. It is forever." In an era when few Mexican American children in Texas completed elementary school, all of the Cavazos siblings earned college degrees and went on to careers in the military, education, business, and scientific research.[42]

As the children of a King Ranch official, the Cavazos offspring lived a different life than most Mexican American children in Texas. They were members of a prominent family, with impeccable credentials in the community. Still, they did not escape all manifestations of discrimination and stereotyping and felt aspects "of the discrimination suffered by Mexican Americans in Kingsville." In his 1987 work, *Anglos and Mexicans in the Making of Texas, 1836–1986*, noted historian David Montejano summarized the obstacles even "well respected" Mexican Americans faced during the first half of the 1900s:

> In the ranch counties, the *patronismo* [fraternity] allowed a certain type of friendship to develop between owner and worker . . . [but] Mexican vaqueros and other hands . . . needed no instruction on the

Kingsville High School building, which both E. C. Lerma and Bobby Cavazos attended, Kingsville, Texas. The building is no longer in use, as a new school has been constructed for the city's students.

> limits of their friendship with the *patron* [master] . . . familiarity or life-long association did not mean equality.[43]

Given the reality of life in southern Texas during the 1940s, the stellar performances of Bobby Cavazos helped change the perception of many Anglos regarding a Mexican American's physical and intellectual capabilities.

Bobby began his Kingsville High School Brahma career in the fall of 1946 and quickly established himself as a superior athlete. During his freshman year he lettered in football, basketball, and track. He impressed his coaches with speed and agility that paved the way for a move to the varsity squad as a sophomore. Nelson Sharpe, a local sports reporter, predicted great benefits for the town's gridiron team once Bobby moved beyond junior varsity because "he is a speedy and elusive breakaway runner—a threat to score every time he has the ball in the open field. Tall and loosely built, he weighs 155 pounds and does not carry an ounce of fat." By August 1947 Bobby was battling for the starting left halfback position on the squad; he was starting after the second game of the season. That edition of the Brahmas recorded eight wins and two losses, the best record in school history until then, finishing second in district play. Cavazos was a significant part of this accomplishment and earned honorable mention on the *Kingsville Record*'s All South Texas Football Team.[44]

The 1948 football season, Bobby's last at Kingsville, generated both disappointment and individual success. During a practice session before the opening of school, Cavazos injured an ankle, which slowed him down during the first three games of the year. Although hobbled, he contributed on both sides of the ball, breaking up several passes in the secondary and scampering for a seventy-seven-yard touchdown run in a game against Laredo High. Reporter Jake Trussell complimented Bobby by stating that "There's no doubt about it, Cavazos means a terribly lot to Kingsville's 1948 gridiron machine." As often happens, once pegged as indispensable to the fortunes of a particular team, the player suffers a serious injury. This is what happened to Bobby on October 6, 1948, when he injured his foot in a game. Although the injury was expected to keep him out for the remainder of the season, he returned by the middle of November and helped the Brahmas with their final two games. Once again, the press in southern Texas was impressed with Bobby's talent and work ethic, selecting him for honorable mention to the All-South Texas Football Team.[45]

During the first few months of 1949 Cavazos rounded out his high school career with a flourish. In February he was named an alternate to the District 14 AA Basketball Team. In March he finished second in the high jump at the Border Olympics held in Laredo. Additionally, he was part of the winning 440-yard relay team. In April he was second in total points at the district track and field meet, helping lead the Brahmas to a district title.[46]

Bobby left Kingsville High School after the spring of 1949 and enrolled at John Tarleton Junior College at Stephenville, Texas. Although he had not yet graduated, by law he could no longer play high school football because he had passed his eighteenth birthday. During one season in the Tarleton Plowboys' backfield, Bobby often competed against players who were several years older than he was. It made little difference to this talented Chicano. He distinguished himself by finishing as the third-leading scorer in the Southwest Junior College Conference. This impressive performance helped open the door for Cavazos to attend Texas Tech University in 1950.

At the Lubbock school Cavazos continued his stellar play, running for 706 yards and nine touchdowns in 1951, 674 yards and ten touchdowns in 1953, and 757 yards and thirteen touchdowns in 1953. Bobby's ethnic background did not generate negative statements from Red Raider supporters or the local media. He was helping Tech win, which was all that mattered. This trend is clearly visible in an August 1951 column by Don Oliver, sports editor of the *Lubbock Avalanche-Journal*. "We don't care where the boys come from as long as they're the 'right kind' of boys and can play winning football." Clearly, Oliver and others at Texas Tech came to believe that Cavazos was one of the "right kind" of boys who could lead the Red Raiders to victory, national recognition, and eventual membership in the Southwest Conference. Oliver's musings present an example of sports' power to "destabilize" the perceptions of some in the majority population.[47]

Bobby topped off his college career by being named second-team All American and winning the MVP trophy, while rushing for 141 yards and three touchdowns, in the Red Raiders' 35-13 victory in the 1954 Gator Bowl game against the Auburn University Tigers.[48]

Between 1950 and 1954, Bobby's English-language hometown newspaper, the *Kingsville Record*, published a constant stream of information on his athletic prowess.[49] These sports-page materials presented a dramatically different picture of Mexican American life to thousands of readers in southern Texas. The articles contained a story of a Spanish-surnamed individual who stood proud, successful, and victorious in an endeavor that most Texans respected and glorified. Contrast this with the daily life of most of the region's Mexican Americans: segregation, racism, substan-

Publicity photo of Bobby Cavazos in his Texas Tech University uniform, c. 1954.
Courtesy of TTU Athletics.

dard schooling for their children, and dominance by corrupt Democratic political machines. Unintentionally, the articles on Bobby Cavazos's athletic brilliance provided a form of resistance against Anglo perceptions and dominance. In these stories a Mexican American individual helped bring athletic glory to Kingsville and showed his mettle in the game that instilled the "keystones of character" into the lives of Texas males.[50]

The athletic and coaching careers of E. C. Lerma and Bobby Cavazos lend support to Cashion's contention that football did provide some Spanish-surnamed individuals in Texas with an opportunity to exist within a "further leveled social playing field." Further research is necessary to determine whether these results are isolated or more generalized. While athletic competition, and the ties created thereby, did not eliminate all racist preconceptions about Spanish speakers, their success did present some Anglos in southern Texas with a different archetype of the Mexican American. Instead of the stereotypical views with which many Texans regarded persons of Mexican descent, here were two men succeeding on the gridiron and bringing athletic glory to their hometown and schools.

The area of sport history, then, is a potentially profitable vein of Mexican American life that scholars in the field have only begun exploring. Students of Italian American, Asian Pacific American, Jewish American, and Native American history have provided some models that colleagues in Mexican American studies/history would be wise to apply in a number of locales. As Nicholas P. Ciotola argued recently in his essay "Spignesi, Sinatra, and the Pittsburgh Steelers: Franco's Italian Army as an Expression of Ethnic Identity, 1972–1977," minorities have often used sport "to make a public statement documented." It is time to insert a missing piece—the Mexican American athlete—into the study of this important aspect of American minority life.[51]

Notes

1. Samuel O. Regalado, "Baseball in the Barrio: The Scene in East Los Angeles since World War II," *Baseball History* 1 (Summer 1986): 47–59.
2. Jeffrey T. Sammons, "'Race' and Sport: A Critical, Historical Examination," *Journal of Sport History* 21 (1994): 203–78.

3. Joel S. Franks, *Crossing Sidelines, Crossing Cultures: Sports and Asian Pacific American Cultural Citizenship* (Lanham, MD: University Press of America, 2000).

4. Steven A. Riess, "Introduction: Sports and the American Jew," *American Jewish History* 74 (1985): 211.

5. Gary Ross Mormino, "The Playing Fields of St. Louis: Italian Immigrants and Sports, 1925–1941," *Journal of Sport History* 9 (1982): 5–19.

6. Anthony A. Yoseloff, "From Ethnic Hero to National Icon: The Americanization of Joe DiMaggio," *International Journal of the History of Sport* 16 (1999): 1–20.

7. David Wallace Adams, "More Than a Game: The Carlisle Indians Take to the Gridiron, 1893–1917," *Western Historical Quarterly* 32 (2001): 37–53.

8. Gerald R. Gems, "The Construction, Negotiation, and Transformation of Racial Identity in American Football: A Study of Native Americans and African Americans," *American Indian Culture and Research Journal* 22 (1998): 145.

9. Mary Lou LeCompte and William H. Beezley, "Any Sunday in April: The Rise of Sport in San Antonio and the Hispanic Borderlands," *Journal of Sport History* 13 (1986): 128–46.

10. Arnoldo De Leon, *They Called Them Greasers: Anglo Attitudes toward Mexicans in Texas, 1836–1900* (Austin: University of Texas Press, 1983); David Montejano, *Anglos and Mexicans in the Making of Texas, 1836–1986* (Austin: University of Texas Press, 1987).

11. De Leon, *They Called Them Greasers*, 34, 67.

12. Guadalupe San Miguel, *"Let Them All Take Heed": Mexican Americans and the Campaign for Educational Equality in Texas, 1910–1981* (Austin: University of Texas Press, 1987), 55.

13. James Kilbourne Harris, "A Sociological Study of a Mexican School in San Antonio, Texas" (master's thesis, University of Texas, 1927), 97.

14. Genevieve King, "The Psychology of a Mexican Community in San Antonio, Texas" (master's thesis, University of Texas, 1936), 62.

15. Roberta Muriel Johnson, "History of the Education of Spanish-Speaking Children in Texas" (master's thesis, University of Texas, 1932).

16. King, "Psychology of a Mexican Community in San Antonio," 60.

17. Albert Folsom Cobb, "Comparative Study of Athletic Ability of Latin American and Anglo American Boys on a Junior High School Level" (master's thesis, University of Texas, 1952), 2.

18. San Miguel, *"Let Them All Take Heed"*, 45.

19. Kilbourne Harris, "Sociological Study of a Mexican School in San Antonio," 96.

20. Bruce Walsh Shaw, "Sociometric Status and Athletic Ability of Anglo American and Latin American Boys in a San Antonio Junior High School" (master's thesis, University of Texas, 1951), 18–19.

21. Merrell E. Thompson and Claude C. Dove, "A Comparison of Physical Achievement of Anglo and Spanish American Boys in Junior High School" *Research Quarterly* 13 (1942): 345–46.

22. Francis Edward Meyer, "A Comparison of the Football Programs in Some AAA High Schools in the State of Texas" (master's thesis, University of Texas, 1958), 41.

23. Harold Ratliff, *Autumn's Mightiest Legions: History of Texas Schoolboy Football* (Waco: Texian Press, 1963).

24. Bill McMurray, *Texas High School Football* (South Bend, IN: Icarus Press, 1985).

25. Carlton Stowers, *Friday Night Heroes: A Look at Texas High School Football* (Austin: Eakin Press, 1983).

26. Ty Cashion, *Pigskin Pulpit: A Social History of Texas High School Football Coaches* (Austin: Texas State Historical Association, 1998), 19.

27. H. G. Bissinger, *Friday Night Lights: A Town, a Team, and a Dream* (New York: HarperCollins, 1990); Douglas E. Foley, "The Great American Football Ritual: Reproducing Race, Class, and Gender Inequality," *Sociology of Sport Journal* 7 (1990): 111–35.

28. Ratliff, *Autumn's Mightiest Legions*, 158.

29. Cashion, *Pigskin Pulpit*, 100–102.

30. Ibid., 250.

31. Texas High School Coaches Association press release, August 1, 1968.

32. *McAllen Monitor*, September 26, 1997, 1C, 3C.

33. Ibid., 1C.

34. L. E. Ramey, speech given on April 4, 1989 (copy in author's possession).

35. Ibid.

36. Ibid.

37. *McAllen Monitor*, September 26, 1997, 1C, 3C.

38. Charlie Williams, "South Texas Football," *Texas Coach* (April 1979): 37.

39. *McAllen Monitor*, September 26, 1997, 1C, 3C.

40. *Edinburg Daily Review*, October 9, 1991, 4; *Duval County Picture*, October 16, 1991; *McAllen Monitor*, October 6, 1991, B2.

41. Tom Lea, *The King Ranch*, 2 vols. (Boston: Little, Brown and Co., 1957), 1:301, 380, 461; 2:497, 584, 587, 638. Estimates for the size of the Cavazo land grant were drawn from *Houston Chronicle*, April 23, 1982, sec. 6, 48; and Jane Clements Monday and Betty Bailey Colley, *Voices from the Wild Horse Desert: The Vaquero Families of the King and Kenedy Ranches* (Austin: University of Texas Press, 1997), xx.

42. *Houston Chronicle*, April 23, 1982, sec. 6, 48; *Corpus Christi Caller*, March 17, 1980, B2.

43. *Laredo Times*, March 14, 1982, A3; Montejano, *Anglos and Mexicans*, 249–50.

44. *Kingsville Record*, June 11, 1947, 10.

45. *Kingsville Record*, August 25, 1948, 9; September 1, 1948, 9; September 8, 1948, 8; September 22, 1948, 13; October 13, 1948, B2, B7; November 11, 1948, B5; November 24, 1948, B1; December 1, 1948, B1.

46. *Kingsville Record*, December 15, 1948, B4; February 16, 1949, B3; March 16, 1949, 11; March 23, 1949, B12; April 13, 1949, B5.

47. Don Oliver, *Lubbock Avalanche-Journal*, August 15, 1951, sec. 2, 4.

48. *Kingsville Record*, October 19, 1949, B7; January 25, 1950, B3. For a complete record of Cavazos's college career, see Jorge Iber, "A Vaquero in the Backfield: The Career of Bobby Cavazos, Texas Tech's First Hispanic All American," *College Fottball Historical Society* 14 (2001): 1–5.

49. *Kingsville Record*, November 21, 1951, B3; November 28, 1951, 6; March 19, 1952, B2; August 19, 1953, C3; December 2, 1953, C4; February 3, 1954, B2.

50. Cashion, *Pigskin Pulpit*, 15.

51. Nicholas Ciotola, "Spignesi, Sinatra, and the Pittsburgh Steelers: Franco's Italian Army as an Expression of Ethnic Identity, 1972–1977," *Journal of Sport History* 27 (2000): 285.

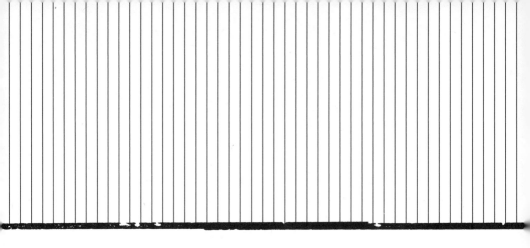

CHAPTER 8

Friday Night Rights: South Texas High School Football and the
Struggle for Equality, 1930s–1960s

Joel Huerta

etween the 1930s and the 1960s, American-style football became a highly visible arena for the construction, performance
and also dismantling of an Anglo-American quasicolonialist
sociology. The situation in South Texas, a region bordering Mexico with a
majority Mexican American population, was not unlike that of the British
colonies, where cricket was both an important instrument for the social-
ization and edification of the English and also a cultural production that
served to transmit the Victorian ideals of manliness, stamina, and vigor to
native groups commonly viewed as lazy, crude, undisciplined, or effete.[1]

This article gives a short history of high school football and race relations in South Texas and begins with a discussion of the early game and
the role and vision of the University Interscholastic League (UIL) and Roy
Bedicheck, its early director, in shaping the game, ethos, and popular culture. The balance of the article, however, focuses on a player and coach
named Everardo (E. C.) Lerma. One of the first Mexican Americans to
play and coach in Texas, Lerma was a key figure in the dismantling of segregated scholastic athletics. Lerma's career gives us a glimpse of the world
of scholastic athletics in the 1930s and 1940s, its ideals and hypocrisies,

and the struggles by Mexican American and Texas Anglo progressives to open the coveted game and folk spectacle to all.

The Mania for American Football

Football stirred up huge clouds of discursive dust in the late nineteenth and early twentieth centuries. The rhetoric and metaphors of the game percolated through writings, speeches, and illustrations in everything from politics, business, higher education, and management to social engineering, and, most saliently, discourse on the (re)making of righteous young men.

In print culture, sensationalistic stories about brutality, violence, and fatalities in publications like the *National Police Gazette* and *Harper's Weekly* spurred interest and controversy nationwide. Hypermasculine celebrities like artist Frederic Remington and Theodore Roosevelt celebrated the game, painting the gridiron heroics of Ivy Leaguers as the very symbol of American imperial masculinity. Roosevelt, for example, recruited western cowboys and college football players for his celebrated Rough Riders. While at Yale, Remington is said to have dipped his jersey in slaughterhouse blood to make it "more business-like."[2]

From the late 1880s through the 1920s, a stream of articles and books chronicle the fun and pageantry of the football weekend and the exploits of real-life stars like Red Grange and Jim Thorpe and Coach Knute Rockne. Fictional characters like Walter Camp's Jack Hall and Gilbert Patten's Frank Merriwell entertained young readers and modeled the virtues of pluck, teamwork, and fair play. Even the gritty and ubiquitous dime novel dropped its "mechanic" and frontiersman protagonists and replaced them with detectives and athletes; the new settings and themes focused on "sports, schools, and empire," writes Michael Denning. One should not underestimate the influence of these symbols and narratives. The Frank Merriwell books alone sold in the millions, and episodes ran in serialized form in the *Tip Top Weekly* for seventeen years. The majority of Americans came to know football first as narratives and symbols and only later as actual practice.[3]

"Touch-down Extraordinario," a satirical essay from the 1920s, provides a rare glimpse of American football as interpreted by the Mexican

American. Penned by Jorge Ulica, "Touch-down" is a picaresque *crónica* (sketch/dispatch) that describes a Mexican pelado's (ragged fellow) encounter with American college football. The *crónica* is structured as a string of observations, dialogues, puns, and mistranslations. Like Thorstein Veblen and other North American critics of the day, Ulica marvels at the college game's pomp and ritual, while also lambasting the culture's violence, disorder, tribalism, and excesses. In Ulica it is not so much the game or fan that are in the crosshairs but rather the Mexican who is seduced by football's vulgarity.[4]

Hampered by bad roads, vast distances between settlements, and poorly funded or nonexistent public education, the football craze did not strike Texas until well after it had swept through the East, South, and Midwest. John F. Rooney, a cultural geographer, ventures that the football boom in Texas was tied to the early-twentieth-century oil boom. He posits that transplanted "oilers" from the football mecca of western Pennsylvania, northern West Virginia, and eastern Ohio brought their enthusiasm for the game to Texas and Oklahoma.[5] In the case of South Texas, the game's origins are also tied to agriculturists from the American Midwest and North who settled in the region in the early twentieth century, and the presence of the US Army in the militarization of US-Mexico border during World War I and the Mexican Revolution (1911–1920).

The Dallas Foot Ball Club was the first group to play regularly, beginning in the 1880s. In December 1893 the *San Antonio Express* mentions South Texans trying the new game of "rugby football," and by the turn of the century, high school football teams had sprung up in larger cities, such as San Antonio and Corpus Christi. High school football did not make it to the border until December 1909. The game gained momentum in the 1910s, but until the formation and intervention of the University Interscholastic League (UIL) in the 1920s, it remained both unregulated and dangerous. It was not uncommon to find hardened men in their twenties playing boys ten years younger. Moreover, games were played at rudimentary stadiums run by local boosters and impresarios, who made a business of gate receipts. The game's violence and unscrupulous parasites earned football few supporters among educators.[6]

School yearbooks and photos taken by South Texas photographer Robert Runyon between 1912 and 1920 give us a sense for the early border game. In a series of towns that sprung up along new rail lines, the contests were Spartan affairs. Carved out of mesquite and cactus thickets, the fields were *fields*, literally—dusty clearings with patches of coastal grass, burrs, and a sprinkling of squinting spectators on the sidelines. In this outback the boys looked more like aviators dropped from the sky than proper athletes. In fact, much of what passed for a uniform was merely discarded gear from regional military installations. Larger towns like Brownsville, Harlingen, and McAllen drew respectable crowds and enjoyed more refined facilities, but up through the 1930s only a few cities enjoyed proper seating, lights, press boxes, scoreboards, and field houses.[7]

The game of football itself was novel, but physical, violent male sport had long been an established part of both Anglo and Mexican American cultures in southern Texas. The violence (or carnivalesque license) that marked early football was, in many ways, a carryover of the agonistic and initiation rites that had defined nineteenth-century masculinity. The game's rituals and ceremonies also had analogues. Pageants, parades, and agricultural fairs were very popular in the region. Non-elite Mexican Americans were relegated to mere spectators at Anglo events, but, of course, they held their own celebrations and performances. Spanish-language periodicals abound with announcements of the coronation of young women as "*reinas*" (queens) of fairs, clubs, schools, and school grades, for example. Mexican Americans also performed in marching and company brass bands. To stroll San Antonio's Near West Side, the social and cultural center of Mexican South Texas, was to hear "the ever present music of the military band," a sociologist noted in 1931.[8]

Roy Bedicheck and the UIL

The influx of northerners and the circulation of print media introduced the game to Texas, but it was school reform during the Texas Progressive Movement (1898–1910) that planted it firmly in local civic life. Reforms and governmental intervention led to a boom in road and school building and consolidations. Under Governor Thomas Campbell (1907–1911), a progressive Democrat, a more aggressive system of taxation pumped millions of new monies into state coffers. Public education in pre–World War I Texas was still rudimentary, but such developments together with revenues from oil, facilitated the growth of more expensive school activities like football teams and marching bands.[9]

The formation of the University Interscholastic League (UIL) in 1911 was instrumental in the growth and institutionalization of scholastic sports. Though not officially tied to the Progressive movement, in the spirit of reform the UIL organized and standardized scholastic competition in the state. The UIL's drawing of districts and eligibility rules, and its ethos of "educational competition" gave Texas its own distinct articulation of the sport.

John Avery Lomax, the folklorist, created the league in 1911 as an extension program at the University of Texas. Its immediate goals were to draft eligibility restrictions, which meant disbanding the town football free-for-all. The league also organized intermediate and high school competitions by creating districts, grouping schools according to size, and sponsoring tournaments and meets. Initially, the UIL sponsored competitions in track and field, debate, and rhetoric—a decidedly neoclassical repertoire. But the league quickly grew to include a wide range of activities, everything from football to math and poetry interpretation. Virtually every public school in the state joined.

Under the guidance and vision of Roy Bedicheck, a homespun intellectual, naturalist, and student of Lomax's, the UIL grew into an important and emulated institution. A man who had worked countless odd jobs and tramped across North America and Europe for fifteen years before settling in the state capital of Austin, Bedicheck was of the conviction that the classroom was but one arm of pedagogy. In the experimentalist spirit of John Dewey and Henry George, Bedicheck saw participation in recreation and competition as key instruments for developing critical thinking skills and instilling moral and civic virtue. Like Dewey, Bedicheck felt that education should be oriented toward the future; it should develop the habits of mind and confidence to assess complex problems and meet the challenges of this mercurial new thing: modernity. Set within a structured and supervised program of competition, the pupil learned not only the fundamental workings of citizenship, democracy, fair play, and sportsmanship but, more importantly, through practice and experience he or she would come to embody these traits. Competition, be it in debate, athletics, or the arts, offered both "practice in democracy" and "emotional conditioning"—the very experience needed to thrive in a rapidly changing, competitive world. Whether one won, lost, placed, or not, was irrelevant; what mattered were process, experience, and reflection. "I believe it the duty of the public school in a competitive society such as ours to offer every child the opportunity of winning and losing, either personally or vicariously, or both, time and again, hundreds of times during his scholastic career," Bedicheck exclaimed.[10]

Though football had become the most popular program in the UIL—tiny schools even forming six-man teams in order to compete—Bedicheck never quite embraced it. In fact, the game was a source of perpetual frustration; "schoolboy" football was an overpowering, thick-necked adolescent and he the bookish father. While the UIL's problems paled in comparison to the corruption and commercialism that had compromised the major college game, football was easily the most problem-wracked area in the league. Unlike the league's debaters, thespians, and their coaches, footballers constantly threatened to secede when rules were enforced or tightened. And contrary to the popular myth painting Texas high school football as the picture of good old-fashioned, clean-cut values, Bedicheck and many a teacher-on-stadium-duty waged a decades-long battle with the adult brawlers and drinkers who defiled the sanctity of this "open-air classroom," season after season.

Gambling and bribery also plagued the project. "Both professional and small-time gamblers are moving in on high-school football, and no protests seem to be heard," Bedicheck wrote in frustration. "Gambling on the outcome of a football game is becoming as common as eating peanuts. . . . Stadiums were never designed as branch offices of bookie shops." Corruption sullied even that preternaturally wholesome symbol of town and alma mater—the marching band. Administrators and directors were said to line their pockets with kickbacks from the sale or rental of uniforms, sheet music, and instruments. Sales executives from large music firms openly bribed judges at state competitions.[11]

Brutality. Raucous fan behavior. Sleazy dealings. Even through this Cabeza de Vacan morass, Bedicheck felt that football could improve Texan boys. Of course, the discourse of football as fortifying agent had circulated on English and American campuses for years. Yankee educators and reformers of a previous generation had sought to invigorate a supposedly feminized, "overcivilized," WASP male through strenuous tests like football. In the urban colleges of the North, a cold, wet game and a little blood had given the young man a needed shot in the arm. It was a test, a slap, an infusion of the pluck and vigor that had built and steeled their nation, that had established white Anglo-Saxon prosperity and dominance. Educators and reformers saw strenuous sports like football as functioning as a sort of artificial frontier. Where the western frontier—dangerous, wild, "the meeting between savagery and civilization," as Frederick Jackson Turner famously framed it—had produced a restless, nervous energy; strength and exuberance; and a common national experience, for the postfrontier WASP male, urbanization, material success, and "brain work" had emasculated him. Success had made him soft, literally, and the waves of immigrant laborers, Jews, and Catholics threatened to muscle the lad from the helm. Manly, strenuous sports like football were antidotes; they injected a "careful primitivism," a sort of compensation. Historian T. J. Jackson Lears writes that the notion that sports regenerate and toughen "the leaders of tomorrow, by now a television cliché, originated in the *fin-de-siécle* worship of force."[12]

The backwater Texan was many things, but overcivilized he was not. With the Mexican Revolution to the south, protracted Texas-Mexican resistance in the borderlands, and the chaos of the oil boom, much of early-twentieth-century Texas retained the restless and nervous energy of the frontier. Mobs still lynched, trains were still ambushed and derailed. Bandits, posses, rebels, smugglers, wildcatters, and lawmen still shot it out in saloons, on courthouse steps, and in sun-drenched middles-of-nowhere. The pistons of frontier democracy still fired and misfired. What the Texan needed was some taming. He needed a controlled outlet for aggression and energy. Something like (reformed) football could teach the Texan boy how to cooperate, how to win and lose honorably; it could give the rustic boy structure, polish, and a public role without making him soft

and sweet. Where the Yankee bourgeoisie had employed strenuous competition to toughen, Bedicheck and the UIL saw in it a tonic to sublimate
"the fighting instinct."[13]

An anecdote Bedicheck told while delivering a speech to parents and
teachers illustrates his aim for sport in pedagogy and reform. The story goes that a group of teenage boys from Longview (Texas) had broken
into a department store on a Saturday night. Quite ingeniously, the thieves
had climbed onto the roof, pried open a skylight, and shimmied down on
a rope. The boys then helped themselves to some three hundred dollars
worth of merchandise.

Bedicheck explained that these were not *bad* kids; they were "from the
best families" of the city, after all. No, they were bored kids. They simply
lacked outlets for their physical and mental energies, their creative fac-
ulties. "Did the superintendent assemble a group of sleuths to ferret out
the miscreants and a group of ex–prize fighters to administer the punishment?" he asked the assembly:

> Fortunately, he was wiser than that. What he did was to go out in
> search of the best athletic coach he could find. It was not long before
> the yen for adventure was finding satisfaction on the athletic field, and
> athletic achievements turned from porch-climbing to pole-vaulting,
> and the great sport of outwitting the peace officers was turned into
> outwitting the opposing team on the football field.

Bedicheck was too astute to see things in black and white, but when
pitching his programs to the masses, he simplified the message. One either
allowed "the competitive impulse to vent itself in a way that is subversive
to school discipline," or one directed that "competitive spirit" toward more
orderly and constructive ends. Longview, said Bedicheck, had gotten it
right.[14]

While Yankee reformers had sought to reinvigorate WASP masculinity,
and Bedicheck's UIL to channel youthful energies toward constructive
ends, they both shared the conviction that organized competition provided a useful apparatus for teaching democratic principles and for equip-
ping youth for the challenges of modernity. The most glaring problem

with these projects was that many women and minorities were marginalized within, if not outright omitted from, the enterprise. In Texas, for
example, the UIL would not sponsor women's athletics competition, with
the exception of tennis, until 1949. Mexican and African Americans fared
no better. African American schools were not welcome in the league; to
comply with *Plessy v. Ferguson*, the UIL formed the Prairie View League
in 1920 to accommodate them. Mexican Americans were not specifically
excluded from UIL activities; still, one had to be an active student to compete. Attrition, poverty, and cold receptions at many schools kept out all
but a few brown students.

A combination of extreme poverty, Jim Crow laws, anemic political
muscle, and an agribusiness economy that ran on cheap, uneducated labor
meant that few Mexicans ever advanced to the secondary public school
level in South Texas. In 1928 University of Texas professor Herschel T.
Manuel found that 40 percent of Mexican American school-age children
were without educational facilities or instruction. Of the region's schools,
nine out of ten schools were segregated (1930), and fewer than 4 percent
of brown children made it to the junior high or high school level where
football was played.[15]

Texas's method for apportioning school funds certainly exacerbated the gross inequality. Legislators allotted money on a per capita basis,
whether the child attended school or not. This system led to many abuses.
Administrators diligently rounded up and counted Mexican children but
then failed to serve and retain them. In the most egregious cases, they
even *encouraged* seasonal attrition to dovetail with the labor needs of
the agribusiness sector. Essentially, administrators garnished funds from
brown students to the benefit of Anglo students.[16]

The situation was a bit less grave in older southern Texas cities like
Brownsville, Rio Grande City, and Corpus Christi, the home base of the
increasingly influential League of United Latin American Citizens (LU-
LAC), the civil rights organization that was founded in 1929. In these
locales middling and elite Mexican American and Mexican expatriates
wielded some power. According to Brooks Conover, a coach at Brownsville High School in the 1930s, students from these families, "mixed freely
with Anglos." They "demanded certain privileges," folklorist Jovita Gonzalez wrote in 1930.[17]

Indeed, of the handful of the Spanish-surnamed students who appear in valley high school yearbooks and team rosters from the 1910s through the 1930s, virtually all have the surnames of the old Texas-Mexican ranching families and original Spanish grantees. Their physical appearance and complexion were also more typically European than Indian.

In the eyes of the US Census Bureau, all Mexicans were Caucasian. But Washington's taxonomies wilted down in South Texas. Mexicans and Mexican Americans were Caucasian "only in some legal, pseudo-scientific, and ethnographic sense," writes historian Neil Foley. Instead, they traversed an "ethnoracial middle ground between Anglo Americans and African Americans"; they may have been white enough to escape some depredations, yet not white enough to claim equality with Anglos.[18] The poetics of a passage from a *School History of Texas*, a long-lived, standard textbook, are revealing. Here, historian Eugene Barker describes the state's "thoroughly cosmopolitan" population:

> About four-fifths of the people are white, and most of these are made up of native Texans or immigrants from other states of the Union. There are, however, a good many foreign immigrants, and of these the Mexicans, scattered through the Rio Grande region from El Paso to San Antonio and Brownsville, are the most numerous. Less numerous, but far more important than the Mexicans, are the Germans. . . .[19]

Mexican Americans countered subordination in many ways. They wrote, formed mutual aid societies and political organizations, and negotiated legal and governmental systems. They also challenged the status quo in areas like popular culture and sports.

Tackling Jim Crow

It was simple enough. Everardo Lerma wanted to play high school football. The year was 1932, the place Kingsville, Texas, a small city on the fringe of the duchy that is the King Ranch. Young Lerma had watched the practices from the fence and had attended games at Henrietta King High, the local school named after the ranching dynasty's matriarch. In the papers and on the radio he followed the major collegiate programs of the era: Notre Dame, Southern Methodist University, Texas Christian University, and the University of Texas. And with a big frame, hardened by cotton picking and baseball, he had a hunch the game would suit him well.

Getting on the team roster was not difficult; Coach issued him equipment and told him to report after school. On the practice field, however, Lerma quickly discovered that he was not welcome. "Nobody would talk to me . . . rarely a conversation. When they did talk to me, it was to insult. So I would just do what he told me to do. To the players I was like a ghost, or the brunt of jokes."[20]

Ostracized, frustrated, Lerma would quit, and further frustrated would rejoin. His play was solid, but all things considered, freshman season was a disaster. Lerma returned again the following fall. This time he had a little help. While working in the cotton fields, he had convinced his good friend Gerald Alvarez to come out for the team. "It wasn't a plot or anything, I simply wanted somebody to talk to out there."[21]

Out on the practice field Lerma got a pleasant surprise. Coach had done some thinking over the summer. He would start Lerma on both offense and defense. "Even as a sophomore, I was one of the biggest guys. He knew he needed me, if we wanted to stand a chance."[22]

Lerma didn't disappoint, he was a formidable defender and capable receiver. His exploits could not be overlooked. Hugh Boyd, a local sportswriter announced, "Llerma [sic], big end of the Brahma team, made himself a name in the Sinton game. Time after time he piled the Sinton attack in a big heap on top of himself." In another article Boyd declared Lerma one of the "best high school ends this town has seen in several years. His defensive play is brilliant, and his offensive play stacks up with the best in South Texas."[23]

According to Lerma, his athletic prowess helped whittle away some of the animosity. The world out there hadn't changed, but it seemed that with every yard gained and tackle made, he garnered respect from some of his teammates. By season's end he had even made a few lifelong friends.[24]

In 1934 Texas Christian University in Fort Worth offered Lerma a full athletic scholarship. The scholarship was quite an honor for Lerma and King High—TCU being a powerhouse that would win the Cotton Bowl Classic (1937), a precursor to the modern end-of-season bowl game, and the national title in 1938. Lerma declined. Instead, he decided to play with the

Javelinas of the newly built College of Arts and Industries of Kingsville, or Texas A&I College. The decision was difficult, but because he had been orphaned, he felt some obligation to remain close to home. By staying in Kingsville he could watch over his younger siblings and tend to their needs with earnings from part-time work. Responsibility and altruism aside, the sense one gets from listening to Lerma in interviews was that his work in South Texas's arenas of masculinity was far from complete at this juncture in his life.[25]

A small group of Mexican Americans attended A&I, but the racial climate on campus was no more hospitable than at King High. As a freshman Lerma had to prove himself worthy of promotion to the varsity, and more importantly, deserving of a scholarship. According to L. E. Ramey, a teammate, much of the ire directed at Lerma stemmed from bitterness and resentment concerning scholarships. It being the Depression, scholarships were especially dear; many Anglos could not stand the idea that "a brown-skinned Mexican" would take a scholarship, talented as he may be, from a "real" American. This being the case, Lerma endured repeated abuse. He was thrown into the pool, his teammates knowing he could not swim. He took cheap shots on the field. And he had to tolerate venomous remarks like "Kill that Mexican!" not from opponents or hecklers, but from certain members of his team.[26]

Through much of his athletic career, Lerma's coaches were largely indifferent and intransigent. Sometimes a coach would push a player to apologize, or he'd have Lerma and the offending teammate don boxing gloves and work things out in blunt, manly fashion. More often, coaches and teachers propped up the sociopolitical status quo—one that saw Mexicans as passive, inferior interlopers.

One must remember that in the Anglo-American imagination of the time, the Mexican was an embodiment of laziness, docility, inferior genetics, and dirtiness; and there was no shortage of eugenicists to lend a pseudo-scientific authority to these views.[27]

Citing Spencer, Haeckel, Huxley, and Mill for authority, a eugenicist writing in the *Saturday Evening Post* described the Mexican as a "white elephant" doomed to extinction because of miscegenation. In more learned circles such as the University of Texas, historian Walter Prescott Webb described Mexicans as cowardly in battle and genetically polluted. Unlike the Plains Indian and the "pure American stock," the Mexican had blood like "ditch water." In researching the now-classic *North from Mexico: The Spanish-Speaking People of the United States* (1948), Carey McWilliams wrote of encountering

> a mountainous collection of master's theses [that] "proved" conclusively that Spanish-speaking children were "retarded" because, on the basis of various so-called intelligence tests, they did not measure up to the intellectual caliber of Anglo-American students. Most of this theorizing was heavily weighted with gratuitous assumptions about Mexicans and Indians. Paradoxically, the more sympathetic the writer, the greater seems to have been the implied condescension.

As late as the 1960s the mainstream press described Texas-Mexicans as "slow-burning" and :apathetic . . . excelling only in joblessness, illiteracy, substandard housing and mortality rates for infantile diarrhea and TB." Paul Taylor's ethnography, *An American-Mexican Frontier, Nueces County, Texas* (1934), details the racist views and policies in the region where Lerma resided. Schools offered no refuge, and administrators few concessions.[28]

A poem published in 1936 in the local newspaper, the *Kingsville Record*, illustrates the smug voice of white supremacy in 1930s South Texas. In a posture akin to what the anthropologist Renato Rosaldo dubbed "imperialist nostalgia" (lament and desire for that which one has helped destroy), we see the poet praise the uber-masculinity and pioneer mettle of the Mexican-of-old, while pronouncing his modern incarnation "Pancho"—emasculated, servile, finished.[29] The poem ends with the stanza,

> The youthful Pancho had his fling!
> Now he dreams of other days,
> Before the great migration,
> And listens for the master's call
> With perfect resignation.

Institutionalized, normalized, the subordination of common Mexicans blinded even well-intentioned educators to the severity of discrimination.

While coaching at McAllen High School in the 1930s, Chatter Allen found himself baffled by the lack of enthusiasm among Mexican Americans for football. Was it something cultural? Was there something about football that the Mexican mind did not find conceptually interesting—they were mad about baseball after all? Finally, it clicked. In the stands and on the field, brown athletes faced a racist, vocal crowd. What attraction did that hold?[30]

Despite the objections, hassles, anxieties, and racist salvos, Mexican Americans made teams. To be on the team was one thing; to play was another. Favoritism has always plagued high school coaching; too often, the wealthy and connected influence whether they wish to or not. Before the school reforms of the 1960s and 1970s, whiteness also bestowed certain privileges. A fellow who played nearby Hidalgo County in the 1940s summarized the attitude, "Who in the hell was going to play a Mexican when they had an Anglo? That was an absurd idea. Anglos came first; that's just the way it was." A player from the 1950s told of sidelined players staging a small act of resistance to the de facto policy. "Well, we decided to pull out comic books and read them on the bench. Hey, you ignore us. You don't play us. We'll do something else. Well, Coach blew up when he saw this. 'What the hell are you doing!' We didn't want to quit. We just wanted to make a point." Skin color and surnames complicated prejudice. Lydia Campbell Lerma, the first Mexican American elected to the drill team at Corpus Christi High School in the 1930s, explained the advantage of being a Campbell rather than, let's say, a Dominguez or Martinez. "They knew I was Hispanic. I was dark from working out in the fields! But my name was Campbell. Somehow, that softened things."[31]

National and state organizations and leaders did little to ameliorate the situation. The UIL certainly disappointed. Granted, most of the league's business involved technical matters, rules, and procedures. But under Bedicheck, the league had done much more; it discoursed on intellectual problems and relevant social issues: What is the role of athletics and extracurricular activities in the war effort? Can experience in sports save a soldier's life? Do extracurricular activities teach democratic values and citizenship, and if so, how? What else could they teach; could they teach or reinforce the negative? When would women get a fair shake in school programs and society in general? Do sports masculinize women? What could modern Americans learn from the "civilized" Greeks, the austere Spartans, or the "decadent" Romans? How could the league balance modernity's rationalism with the timeless and universal *jouissance* of play? How could the League keep the crass commercialization that had cheapened big college athletics out of the high school? The issue of race and equality—*the* overarching issue in Texas—could or would not be broached by coaches, directors, and team sponsors, in official forums, at least.

There was a glimmer of hope in 1947. Inspired by baseball executive Branch Rickey's signing of African American Jackie Robinson to the Brooklyn Dodgers, Bedicheck suggested that student competition could serve as a mitigating force for softening racism. But Roy Bedicheck was no Branch Rickey; he passed up the chance to steer a new course. The *Brown v. Board of Education* decision in 1954, modern American education's watershed event, registered with a mere blip in the post-Bedicheck UIL. All the state executive committee could muster in the *Leaguer*, its newsletter, was the announcement of yet another rule change: white public schools that admitted Negro students would remain eligible for membership in the league. Negro schools together with schools "for defectives and correctives" remained ineligible. Not until 1964 would the UIL remove the phrase "white public schools" from its charter and membership requirements. Moreover, Jim Crow's UIL, the all-black Prairie View Interscholastic League, would not be dissolved until late in the decade.[32]

What kept Everardo Lerma going in those difficult, lonely days in Kingsville? There was, of course, the chronic irritant—the thorn of Anglo-Texan male hegemony glorified and magnified in the manly sport of football—and there was the corporeal element: a deep-seated love of the physical pleasures of sportive tests and competition. "I cried many times, not because of the blows, but because of the discrimination. It was very hard to take, but I just loved playing sports. I loved baseball. I loved football. To me there was nothing better. I was an athlete."[33]

Lerma also possessed all the attributes that make a good player: strength, mass, and speed. On offense he drove; on defense he stopped. With a passion for the game and superior athleticism, playing football—

in the technical and mechanical sense of moving the ball and stopping bodies—rewarded and sustained Lerma. It was an antidote to, an interruption of, the ideological, verbal, and structural oppression that so suffused his world. To play football was to struggle and brawl, but also escape and dance.

During one of our interviews Lerma's wife, Lydia, reminded him that all the attention he received within the Mexican American community also helped mitigate the negative. "I first saw him at a dance. The girls sat on one side of the hall and the boys on the other, with the grown-ups watching us like hawks. All the girls were just taken by him. He was this tall, handsome, college man—shy and a little cocky at the same time. None of us girls had ever met a college athlete." But there was more to it than popularity. Lerma knew that his successes and failures affected how local Anglos viewed Mexicans and how Mexicans viewed themselves. It was more than a mere awareness or knowledge; it was a burden.[34]

It had also become clear to Lerma that Mexican Americans, especially kids, were watching him. If he succeeded he might encourage them to claim their rightful place on the playing fields, classrooms, marching bands, and drill teams—the heart of South Texas youth culture.

If Lerma had doubts about his role as trailblazer and symbol, they were dispelled in the spring of his sophomore year. In a suspiciously sadistic scheme, coaches elected Lerma to fight for the heavyweight title of the college. His opponent, "Wild Bill" Farish, was a big and capable boxer. Having tangled repeatedly on the football field, Wild Bill and Lerma knew each other all too well. It wasn't Joe Lewis vs. Max Schmelling, but in the cotton fields and ranchlands of Kleberg County, the match was big deal enough. Race mattered. Predictably, the majority of spectators divided themselves along racial lines. Anglos called for the merciless pummeling of the Mexican, and Mexicans relished their *chamaco*'s (lad's) counterhegemonic jabs. For Lerma, the fight was a long, loud, brutal hell. "Nobody thought that I had a chance, but I gave him a very good fight." Of the match a journalist wrote, "It looked as if Lerma had piled up enough lead to have won the match, but the judges couldn't agree. The writer's scorepad gives Lerma the edge, but it was close." Quite wisely, referee Willie Jones called the bout a draw.[35]

Lerma's junior and senior years brought more challenges, respect, and even glory. Ironically, the peak moment in his athletic career came not on a Texas gridiron or in some storybook goal-line stand; it wasn't an athletic feat at all.

In 1937 Lerma found himself hailed as a celebrity during a routine pregame stretch on the occasion of A&I playing the National University of Mexico. During the week, Mexico City's sportswriters had reported on the player's prowess, size, and statistics. Impressive, certainly, but what *really* distinguished him in their eyes was his Mexicanness. An American reporter recounts Lerma's reception:

> Right after noon the squad commenced preparation for the game and went out to the field to find that a big crowd had assembled to enjoy a preliminary game. E. Lerma, Javelina utility man and captain for the day, was mobbed by fans wanting his autograph. He could escape from one crowd only to be surrounded by another. Other players were in for the same treatment but Lerma was the favorite. After the football game the Javelinas visited several night clubs in Mexico City – all except for Lerma. He was the special guest at a Mexican fiesta.[36]

What a difference a border makes. Lerma had had his shining moments in Texas, but it was in Mexico City that he first experienced loud, seemingly unqualified praise and support.

It was here—facing a squad of brown players on the field; hearing songs, cheers, and curses in Spanish; talking game for hours—that he glimpsed what could have been had things been played better back home. It was here that he glimpsed what he, as a coach and administrator, would help realize in South Texas—a plain, lovely thing: vigorous competition unencumbered by the hackles of prejudice and ignorance.

The Eagles of Benavides

In the fall of 1938 the newly minted college graduate got a job as an assistant coach in Benavides, Texas, a small town in the heart of the South Texas brush country. With Lerma at Benavides, Texas now had three Mexican American coaches in the public schools. The greenhorn joined Nemo "El Viejo" ("Old Man") Herrera of San Antonio Lanier and Lino "Gramps"

Perez of Rio Grande City. Gramps was more phys-ed teacher than coach, and El Viejo was known for his basketball teams, winning the state title three times at San Antonio Lanier and El Paso Bowie. E. C. Lerma would make his name on the gridiron.

Work went well. He had a regular paycheck, a new wife, and enthusiastic pupils. In 1940 the head coach position opened up, and Lerma found himself on the short list. Once again, he had to run the gauntlet of Anglo-controlled public education; this time he faced the chain-smoking Benavides School Board and one Hilda Parr, sister-in-law of local political boss George Parr. Like every South Texan, Lerma knew of the Parrs' wealth, power, and shenanigans. (Recall the infamous "found missing ballot box" in Lyndon Johnson's senatorial election?) The Parrs were the Tweeds, the Longs, of the South Texas brush country. And George, the "Second Duke of Duval County," or "La Tlacuacha" (possum), as the Tejanos called him, had his paw in everything. The Parr machine controlled every public sector job. But Lerma, a straight-arrow outsider, neither owed nor had no favors due.[37]

There was also the issue of race. "There was no precedent. They just couldn't believe that a Mexican could do as good a job as an Anglo. They didn't tell me that, but it was written across their foreheads. They were in a bind, though. They needed a coach and there I was."[38] After his promotion to head coach, Lerma soon proved doubters wrong. The Eagles of Benavides improved dramatically. In 1942, his second year as head, the Eagles went 7-0-1 and took the district championship for the first time. It was the biggest thing to hit Benavides since the Tex-Mex Railroad had put it on the map. With uncommon expeditiousness, the Parr school board built Coach a modern stadium, turf and all. The 1943 season saw the Eagles go undefeated yet again.

According to Lydia Lerma, the championship years boosted and roused Benavides. The football season became the highlight of the year. "They would have pep rallies . . . and parade around town. The enthusiasm was fantastic. Little old ladies would sit in the stands . . . with rosary beads . . . praying for Benavides."[39]

Everybody loves a winner, but something else was at work. In the shadows of a declining ranch economy, the young and attractive Lermas engendered optimism, pride. The war in Europe and the Pacific had also thrown youth into a different light—more appreciated, their play and contests semiotically richer and weightier, their stout bodies frangible. The struggles on the field echoed national purpose.

Lerma's strict, paternalistic coaching style also dovetailed with the South Texas ranch country ethic. His practices were long and arduous. He closely monitored academic performance and enforced strict curfews, but he knew when to let up. In short, he was one of them. "Balo" drank a little beer, knew how to tell a joke, went to church, and worked just about every day.

"We had to set positive examples with our behavior and that of our own children," Lydia Lerma said.

> Oh, to be the coach's wife was a lot of work. She had an image to uphold. She had to be a lady. She had to be charming, whether talking to wealthy ranchers or the humblest people. At the annual coach's conventions the women held shows and workshops on how to entertain and dress. We learned the rules of football and how to deal with parents and the public. We were under a microscope, but we were very respected.[40]

The Lermas' recipe worked. They were on everyone's guest lists for weddings, *quinceaneras* (girls' fifteenth-birthday celebrations), and First Communions. Along with showing gratitude with the usual ranch country gifts of tamales, *cabrito* (roasted kid goat), and bundles of fresh beef, game, and jerky, folks in tiny Benavides pooled together and bought them a new sedan when their old car failed. Benavides never forgot them. Upon learning of Lerma's upcoming retirement in the 1980s, for example, former athletes raised enough funds to send the Lermas on a six-week-long, all-expenses-paid trip to Europe. In one last tribute, Benavides named the stadium after Mr. Lerma.[41]

After his stint at Benavides, Lerma rounded out his coaching career in the old border town of Rio Grande City, where he arrived in 1955. In Starr County and at Rio Grande City High, Lerma found a poor and working-class community with deep roots and a long tradition of integrated schooling—the legacy of Don Manuel Guerra, a prominent rancher and indomitable political boss. An anomaly in modern Texas, Starr County

had an established Mexican American teacher population that included
Roque Guerra, Jr., a veteran band director. For twenty-five years thereafter,
Lerma worked as a coach, principal, and superintendent of schools in
South Texas cities. Up to his death in 1998, Lerma remained active in re-
gional athletics and coaching; he was inducted into several regional halls
of fame.

Coach Lerma's success with the Eagles of Benavides is impressive. In fifteen years he snatched thirteen titles. But coaches are more than records.
Here is a parent, educator, community leader, and a tough-minded bull of
a man who simply refused to acquiesce to Anglo male controls. A leader
in the schools and community, Lerma was an exemplar of what historian Mario Garcia called "the Mexican American generation." This group
came of political age between the Great Depression and the 1950s. This
generation served in the military in disproportionate numbers and had
educational reforms as their chief and perpetual cause. A sort of double
consciousness was at the core of their politics. They sought to maintain
loyalty and respect for things Mexican while simultaneously asserting
their rights as Americans and loyalties to the United States.[42]

In Américo Paredes's "Folk Medicine and the Intercultural Jest," a brilliant essay that mines jokes about folk healing (*curanderismo*) for clues on
Mexican American identity in the face of rapid social change, he describes
the men of Lerma's social group as seemingly

> completely acculturated, having adapted to American culture and
> functioning in it in a very successful way. At the same time, when they
> are away from the courtroom, the school, the office, or the clinic and
> congregated in a group of their own, they think of themselves as *mex-
> icanos*. Not only will they speak Spanish among themselves, but it is
> quite obvious that they place a high value on many aspects of Mexican
> culture and are proud of the duality of their background. They do in a
> sense live double lives, functioning as Americans in the affairs of the
> community at large and as Mexicans within their own closed circle.[43]

Of course, much of the Chicano generation saw acculturation as a
slippery slope resulting not in the hybridity or *mestizaje* touted today
but in assimilation. Acculturation undermined the struggle for self-

225

determination and cultural survival. But the "Mexican American" position also interpellated American discourses that drew Mexicans in the United States, no matter how established or patriotic, as outsiders. I generalize here, but in essence, theirs was a politics of negotiation. They consented to certain Anglo controls and rationalizations, and in the process internalized various strains of white supremacist logic, capitalist blind faith, and myopic patriotism. We saw (and see) these articulated in the Anglicization of names and naming, for example; brooding and vexation on the subject of new immigrants; and ambivalent views on skin color. Juan Gómez-Quiñones, one of the most influential intellectuals of the Chicano movement, later conceded that differences between the Chicano youth movement and "the middle-class element" were based on "tactics" rather than "issues."[44]

All that said, Mexican Americans like Lerma—the big-wheel politicos and the smaller gears both—doggedly forced compromises and concessions. Historian Jorge Iber writes, "The athletic (and later coaching) career of E. C. Lerma presented a dilemma for Texans who believed in the athletic and intellectual inferiority of Mexican Americans. Clearly, here was an individual who did not fit the perception of a typical 'greaser.' If a Spanish-surnamed individual helped the local team win, perhaps he could be accepted as an equal."[45]

The 1940s and 1950s saw increased racial contact and a slow and steady dismantling of segregation in sports, schools, and the broader society—often, *in that order*. Lerma and his Eagles and Rattlers were trigger points, bellwethers of the changes afoot in this football-obsessed province of Mexican America.

With the growth of the middle class, gains in political power, and a reinvigoration of ethnic and cultural pride spurred by the Chicano movement of the 1970s, Mexican Americans in South Texas began to transform town football culture in unique ways. Attendance surged as more brown students occupied high-status positions like captain, quarterback, or cheerleader. Spanish-language radio took to the game. In the 1970s KGBT's *Football Scoreboard*, a Spanish-language show, quickly grew into a forum where garden-variety sports discourse merged with traditional ethnic verbal arts—for example, ritual insult, doggerel, and proverbs. An anomaly in sports fandom, Mexican American women became and remain today the most vocal fans. In the 1970s fans also began composing heroic and mock-heroic ballads in the markedly ethnic and beloved Mexican ballad form called the "*corrido*," a genre with roots in medieval Spain. The football *corridos* sing the praises of coaches, teams, the fighting boys, and the true fans. The expressive culture that grew around borderlands football in the 1970s and 1980s in many ways resembles the vibrant fan culture found in European and Latin American rugby and soccer.[46]

Conclusion

Writing in the early 1990s, historian George Sanchez lamented the fact that historians had largely ignored adolescents and young adults in American society. "This is especially true for Mexican American youth," he emphasized. "More attention has been paid to Chicano intellectual history and political history for the post–World War II era." More recently, historian Jorge Iber observed that the subject of sports in Mexican American studies was "profitable" but "largely untapped." Political and intellectual history is more central than ever in the field, but scholarship on brown youth has seen modest gains. With the contributions of scholars like Douglas Foley, Mary Lou LeCompte, Kathleen Sands, Sam Regalado, Mario Longoria, Gregory Rodriguez, Iber, and others, this branch of sports history is beginning to take shape.[47]

This article helps fill these voids. It describes the maturation of modern institutional sports in South Texas, the struggles and victories. It shows how Anglo colonization and Western modernity in general changed sports and leisure. It sketches how an embattled, largely rural populus, pushed to the margins by Anglo-American power and capital, takes the popular sports of the new order and uses it for expression and recreation. It shows how institutional sports acculturated and disciplined, and also how they opened spaces for expression, resistance, and repair.

A part of a larger ethnography project, this history is by necessity highly localized; it cuts but one swath through a broad field. However, much of what transpired in South Texas mirrors the experience of other borderlands and ethnic American communities, other Bedichecks and Lermas.

Notes

1. C. L. R James, *Beyond a Boundary* (Durham: Duke University Press, 1993), 1963.

2. T. J. Jackson Lears, *No Place of Grace: Antimodernism and the Transformation of American Culture 1880–1920* (New York: Pantheon, 1981); Gail Bederman, *Manliness and Civilization: A Cultural History of Gender and Race in the United States* (Chicago: University of Chicago Press, 1995); Michael Oriard, *Reading Football: How the Popular Press Created an American Spectacle* (Chapel Hill, University of North Carolina Press, 1993), 191.

3. Michael Denning, *Mechanic Accents: Dime Novels and Working-Class Culture in America*, Haymarket Series, (London: Verso, 1987), 192; Smith, Ronald, *Sports and Freedom: The Rise of Big-Time College Athletics* (New York: Oxford University Press, 1988), 81–85; Oriard, *Reading Football*, 192; Higgs, Robert, *God in the Stadium: Sports and Religion in America* (Lexington: University of Kentucky Press, 1995), 154–56.

4. Jorge Ulica, "Touch-down Extraordinario." *Crónicas Diabólicas de "Jorge Ulica"/Julio B. Arce*, ed. J. Rodriguez, (San Diego: Maize Press, 1982).

5. Rooney, *A Geography of American Sport from Cabin Creek to Anaheim* (Reading (PA): Addison-Wesley, 1974), 139.

6. "Rugby Football," *San Antonio Express*, December 23, 1893, 6; E. C. "Doc" Osborn, "The History of Sports in the Rio Grande Valley," *Brownsville Herald*, December 6, 1942, 1; Rodney Kidd, "Molding the Character of Youth: The Texas Interscholastic League and Friday Mountain Boys Camp.," New York Times Oral History Program, University of Texas Regional History of Business in the Southwest, No. 5, ed. Meyer, I. (Austin: University of Texas, 1971); James Creighton, *The Buccaneers: Corpus Christi Football, 1904–1974* (Corpus Christi (TX): self-published, 1975); Bill MacMurray, *Texas High School Football* (South Bend: Icarus Press, 1985), 3.

7. Robert Runyon, "Rio Grande Valley Photographs, 1912–1949," Robert Runyon Collection, Center for American History, Austin, Texas; Kidd, "Molding the Character," 14.

8. Laura Hernandez-Ehrisman, *Inventing the Fiesta City: Heritage and Carnival in San Antonio* (Albuquerque: University of New Mexico Press, 2008); Max Handman, "San Antonio: The Old Capital City of Mexican Life," *The Survey* 66 (1931): 161.

9. Eugene Barker, Charles Potts, and Charles Ramsdell, *A School History of Texas* (Chicago: Row, Peterson, 1918), 276–315; Douglas Foley, *From Peones to Politicos: Class and Ethnicity in a South Texas Town*, Mexican American Monographs (Austin: University of Texas Press, 1988), 36; Ty Cashion, *Pigskin Pulpit: A Social History of Texas High School Football Coaches* (Austin: Texas State Historical Association, 1998), 54.

10. Roy Bedicheck, Brief article, *Interscholastic Leaguer* 32, no. 2 (1948): 2; Roy Bedicheck, *Educational Competition: The Story of the University Interscholastic League of Texas* (Austin: University of Texas Press, 1956), 69–79.

11. Roy Bedicheck, "Editorial," *Interscholastic Leaguer* 30, no. 2 (1946): 2; Kidd, "Molding the Character," 22.

12. Drinnon, *Facing West: The Metaphysics of Indian Hating and Empire Building* (New York: Schocken, 1980), 460; Oriard, *Reading Football*, 191; Bederman, *Manliness and Civilization*; Lears, *No Place of Grace*, 108.

13. Roy Bedicheck, "Bedicheck Papers," Center for American History, Austin, Texas, Box 3q44.

14. Bedicheck, *Educational Competition*, 24.

15. Herschel Manuel, *The Education of Spanish-Speaking Children in Texas* (Austin: University of Texas Press, 1930), 103; Paul Taylor, *An American-Mexican Frontier: Nueces County, Texas* (Chapel Hill, University of North Carolina Press, 1934), 194.

16. Guadalupe San Miguel, *Let All of them Take Heed: Mexican Americans and the Campaign for Educational equality in Texas, 1910–1981*, Mexican American Monographs (Austin: Center for Mexican American Studies, 1987), 53–54.

17. Cashion, *Pigskin Pulpit*, 101; Jovita Gonzalez, *Social Life in Cameron, Starr, and Zapata Counties* (master's thesis, University of Texas at Austin, 1930), 115.

18. Neil Foley, *The White Scourge: Mexicans, Blacks, and Whites in Texas Cotton Culture*, American Crossroads (Berkeley: University of California Press, 1997), 41.

19. Barker et al., *School History of Texas*, 277.

20. Everardo Lerma, interview by author, McAllen, Texas, 1995.

21. Ibid.

22. Ibid.

23. Boyd, Hugh, "Brahmas Tie," *Kingsville Record*, October 11, 1933, 2; Boyd,

Hugh, "Sideline Chatter," *Kingsville Record*, October 18, 1933, 2.

24. One teammate, L. E. Ramey, would honor Lerma by cofounding and endowing the E. C. Lerma Scholarship at Texas A&I University, for example.

25. Rosaldo, Renato, *Culture and Truth: The Remaking of Social Analysis*, Boston: Beacon, 68–87. Notions of racialized masculinity were not uniform. For example, historian Neil Foley discusses the view among white Texas Socialist Party and labor leaders that Mexican males, many of whom were political radicals, exhibited a pure, vigorous manliness that put white men to shame (*White Scourge*, 141–62).

26. Everardo Lerma, interview, 1995; Jorge Iber, "Mexican Americans of South Texas Football: The Athletic and Coaching Careers of E.C. Lerma and Bobby Cavazos, 1932–1965," *Southwestern Historical Quarterly* 105, no. 4 (2002): 626.

27. Historian David Montejano points out that the racial views of South Texas Anglo "old-timers" were rooted in frontier memories of conflict with Mexicans and Indians, and narratives of Anglo revenge and victory. The ideas of newcomers and latter-day homesteaders at the turn of the century were rooted in germ theories and racialized views of hygiene. The views of the old and new stock eventually mixed into a particularly noxious cocktail. *Anglos and Mexicans in the Making of Texas, 1836-1986* (Austin: University of Texas Press, 1987), 82–84, 103–12.

28. Kenneth Roberts, "The Docile Mexican," *Saturday Evening Post* 200, no. 37 (1928), 41; Walter P. Webb, *The Texas Rangers* (Cambridge: Houghton-Mifflin, 1935), 125–26; Carey McWilliams, *North from Mexico: The Spanish-Speaking People of the United States* (New York: Greenwood, 1968 (1948)), 206–7; Thomas Morgan, "The Texas Giant Awakens," *Look* 27, no. 19 (1963): 71–75; Taylor, *An American-Mexican Frontier*.

29. Jay Ashton, "Pancho Dreams of Other Days," *Kingsville Record*, May 20, 1936, 4.

30. Cashion, *Pigskin Pulpit*, 101.

31. Rene Hinojosa, interview by author, McAllen, Texas, 1999; Lydia Campbell Lerma, interview by author, McAllen, Texas, 1996.

32. Bedicheck, "Brief Article," 2; Bedicheck, "Official Notes," *Interscholastic Leaguer* 29, no. 1 (1955): 2; University Interscholastic League, "A Brief History of the University Interscholastic League," Austin, Texas, 1985.

33. E. Lerma interview, 1995.

34. L. Lerma interview.

35. "College Champion Vacant at A&I Boxing Show," *Kingsville Record*, May 13, 1936, 6; E. Lerma interview, 1995.

36. "A&I Javelinas Loud in Praise of Old Mexico," *Kingsville Record*, December 1, 1937, 2B.

37. Lynch, *The Duke of Duval: The Life and Times of George B. Parr* (Waco: Texian Press, 1976); E. Lerma interview, 1995.

38. E. Lerma interview, 1995.

39. May, Mark, "Legend by Example," *Monitor* (McAllen), September 9, 1997, 1–3C.

40. L. Lerma interview.

41. E. Lerma interview, 1995.

42. Garcia, Mario, *Mexican Americans: Leadership, Ideology, and Identity, 1930–1960* (New Haven: Yale University Press, 1989).

43. Paredes, *Folklore and Culture on the Texas-Mexican Border* (Austin: CMAS Books, University of Texas Press, 1993), 58.

44. Juan Gómez-Quiñones, *Chicano Politics: Reality and Promise, 1940–1990*, The Calvin P. Horn Lectures in Western History and Culture (Albuquerque: University of New Mexico Press, 1990), 175.

45. Iber, "Mexican Americans of South Texas Football," 628.

46. Joel Huerta, *Red, Brown, and Blue: A History and Cultural Poetics of High School Football in Mexican America* (PhD dissertation, University of Texas at Austin, 2005).

47. Sanchez, *Becoming Mexican American: Ethnicity, Culture, and Identity in Chicano Los Angeles, 1900-1945* (New York: Oxford University Press, 1988), 256; Iber, "Mexican Americans of South Texas Football," 620.

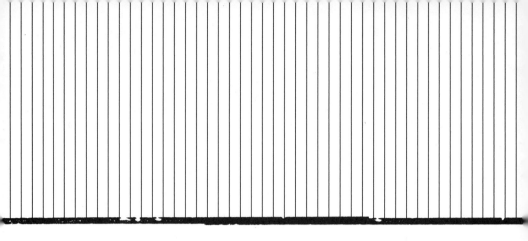

CHAPTER 9

Baseball Players, Organizational Communication, and
Cultural Diversity: Organizational Citizenship Behavior in
Minor-League Clubhouses

William Harris Ressler

A s baseball attracts players from more and more cultures,
players are called on to function in an increasingly diverse
environment. Scholars of baseball and culture have been following these changes from various perspectives. Several presentations at
the Nineteenth Annual NINE Spring Training Conference on the Historical and Sociological Impact of Baseball, for example, looked at the roles of
owners, media, league officials, and governments in promoting or stifling
diversity in baseball.[1] One presentation, however, alluded to players' approaches to diversity: Ila Borders described how her on-field performance
improved following her move to a culturally diverse minor-league team.
She attributed much of her improvement to the communication among
team members, which she characterized as supporting and embracing
cultural differences.[2]

Her story was thought-provoking and leads to a number of questions.
What aspects of being in a multicultural context influence communications among team members? What significance does cultural identifica-

tion hold for professional baseball players? In what ways might culture affect performance? In an initial effort to address questions such as these, prior interviews with culturally identified minor-league players were analyzed and results were interpreted with reference to relevant and instructive approaches from the field of organizational communication.

Methods

To explore what culture means to players, thirty-seven minor-league players were interviewed during the 2011 season. Of the thirty-seven players interviewed, six were playing Class AAA ball, eleven were playing Class AA ball, an additional player was interviewed twice—at both the AA and AAA levels—and nineteen were playing Class A Short Season ball. They included seventeen Jewish players, fifteen African American players, and three Spanish-speaking players born in the United States; two additional players, native speakers of neither Spanish nor English, were born outside the United States.

The predominance of Jewish and African American interviewees reflects the original goals of the study: to understand the phenomenological meanings of cultural identification in baseball among members of two minorities, one visible (African American), one not (Jewish). During the course of the interviews, and in light of Ila Borders's story, players' comments suggested a different research question: How do players react to cultural diversity within their teams? To help address this question, data from interviews with an additional thirty Spanish-speaking minor-league players were also included in the analysis. These latter interviews were conducted in Spanish during the 2009 and 2010 seasons as part of a separate study.[3]

Semistructured interviews were conducted with players individually, with the exception of three two-player interviews and one three-player interview that included two players who had previously been interviewed separately. Indeed, four of the thirty-seven players were interviewed on two separate occasions. All players were at least eighteen years old, and all were informed that (a) the researcher was affiliated with a college and not with any team or league, (b) participation was voluntary, and (c) no information would be shared that could identify a particular player or team. The inferred trustworthiness of responses is also based on observations that players were accessible and generous with their time and expressed interest in the research; many actually thanked the researcher for addressing the topic of culture in minor-league baseball. Many players requested contact information to obtain a copy of the results or additional information related to cultural identification. In addition, it was possible to observe a number of the players' interactions with other culturally diverse teammates, and thus to validate their statements.

Players gave their consent to have the interviews audio recorded. All interviews were transcribed, and players' comments about cultural groups were coded. After a series of meetings and exchanges of memos, the researcher and three graduate research assistants grouped players' statements into emergent categories, including,

representations of culture

forms of cultural identification, past and present

meanings and salience of cultural identification

within-group relations

approaches to cultural diversity

The analysis focused on players' comments specifically regarding approaches to cultural diversity. The main theme that emerged captured players' natural and genuine interest in cultures and cultural diversity, along with the discretionary, inconspicuous, informal nature of their actions to embrace diversity. Six additional themes included players' reasons for this interest.

Results: Players Embrace Diversity Even When Management Does Not

In organizations, any given internal communication or inwardly directed action, including approaches to diversity, can be formal, top-down, and driven by management, or informal, bottom-up, and initiated by individuals.[4] The latter is captured in the concept of organizational citizenship behavior (OCB): discretionary actions taken by an organization's individual members, at their own initiative, that are not formally rewarded by management, involve interpersonal communication and specifically interpersonal helping, and promote the internal functioning as well as the external image of the organization.[5]

A complementary concept, self-perception theory recognizes that being rewarded for performing a task or disciplined for not performing it reduces internal motivation to perform that task. Top-down, formal requirements to perform a task make the task less likely to be performed when the reward or threat is no longer present.[6] Seeing their actions as voluntary, without formal demands or rewards, reinforces individuals' self-perceptions and sustains helping behaviors, because it focuses individuals' attention on their personal reasons for helping. For example, one of the players explained why he enjoys visiting children's hospitals throughout the season on his own, outside the framework of team-mandated community service, and without receiving credit: "The honest truth—do you want me to go deep down inside? Baseball's a selfish game. . . . Minor-league baseball is spent mainly as the most selfish game you could ever play. . . . It's such a selfish, cut-throat thing, that I feel like, maybe subconsciously, I need a balance. . . . [Visiting sick children spontaneously] is just stuff that really makes you feel good about yourself."

Consistent with the concepts of OCB and self-perception theory, players tended to say that helping each other across cultural lines was perhaps encouraged but generally not mandated by their organizations. As a result, players took the initiative in helping other culturally diverse players and saw their actions as internally motivated. For example, after describing the process of helping different groups of players on the team, one of the players was asked who initiates those contacts. He explained, "I think it's something that's dealt with among [players in] the locker room between ourselves—communicating and stuff." Another player echoed this idea, explicitly downplaying the role of team officials: "The players take it on themselves to introduce themselves to a new guy and try to communicate with them as much as they can. . . . I don't think it has anything to do with the staff." A third explicitly reflected the idea of self-perception theory— and OCB—that without strong external influences, individuals are more likely to internalize a sense of personal responsibility to initiate prosocial, internal, cross-cultural communications: "As players we should take it on ourselves to get to know the guys."

Asked directly if the organization encourages him or other players to interact with the team's Spanish-speaking players, for example, a player replied, "That was my personal goal, the day that I signed . . . and I am still living it every single day."

Many of the Spanish-speaking players said they actually did not expect to receive a great deal of assistance from team officials—and many did not. As one Spanish-speaking interviewee noted, "It is not like the team is obligated to help you."

None of this is meant to suggest that organizations and individual minor-league teams do not use policy or programming to promote cross-cultural communication. Players acknowledged that they do. One of the players even admitted that he was not always enthusiastic about interacting with the multitude of cultural groups and languages spoken on his team; he also conceded that he was initially skeptical about his organization's efforts to force different cultural groups into close contact. At the same time, however, he described his personal efforts and successes— and the satisfaction he felt—interacting socially with members of different cultural groups. He made the point that, while the team created an initial opportunity, successful internal communication across cultures was up to the players themselves.

Furthermore, the preceding analysis is not meant to imply that all interactions are cross-cultural or that players eschew social interactions driven by common cultural identification. The same player acknowledged, for example, that even when he would go out to eat with one member of another culture, the other members of that cultural group would invariably all come along as well. Players' initiatives are meant to bridge but not to erase the boundaries between groups. Their reactions to diversity were a recognition, not a negation, of social categories.

When players' communication activities surrounding cultural diversity were internally motivated, what did those motivations include? Players' explanations can be categorized into six separate but related reasons for their choosing to help their culturally diverse teammates.

Six Reasons for Helping Culturally Diverse Teammates

Players Embrace Diversity Because Cultures Matter

Players expressed an appreciation for cultural diversity on their teams, because culture is meaningful to most of them. Many players, however, initially said that culture does not matter, that they all play the same game, on the same team, with the same goals. Nevertheless, their further statements—and at times their actions—showed that culture really is important to them. In one representative example, an African American player began to explain why culture is irrelevant: "When you get on the field, baseball is baseball. No matter where you're from. You still play it the same—" In the middle of that sentence, an African American player from the visiting team called to the interviewee by name, who responded, using the opposing player's nickname. Returning to the interview, the interviewee continued the sentence exactly where he left off, "—base paths ninety feet, the mound is the same—sixty-feet-six—still got the fence, still got a guy throwing the ball, and people got to make plays." At the end of the interview, with the microphone off, he was asked how he knew the player from the visiting team. He replied matter-of-factly that there are not many African American baseball players, so when they see each other, they notice. He made it clear that this is something that he does regularly and that other players do as well: African American minor leaguers notice each other, form friendships, and follow each others' progress. In other words, culture does not matter—except when it does.

Most of the culturally identified players responded similarly, as if they felt that they ought to say that cultural identification should be irrelevant. Thus, many players first asserted that culture was no longer significant or noticeable, then gave examples of noticing and even actively looking for other members of their own culture, making efforts to meet them, helping them when possible, following their careers, and rooting for them to succeed. Almost all said that being baseball players who belong to a particular culture made them feel special.

Culture, however, included much more than race, religion, or language. For example, meaningful cultural identification was frequently geographical—not just being from a particular country, but being from a given region, city, or even neighborhood. Age and tenure in organized baseball formed bases for meaningful group membership and identification. So did draft order, as reported by one player who said he befriends, follows, and identifies with other players who were selected in the latter rounds of the amateur draft. Culture also included physical condition, such as being a member of deaf culture or having a noticeable skin condition, both of which were cited as having created bonds of identification with others with the same condition. Culture, then, was defined to include any meaningful social category membership.[7] In turn, meaningful social identity was often defined by whatever a player felt made him different.[8] As one player observed, "Everything is culturally related."

This juxtaposition of ignoring culture while noticing different aspects of culture and using them as a basis for socially meaningful identification was summed up by one of the players. "I don't think people are saying, 'Hey, this is what I am, listen to my story,' but if you look, you can see it. . . . Music, dress, food choices . . . where people are, what they like, what they do, who they hang out with, who they speak to, what language they speak in, what religion they are, what they're wearing, what they're doing before games." Culture is pervasive in the clubhouse, and players acknowledged its significance in their daily lives. This, in turn, led players who felt different to empathize with players from other cultures who also felt different.

Players Embrace Diversity Because They Feel Empathy

Daniel Batson has presented extensive empirical evidence supporting the important mediating role of empathy in helping others.[9] It is not surprising, therefore, that taking the initiative to help others across cultural boundaries could potentially be moderated by empathy. Indeed, players' comments suggested that some embrace diversity out of feelings of empathy for members of other minority cultures. Asked where these feelings of empathy come from, players' answers reflected a diversity of sources: parents, culturally diverse youth baseball teams, or playing in Spanish-speaking countries in the off-season. Even American-born, Spanish-speaking players noted that playing in South and Central America fostered a greater empathy for diversity.

In addition, some players suggested that identifying as a member of a minority culture was a source of the empathy they felt toward players from other minority cultures. One of the Spanish-speaking players, referring to an African American teammate who makes more effort to learn Spanish than other players on his team (a pattern repeated on other teams as well), said, "Maybe he understands both minorities, I guess."

One player, when asked what he would want to know about players from other cultures if he were conducting this research, replied, "I guess I'd just want to know, really, do they feel somewhat left out or kind of set aside? I feel like that at times, being the only African American. I feel like—that I'm left out sometimes from some things. . . . You know?" He explained that he was not implying racism or intentional exclusion from activities, but that the other players simply had other culturally driven values and interests and that he was unable to find anyone else on the team who enjoyed spending free time the way he did—because of his cultural uniqueness on the team. A second player, after the recorder was turned off, admitted that he has tried to help members of other cultures because he has known what it is like, in his words, "to be a stranger."

A third player noted, in reference to teammates from other minority cultures, "They interact with everyone else but for the most part they stick with each other, and me being on the outside and seeing that, I immediately want to cling to them, because I know that all they want is for someone to go that extra mile just to know them even more."

A fourth player directly connected empathy with OCB. He noted that players understand the challenges teammates face and choose to help, without prodding or rewards from management, and without recognition for their good deeds: "We do more than what people think. I mean, a lot of people don't understand how extremely tough it is to come to a completely different country and be involved with people who don't speak the same language and try and be successful."

Thus, players who felt like outsiders expressed a certain empathy for other players whose distinctiveness could have led to their exclusion. None of this is to suggest that players' communication activities surrounding cultural diversity were motivated entirely by altruism, however. Indeed, these same players recognized the inherent self-interest in selflessness.

Players Embrace Diversity to Affiliate and to Achieve

The concept of group cohesion is expressed through sharing common goals, taking collective responsibility for outcomes, valuing group membership, using "we" more than "I" in discussing their roles, and building a culture of teamwork and mutual support.[10] Not surprisingly, because these are many of the defining components of OCB, members of more cohesive work teams tend to be more likely to adopt a pattern of OCB.[11] Group cohesion can take the form of social or task cohesion, and both types of cohesion can work together to help build successful sports teams.[12] More generally, this is also true for any work team.[13] At the same time, stronger group cohesion has been shown to reinforce group members' social (cultural) identities.[14] In other words, when team members identify with each other more strongly, it becomes easier to express and to accept cultural differences.

Players are therefore not disinterested parties when they take initiatives to help each other. Rather, when players approach diversity, they appear to recognize the opportunities for improved social affiliation and professional achievement that embracing diversity offers. The difference between this set of rewards and externally (organizationally) generated rewards is that internally generated rewards are potentially more long-lasting, more meaningful, and more likely to sustain prosocial behavior.

One internal motivation comes from the anticipated satisfaction derived through improved social interaction, consistent with the concept of social cohesion. Players indicated that, given the need to spend so much time together, on and off the field, improved social ties have intrinsic value.

Another internal motivation comes from the anticipated benefit to a player's professional achievement, consistent with the concept of task cohesion. Players' beliefs that cultural diversity can affect their professional achievements appear to be an expression of what organizational communication refers to as "value in diversity."[15] The basic tenet underlying this concept is that diversity among organization members can result in more varied ideas, perspectives, knowledge, and skills becoming available for accomplishing work-related goals more effectively.[16]

Thus, a number of players implied that their desire to affiliate with teammates across cultural boundaries was driven by their motivation to succeed professionally. A player remarked in this context, "They learn from us and we learn from them." Players from Spanish-speaking countries noted specifically that they learn English as they share baseball skills with English speakers.

Consequently, a player explained that he advised his brother to reach out to Spanish-speaking peers, partly for the potential professional profit: "He is down in rookie ball right now, and there's a lot of Latins down there, and I told him, 'You have to get to know those guys because those are the guys that are going to help you more than anyone else out there.'"

Another player noted that taking the initiative to affiliate across cultures builds trust, and that "once you have that trust, guys are going to play better. Not just playing—people operate better when they're around people they trust. . . . I feel more comfortable playing with that guy because I trust him." The player went on to give specific examples of cross-cultural communication leading to trust and yielding better performance on the field. Not surprisingly, OCB has been shown in other settings to be a function of trust.[17]

Benefits can even extend beyond baseball. One player, who spoke neither Spanish nor English before entering professional baseball, talked about his options once his playing days ended. He connected the multicultural experiences he has embraced as a player to his future success as a business owner. "I can speak English now, and I can speak Spanish now, so it's two languages that I picked up while I was here doing baseball, and it's going to help me going up."

Internally generated motivations for embracing cross-cultural interactions can thus reflect enlightened self-interest and the anticipation of benefit. Players' prosocial behaviors, however, can also be motivated by an inherent interest in culture and cultural diversity.

Players Embrace Diversity Because They Enjoy Different Cultures

The concept of cultural intelligence (CQ) has been developed in an effort to capture the tendency for some individuals to have a greater interest in and facility with cultural diversity. It includes four elements: drive, strategy, knowledge, and action.[18] Of the four, CQ-Drive—wanting to experience other cultures—offers the most insight into players' reasons for their communication activities across diverse cultural backgrounds.

CQ-Drive represents not only individuals' interest in experiencing other cultures but also the extent to which they think they are capable of interacting effectively with people from different cultural backgrounds and their confidence in being able to navigate culturally diverse environments. It includes the anticipation of both types of internally generated rewards discussed above: the personal enjoyment and sense of satisfaction that come from interacting with others from diverse cultures as well as the instrumental benefits that those different cultures offer.

CQ-Drive can be seen in players' comments, such as a player who said simply, "I love their culture," or another player who said, "When I go to a different culture, I want to be part of their culture as well." It was reflected in expressions of personal gratification, such as when a Jewish player said, "It's fun interacting with different cultures," and when another Jewish player noted, "You get to know different people. You get to learn a different culture." Their interest was reciprocated: African American and Spanish-speaking players occasionally asked their Jewish teammates detailed questions about being Jewish, such as what "kosher" means. Players from Spanish-speaking countries further expressed the desire to learn about English-speaking cultures, especially through the personal, cross-cultural interactions that being in the United States affords them: "They learn from you and you learn from them, how to treat a person . . . in a different way, whether it be because of race or anything else."

A connection between CQ and OCB was actually made by players. One player recalled, "It has been a great experience getting to meet many players from all around and getting to know them real well and just being able to help whoever I can." Another player, when asked what he would study if he were conducting this research (most of the players were asked this question), replied, "I would ask, do you feel that having people with ability from many different cultures is a positive or a negative for the game? . . . I think it's a positive, because baseball is worldwide. . . . I think it adds something that you have to have. You have to have people from many different cultures to make the game great." This was not only a reflection of the perceived instrumental benefits of cultural diversity, it was an acknowledgment of an additional motivation for players' taking the initiative in embracing cultural diversity: their love of the game itself and their belief that cultural diversity benefits the game of baseball.

Players Embrace Diversity Because They Love Baseball

It is not surprising that players' love of the game would be related to their tendency toward OCB. After all, organizational identification and commitment are related to OCB.[19]

To the players interviewed, embracing culture helps to promote the game. While organizations should play a role, they felt ultimately that the responsibility rests with players, especially if players feel organized baseball is not doing enough to promote the game to culturally diverse audiences. In the words of one player, "Basketball does a great job of promoting its players and promoting the game to different cultures, and I think baseball could do a better job of that. . . . I feel like it's my responsibility, you know? . . . That's how the game grows. I feel like it's handed down from one generation to the next, and I feel like it's your responsibility. I enjoy it, but at the same time, I feel like it's something I should do" (player's emphasis).

This quote is typical of comments that many players made. Culturally identified players appear to perceive, within their fidelity to their cultures, an opportunity to pass along their love of baseball and to help sustain and even bolster the popularity of the game. Thus, one player pointed out that culture, overall, is a way to increase fan identification with the players and therefore with baseball: "Most people will be like, 'How can I relate to that guy? He's a baseball player,' but if you have the middle ground of being Jewish, or black, or Asian, I feel that helps. . . . It is kind of like an icebreaker. . . . It makes you more approachable."

One player said that sharing a common cultural identity with fans not only draws fans to him, it ultimately draws him closer to fans: "I'm not gonna lie. . . . Whenever I see a young black kid, I always make sure I try to toss him a ball or sign an autograph or just go shake his hand or something, because I feel like it helps them to identify with you and identify with baseball, and hopefully they'll want to come out again." Despite the seeming particularism of this quote, he—and other players—repeatedly said that all cultures offer a bridge to greater fan engagement, that cultural diversity benefits the sport as a whole, and this realization enhances players' appreciation of diversity. Their desire to give back to a new generation, moreover, reflects appreciation not only for the game but also for the communities the players came from.

Players Embrace Diversity Because Communities Matter

African American, Jewish, and Spanish-speaking players discussed various needs within their own communities and pointed out the benefits that playing baseball offers to young members of their respective communities, benefits that they believed they, as culturally identified baseball players, could bring back to their communities. One African American player said, "It's just something that motivates me . . . just because I want to and I love giving back and can help change a kid's life or make him feel like, 'Hey, I can do anything I want.' It's just a very great feeling to have that effect on young people, . . . especially African American kids."

African American, Jewish, and Spanish-speaking players asserted that they can be especially influential when interacting with members of their own communities. One player's representative comments captured this: "When I do have the opportunity, I jump at it, because I know that, coming from an African American background, if you hear it from somebody that looks like you, it's a little bit easier to relate to what's coming out of that person's mouth."

The latter quote also contains a clue for understanding players' voluntary choices to embrace culture and cultural diversity. Understanding the importance of community within their own cultures also makes players more understanding of the importance of community to all cultures. It thus represents an additional source of players' appreciation for cultural diversity, one that finds expression in the voluntary acts that players perform. It brings the results back to Ila Borders's reflections on her own experiences. Perhaps her teammates were better at embracing cultural diversity, and therefore at accepting her, because they understood the contribution of cultural identification to effective communication, based on their experiences connecting to their own communities. If anything, having a strong connection to one's own community actually facilitates cross-cultural communication. This was noted by individual Spanish-speaking players and has support in psychological concepts of in-group identification, going back to Kurt Lewin's work on core versus marginal identification.[20]

Discussion: What Organizational Communication Can Learn from Baseball Players; What Organized Baseball Can Learn from Organizational Communication

What began as a study of baseball players' own cultural identifications ended up as an exploration of players' reactions to each others' cultural identifications, with the realization that appreciation for diversity and accompanying communication activities originate in the voluntary decisions of players themselves. A number of related lessons can benefit both organized baseball and organizational communication practitioners. The relationship between OCB and culture, especially diversity, is still being studied; minor-league baseball can offer fertile ground for exploring possible connections.

Opportunities, Not Demands

One of the lessons for baseball and other organizations seems to be that organizations are well served when they offer their members opportunities to embrace diversity. Results of the current study suggest that the emphasis should be on opportunities. Meaningful approaches to diversity seem to come from individual choice, flowing organically from the bottom up, not from organizational policy, dictated from the top down. To use a baseball analogy, Branch Rickey could communicate the value of diversity by hiring Jackie Robinson, but it was up to players like Pee Wee Reese to take advantage of the opportunity and embrace diversity. Bill Veeck could move spring training to Arizona so Larry Doby could stay in the same hotel with the rest of team, but after that the players were on their own, in the hotel and in the clubhouse.

One opportunity involves starting early in players' careers.[21] Lower organizational levels tend to involve higher task interdependence, which has possible links to OCB.[22] Moreover, some of the concomitant aspects of being at a lower organizational level, such as having limited resources, can lead to higher OCB as well.[23] One player noted, in this context, "From talking to people, I have heard that as you get higher up and closer to the majors, when it becomes more real that it is so close, within reach, I think that it is a little more competitive. I feel at this point [Class A Short Season] we are far away from there, so it's slightly more team-oriented."

How, then, should players be given the opportunities to embrace diversity, especially at these lower organizational levels? Their comments during the interviews (and self-perception theory) suggested that, left on their own, players can initiate multiculturally inclusive communication activities. Giving players a certain latitude in creating roles within the organization rather than having formally defined expectations can go a long way toward creating these opportunities.

Roles, Not Rules

CQ is related to the ability to negotiate culture and conflict.[24] Thus players with higher CQ should be more likely to initiate prosocial internal communications—to adopt an OCB orientation. One player said, "I like to be kind of in the middle and try to help out a little bit if problems come up. Like if Spanish people have problems with the American guys or the other way around, I try to [explain], 'You got to understand . . . that's how these guys are' . . . because I am not really American, I am not really Spanish. But I am speaking English and a little bit of Spanish. So, yeah, it kind of helps to be in the middle sometimes."

Flexible, informal organizational styles can facilitate OCB.[25] Perhaps, then, simply letting players take leadership roles in internal communications allows those with higher CQ to engage in cross-cultural OCB. CQ approaches, however, suggest that individuals are more likely to initiate those activities if they are given the confidence that their efforts will succeed. This is one area in which top-down approaches can bear fruit.

Cultural Satisfaction, Not Awareness Training

Asked what organizations could do to promote cultural diversity, players offered ideas that went beyond hackneyed cultural sensitivity workshops or diversity training seminars. A player suggested that celebrations of heritage nights could be used to showcase culture—not to attract more fans, but to let the players on the diamond know that the organization values culture. He said, "They could do different cultures on different nights. So you can make everybody on the field feel like they are part of it, and everybody in the world is part of this game, regardless of what country, what race you are, and what background you come from." Other players also expressed an appreciation for heritage nights, while admitting that they derived the greatest pleasure from events that celebrated their own culture. Studies have shown that an increase in perceived support for members' culture by their organization seems to increase the probability of members adopting an OCB orientation.[26]

Similarly, opportunities for fostering CQ also include a range of non-work experiences.[27] These can include community service, for example, which has been shown to bolster minor-leaguers' positive perceptions of culture and comfort with cultural diversity.[28]

So, too, community service and other socially responsible communication activities can be related to OCB. Athletes derive personal satisfaction from helping others; they also report stronger feelings of attachment to their team when the team is involved in socially responsible acts, such as promoting or raising money for a prosocial cause.[29] These outcomes are related to the clear, immediate, positive feedback that can accompany these activities, and that feedback can come from the organization. This can help raise individuals' feelings of self-worth, which is in turn related to the tendency to initiate OCB.[30] Thus, organizational expressions of appreciation, while avoiding the use of incentives, can encourage players' spontaneous acts of embracing cultural diversity.

Selfish Interests, Selfless Acts

Doing good can come from the anticipation of feeling good, but players can also perform selfless acts while motivated by more tangible forms of personal self-interest. One player, for example, described why he helps members of all groups: "One thing that my father always told me is that you never know who you are going to need. So it doesn't matter who you come across, you know, white, black, tall, skinny, it doesn't matter. You may need them one day."

Rather than appealing to self-sacrifice, then, encouraging players' enlightened self-interest may be a more effective way to stimulate OCB. Organizations can frame diversity as being in individuals' interests; this approach can offer greater potential for success in encouraging OCB by its being consistent with players' nascent perceptions. One of those seemingly selfish interests can be acquiring better skills; greater cultural diversity can mean greater access to diverse and innovative approaches to playing the game.

More Cultures, More Innovation

As noted above, players can perceive professional benefit when linking OCB with diversity. One player said, "It's fun learning how to communicate with them, but it's also—hey, this isn't just the American game now, this is the Latin game as well." Another said, "In the process of me doing that for them, they've taught me so much about the game."

These comments—and others, some of which were quoted above—

suggest that increased diversity leads not only to increased knowledge (of language, customs, or style of play) but also to increased appreciation for the value of diversity as a resource offering innovative professional and communication skills.[31] In turn, comments like these and others quoted above suggest that players might see the game as moving toward a tipping point, in which so many cultures interact that the concepts of majority and minority are rendered increasingly less meaningful.[32]

Is Multicultural the New Majority?

One lesson from minor-league baseball seems to be that, as the numbers of culturally diverse players continues to grow, the divide between majority and minority cultures becomes increasingly blurred. One player commented, "The world grew together so much, everybody has to live together. And the clubhouses are the same way. Everybody in the world plays baseball. You have Asian people, you have Latin American people, European people nowadays, American people. . . . And if you just build groups and just separate yourselves from the other cultural groups, then that is not going to work out in the end."

Comments such as this—and others—seem to suggest that because so many different groups play baseball, the mosaic of cultural minorities together constitute the majority—or soon will. As cultural diversity becomes the new majority, then, professional success could become intertwined with a player's motivation and ability to navigate a multicultural environment. If so, then perhaps an individual player's approaches to culture could factor into estimations of the overall value of that player to the organization.

Is Culture the New "Moneyball"?

In Moneyball, Michael Lewis described an approach through which advanced statistical analysis of player performance is used to identify previously undervalued players.[33] As cultural diversity is rapidly becoming the norm, communication skills might serve as an additional means for determining player value and identifying undervalued players. Perhaps CQ and a predisposition to engage in OCB can be used to identify undervalued players with the potential to contribute to team success in a growing multicultural environment. The essence of this idea was originally suggested by the culturally identified broadcaster of one of the Class A Short Season teams, who, although he did not specifically address OCB or CQ, referred to "that next inefficiency. Moneyball, Oakland, the whole thing. That's the inefficiency, how many guys are going by the wayside because they just didn't have the resources to deal with certain things." Those "things" can include the challenges of cultural diversity, and those valued resources can include the ability and motivation of players to take the initiative in addressing those challenges.

Some organizations, such as IBM, Lloyd's, Novartis, and Nike, have used CQ in some form as a criterion for hiring. CQ has been related to working smarter and learning faster while also being more patient—for example, being able to delay gratification in receiving workplace rewards—skills demanded of baseball players working their way up through the minor leagues.[34] Moreover, research has suggested that CQ-Drive is correlated with successfully identifying with a multicultural group, such as a culturally diverse baseball team.[35] High CQ of individual team members, then, might relate to increased team cohesion and even enhanced team performance, and could add to a player's value to the team.

OCB has also been suggested as a possible criterion for selection, retention, and promotion within an organization.[36] OCB has been shown to improve organizational productivity and efficiency.[37] While feelings of collective group potency (such as winning) have been shown to increase the tendency toward adopting an OCB orientation, OCB could conceivably enhance feelings of group efficacy, which in turn can increase the probability of success, on a baseball team or any work team.[38] In that case, a tendency toward OCB could be used in baseball as a criterion for evaluating potential team members.

Attention is often directed to what organized baseball has or has not done sufficiently in addressing and promoting cultural diversity. Typically, however, the conversation ignores players' contributions, perhaps because their actions tend to be private and informal. Nonetheless, minor-league baseball players appear to initiate meaningful, cross-cultural communication in ways that embrace cultural diversity, and organized baseball can benefit from these self-motivated choices to span cultural boundaries, when teams

1. Recruit and promote individuals who have the motivation to initiate and sustain cross-cultural communication.

2. Nurture those motivations by demonstrating that cultural diversity is valued, using carefully planned external and internal communications that celebrate cultures.

3. Give those individuals latitude to explore culture in their own personally meaningful ways, taking care to avoid imposing external, organizational incentives that undermine internal, individual motivations to embrace diversity.

Players' comments indicated that the point is being reached where management can focus on encouraging and trusting individual players' initiatives, by actively listening to the players' reasons for embracing cultural diversity. It would therefore be worth testing players' beliefs that were expressed in the interviews. Future research could examine, for example, to what extent and in what ways events such as heritage nights affect players' perceptions of cultures and their perceptions of how their organizations value cultures. Studies could evaluate how different ways of planning and promoting those events have an effect on players. It would be instructive, as well, to analyze the roles that cultural diversity plays in community relations, or the extent to which culture-specific community service influences players' reactions to culture and cultural differences; planning and evaluating these activities could both incorporate an experimental approach, to try to understand what aspects of the activities have the greatest influence on the players. Observation and interviews can help provide more detail regarding ways in which socially responsible communication activities can impart greater appreciation for culture and increase players' motivation to explore diverse cultures.

Interactions among OCB, CQ, communication, and cultural diversity warrant further study.[39] Minor-league baseball offers a promising environment for studying those interrelations. Studying the effects of these interconnected variables among baseball players represents a potential contribution to the growing understanding of cultural diversity and communication. The outcomes can have implications not only for baseball teams but for any organization with a multicultural, team-based workforce and an interest in understanding what motivates its members to build working relationships that cross cultural boundaries.

Notes

1. Raymond Doswell, "19 for 31: Jackie Robinson Steals Home and History";
   Andy McCue, "Barrio, Bulldozers, and Baseball: The Clearing of Chavez Ra-
   vine"; Samuel Gale, "'It's a Press Victory': The Role of the African American
   Press in Desegregating Major League Baseball"; Mitchell Nathanson, "Race,
   Rickey, and 'All Deliberate Speed'"; Robert F. Garratt, "Horace Stoneham:
   The Neglected Pioneer"; John Sillito, "'Building the Pirates of Tomorrow':
   Race, Mr. Rickey, and R. C. Stevens, 1952–55"; Maureen Smith, "Construct-
   ing History and Heritage 21st-Century Style: Major League Baseball and
   Statues"; Rebecca Alpert, "Bud Selig: The First Jewish Commissioner of
   Baseball"; Bill Staples, Jr., "From Internment to Hope: Celebrating Japa-
   nese American Baseball in Arizona"; Steve Treder, "The Pioneer's Pioneer:
   Masanori Murakami"; Scott D. Peterson, "'A Novelty in Baseball Literature':
   Ella Black and the 1890 Pre-Season"; Willie Steele, "Poetic Players: Baseball
   Poetry from within the Game" (presented papers, Nineteenth Annual NINE
   Spring Training Conference on the Historical and Sociological Impact of
   Baseball, Tempe, AZ, March 8–11, 2012).
2. Ila Borders, "Baseball: My Past and the Present and Future of Women in the
   Game" (presented paper, Nineteenth Annual NINE Spring Training Con-
   ference on the Historical and Sociological Impact of Baseball, Tempe, AZ,
   March 8–11, 2012).
3. William Harris Ressler, Sebastian Itman Bocchi, and Patricia Rodríguez
   María, "English- and Spanish-Speaking Minor League Baseball Players'
   Perspectives on Community Service and the Psychosocial Benefit of Helping
   Children," *NINE: A Journal of Baseball History and Culture* 20, no. 1 (2011):
   92–116.
4. John W. Berry, "Acculturation: Living Successfully in Two Cultures," *International Journal of Intercultural Relations* 29 (January, 2005): 697–712.
5. Dennis W. Organ, *Organizational Citizenship Behavior: The Good Soldier Syn-
   drome* (Lexington, MA: Lexington Books, 1988).
6. Daryl J. Bem, "Self-Perception Theory," in *Advances in Experimental Social
   Psychology*, ed. Lawrence Berkowitz, vol. 6 (New York: Academic Press,
   1972), 1–62.
7. Henri Tajfel, *Human Groups and Social Categories* (Cambridge: Cambridge
   University Press, 1981); Henri Tajfel and John C. Turner, "Social Identity
   Theory of Intergroup Behavior," in *Psychology of Intergroup Relations*, 2nd

ed., ed. William G. Austin and Stephen Worchel (Chicago: Nelson-Hall, 1986), 33–47.

8. William J. McGuire, Claire V. McGuire, Pamela Child, and Terry Fujioka, "Salience of Ethnicity in the Spontaneous Self-Concept as a Function of One's Ethnic Distinctiveness in the Social Environment," *Journal of Personality and Social Psychology* 36 (1978): 511–20.

9. C. Daniel Batson, "Prosocial Motivation: Is It Ever Truly Altruistic?" in *Advances in Experimental Social Psychology*, ed. Lawrence Berkowitz, vol. 20 (New York: Academic Press, 1987), 65–122.

10. David M. Paskevich, Lawrence R. Brawley, Kim D. Dorsch, and W. Neil Widmeyer, "Relationship between Collective Efficacy and Team Cohesion: Conceptual and Measurement Issues," *Group Dynamics: Theory, Research, and Practice* 3 (1999): 210–22; H. Prapavessis and Albert V. Carron, "Sacrifice, Cohesion, and Conformity to Norms in Sports Teams," *Group Dynamics: Theory, Research, and Practice* 1 (1997): 231–40; Kevin S. Spink, "Mediational Effects of Social Cohesion on the Leadership Behavior-Intention to Return Relationship in Sport," *Group Dynamics: Theory, Research, and Practice* 2 (1998): 92–100; and David Yukelson, "Principles of Effective Team Building Interventions in Sport: A Direct Services Approach at Penn State University," *Journal of Applied Sport Psychology* 9 (1997): 73–96.

11. Roland E. Kidwell, Jr., Kevin W. Mossholder, and Nathan Bennett, "Cohesiveness and Organizational Citizenship Behavior: A Multilevel Analysis Using Work Groups and Individuals," *Journal of Management* 23 (1997): 775–93; Philip M. Podsakoff, Michael Ahearne, and Scott B. MacKenzie, "Organizational Citizenship Behavior and the Quantity and Quality of Work Group Performance," *Journal of Applied Psychology* 82 (1997): 262–70.

12. Albert V. Carron, Steven R. Bray, and Mark A. Eys, "Team Cohesion and Team Success in Sport," *Journal of Sports Sciences* 20 (2002): 119–26; Albert V. Carron, Michelle Coleman, Jennifer Wheeler, and Diane Stevens, "Cohesion and Performance in Sport: A Meta Analysis," *Journal of Sport and Exercise Psychology* 24 (2002): 168–88; Albert V. Carron and Kevin S. Spink, "Team Building and Cohesiveness in the Sport and Exercise Setting: Use of Indirect Interventions," *Journal of Applied Sport Psychology* 9 (1997): 61–72; L. Hodges and Albert V. Carron, "Collective Efficacy and Group Performance," *International Journal of Sport Psychology* 23 (1992): 48–59; Stephen

A. Kozub and Justine F. McDonnell, "Exploring the Relationship between Cohesion and Collective Efficacy in Rugby Teams," *Journal of Sport Behavior* 23 (2000): 120–29; Kevin S. Spink, "Group Cohesion and Collective Efficacy of Volleyball Teams," *Journal of Sport and Exercise Psychology* 12 (1990): 301–11; Mike Voight and John Callaghan, "A Team Building Intervention Program: Applications and Evaluations with Two University Soccer Teams," *Journal of Sport Behavior* 24 (2002): 420–30.

13. R. Edward Freeman, "The Politics of Stakeholder Theory," *Business Ethics Quarterly* 4 (1994): 409–21; and R. Edward Freeman, Andrew C. Wicks, and Bidhan Parmar, "Stakeholder Theory and 'The Corporate Objective Revisited,'" *Organization Science* 15 (2004): 364–69.

14. Audrey J. Murrell and Samuel L. Gaertner, "Cohesion and Sport Team Effectiveness: The Benefit of a Common Group Identity," *Journal of Sport and Social Issues* 9 (1992): 1–14.

15. Taylor H. Cox, Jr., *Cultural Diversity in Organizations: Theory, Research, and Practice* (San Francisco: Berrett-Koehler, 1993).

16. It should be noted that empirical support for this has been mixed; see Katherine Williams and Charles O'Reilly, "Demography and Diversity in Organizations: A Review of 40 Years of Research," *Research in Organizational Behavior* 20 (1998): 77–140.

17. Prithviraj Chattopadhyay, "Beyond Direct and Symmetrical Effects: The Influence of Demographic Dissimilarity on Organizational Citizenship Behavior," *Academy of Management Journal* 4 (1999): 273–87; Dennis W. Organ and Katherine Ryan, "A Meta-Analytic Review of Attitudinal and Dispositional Predictors of Organizational Citizenship Behavior," *Personnel Psychology* 48 (1995): 775–802; Dennis W. Organ, Philip M. Podsakoff, and Scott B. MacKenzie, *Organizational Citizenship Behavior: Its Nature, Antecedents, and Consequences* (Thousand Oaks, CA: Sage, 2006).

18. Soon Ang and Linn Van Dyne, "Conceptualization of Cultural Intelligence: Definition, Distinctiveness, and Nomological Network," in *Handbook of Cultural Intelligence: Theory, Measurement, and Applications*, ed. Soon Ang and Linn Van Dyne (Armonk, NY: Sharpe, 2008), 3–15.

19. Philip M. Podsakoff, Michael Ahearne, and Scott B. MacKenzie, "Organizational Citizenship Behavior and the Quantity and Quality of Work Group Performance," *Journal of Applied Psychology* 82 (1997): 262–70; Philip M.

Podsakoff, Scott B. MacKenzie, Julie Beth Paine, and Daniel G. Bachrach, "Organizational Citizenship Behaviors: A Critical Review of the Theoretical and Empirical Literature and Suggestions for Future Research," *Journal of Management* 26 (2000): 513–63.

20. Kurt Lewin, "Field Theory and Experiment in Social Psychology: Concepts and Methods," *American Journal of Sociology* 44 (1939): 868–96.

21. Christopher Early, Soon Ang, and Joo-Seng Tan, *CQ: Developing Cultural Intelligence at Work* (Stanford, CA: Stanford Business Books, 2006).

22. Sheila S. Webber and Lisa M. Donahue, "Impact of Highly and Less Job-Related Diversity on Work Group Cohesion and Performance: A Meta-Analysis," *Journal of Management* 27 (2001): 141–62; C. Ann Smith, Dennis W. Organ, and Janet Near, "Organizational Citizenship Behavior: Its Nature and Antecedents," *Journal of Applied Psychology* 68 (1983): 653–63.

23. Steve M. Jex, Gary A. Adams, Daniel G. Bachrach, and Sarah Sorenson, "The Impact of Situational Constraints, Role Stressors, and Commitment on Employee Altruism," *Journal of Occupational Health Psychology* 8 (2003): 171–80.

24. Organ, Podsakoff, and MacKenzie, *Organizational Citizenship Behavior.*

25. You-Ta Chuang, Robin Church, and Jelena Zikic, "Organizational Culture, Group Diversity, and Intra-Group Conflict," *Team Performance Management* 10 (2004): 26–34; Michele J. Gelfand, Miriam Erez, and Zeynep Aycan, "Cross-Cultural Organizational Behavior," *Annual Review of Psychology* 58 (2007): 479–514.

26. James W. Bishop, K. Dow Scott, and Susan M. Burroughs, "Support, Commitment, and Employee Outcomes in a Team Environment," *Journal of Management* 26 (2000): 1113–32; Jarrod Haar and David Brougham, "Consequences of Cultural Satisfaction at Work: A Study of New Zealand Maori," *Asia Pacific Journal of Human Resources* 49 (2011): 461–75.

27. Ibraiz Tarique and Riki Takeuchi, "Developing Cultural Intelligence: The Roles of International Nonwork Experiences," in *Handbook of Cultural Intelligence: Theory, Measurement, and Applications,* ed. Soon Ang and Linn Van Dyne (Armonk, NY: Sharpe, 2008), 56–70.

28. Ressler, Itman, and Rodríguez, "English- and Spanish-Speaking Players."

29. Ibid.

30. Linn Van Dyne, Jill W. Graham, and Richard M. Dienesch, "Organizational

Citizenship Behavior: Construct Redefinition, Measurement, and Validation," *Academy of Management Journal* 37 (1994): 765–802.

31. See, e.g., Thomas Rockstuhl and Kok-Yee Ng, "The Effects of Cultural Intelligence on Interpersonal Trust in Multicultural Teams," in Ang and Van Dyne, *Handbook of Cultural Intelligence*, 206–20.

32. Cf. Dora C. Lau and J. Keith Murnighan, "Demographic Diversity and Faultlines: The Compositional Dynamics of Organizational Groups," *Academy of Management Review* 23 (1998): 325–40.

33. Michael Lewis, *Moneyball: The Art of Winning an Unfair Game* (New York: Norton, 2003).

34. Early, Ang, and Tan, *CQ*.

35. Efrat Shokef and Miriam Erez, "Cultural Intelligence and Global Identity in Multicultural Teams," in Ang and Van Dyne, *Handbook of Cultural Intelligence*, 177–91.

36. Organ, Podsakoff, and MacKenzie, *Organizational Citizenship Behavior*.

37. Nathan Podsakoff, Steven W. Whiting, Philip M. Podsakoff, and Brian D. Blume, "Individual- and Organizational-Level Consequences of Organizational Citizenship Behaviors: A Meta-Analysis," *Journal of Applied Psychology* 94 (2009): 122–41.

38. Michael Ahearne, Narasimhan Srinivasan, and Luke Weinstein, "Effect of Technology on Sales Performance: Progressing from Technology Acceptance to Technology Usage and Consequence," *Journal of Personal Selling and Sales Management* 24 (2004): 297–310.

39. Organ, Podsakoff, and MacKenzie, *Organizational Citizenship Behavior*.

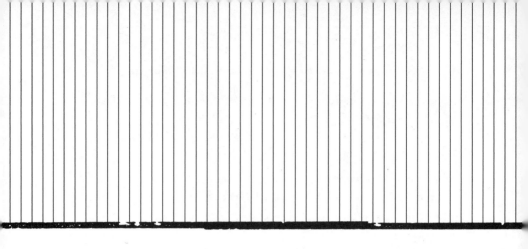

CHAPTER 10

Major League Soccer Scores an Own Goal in Houston:
How Branding a Team Alienated Hispanic and Latino Fans

Ric Jensen and Jason Sosa
Montclair State University and Rice University

The intent of new professional sport franchises is to increase public awareness, build a brand, and provide opportunity for positive media reports. Houston's new Major League Soccer (MLS) franchise, the Houston Dynamo—formerly known as Houston 1836—failed to do this. In this essay we cover a number of social issues, such as the attitudes of Anglo-Americans and Hispanics to professional soccer within the United States and how the MLS promotes its product to Hispanic audiences; we use the efforts of the MLS to relocate its San Jose franchise to Houston for the 2006 season as an example. Additionally, we further analyze the extent to which the Houston franchise successfully used crisis communications methods to deal with this public relations challenge. Finally we attempt to reinforce the idea that MLS franchises must develop strategies to get Hispanics excited about the league in order to succeed.

Introduction

Since its creation, Major League Soccer (MLS) has become one of the success stories of American professional sports. The league now includes twenty-one teams, and its teams average 17,872 fans per game, more than such established leagues as the National Basketball Association and the National Hockey League.[1] In 2014 MLS signed its most lucrative television broadcasting package; ESPN, Fox, and the Spanish-language network Univision will pay $90 million a year over the next eight years.[2] With the recent spike in enthusiasm generated by the large numbers of fans in the United States who cheered for the American national team in the 2014 World Cup, advocates of the league suggest that interest in soccer overall and in MLS specifically should rise; the league experienced a 11 percent increase in attendance following the 2010 World Cup tournament.[3] In fact, television ratings for the United States vs. Portugal match in the group stage of the 2014 World Cup drew significantly more viewers than the NBA finals or the MLB World Series; soccer drew more than 25 million viewers, while baseball and basketball each garnered only 15 million.[4] Even after the Americans were eliminated, fans were compelled to watch; the 2014 World Cup Final between Germany and Argentina received a higher television rating than any World Cup since 1994, when the United States hosted the event.[5]

A few unique trends suggest that MLS might be on the precipice of a huge boon in popularity in the United States Young people, many of whom grew up playing the sport in youth leagues or in public schools, were much more interested in the 2014 World Cup than any other age group; 40 percent of people between the ages of eighteen and twenty nine said they were especially looking forward to the tournament, compared to only 23 percent of those ages thirty to forty-nine and 13 percent of people fifty or older.[6] Second, MLS is benefiting from the growing number of Hispanics in the United States, many of who grew up in countries or cultures where soccer is the most favorite sport by a wide margin; the number of Hispanics in the nation rose from 37 million persons in 2002 to 53 million individuals in 2012.[7]

MLS has been successful in several areas. Since 2007 the MLS expanded internationally, placing teams in in Toronto, Vancouver, and Montreal. The league is attracting prominent investors with ties to soccer; Manchester City of the English Premier League has joined forces with the legendary New York Yankees to create a new franchise that begins play in New York City in 2015; British soccer legend David Beckham is leading efforts to create a new MLS franchise in Miami. Sponsors are paying for stadium naming rights, advertising on team uniforms, and other promotional events, and revenue from corporate sponsorship has increased substantially since 2010.[8] Several of the league's franchises have recently built or are now planning soccer-only stadiums in Los Angeles, Columbus, Dallas, Chicago, Salt Lake City, New Jersey, Kansas City, Houston, and Portland (among others).

Although soccer had for some time struggled to achieve a foothold in the United States, there are now signs that the sport has finally emerged on the national stage. Smith reports that the average MLS franchise is now worth a minimum of $103 million, an increase of 175 percent since 2010; ten of the league's franchises are now making a profit, led by the Seattle Sounders and Los Angeles Galaxy.[9]

But in spite of the growing optimism, there are still causes for concern.

Collins reports that 3.2 million youth play the game and 75 percent of league matches are televised, MLS is yet to attain the status of a popular spectator sport in the United States, lagging far behind professional football, baseball, and basketball. A 2014 survey of sports fans revealed that only 18 percent of those surveyed said MLS was their favorite American-based sports league, behind the NFL (23 percent) and the NBA (21 percent) but ahead of MLB, the NHL, and NASCAR;[10] that survey also showed that these fans were more interested in following the US Men's National Team and the English Premier League than MLS. The league also has failed so far to attract large numbers of viewers to tune in for MLS matches, even despite the increased interest in soccer as a whole; Osham reported that the 2013 league championship game suffered its worst rating ever and that no MLS match broke into the ten most-watched televised soccer games that year.[11] Markovits and Hellerman suggest that, although much of the American public may follow the United States national team during the World Cup once every four years, a much smaller group of fans regularly keeps up with and attends MLS matches.[12] TV ratings for MLS matches are typically low, described as "just short of invisible."[13] Brown suggests that MLS is often unable to match the salaries the best players in Mexico are paid by their club teams.[14]

On a broad level, there is a sense that the league's potentially largest market, Mexican Americans, Hispanics, and Chicanos, have yet to fully embrace the sport and pack the league's stadiums.[15] Faflik describes efforts by some MLS franchises, especially the Los Angeles Galaxy and Chivas USA, to build and market these teams to Hispanic audiences, but also criticizes the league for restricting the numbers of international players who can be on each team.[16] If that limit was lifted, Faflik suggests that most MLS teams would feature rosters with far more players from various nations throughout the Western Hemisphere. In 2000 Cohen wrote that MLS "is considered a second-tier sport by American sports fans and a second-tier league by the world's soccer aficionados."[17] There are signs that this trend may be changing for the better; Osham reported that while TV ratings for MLS among all fans are still low, the numbers of Hispanic and Latino fans who are tuning in has increased over the past five years.[18] Cassidy (2014) describes how the American public was captivated with the Men's National Team's performance at the 2014 World Cup and fell in love with soccer;[19] whether this excitement will extend to MLS remains to be seen.

In broad terms, some marketing and public relations experts suggest that several MLS teams are choosing international-sounding names (i.e., FC Dallas, Real Salt Lake, Chivas USA, New York City FC, etc.) to appeal to ethnic groups of fans that follow long-established international soccer leagues, including Mexican Americans, Hispanics, and Chicanos.[20] According to Brown, in order to survive, MLS needs to secure a more lucrative TV contract and bring the world's best players to America instead of sending the most promising young players from the United States to play overseas and succeed in the World Cup.[21] As mentioned previously, the league is succeeding in many of these areas. More elite international soccer players are signing with MLS;[22] the league recently signed its most lucrative-ever television rights deal.[23] In the 2014 World Cup, the United States exceeded all expectations by advancing to the knockout round after surviving "the Group of Death" in the opening round that featured legendary soccer powers Germany and Portugal as well as a Ghana squad that eliminated the United States in the last tournament; the result was that American fans became enamored of the Men's National Team, and interest in the World Cup soared in cities throughout America [24]

Methodology

This essay is based on a content analysis of articles presented by the mass media in Houston as well as national news outlets during the spring of 2006. The articles were taken from news websites and blogs. Content analysis consists of systematically categorizing content from media coverage to identify critical topics and themes reported on during a news event.[25] Additional information was gleaned from interviews with team officials, members of the Houston mass media, scholars, and other sources.

Public Relations and Sports

Several recent studies have examined public relations focused on public relations issues related to professional soccer. Boyle, Dinan, and Morrow described how public relations efforts could increase newspaper coverage of soccer in the United Kingdom.[26] Giulianotti discussed how public relations and marketing professionals will have to adapt to changes in the demographics of international soccer fans as the sport becomes followed more closely throughout the globe.[27] Ferrand and Pages studied how public relations and marketing activities can be used to improve the image of European professional soccer clubs.[28] Bennett analyzed the extent to which soccer fans at soccer matches in the United Kingdom remembered firms that paid to advertise at these events.[29]

Similarly, several writings have recently described how public relations principles can be used to publicize and market the organization. Irwin, Zwick, and Sutton assessed the American professional sports franchises to identify excellent public relations and marketing practices used by these organizations.[30] The authors suggest that fielding a winning team, developing close relationships with fan bases and concentrating on building core areas of excellence most help sports franchises succeed. Mason identified four different groups that need to be addressed in sports PR and marketing efforts: fans, people who watch the sport on TV, communities that host the franchise, and corporations that sponsor and advertise the team and its events.[31] Stoldt, Dittmore, and Branvold presented a comprehensive overview of public relations issues specifically related to sports and describe how to develop and implement strategic public relations programs.[32] Quirk and Fort discussed the business of professional team sports in the United States, including marketing, public relations, and promotion.[33]

A few studies have addressed the time frame needed to adequately plan to market and publicize a team that has recently moved to a new city. For example, the Carolina Hurricanes' franchise of the National Hockey League spent more than a year developing its public relations and marketing strategy after the franchise relocated from Hartford in 1997.[34] A Houston public relations consultant recommends that teams should ideally plan initial public relations and marketing programs in a period of up to eighteen months.[35] The need to have a significant window of time to develop public relations plans is especially salient to Houston 1836 since the franchise had little time to create and implement its initial marketing campaign.

Public Relations during a Crisis

A key role for public relations professionals is to help organizations manage crisis events that have the potential to harm their reputation. Wrigley, Salmon, and Park define *crises* as events that can disrupt everyday business activity, draw unwanted attention to the organization, and threaten the financial viability and reputation of an entity.[36] Wilcox and Cameron suggest a crisis management strategy that consists of scanning the environment to identify potential public relations problems, taking preventive actions that lessen the likelihood the crisis will occur, resolving conflicts as soon as possible, and then working to restore the organization's reputation.[37] By managing a public relations crisis properly, an organization can lessen the damage to its reputation that might otherwise result. For example, NASA was able to maintain confidence and trust in the space agency after the 2003 *Columbia* explosion because the organization handled the crisis so effectively.[38]

Hispanics, Mexican Americans, and Chicanos

The Hispanic community, especially within the state of Texas, has grown significantly with each passing year.[39] Hispanics (most of whom are Mexican Americans) are the largest single ethnic group in Houston and now constitute 42 percent of the city's population.[40] In the year 2000, more than

6.66 million Hispanics were living in Texas, which represents a 55 percent increase from 1990.[41] On a national level, 27 million of the 42 million Hispanics in the United States in 2006 are Mexican American.[42] Further, Hispanics are becoming younger as the average household consists of three children. Due to the increase in youth and the growth of the population, the spending power of Hispanics has increased to an estimated $171 billion.[43] Generally, the Hispanic population is seen as an impoverished group, but realistically speaking it is a group with much affluence that is rising every year.[44] As such, many businesses have created marketing plans aimed at the Hispanic market. Within a sports context, many professional sports franchises in the United States have created marketing arms that target the Hispanic communities. Further, within the context of this study, MLS has invested much of its resources in attempts to capture this potential "gold mine."[45]

To date, none of the major professional leagues in the United States have successfully captured this growing segment of the market, although Major League Soccer is trying to build this connection.[46] Traditionally across the United States, the Hispanic culture has considered itself different from the total population and potentially falling prey to discriminatory acts rather than being a target demographic that is sought after and desired.[47] Faflik describes how Chivas USA is embracing a Mexican American identity that suits the Mexican American and Chicano culture of Los Angeles. When the team was introduced, the marketing message was broadly disseminated in Spanish and English: the slogan emphasized that Chivas USA was a new player in the international sport of "futbol."[48] To create a closer connection between Chivas USA and Mexican American and Chicano fans, the club borrowed the colors and tradition, and traded on the passion of Chivas's club in the Mexico Premier League, which has a legendary fan following since the team emphasizes its Mexican roots and heritage. Mariscal discusses the importance of differentiating between Chicanos (US citizens of Mexican descent) and recently arrived Mexican immigrants when trying to understand Hispanic attitudes related to sports.[49] For example, Mariscal notes how Mexican Americans generally supported prizefighter Julio Cesar Chavez (a resident of Mexico) while Chicanos typically cheered for Oscar de la Hoya (who was born in

East Los Angeles). Similarly, Braysmith describes the Chicano culture as mostly working-class Mexican Americans who do not view themselves through the lens of the Anglo-American culture.[50] In contrast, the focus of Chicano culture is on building cultural connections that explain the history and ethnicity of Mexico. Pescador describes how the Mexican national team as well as professional soccer clubs from Mexico have played exhibition and tournament matches in the United States since the 1970s and have thus developed a large fan base in this country.[51]

In order to be successful, public relations and marketing professionals must create campaigns that are socially acceptable to diverse groups of Latin Americans. With regard to consumer marketing, Hispanics may feel as if their culture is not valued by the greater population as marketers use stereotypes to increase awareness of their products at the expense of defaming cultural pride.[52] In the context of this study, the Houston Dynamo exacerbated simmering conflicts between the Anglo and Hispanic communities when they named the new soccer team '1836'— a name with vastly different connotations in the Anglo-American and Hispanic communities.

How Major League Soccer Came to Houston

In December 2006 MLS and the Anschutz Entertainment Group (AEG; owner of several of the league's franchises) announced that its San Jose Earthquakes franchise would relocate to Houston. The move occurred because the city of San Jose failed to develop a plan to fund and build a soccer-specific stadium.[53] Dynamo played its first home game on April 2, 2006, when they beat the Colorado Rapids in front of 25,462 fans.

AEG was faced with the challenge of choosing a team name, team colors, and a public relations and marketing scheme in a very compressed time frame because the first game of the season was so soon after the franchise move was announced. AEG supplied a list of potential team names and ran a promotion with the *Houston Chronicle* and its Spanish-language edition (*La Voz*) to let people in the community vote on which name would be given to the team. Houston public relations consultant John Wagner suggests the franchise may have been working under a compressed time frame to make these important choices. Shortly after the franchise relocated to Houston, more than thirty-five hundred fans had paid deposits for season tickets, and team officials anticipated selling as many as seven thousand season tickets for the inaugural campaign.

The Choice of Houston 1836

Before the team name was announced, team president Oliver Luck met with the Hispanic Chamber of Commerce and several Latino business leaders and politicians to obtain feedback about whether the 1836 name would be acceptable to the Houston Hispanic community, which includes individuals from Peru, Ecuador, and several Latin American nations in addition to Mexico.[54] After the vote, the Anschutz Entertainment Group and MLS decided on the Houston 1836 name. Quoted on the website for Fox Sports, Luck said, "We were aware of the dual meaning of the name. We vetted the name with the [Houston] Hispanic Chamber of Commerce, and they thought it would be a good name and a way to unify Houston. In our polls and focus groups we found a very small group—[in the] single digit[s]—took offense."[55] When the team name was introduced on January 26, 2006, Luck said, "The beauty we have as an MLS franchise is we can be a little riskier [in choosing a team name] than some of the more established leagues. We're not bound by something that maybe an NFL team or an NBA team is tied to."[56] Luck also commented that a blessing of choosing such an unusual team name was that it sparked conversation in the media and among fans, thus ensuring that the team would be in the public eye.[57]

At that press conference, Houston councilman Adrian Garcia appeared onstage alongside Luck and addressed the crowd in Spanish to endorse the choice. Romero reports that the Houston 1836 name was selected by the Anschutz Entertainment Group, which owns the franchise and conducted its own polling and development of the brand. Participants were asked to identify the nickname they most preferred from among the following choices: Buffalos, Ravens, Generals, Apollos, Patriots, Lonestars, Eagles, Gatos, Toros, Stallions, Mustangs, Stars, and 1836.[58] The 1836 team name follows an international tradition where some soccer franchises are identified by the year they were organized. German clubs that fit this mold include Hannover 96 (for the year 1896), Bayer 04 (1904), and FSV Mainz

05 (1905). Australia's Adelaide 36ers was named after the year the host city was founded, ironically also in 1836.

The intent of choosing Houston 1836 as the team name was to honor the year the city of Houston was founded. That same year, Texas won independence from Mexico by defeating General Santa Ana's troops at the battle of San Jacinto. The theme of Houston 1836 featured the profile of General Sam Houston riding a horse into battle. Ironically the 1836 was name was chosen in spite of the fact that Mexican Americans were identified as one of the franchise's key target audiences and perhaps its most loyal local fan base. One of the reasons Houston landed an MLS franchise was the fact that more than thirty-five thousand fans attended a match between the Mexican and Bulgarian national teams in November 2005, and games in Houston between professional teams from Mexico drew some of the biggest crowds in the InterLiga tournament.

The Controversy about the Team Name

At the time the Houston 1836 name was introduced, some Anglo-American commentators in the mass media suggested that any controversy that might arise would be short lived. John Lopez, a *Houston Chronicle* columnist, wrote on January 26, 2006, "All of you who have your soccer shorts in a bunch because you think 1836 is some kind of insulting reference to Mexico's defeat by Gen. Sam Houston's Texas patriots . . . Get over it." Lopez awarded the team a grade of A for uniqueness in choosing the name. However, the naming of Houston 1836 seemed to strike an especially raw nerve because it was perceived by some in the city's Hispanic community as being racist and derogatory toward Mexican Americans and Chicanos.[59] Shortly after 1836 was chosen as the team name, columnist Jamie Trecker of the Fox Soccer Channel published a column titled "What's in a Name? Plenty of Controversy" that featured the comments by many leaders in the Houston Hispanic community who were critical of the choice of 1836. Shortly after the column was published, Trecker said he received more than eighteen hundred emails and two death threats from people who supported and opposed the naming of team as Houston 1836.[60]

One of the first signs that the name might be causing a public relations problem occurred when MLS spokesman Dan Courtemanche admitted he had concerns about the name. He said, "We've heard from a very vocal audience that some people are upset about the name. At no time did we want to offend people with the choice of the name . . . so we have had to look closely at changing the name."[61] Sylvia Garcia, a Hispanic who serves as a Harris County commissioner, rallied Mexican Americans to boycott the team name.[62] She stated that many constituents called, emailed, and approached her to express concerns about the Houston 1836 name. Garcia was quoted by KTRK-TV as saying, "[I understand] . . . concerns that people might have with marketing, [Houston's] image . . . and [its] image as an international trading partner as a gateway to the Americas." In the *Houston Chronicle*, Garcia said, "I can understand that [1836] was also a sad time for the people of Mexico and their descendants . . . in a conflict that sometimes pitted families against their own people."[63] Paco Bendana, the Latino geographic marketing and community relations manager for Anheuser-Busch in Houston, commented, "Clearly, not enough homework was put into this. Historically speaking, 1836 is not something [Hispanics] celebrate."[64] In contrast, Houston public relations practitioner John Wagner questions how many Mexican Americans, Chicanos, and other Hispanics were offended by the team name choice. He wrote, "When the name was released there was a small outcry. A few complaints . . . never a huge rallying force. Just a couple of very visible folks saying, 'Change the name.'"[65]

Much of the controversy surrounding the selection of Houston 1836 was sparked by the comments of two professors at the University of Houston. In January 2006 Dr. Raul Ramos of the history department wrote a guest editorial in the *Houston Chronicle*, sharply criticizing the name:

> By naming the team Houston 1836, the newly arrived Major League Soccer franchise has chosen to identify with a year that may divide the city rather than unite it. . . . Naming the team 1836 smacks of nostalgia for a time when Mexican people were absent [from the Houston region] or at least knew their place. . . . Short of changing the name, the team needs to make extra efforts to appear open to Latino Houstonians. Only then, and by removing Sam Houston from the logo, will the team come to symbolize the promise of a global capital. . . . The team compounds the connection [of celebrating Texas' military

victory against Mexico] by depicting Sam Houston on horseback, leading the charge against Mexican troops. What other conclusion can we draw?[66]

Columnist Jamie Trecker interviewed Ramos for an article published by the Fox Soccer Channel.[67] In the interview, Ramos said,

> The team wants Latino [fans] but only on their terms . . . leaving your heritage, identity, and family at the door. The team chose a date that has [more than] one meaning and, unfortunately, you can't put an asterisk in a logo. The team's name is something of a litmus test. If you disagree with this singular notion of Texas Independence, then you're not a good American. But in a multicultural America, Americans can hold differing views of the same event.

In addition, Dr. Tatcho Mindiola, who leads the Center for Mexican-American Studies at the University of Houston, said he believes the 1836 name could be "gung-ho" for Anglos but insulting to Hispanics: "It's unfortunate because sport is an integrating mechanism in society, and unintentionally or not, this is a PR blunder. . . . Do they think [Hispanics] are going to wear a T-shirt with the year 1836 on it?"[68]

In the *Houston Chronicle*, Mindiola was quoted as saying,

> Maybe Anglos find a lot of bravado in 1836. To us, it conjures all this bad history. Why should we put up with this? This community has to change. They could have pulled off the 1836 name years ago, but they sure can't now. We now have a very significant Mexican-American intellectual class that does its own research and isn't going to put up with this.[69]

The Hispanic mass media in Houston also criticized the Houston 1836 name choice. Carlos Puig, the editor of Houston's Spanish newspaper, *Rumbo de Houston*, said his email inbox filled with messages from angry readers who were "going crazy with the name."[70] On the front page of *Rumbo de Houston*, Puig lambasted the choice of Houston 1836, calling it a public relations "own goal," when you put the ball in your own goal and score a point for the opposition.[71] Puig charged that the name would discourage Hispanic fans in the Houston area from being as enthused about the team as they would be if a less offensive name had been selected. He wrote, "The team does not understand the negative connotation of the name, or it understands it and chose it (in spite of how Mexican fans would react)."[72]

A few public relations professionals that practice in Texas and work with sports PR also weighed in on the choice of the team name. Public relations specialist Dan Keeney questioned whether an online poll was the best process to measure the attitudes of Latinos in Houston since many of them were still not online at the time. Kenney criticized the choice of Houston 1836 as a public relations error and wrote,

> It's incredible that the team's owner . . . failed to fully consider how the name would be received by the soccer-crazy fans they were hoping to lure. After all, they are basing the venture in part on the crowds of Spanish-speaking futbol aficionados who regularly fill stadiums here to attend the matches of visiting clubs from Mexico. . . . Don't insult your core customer and show yourself to be disconnected at best and callous and uncaring at worst by failing to fully consider their point of view.[73]

Dynamo—A New Name and a New Controversy

On March 2, 2006, the team name was changed from Houston 1836 to Houston Dynamo. At the press conference announcing the name change, Luck said,

> At no time did MLS or AEG ever want to offend any members of the community in Houston. We want everyone to feel welcome and become a part of professional soccer in Houston. Similar to soccer around the world and in our other MLS markets, the sport embraces all cultures and unites the communities.[74]

Even with the name change, things took a turn for the worse, in the eyes of some, when the Dynamo name was unveiled.[75] Houston public relations professional John Wagner suggests that removing the Houston 1836 name alienated large numbers of Anglo-Americans and created a greater PR nightmare than the initial naming of the franchise. In addition, several people were upset that the choice of the new name, "Dynamo," evokes sinister memories on the part of many Eastern Europeans. Dynamo was the name given to soccer teams fielded by the secret police departments in the former Soviet Union, by the repressive police force in Hungary, and by the Stasi secret police of East Germany.[76] During the 1940s, Stalin's secret chief of police, who served as the chairman of Dynamo Moscow, ordered that players of rival clubs in the Soviet Union be sent to Siberia.[77]

How MLS Tries to Woo Hispanic Fans

The idea that Houston 1836 chose a name that had the potential to worsen relations with Mexican American, Chicano, and Latino fans is surprising since MLS has identified Hispanics as one of its largest fan bases. Since it was created in 1996, MLS has tried to learn marketing lessons associated with the failure of its predecessor, the North American Soccer League (NASL).[78] The NASL strategy was to place large numbers of older European players on teams in the league while few Latinos were recruited, except for the great Brazilian Pelé, who played for the New York Cosmos.[79] As a result, NASL failed to draw large numbers of Hispanic fans.

According to Delgado, Latinos are viewed by MLS as necessary economic and community assets that are keys to the sport's success. He asserts that this is one of the first times that a professional sports league in the United States has targeted the Hispanic market. In the initial stages of MLS, the league allocated Mexican players to Dallas and San Jose and Colombian players to Tampa Bay to provide Hispanic stars that Latino fans in those cities would pay to see play. Later, such Latino stars as Tab Ramos, Marcelo Balboa, and Jorge Campos were featured prominently in the league's bilingual sponsorship, licensing, and promotions programs.[80] Faflik contends that MLS has the potential to draw fans from throughout the Americas by capitalizing on growing intercultural ties now flourishing in the "transnational megaregion" of the Western Hemisphere. Brown describes how MLS is working to tap into the passion of Mexican Americans and Hispanics to help grow professional soccer in the United States.[81] Dan Courtemanche, the senior vice president of marketing for the league, expressed the marketing effort this way:

[The Hispanic audience is] a huge opportunity for us, something each team recognizes and tries to respond to. Every [MLS] team has at least one bilingual member of the public relations staff. . . . We have play-by-play of our games on Spanish radio. Our Hispanic stars . . . are filming spots for Spanish television.[82]

Courtemanche points out that MLS has struggled to make Mexican Americans and Hispanics fans of the league. One columnist suggested that MLS showed its concern for the Hispanic market when it changed Houston 1836 to something less offensive to Mexican Americans. Delgado describes how the 1994 World Cup, held in the United States, was marketed heavily to Hispanics.[83] Cup organizers identified specific "Hispanic marketing activities" that utilized the Spanish-language Univision television network and the Cadena Spanish-language radio network. In 1998 the Univision TV network aired Budweiser commercials in Spanish promoting the Mexican national soccer team. During the 2006 World Cup, the Univision TV network drew more than 50 million viewers—more than ESPN or ABC—because of the passion of Hispanics for soccer.[84] In 1996 MLS commissioner Doug Logan said, "We opened our arms to new Americans and they responded with glee. Forty percent of our audience is ethnic first- or second-generation American, and most (of them are) Latinos."[85] Pratt suggests that many Hispanic groups in the United States care deeply about soccer because they are proud of the success of people from their home countries.[86] Even if much of life in America is confusing for recent immigrants, they understand how the game should be played and are passionate about the sport. Brown adds, "For almost all of them, soccer is the sport they grew up on."[87] Kuper stated that soccer "arouses in the rest of the world collective passions that are matched by nothing short of war," especially in nations that are poor and suppressed.[88] One of the key issues is whether Mexican Americans, Chicanos, and other Hispanics in the United States can be converted into MLS fans. Faflik suggests that MLS is slowly winning the battle to develop a fan base among Mexican Americans, Chicanos, and Hispanics, stating, "MLS has discovered a way to turn multicultural without compromising its policies: Quite simply, Major League Soccer has crossed the border."[89] Brown reports that while it is common for fifty thousand or more Hispanic fans to come to attend exhibition matches of the Mexican national team in the United States, many Mexican American and Chicano fans may be much more likely to follow the national team than an MLS team that features Latino stars. At the same time, Brown suggests that the success of the US national team in friendly matches against Mexico has helped legitimize the stature of MLS in the eyes of Mexican American fans. To increase the credibility of MLS among Mexican American fans, Holtzman described discussions to create a champion's league tournament between MLS and Mexican Premiere Division teams in 2007, suggestinge that this type of event could help MLS tap a latent market of Hispanic fans who may have believed that American professional soccer is an inferior product. MLS teams have competed in the CONCACAF Champions League competition versus professional clubs from throughout North America, but so far this event has yet to capture the imagination of soccer fans in the United States.[90] Jewell and Molina comment that Mexican Americans and Chicanos may be more inclined to support and follow professional teams in Mexico than attend MLS games.[91] Their research suggests that fans who moved from El Salvador to Dallas (not Mexican Americans) are the largest group of supporters of the Dallas FC MLS team, while many potential Mexican American fans are more likely to stay home watching a Mexican Premiere Division game on TV than pay to attend an MLS match. As a result, MLS has intentionally scheduled many of its matches that are broadcast over the Telemundo TV network for Saturday afternoons to avoid being in the same time slot when Mexican professional league games are shown. Data from Jewell and Molina show that MLS teams in Hispanic markets had lower attendance than other franchises in the first six years of the league's existence.[92]

Herbig and Yelkur describe how a Hispanic promotion for Surf laundry detergent that used baseball themes was very successful in South Florida (where baseball is the favorite sport of Cuban-Americans), but did poorly in Texas and the Southwest (because Mexican- Americans in this region favor soccer).[93] They note how AT&T contracted with MLS to promote and advertise its products to markets with large numbers of Mexican Americans and Hispanics from nations where soccer is most popular. Even political parties are recognizing the affinity that many Hispanics in the United States have toward soccer and are also trying to capitalize on it.[94] The national Democratic Party paid to advertise on the Spanish language Univision TV network during the 2006 World Cup in an attempt to court Hispanic voters and developed a website to support the effort, http://www.ndnfutbol.org. The ads were targeted to markets with large Hispanic populations, including Houston, El Paso, Albuquerque, and Denver (among others). Joe Garcia, spokesman for this campaign, said, "The highest-rated broadcast ever on Univision has been the World Cup. The numbers are just outstanding. The audience is huge."[95]

Are the Team's Public Relations Efforts Repairing the Damage?

One of the key questions that must be asked in this case study is how well did Houston Dynamo handle this public relations crisis? By comparing the actions of Houston Dynamo to the public relations crisis management strategy set forth by Wilcox and Cameron,[96] one can briefly examine how well the team did in each step of the process.

(1) *Scanning the environment to identify potential public relations problems.* Club officials had some knowledge that the Houston 1836 team name might be controversial. Still, they went ahead with that choice. In part, the team chose the 1836 name with the knowledge that it would create conversation in the press and among the public. The Houston 1836 name was not an accident but instead a strategic choice meant to generate media buzz about the franchise.

(2) *Taking preventative actions to lessen the likelihood a crisis will occur.* The team seems to have done very little to plan how to deal with hostility toward the Houston 1836 name even though they should have known it would create some controversy.

(3) *Resolving conflicts as soon as possible.* The media and public relations practitioners both give Houston Dynamo high marks in this regard. The team acted swiftly, perhaps motivated by political pressure, to change the name. They apologized and met with Hispanic and Mexican American groups that were offended.

(4) *Working to restore the organization's image.* Media reports and anecdotal evidence suggest that Mexican Americans and other Hispanic groups are now supporting the team. The franchise seems to be taking steps to win friends in the community.

Public relations expert John Wagner praises how Houston Dynamo survived the controversy.[97] He wrote,

> Oliver Luck and other team officials were honest and upfront with groups who felt offended. When they found people were upset, they took actions to show they cared. Team officials met with several people, both in the Latino and Anglo-American community, who were concerned about the naming process. I think the bottom line is that even though Houston Dynamo may have made an initial PR mistake, they were totally honest, owned up to their error quickly, and tried to repair the damage.

In addition, public relations consultant Dan Keeney said this incident contains insights on how sports franchises should treat their fans. He wrote,

> It will be interesting to see if this ends up being a small issue that blows over quickly or if it leads to a reassessment of the franchise name. In the meantime, it offers an important lesson for businesses entering ethnically diverse areas. Don't insult your core customer and show yourself to be disconnected at best and callous and uncaring at worst by failing to fully consider their point of view.[98]

Other studies suggest public relations strategies that may help MLS succeed and prosper. Mahony and Howard suggest that developing marketing and promotions tied to major events and working to gain the support from a very loyal fan base are key concepts that will affect the success of sports public relations efforts in the future.[99] Houston Dynamo might consider promoting MLS during the World Cup and other international events. Kelley, Hoffman, and Carter offer advice for sports teams that have recently relocated.[100] They stress the importance of building meaningful relationships with target audiences and the community. Unfortunately, the introduction of Houston 1836 may have alienated the Mexican American and Hispanic audiences the team was trying to capitalize on as a core fan base.

As a postscript, Houston Dynamo ended up winning the 2006 and 2007 Major League Soccer championships and reached the finals in 2011 and 2012. The Hispanic community embraced the team, as did other ethnic groups, and the team's success has been celebrated throughout the Houston region. Growing support for the team in the Houston area increased popular support for a publicly funded soccer-only stadium that was built in 2012.[101] Apparently, winning and winning big can make it easier for fans to forget and forgive. It's possible that many of those same Hispanic fans who cheered the Dynamo during their championship run may be some of those who were most upset by the Houston 1836 name.

Summary

A few lessons can be derived from this case study. First, leaders of MLS franchises (including public relations professionals) need to fully contemplate how all the actions of the organization will be received by Mexican Americans, Hispanics, and Chicanos, who are essential to the league's success. It seems likely that the best way to help MLS grow into a major presence in American sports is by cultivating positive relationships among Mexican American, Chicano, and Hispanic fan bases throughout the Americas. Alienating Hispanic fans may cause problems for MLS franchises. Perhaps the Houston franchise should have done much more in advance to anticipate how Mexican Americans would react to the "1836" name. On the other hand, if the 1836 name was chosen intentionally to make sure the team name would be discussed for weeks in the Houston media, perhaps the club's leaders knew exactly what they were doing and achieved the desired results.

This study reinforces the importance of using distinct public relations and marketing efforts to reach different Hispanic, Mexican American, and Chicano groups in the community. Each Hispanic ethnic group has its own distinct culture and connection with sports. To increase fan loyalty, MLS franchises should consider recruiting top players from the dominant Latin American nations represented in their market. This may be especially true since soccer evokes a great sense of national pride within its most loyal followers.[102] Houston Dynamo may want to stock the team with prominent Mexican professional soccer players in order to be accepted by the Mexican American community in Houston.

Notes

1. Chris Smith, "Major League Soccer's Most Valuable Teams," *Forbes*, November 20, 2013, http://www.forbes.com/sites/chrissmith/2013/11/20/major-league-soccers-most-valuable-teams/.

2. John Ourand, Christopher Botta, and Tripp Mickle, "Legacy of the Cup," *Sports Business Journal*, July 14, 2014, http://www.sportsbusinessdaily.com/Journal/Issues/2014/07/14/Events-and-Attractions/World-Cup.aspx.

3. Jim Peltz, "A World Cup 'Bump' for Major League Soccer? Not yet," *LA Times*, July 9, 2014, http://www.latimes.com/sports/soccer/worldcup/la-sp-mls-world-cup-20140709-story.html.

4. Graeme Yorke, "USA's draw with Portugal the most watched football match ever in United States with 24.7million viewers... more than NBA Finals," *Daily Mail*, 2014, http://www.dailymail.co.uk/sport/worldcup2014/article-2666772/USAs-draw-Portugal-watched-football-match-United-States-24-7million-viewers.html#ixzz3AlsltlAF.

5. Maury Brown, "U.S. Vs. Germany On ESPN Second-Highest World Cup Game Watched With 10.77M Viewers," *Forbes*, 2014, http://www.forbes.com/sites/maurybrown/2014/06/27/tv-ratings-for-u-s-vs-germany-world-cup-game-on-espn-third-highest-ever/.

6. Mike Mikho, "Brazil's World Cup Is a Marketer's Dream, but Also a Potential Nightmare," *AdWeek*, http://www.adweek.com/news/advertising-branding/brazil-s-world-cup-marketers-dream-also-potential-nightmare-152890.

7. Amol Sharma, Keach Hagey, and Lauren Stevens, "Is This Soccer's Moment in America? Ratings Have Soared During the World Cup; Olympic-Level Audiences," 2014, http://online.wsj.com/articles/is-this-soccers-moment-in-america-1403819659.

8. Ronald Blum and Janie McCarthy, "After the World Cup, MLS Looks to Steady Growth," *The Associated Press*, 2014, http://bigstory.ap.org/article/after-world-cup-mls-looks-steady-growth.

9. Chris Smith, "Major League Soccer Announces New TV Deals with ESPN, Fox, Univision," *Forbes*, May 12, 2014, http://www.forbes.com/sites/chrissmith/2014/05/12/major-league-soccer-announces-new-tv-deals-with-espn-fox-univision/.

10. Bill King, "Soccer's Growing Reach: You've Heard It Before, But Has Soccer's Time Finally Arrived in the U.S.?" *Sports Business Journal*, June 2, 2014,

http://www.sportsbusinessdaily.com/Journal/Issues/2014/06/02/In-Depth/Main.aspx?hl=Bill%20King&sc=0.

11. Jeremiah Oshan, "MLS attendance down in 2013, but only slightly off 2012's record high." SBNation, October 31, 2013, http://www.sbnation.com/soccer/2013/10/31/5047982/mls-attendance-2013-report.

12. Markovits and Hellerman, "'Olympianization' of Soccer in the United States."

13. Gardner, "MLS Puts Heads Together for New Game Plan."

14. Brown, "Can European Football Spur Interest in American Soccer?"

15. Pescador, "¡Vamos Taximaroa!"

16. Faflik, "Futbol America."

17. Cohen, "Soccer Madness!," 45.

18. Jeremiah Oshan, "The 2014 World Cup Made Soccer Mainstream," SBNation, July 15, 2014, http://www.sbnation.com/soccer/2014/7/15/5899727/world-cup-2014-ratings.

19. John Cassidy, "How Far Can Soccer Go in the U.S.A.?" *The New Yorker*, 2014, http://www.newyorker.com/news/john-cassidy/how-far-can-soccer-go-in-the-u-s-a.

20. Wagner, "A Living Case Study on Multi-Cultural Communications."

21. Brown, "Can European Football Spur Interest in American Soccer?"

22. Barbara Liston, "Foreign players attracted to MLS, says Brazilian Kaka," *Yahoo Sports*, 2014, http://sports.yahoo.com/news/foreign-players-attracted-mls-says-brazilian-kaka-195623208--sow.html.

23. Ourand, Botta, and Mickle, "Legacy of the Cup."

24. Cassidy, "How Far Can Soccer Go in the U.S.A.?"

25. Wilcox and Cameron, *Public Relations Strategies and Tactics*.

26. Boyle, Dinan, and Morrow, "Doing the Business?"

27. Giulianotti, "Supporters, Fans, and Flaneurs."

28. Ferrand and Pages, "Image Management in Sports Organizations."

29. Bennett, "Sports Sponsorship, Spectator Recall, and False Consensus."

30. Irwin, Zwick, and Sutton, "Assessing Organizational Attributes."

31. Mason, "What Is the Sports Product and Who Buys It?"

32. Stoldt, Dittmore, and Branvold, *Sport Public Relations*.

33. Quirk and Fort, *Pay Dirt*, 25–32.

34. Kelley, Hoffman, and Carter, "Franchise Relocation and Sport Introduction."

35. Personal communication with John Wagner, June 2006.

36. Wrigley, Salmon, and Park, "Crisis Management Planning."

37. Wilcox and Cameron, *Public Relations Strategies and Tactics.*

38. Kauffman, "Lost in Space."

39. US Census Bureau reports.

40. L. Rodriguez, "1836: The Battle Then and Now," *Houston Chronicle*, March 2, 2006.

41. *Hispanics in the State of Texas*, 3.

42. Brown, "Hispanic Community Key for Major League Soccer."

43. Delgado, "Major League Soccer."

44. Herbig and Yelkur, "Differences between Hispanic and Anglo Consumer Expectations."

45. Herbst, "Soccer Gets Some Passing Grades after a Promising First Year."

46. Falfik, "Futbol America."

47. Delgado, "Sport and Politics."

48. Falflik, "Futbol America."

49. Mariscal, "Chicanos and Latinos in the Jungle of Sports Talk Radio."

50. Braysmith, "Constructing Athletic Agents."

51. Pescador, "¡Vamos Taximaroa!"

52. Herbig and Yelkur, "Differences between Hispanic and Anglo Consumer Expectations."

53. B. Fallas, "Hot in Houston," *Houston Chronicle*, February 1, 2006.

54. Wagner, "A Living Case Study on Multi-Cultural Communications."

55. J. Trecker, "What's In a Name? Plenty of Controversy," http://msn.foxsports.com/soccer/story/5296432.

56. John Lopez, "Welcome, MLS Fans, to the Digital Age," *Houston Chronicle*, January 26, 2006.

57. Personal communication with Oliver Luck, December 2006.

58. S. Romero, "What's in a Brand Name? Houston Just Found Out," *New York Times*, January 27, 2006.

59. Ramos, "Editorial," *Houston Chronicle*, February 12, 2006.

60. Personal communication with J. Trecker, 2006.

61. Trecker, "What's In a Name?"

62. "Houston 1836 to Change Their Name," KTRK-TV, February 14, 2006, http://abclocal.go.com/ktrk/story?section=localandid=3907294.

63. Garcia, in Passwaters, "Houston 1836 Logo, Colors, Unveiled."

64. Romero, "What's in a Brand Name?"

65. Wagner, "Living Case Study on Multi-Cultural Communications."

66. Ramos, "Kicking Around Houston 1836."

67. Trecker, "Houston 1836 Close to Name Change."

68. "Can't Stop the Bleeding," January 27, 2006.

69. Rodriguez, "1836: The Battle Then and Now."

70. Romero, "What's in a Brand Name?"

71. Keeney, "Houston Dynamo Introduced as Team Hopes to End Houston 1836 Controversy."

72. Puig in Keeney, "Houston 1836."

73. Keeney, "Houston Dynamo Introduced."

74. Luck quoted in "Houston MLS Unveils Its New Name, Houston Dynamo," Major League Soccer press release, March 6, 2006.

75. Rodriguez, "1836: The Battle Then and Now."

76. Trecker, "Houston 1836 Close to Name Change."

77. S. Kuper, "The World's Game Is Not Just a Game," *New York Times*, May 26, 2002.

78. Delgado, "Major League Soccer."

79. Satterlee, "Making Soccer a 'Kick in the Grass.'"

80. Delgado, "Major League Soccer."

81. Brown, "Hispanic Community Key for Major League Soccer."

82. Trecker, "Houston 1836 Close to Name Change."

83. Delgado, "Sport and Politics."

84. Brown, "Hispanic Community Key for Major League Soccer"; Veiga, "2006 World Cup Gives Univision Ratings a Boost."

85. Logan in Delgado, "Sport and Politics."

86. Pratt, "The Role of Non-Professional Soccer Clubs."

87. Brown, "Hispanic Community Key for Major League Soccer."

88. Kuper, "World's Game Is Not Just a Game."

89. Faflik, "Futbol America."

90. Brian Straus, "CONCACAF Champions League Final Indifference Raises Concern, Questions," *Sports Illustrated*, April 24, 2014, http://www.si.com/soccer/planet-futbol/2014/04/24/concacaf-champions-league-ccl-indifference-cruz-azul-toluca-mexico.

91. Jewell and Molina, "An Evaluation of the Relationship between Hispanics and Major League Soccer."

92. Ibid.

93. Herbig and Yelkur, "Differences between Hispanic and Anglo Consumer Expectations."

94. S. Griffith, "Democrats Launch World Cup Ads to Troll for Latino Votes," http:// news.yahoo.com/ s/afp/20060708/pl_afp/fblwc2006us-vote_060708225016.

95. Garcia in Griffith, "Democrats Launch World Cup Ads to Troll for Latino Votes."

96. Wilcox and Cameron, Public Relations Strategies and Tactics.

97. Wagner, "A Living Case Study on Multi-Cultural Communications."

98. Keeney, "Houston 1836."

99. Mahony and Howard, "Sport Business in the Next Decade."

100. Kelley, Hoffman and Carter, "Franchise Relocation and Sport Introduction."

101. Jose DeJesus Ortiz, "Dynamo Break Ground on New Stadium," *The Houston Chronicle*, 2011, http://www.chron.com/sports/dynamo/article/Dynamo-break-ground-on-new-stadium-1692669.php.

102. Brown, "Hispanic Community Key for Major League Soccer."

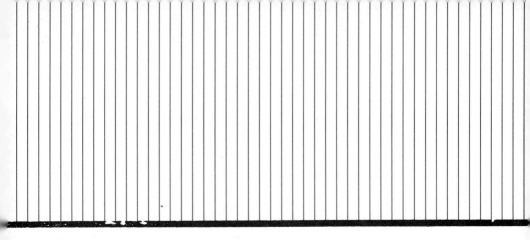

EPILOGUE

From "Quarterbacking While Mexican" to New Horizons in Sports History

Jorge Iber

Texas Tech University

No significant collection comes together swiftly. This one has been no exception. Although each chapter retains its currency and significance for the story it examines, some of the sports figures examined have gone on to capture the nation's attention in new ways. Some have gone on to great success while others have been benched or even fired. The initial version of this collection came together during the collegiate football season of 2008 and discussed particular aspects of the career of a Mexican American quarterback: Mark Sanchez of the University of Southern California (USC) Trojans. The principal reason for detailing some of the events surrounding this young man's career at USC was to provide readers with a sense of both the benefits and pitfalls that currently exist for Latino athletes in US sports in the early twenty-first century. Now that readers have had an opportunity to scrutinize a few essays highlighting important topics/issues that historians are examining, it seems only appropriate to complete the circle and provide an update of Sanchez's activities, both on the field and off.

The autumn of 2008 was typical of the success and heartbreak that

Trojan squads and fans have endured recently. The team's overall record, twelve victories and only one defeat, was no doubt sterling, allowing the cardinal and gold to finish, yet again, with a top-five national ranking at the end of the campaign. Unfortunately, an early-season upset at the hands of the Oregon State University Beavers (for the second time in three years) kept USC from qualifying for the Bowl Championship Series (BCS) National Championship Game, to be held in Miami in early 2009. Though disappointed, the mighty "sons of Troy" took out their frustrations by capping off their year with a decisive crushing of the Big 10 champions, the Penn State University Nittany Lions, 38-24, in the Rose Bowl on New Year's Day.

Appropriately enough (for a school located in Los Angeles), and in an almost Hollywood-like ending, Sanchez was the dominant player of the contest, completing twenty-eight of thirty-five pass attempts (a record 80 percent completion percentage) for 413 yards and four touchdowns, and rushing for another score. After the game Sanchez, as had other USC gridiron heroes of old, led the Trojan band in the playing of the university's fight song to commemorate another victory. Shortly thereafter, rumors began circulating across campus and on the Internet that the USC signal caller had played his final collegiate game and would declare himself available for the upcoming NFL draft. Not surprisingly, on January 15, 2009, Sanchez confirmed that he would indeed seek fame and fortune in the pros. Prognosticators believed that the now-former Trojan signal-caller would be selected in the first round of the April 2009 draft. After signing with a professional franchise (the New York Jets), Mark Sanchez joined approximately two dozen other Latinos on NFL rosters, further enhancing the presence of Spanish-surnamed athletes in America's favorite athletic league.

The articles included in this collection featured stories of US-based Spanish-surnamed competitors playing at levels from amateur to professional, covered a time span from colonial San Antonio to 1930s New York City and Chicago, to twentieth-century Texas, and documented these individuals competing in a wide array of athletic undertakings. While still in its nascent stage, it appears that this field of research is beginning to attract attention within the academic community. The works of authors

Tony Romo in action quarterbacking the Dallas Cowboys.
Courtesy of James D. Smith.

such as Michael Innis-Jimenez, Christine Marin, Jose Alamillo, Frank Jesus de las Tejas, and Jorge Iber (and others who did not contribute to this issue, such as Samuel O. Regalado and Katherine Jaimeson) have now laid a not-insignificant groundwork that should encourage scholars to pursue study on the subject matter.

The popular sports literature, too, is beginning to realize that not only are Latinos becoming more prevalent in various American sports but that this growing population is also coalescing into a larger and larger market for both sporting goods and athletic events. An issue of the popular magazine *Sports Illustrated* helps make this trend evident. In the October 6, 2008, issue, Melissa Segura authored an article titled "The Latino Athlete Now," presenting a series of snippets regarding the presence of Spanish-surnamed athletes in the contemporary sporting scene. Some of the information contained in this article would not cause much of a stir for the typical US sports fanatic: for example, Segura details the growing number of "Rodriguezes and Garcias on the back of jerseys and at the top of All-Star ballots (in Major League Baseball)," and the significant presence of such individuals on the pitches of Major League Soccer (MLS). No surprises there. However, there was some information that the rest of the US population might have found very astonishing: for example, the University of Oklahoma Sooners football team now broadcasts games in Spanish, hoping to attract the attention of roughly one-quarter of a million Oklahomans of Spanish-speaking background; or that Birmingham (Alabama)'s Department of Parks and Recreation now features a sixty-five-club circuit called the Latin American Soccer League (how far we have come from the night of September 12, 1970!). Finally, Segura also mentions that the very popular video-game *Madden NFL* has now put out a new edition, *Madden NFL En Espanol* to satisfy the demands of a new *segmento* (segment) of video game aficionados.[1]

In this same publication, other *SI* contributors presented articles on the role of Latinos in the growth and development of youth-club soccer (which may eventually feed into the US World Cup team and improve Americans' performance on this stage) and introduced NFL fans to the San Diego Chargers' star defensive end, Luis Castillo, who discussed his Dominican heritage and childhood in the environs of New York City. Most importantly, the piece also focused upon other aspects of Castillo's life, such as his having earned both All-American and Academic All-American status while playing football at Northwestern University (where he earned an undergraduate degree in economics), as well as his charitable work in the community, and his recent visit with American troops serving in Afghanistan.[2] In other words, Castillo is presented to the readers as a complex, educated, and sophisticated individual—a sharp break from how Latinos (athletes and the general population) have often been portrayed in the media of the United States.

The articles featured in this 2008 issue are not the only examples of the coverage of Latino athletes in *SI*. In more recent years, the writers for this magazine have examined subjects such as the importance of Spanish-speaking fans for the MLS[3] and boxing;[4] the rise of Omar Minaya to become the first Latino general manager in the history of the Major Leagues (first with the Montreal Expos and then with the New York Mets);[5] the attempt by the NFL to attract more fans to *futbol Americano* by utilizing players such as Roberto Garza (of the Chicago Bears) and Tony Gonzalez (of the Atlanta Falcons);[6] and finally, the purchase of the Anaheim Angels (now the Los Angeles Angels of Anaheim) by Mexican American businessman Art Moreno.[7] These stories proffer an introduction to Latinos not only as athletes but as consumers, management, and owners of sport franchises, and reveal other potential avenues of research that academicians can and should pursue.

In summary, this collection has sought to acquaint readers to a mostly unmined sector of US athletic history. As this nation's demographics continue to change during the twenty-first century, more and more Latinos will undoubtedly leave their marks on the field (at all levels) and business offices of the American sporting scene. This volume provides but a glimpse of the potential for this topic for a broad academic and popular audience.

Over the past few years, the popular coverage of the story of Latinos/as' involvement in American sport has expanded even further.[8] Indeed, it is difficult to pick up a copy of *Sports Illustrated* or any other national publication that covers sport without reading about Spanish-surnamed athletes and coaches who are breaking new ground by participating and

A former major leaguer (1991–1998), Ruben Amaro, Jr., has served in the front office of the Philadelphia Phillies since 1998, and as general manager of the team since 2009. Courtesy of the Phillies, © 2012.

succeeding at the very highest levels of American collegiate and professional athletics. A sampling of major and more recent stories includes the following: the success of Mark Sanchez in helping to lead the New York Jets to the AFC title game versus the Pittsburgh Steelers at the end of the 2010 NFL season (in 2013 he was replaced as the Jets' starting quarterback by West Virginia rookie Geno Smith and he eventually signed with the Philadelphia Eagles in March 2014); the firing of Omar Minaya as general manager of the New York Mets (he became vice president of baseball operations for the San Diego Padres in 2011); the hiring of Ruben Amaro, Jr., as general manager of the Philadelphia Phillies; the success of Frank Martin as head coach of the Kansas State University Wildcats basketball program (now head coach at the University of South Carolina); the hiring of Manny Diaz as defensive coordinator for the Texas Longhorns (although he was recently fired by Coach Mack Brown after Texas gave up more than five hundred yards on the ground in an early-season 2013 game to BYU; he signed on to become the defensive coordinator with Louisiana Tech University in January 2014); the promotion of Juan Castillo to serve as de-

The first Puerto Rican to be part of a Super Bowl winning team, Ron Rivera previously served as defensive coordinator for the San Diego Chargers before becoming head coach of the Carolina Panthers in 2011. Courtesy of Kent Smith.

fensive coordinator of the Philadelphia Eagles (he was fired in the middle of the 2012 campaign, but was hired by the Baltimore Ravens and was part of their coaching staff when they won Super Bowl XLVII in New Orleans); the appointment of Ron Rivera as head coach of the Carolina Panthers; the success and retirement of Lorena Ochoa from the Ladies Professional Golfers Association (LPGA); and the stellar guard play of Joey "Boo Boo" Rodriguez as the Virginia Commonwealth University Rams made their improbable advance (including their defeat of Kansas) to the NCAA Tournament's Final Four during March Madness in 2011.

In addition to the headline stories noted above, several books, including *The Boys from Little Mexico: A Season Chasing the American Dream* by

Steve Wilson; *American Victory: Wrestling, Dreams, and a Journey toward Home* by Olympic gold medalist Henry Cejudo and Bill Plaschke; and *100 Campeones: Latino Groundbreakers Who Paved the Way in Sport* by Richard Lapchick (and others) have helped to provide further exposure of how men and women of Spanish-speaking backgrounds have used sports to overcome adversity and to bring this particular group to the mainstream of American sport.[9] On the academic side of the ledger, Jorge Iber, Samuel O. Regalado, Jose Alamillo, and Arnoldo De Leon recently published *Latinos in U.S. Sport: A History of Isolation, Cultural Identity, and Acceptance*, marking the first attempt by academic historians to summarize and analyze the significance and totality of the Latino/a experience in American sport. Given the trends that are reshaping the demographics of the US population (with the Census Bureau noting that this group topped the 50 million mark in 2010), it is to be expected that even more Latinos/as will make their mark on American sports in the years to come.[10]

Notes

1. Melissa Segura, "The Latino Athlete Now," *Sports Illustrated*, October 6, 2008, http://vault.sportsillustrated.cnn.com/vault/article/magazine/MAG1145932/index/htm.

2. Peter King, "Hard Charger," *Sports Illustrated*, October 6, 2008, http://vault.sportillustrated.cnn.com/vault/article/magazine/MAG1145946/index.htm.

3. Mark Bechtel, "Are You Ready for Some Futbol?" *Sports Illustrated*, April 7, 2008, http://vault.sportillustrated.cnn.com/vault/article/magazine/MAG1127740/index.htm.

4. Richard Hoffer, "Taking Care of Business," *Sports Illustrated*, December 11, 2006, http://vault.sportillustrated.cnn.com/vault/article/magazine/MAG1114577/index.htm.

5. Gary Smith, "The Story of O," *Sports Illustrated*, June 18, 2007, http://vault.sportillustrated.cnn.com/vault/article/magazine/MAG1105359/index.htm.

6. Bill Sysken, "Bear Nescessity," *Sports Illustrated*, November 13, 2006, http://vault.sportillustrated.cnn.com/vault/article/magazine/MAG1108797/index.htm.

7. Phil Taylor, "Pennies from Heaven," *Sports Illustrated*, February 9, 2004, http://vault.sportillustrated.cnn.com/vault/article/magazine/MAG1141486/index.htm.

8. Jorge Iber, ed., "More Than Just *Peloteros* (Baseball Players): Latino/a Athletes in US Sports History," *International Journal of the History of Sport* (regional issue) 26, no. 7 (June 2009).

9. Steve Wilson, *The Boys from Little Mexico: A Season of Chasing the American Dream* (Boston: Beacon Press, 2010); Henry Cejudo and Bill Plaschke, *American Victory: Wrestling, Dream, and a Journey toward Home* (New York: New American Library, 2010); and Richard Lapchick, with Jared Bovinet, Charlie Harless, Chris Kamke, Cara-Lynn Lopresti, and Horacio Ruiz, *100 Campeones: Latino Groundbreakers Who Paved the Way in Sports* (Morgantown: West Virginia University Press, 2010).

10. Hope Yen, "Latinos Reach 50 Million in 2010 Census," http://www.dispatch-politics.com/live/content/national_world/stories/2011/03/25.

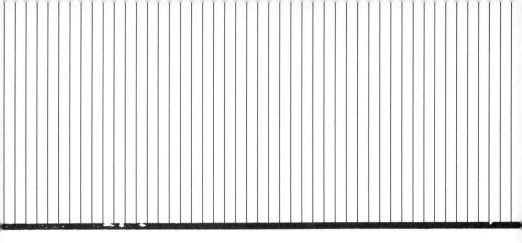

REFERENCES

Books

Abbel-Shehid, Gamal. *Who Da Man? Black Masculinities and Sporting Cultures.* Toronto: Canadian Scholars' Press, 2005.

Acuña, Rodolfo. *Occupied America: A History of Chicanos.* 8th ed. New York: Pearson Longman, 2014.

Adams, James T. *The Epic of America.* Boston: Little & Brown, 1931.

Alamillo, José. *Making Lemonade out of Lemons: Mexican American Labor and Leisure in a California Town, 1880–1960.* Urbana: University of Illinois Press, 2006.

———. "Mexican American Baseball: Masculinity, Racial Struggle, and Labor Politics in Southern California, 1930–1950." In *Sports Matters: Race, Recreation, and Culture,* edited by John Bloom and Michael Nevin Willard. New York: New York University Press, 2002.

———. "Peloteros in Paradise: Mexican American Baseball and Oppositional Politics in Southern California, 1930–1950." In *Mexican Americans and Sports: A Reader on Athletics and Barrio Life,* edited by Jorge Iber and Samuel O. Regalado. College Station: Texas A&M University Press, 2007.

Alexander, Charles C. *Our Game: An American Baseball History.* New York: Henry Holt and Company, 1991.

Alfonso, Jorge. *Puños dorados: Apuntes para la historia del boxeo en Cuba*. Santiago de Cuba: Editorial Oriente, 1988.

Anderson, Dave. *The Return of a Champion" Pancho Gonzalez' Golden Year, 1964*. Englewood Cliffs, NJ: Prentice-Hall, 1973.

Arredondo, Gabriela F. *Mexican Chicago: Race, Identity, and Nation, 1916–39*. Urbana: University of Illinois Press, 2008.

Atkinson, Michael. *Battleground Sports Vol. I*. Westport, Connecticut: Greenwood Press, 2009.

Baldassaro, Lawrence and Richard Johnson, eds. *The American Game: Baseball and Ethnicity*. Carbondale, IL: Southern Illinois University Press, 2002.

Balderrama, Francisco E., Richard A. Santillan, Samuel O. Regalado. *Mexican American Baseball in Los Angeles*. Mount Pleasant, SC: Arcadia Publishing, 2011.

Balibar, Etienne and Immanuel Wallerstein, eds. *Race, Nation, Class: Ambiguous Identities*. London: Verso, 1991.

Barker, Eugene, and Charles Potts, Charles Ramsdell. *A School History of Texas*. Chicago: Row, Peterson, 1918.

Bederman, Gail. *Manliness and Civilization: A Cultural History of Gender and Race in the United States*. Chicago: University of Chicago Press, 1995.

Bedicheck, Roy. "Bedicheck Papers," Box 3q44. Center for American History, University of Texas at Austin.

———. *Educational Competition: The Story of the University Interscholastic League of Texas*. Austin: University of Texas Press, 1956.

Beezley, William H. *Judas at the Jockey Club and Other Episodes of Porfirian Mexico*. Lincoln: University of Nebraska Press, 1987.

Bissinger, H. G. *Friday Night Lights: a Town, a Team, and a Dream*. Reading, Massachusetts: Addison-Wesley Publishing Company Incorporated, 1990.

Boddy, Kasia. *Boxing: A Cultural History*. London: Reaction Books, 2008.

Briley, Ron. "The Black Panther Party and the Revolt of the Black Athlete: Sport and Revolutionary Consciousness." In *Sports and the Racial Divide–African American and Latino Experience in an Era of Change*, edited by Michael E. Lomax. Jackson: University Press of Mississippi, 2008.

Brittan, Arthur. *Masculinity and Power*. New York: Basil Blackwell, 1989.

Brock, Lisa and Digna Castañeda Fuertes, eds. *Between Race and Empire: African-Americans and Cubans before the Cuban Revolution*. Philadelphia: Temple University Press, 1998.

Burgos, Adrian. *Playing America's Game: Baseball, Latinos, and the Color Line*. Berkeley: University of California Press, 2007.

Cackley, Jay. "Organized Sports for a Twentieth Century Invention." In *Learning Culture Through Sports: Explaining the Role of Sports in Society*, edited by Sandra Spickard Prettyman and Brian Lampman. Lanham, Maryland: Rowman & Littlefield Education, 2006.

Cashion, Ty. *Pigskin Pulpit: A Social History of Texas High School Football Coaches*. Austin: Texas State Historical Association, 1998.

Cejudo, Henry and Bill Plaschke. *American Victory: Wrestling, Dreams and a Journey Toward Home*. New York City: New American Library, 2010.

Cengel, Katya. *Bluegrass Baseball: A Year in the Minor League Life*. Lincoln, NE: University of Nebraska, 2012.

Chicago Recreation Commission. *Leisure Time Directory; Chicago Public and Semi-Public Recreation and Auxiliary Agencies*. Chicago: Chicago Recreation Commission, 1936.

——. *The Chicago Recreation Survey, 1937*. 5 vols. Chicago: Chicago Recreation Commission, 1937.

Creighton, James. *The Buccaneers: Corpus Christi Football, 1904–1974*. Corpus Christi, TX: self-published, 1975.

Currell, Susan. *The March of Spare Time: The Problem and Promise of Leisure in the Great Depression*. Philadelphia: University of Pennsylvania Press, 2005.

De León, Arnoldo. *The Tejano Community, 1836–1900*. Albuquerque: University of New Mexico Press, 1982.

——. *They Called Them Greasers: Anglo Attitudes Toward Mexicans in Texas, 1836–1900*. Austin: University of Texas Press, 1983.

Del Pino, Willy, ed. *Enciclopedia del boxeo cubano*. Miami: Manolo de la Tejera and Willy del Pino, 1988.

Denning, Michael. *Mechanic Accents: Dime Novels and Working-class Culture in America*. Haymarket Series. London: Verso, 1987.

Deutsch, Sarah. *No Separate Refuge: Culture, Class, and Gender on an Anglo-Hispanic Frontier, 1880–1940*. New York: Oxford University Press, 1987.

Dobrow, Marty. *Knocking on Heaven's Door: Six Minor Leaguers in Search of the Baseball Dream*. Amherst: University of Massachusetts Press, 2010.

Drinnon, Richard. *Facing West: The Metaphysics of Indian Hating & Empire Building*. New York: Schocken, 1980.

Dunning, Eric. *Sports Matters: Sociological Studies of Sport, Violence, and Civilization*. London: Routledge, 1999.

El Paso City Directory.

Encinosa, Enrique. *Azúcar y chocolate: Historia del boxeo cubano*. Miami: Ediciones Universal, 2004.

Estes, Steve. *I Am A Man! Race, Manhood, and the Civil Rights Movement.* Chapel Hill and London: University of North Carolina Press, 2005.

Fatsis, Stefan. *Wild and Outside.* New York: Walker and Company, 1996.

Fink, Rob. *Playing in Shadows: Texas and Negro League Baseball.* Lubbock: Texas Tech University Press, 2010.

Fleischer, Nat. *The Three Colored Aces: Story of George Dixon, Joe Gans and Joe Walcott and Several Contemporaries.* Vol. 3 of *Black Dynamite: The Story of the Negro in the Prize Ring from 1782 to 1938.* New York: The Ring Athletic Library, 1938.

Foley, Douglas E. *From Peones to Politicos: Class and Ethnicity in a South Texas Town, 1900–1987.* Mexican American Monographs. Austin: University of Texas Press, 1988.

Foley, Neil. *The White Scourge: Mexicans, Blacks, and Poor Whites in Texas Cotton Culture.* American Crossroads. Berkeley: University of California Press, 1997.

Franks, Joel S. *Crossing Sidelines, Crossing Cultures: Sport and Asian American Cultural Citizenship.* Lanham: University Press of America, 2000.

Gabaccia, Donna R. *From the Other Side: Women, Gender, and Immigrant Life in the U.S., 1820–1990.* Bloomington: Indiana University Press, 1994.

Gamio, Manuel. *The Mexican Immigrant His Life-Story.* Chicago: University of Chicago Press, 1931.

García, Juan R. *Mexicans in the Midwest, 1900–1932.* Tucson: University of Arizona Press, 1996.

Garcia, Maria Cristina. *Havana USA: Cuban Exiles and Cuban Americans in South Florida, 1959–1994.* Berkeley: University of California Press, 1996.

García, Mario T. *Desert Immigrants: The Mexicans of El Paso, 1880–1920.* New Haven: Yale University Press, 1981.

———. *Mexican Americans: Leadership, Ideology, and Identity, 1930–1960.* New Haven: Yale University Press, 1989.

García, Richard A. "The Mexican American Mind: A Product of the 1930s." In *History, Culture and Society: Chicano Studies in the 1980s,* edited by Mario T. García and Francisco Lomeli. Ypsilanti, Michigan: Bilingual Press, 1983.

Gilbert, Bill. *They Also Served: Baseball and the Home Front, 1941–1945.* New York: Crown Publishers, Incorporated, 1992.

Gilmore, Al-Tony. *Bad Nigger: The National Impact of Jack Johnson.* Port Washington, NY: Kenikat Press, 1975.

Gmelch, George. *Inside Pitch: Life in Professional Baseball.* Lincoln, NE: University of Nebraska, 2006.

Gomez-Quiñones, Juan. *Chicano Politics: Reality and Promise, 1940–1990*. Calvin P. Horn Lectures in Western History and Culture. Albuquerque: University of New Mexico Press, 1990.

Gonzales, Doreen. *Richard Pancho Gonzalez: Tennis Champion*. Springfield, NJ: Enslow Publishers, 1998.

———. *Tennis Legend: Pancho Gonzales*. Gregory Gonzalez Publishing, 2007.

Gonzales, Pancho, and Cy Rice. *Man with a Racket: The Autobiography of Pancho Gonzales*. New York: A.S. Barnes and Company, 1959.

González-Echevarría, Roberto. *The Pride of Havana: A History of Cuban Baseball*. New York: Oxford University Press, 1999.

Grimsley, Will. *Tennis: Its History, People and Events*. Englewood Cliffs, NJ: Prentice Hall Inc., 1971.

Grossman, James R. *Land of Hope: Chicago, Black Southerners, and the Great Migration*. Chicago: University of Chicago Press, 1989.

Grundy, Pamela. *Learning to Win: Sports. Education, and Social Change in Twentieth-Century North Carolina*. Chapel Hill: University of North Carolina Press, 2001.

Guridy, Frank Andre. *Forging Diaspora: Afro-Cubans and African-Americans in a World of Empire and Jim Crow*. Chapel Hill: University of North Carolina Press, 2010.

Gutierrez, David. *Between Two Worlds: Mexican Immigrants in the United States*. Jaguar Books on Latin America. Wilmington, DE: Scholarly Resources, 1996.

———. *Walls and Mirrors: Mexican Americans, Mexican Immigrants, and the Politics of Ethnicity*. Berkeley: University of California Press, 1995.

Guttmann, Allen. *From Ritual to Record: The Nature of Modern Sports*. Updated with a New Afterword. New York: Columbia University Press, 2004.

———. *Games and Empires: Modern Sports and Cultural Imperialism*. New York: Columbia University Press, 1994.

Hawkins, Mike. *Social Darwinism in European and American Thought, 1860–1945: Nature as Model and Nature as Threat*. Cambridge: Cambridge University Press, 1997.

Hayhurst, Dirk. *The Bullpen Gospels: Major League Dreams of a Minor League Veteran*. Sacramento, CA: Citadel, 2010.

Hernandez-Ehrisman, Laura. *Inventing the Fiesta City: Heritage and Carnival in San Antonio*. Albuquerque: University of New Mexico Press, 2008.

Hietala, Thomas R. *The Fight of the Century: Jack Johnson, Joe Louis and the Struggle for Racial Equality*. Armonk, NY: M.E. Sharpe, 2002.

Higgs, Robert. *God in the Stadium: Sports and Religion in America.* Lexington: University of Kentucky Press, 1995.

Hill, Jeff. *Sport, Leisure, and Culture in Twentieth-Century Britain.* New York: Palgrave, 2002.

Hispanics in the State of Texas: Trends from the 2000 Census. Texas: The Hispanic Research Center, University of Texas at San Antonio, 2002.

Hoffman, Abraham. *Unwanted Mexican Americans in the Great Depression: Repatriation Pressures, 1929–1939.* Tucson: University of Arizona Press, 1974.

Honor the Past, Mold the Future. Globe, AZ: Gila Centennials, Inc., 1976.

Iber, Jorge and Samuel O. Regalado, eds. *Mexican Americans in Sports: A Reader on Athletics and Barrio Life.* College Station: Texas A&M University Press, 2007.

Iber, Jorge, Samuel O. Regalado, Jose Alamillo and Anroldo de Leon. *Latinos in U.S. Sport: A History of Isolation, Cultural Identity, and Acceptance.* Champaign, Illinois: Human Kinetics, 2011.

Ingram, Bob and Ray Sánchez. *The Miners: The History of Sports at the University of Texas at El Paso.* El Paso: Mesa Publishing Corporation, 1997.

Ingram, Bob. *Baseball from Browns to Diablos.* Paul Brothers Publishing, 1991.

Innis-Jiménez, Michael. *Steel Barrio: The Great Mexican Migration to Chicago.* New York: New York University Press, 2013.

James, C. L. R. *Beyond a Boundary.* Durham: Duke University Press, 1993 (1963).

Karlen, Neal. *Slouching Toward Fargo.* New York: Avon Books, 1999.

Kendall, Dorothy Steinbomer. *Gentilz, Artist of the Old Southwest.* Austin: University of Texas Press, 1974.

Kent, Graeme. *The Great White Hopes: The Quest to Defeat Jack Johnson.* Gloucestershire, England: Sutton Publishing, 2005.

Keys, Barbara J. *Globalizing Sport: National Rivalry and International Community in the 1930s.* Cambridge, MA: Harvard University Press, 2006.

Kimmel, Michael S. "Baseball and the Reconstruction of American Masculinity, 1880–1920." In *Sport, Men, and the Gender Order: Critical Feminist Perspectives,* edited by Michael A. Messner and Donald F. Sabo. Champaign, Illinois: Human Kinetic Books, 1990.

Klein, Alan M. *Baseball on the Border: A Tale of Two Laredos.* Princeton, NJ: Princeton University Press, 1997.

———. *Growing the Game.* New Haven, CT: Yale University Press, 2006.

———. *Sugarball: The American Game, the Dominican Dream.* New Haven, CT: Yale University Press, 1991.

Kleinberg, S. J. *The Shadow of the Mills: Working-Class Families in Pittsburgh,*

1870–1907. Pittsburgh: University of Pittsburgh Press, 1989.

Kraus, Rebecca S. *Minor League Baseball: Community Building through Hometown Sports*. New York: Haworth, 2003.

Kurlansky, Mark. *The Eastern Stars: How Baseball Changed the Dominican Town of San Pedro de Macoris*. New York: Riverhead Books, 2010.

Lamb, David. *Stolen Season: A Journey through America and Baseball's Minor Leagues*. New York: Random House, 1991.

Lapchick, Richard with Jared Bovinet, Charlie Harless, Chris Kamke, Cara-Lynn Lopresti, and Horacio Ruiz. *100 Campeones: Latino Groundbreakers Who Paved the Way in Sports*. Morgantown, WV: West Virginia University, 2010.

Lea, Tom. *The King Ranch* (2 Volumes). Boston: Little, Brown and Co., 1957.

Lears, T. J. Jackson, *No Place of Grace: Antimodernism and the Transformation of American Culture, 1880–1920*. New York: Pantheon, 1981.

Lomax, Michael E. *Sports and the Racial Divide–African American and Latino Experience in an Era of Change*, edited by Michael E. Lomax. Jackson: University Press of Mississippi, 2008.

Loubet, Nat and John Ort. *The Ring Boxing Encyclopedia and Record Book*. New York: The Ring Book Shop, 1978.

Lynch, Dudley. *The Duke of Duval: The Life and Times of George B. Parr*. Waco: Texian Press, 1976.

MacMurray, Bill. *Texas High School Football*. South Bend: Icarus Press, 1985.

Mandel, Brett. *Minor Players, Major Dreams*. Lincoln, NE: University of Nebraska, 1997.

Manuel, Herschel. *The Education of Spanish-Speaking Children in Texas*. Austin: University of Texas Press, 1930.

Maraniss, David. *Clemente: The Passion and Grace of Baseball's Last Hero*. New York: Simon & Schuster, 2006.

Martin, Charles H. *Benching Jim Crow: The Rise and Fall of the Color Line in Southern College Sports, 1890–1980*. Urbano: University of Illinois Press, 2010.

McCann, Peggy and Martha Ewing. "Motivation and Outcomes of Youth Participation in Sport." In *Learning Culture Through Sports: Explaining the Role of Sports in Society*, edited by Sandra Spickard Prettyman and Brian Lampman. Lanham, MD: Rowman & Littlefield Education, 2006.

McCarthy, Matt. *Odd Man Out: A Year on the Mound with a Minor League Misfit*. New York: Viking, 2009.

McDevitt, Patrick F. *May the Best Man Win: Sport, Masculinity and Nationalism in Great Britain and the Empire, 1880–1935*. New York: Palgrave MacMillan, 2004.

McMurray, Bill. *Texas High School Football*. South Bend: Icarus Press, 1985.

McWilliams, Carey. *North from Mexico: The Spanish-Speaking People of the United States*. New York: Greenwood, 1968 (1948).

Menéndez, Elio and Víctor Joaquín Ortega. *Kid Chocolate: El boxeo soy yo*. Havana: Editorial Obre, 1980.

Menéndez, Elio and Víctor Joaquín Ortega. *Kid Chocolate: El boxeo soy yo*. 2nd ed. Havana: Editorial Pablo de la Torriente, 1990.

Messner, Michael A. "Masculinities and Athletic Careers: Bonding and Status Differences." In *Sport, Men, and the Gender Order: Critical Feminist Perspectives*, edited by Michael A. Messner and Donald F. Sabo. Champaign, Illinois: Human Kinetic Books, 1990.

———. *Power at Play: Sports and the Problem of Masculinity*. Boston: Beacon Press, 1992.

Messner, Michael A. and David F. Sabo. *Sex, Violence and Power in Sports: Rethinking Masculinity*. Freedom, CA: The Crossing Press, 1994.

Miller, Marilyn Grace. *Rise and Fall of the Cosmic Race: The Cult of Mestizaje in Latin America*. Austin: University of Texas Press, 2004.

Miller, Robert Ryal and William J. Orr, eds. *Daily Life in Colonial Mexico: The Journey of Friar Ilariano da Bergamo, 1761–1768*. trans. William J. Orr. Norman: University of Oklahoma Press, 2000.

Miller, Toby, Geoffrey Lawrence, Jim McKay, and David Rowe. *Globalization and Sport: Playing the World*. London: Sage Publications, 2001.

Monday, Jane Clements and Betty Bailey Colley. *Voices from the Wild Horse Desert: The Vaquero Families of the King and Kenedy Ranches*. Austin: University of Texas Press, 1997.

Monroy, Douglas. *Rebirth: Mexican Los Angeles from the Great Migration to the Great Depression*. Berkeley: University of California Press, 1999.

Montejano, David. *Anglos and Mexicans in the Making of Texas, 1836–1986*. Austin: University of Texas Press, 1987.

Morgan, William J. *Why Sports Socially Matter*. New York: Routledge, 2006.

Mormino, Gary R. and George E. Pozzetta. *The Immigrant World of Ybor City: Italians and Their Latin Neighbors in Tampa, 1885–1985*. Urbana: University of Illinois Press, 1987.

Odem, Mary E. *Delinquent Daughters: Protecting and Policing Adolescent Female Sexuality in the United States, 1885–1920*. Chapel Hill: University of North Carolina Press, 1995.

Oriard, Michael. *King Football: Sport and Spectacle in the Golden Age of Radio and Newsreels, Movies and Magazines, the Weekly & the Daily Press*. Chapel

Hill: University of North Carolina Press, 2001.

———. *Reading Football: How the Popular Press Created an American Spectacle.* Chapel Hill: University of North Carolina Press, 1993.

Pacyga, Dominic A. *Polish Immigrants and Industrial Chicago: Workers on the South Side, 1880–1922.* Columbus: Ohio State University Press, 1991.

Paredes, Américo. *Folklore and Culture on the Texas-Mexican Border.* Austin: CMAS Books, University of Texas Press, 1993.

Payne, Charles M. *I've Got the Light of Freedom: The Organizing Tradition and the Mississippi Freedom Struggle.* Berkeley: University of California Press, 1995.

Pescador, Juan Javier. "*Los Heroes del Domingo*: Soccer, Borders, and Social Spaces in Great Lakes Michigan." In *Mexican Americans and Sports: A Reader on Athletics and Barrio Life,* edited by Jorge Iber and Samuel O. Regalado. College Station: Texas A&M University Press, 2007.

Pratt, Mary Louise. *Imperial Eyes: Travel Writing and Transculturation.* New York: Routledge, 1992.

Quirk, J., and R. Fort. *Pay Dirt: The Business of Professional Team Sports.* Princeton, NJ: Princeton University Press, 1997.

Ramírez, Catherine S. *The Woman in the Zoot Suit: Gender, Nationalism, and the Cultural Politics of Memory.* Durham and London: Duke University Press, 2009.

Ratliff, Harold., *Autumn's Mightiest Legions: History of Texas Schoolboy Football.* Waco: Texian Press, 1963.

Regalado, Samuel O. "Invisible Identity: Mexican American Sport and Chicano Historiography." In *Mexican Americans and Sports: A Reader on Athletics and Barrio Life,* edited by Jorge Iber and Samuel O. Regalado. College Station: Texas A&M University Press, 2007.

———. *Viva Baseball!: Latin Major Leaguers and Their Special Hunger.* Urbana: University of Illinois Press, 1998.

———. *Viva Baseball: Latin Major Leaguers and Their Special Hunger.* 3rd ed. Urbana: University of Illinois Press, 2008.

Ressler, William Harris. "Minor Leaguers: Chasing the Dream and Touching Home." *Chasing Dreams: Baseball & Becoming American,* ed. Joshua Perelman, 212–17. Philadelphia: National Museum of American Jewish History, 2014.

———."How a Baseball Team Gets Its Communications Across the Plate." *Employee Communications Guidebook,* ed. Lane F. Cooper, vol. 4, 30–33. Rockville, MD: PRNews Press, 2013.

Rivera Ayala, Sergio. "Lewd Songs and Dances from the Streets of Eighteenth-Century New Spain." In *Rituals of Rule, Rituals of Resistance: Public Celebrations and Popular Culture in Mexico,* ed. William H. Beezley, Cheryl English Martin, and William E. French. Wilmington, DE: Scholarly Resources, 1994.

Roberts, Randy. *Papa Jack: Jack Johnson and the Era of White Hopes.* New York: The Free Press, 1983.

Rooney, John. *A Geography of American Sport: From Cabin Creek to Anaheim.* Social Significance of Sport. Reading, PA: Addison-Wesley, 1974.

Rosaldo, Renato. *Culture and Truth: The Remaking of Social Analysis.* Boston: Beacon Press, 1989.

Rosengren, John. *The Fight of Their Lives: How Juan Marichal and John Roseboro Turned Baseball's Ugliest Brawl Into a Story of Forgiveness and Redemption.* Guilford, CT: Lyons Press, 2014.

Runyon, Robert. "Rio Grande Valley Photographs, 1912–1949." Robert Runyon Collection, Center for American History, University of Texas at Austin.

Sammons, Jeffrey T. *Beyond The Ring: The Role of Boxing in American Society.* Urbana, IL: University of Illinois Press, 1988.

San Miguel, Guadalupe. *"Let All of Them Take Heed": Mexican Americans and the Campaign for Educational Equality in Texas, 1910–1981.* Mexican American Monographs. Austin: Center for Mexican American Studies, University of Texas at Austin, 1987.

Sanchez Korrol, Virginia. *From Colonia to Community: The History of Puerto Ricans in New York City.* Berkeley: University of California Press, 1994.

Sanchez, George J. *Becoming Mexican American: Ethnicity, Culture, and Identity in Chicano Los Angeles, 1900–1945.* New York: Oxford University Press, 1993.

Sánchez, Ray. *El Paso's Greatest Sports Heroes I Have Known.* El Paso, Texas: The Sunturians Press, 1989.

———. *The Good, the Bad, and the Funny of El Paso Sports History.* El Paso: Mesa Publishing Corporation, 2013.

Santillán, Richard, Mark A. Ocegueda, and Terry A. Cannon. "Mexican Baseball Teams in the Midwest, 1916–1965: The Politics of Cultural Survival and Civil Rights." In *Sports and the Racial Divide–African American and Latino Experience in an Era of Change,* edited by Michael E. Lomax. Jackson: University Press of Mississippi, 2008.

———. *Mexican American Baseball in the Inland Empire.* Mount Pleasant, SC: Arcadia Publishing, 2012.

Sarabia Viejo, María Justina. *El juego de los gallos en la Nueva España.* Seville: Escuela de Estudios Hispanoamericanos, 1972.

Seebohm, Caroline. *Little Pancho: The Life of Tennis Legend Pancho Segura.* Lincoln: University of Nebraska Press, 2009.

Smith, Ronald. *Sports and Freedom: The Rise of Big-Time College Athletics.* Sports and History. New York: Oxford University Press, 1988.

Solomon, Arthur P. *Making It in the Minors: A Team Owner's Lessons in the Business of Baseball.* Jefferson, NC: McFarland, 2011.

Spickard Prettyman, Sandra. "Coaches, Language, and Power." In *Learning Culture Through Sports: Explaining the Role of Sports in Society,* edited by Sandra Spickard Prettyman and Brian Lampman. Lanham, MD: Rowman & Littlefield Education, 2006.

Spielvogel, Jackson J. *World History: The Human Odyssey.* Lincolnwood, IL: National Textbook Company, 1999.

Stoldt, G., S. Dittmore, and S. Branvold. *Sport Public Relations: Managing Organizational Communication.* Champaign, IL: Human Kinetics Publishers, 2006.

Stowers, Carlton. *Friday Night Heroes: A Look at Texas High School Football.* Austin: Eakin Press, 1983.

Sugden, John. *Boxing and Society: An International Analysis.* Manchester: Manchester University Press, 1996.

Taylor, Paul Schuster. *Mexican Labor in the United States: Chicago and the Calumet Region.* University of California Publications in Economics, vol 7, no 2. Berkeley: University of California Press, 1932.

Taylor, Paul. *An American-Mexican Frontier: Nueces County, Texas.* Chapel Hill: University of North Carolina Press, 1934.

Travers, Steve. *One Night, Two Teams: Alabama vs. USC and the Game That Changed a Nation.* Lanham: Taylor Trade Publishing, 2007.

Tyson, Timothy B. *Radio Free Dixie: Robert F. Williams and the Roots of Black Power.* Chapel Hill: University of North Carolina Press, 1999.

Ulica, Jorge. *Crónicas Diabólicas de "Jorge Ulica"/Jorge Arce.* Ed. J. Rodriguez. San Diego: Maize Press, 1982.

Valdés, Dennis Nodín. *Al Norte: Agricultural Workers in the Great Lakes Region, 1917–1970.* Austin: University of Texas Press, 1991.

———. *Barrios Norteños: St. Paul and Midwestern Mexican Communities in the Twentieth Century.* Austin: University of Texas Press, 2000.

Vargas, Zaragosa. *Proletarians of the North: A History of Mexican Industrial Workers in Detroit and the Midwest, 1917–1933.* Berkeley: University of California Press, 1993.

Viqueira Albán, Juan Pedro. *Propriety and Permissiveness in Bourbon Mexico.* Trans. Sonya Lipsett-Rivera and Sergio Rivera Ayala. Wilmington, DE: Scholarly Resources, 1999.

Ward, Geoffrey C. *Unforgivable Blackness: The Rise and Fall of Jack Johnson.* New York: Alfred A. Knopf, 2004.

Webb, Walter P. *The Texas Rangers.* Cambridge: Houghton Mifflin, 1935.

Wendel, Tim. *The New Face of Baseball: The One-Hundred Years Rise and Triumph of Latinos in America's Favorite Sport.* New York: HarperCollins, 2003.

West Davison, James, Brian DeLay, Christine Leigh Heyrman, Mark H. Lyte, and Michal B. Stoff. *U.S. A Narrative History Vol. 2: Since 1865.* Boston: McGraw-Hill, 2009.

Wilcox, D. and G. Cameron. *Public Relations Strategies and Tactics.* 8th ed. New York: Pearson Education, 2006.

Williams, Charlie. "South Texas Football." *Texas Coach* (1979).

Wilson, Steve. *The Boys from Little Mexico: A Season Chasing the American Dream.* Boston, MA: Beacon Press, 2010.

Woodward, Kath. *Boxing, Masculinity and Identity: The "I" of the Tiger.* London: Routledge, 2007.

Periodicals

Ashton, Jay. "Pancho Dreams of Other Days." *Kingsville Record*, May 20, 1936, 4.

Baxter, Kevin. "USC's Mark Sanchez Has More Than Pads on His Shoulders". *Los Angeles Times,* December 29, 2008, http://www.latimes.com/news/printedition/front-la-sp-sanchez29-2008dec29.0.752102.story?page=3.

Bedicheck, Roy. brief article, *Interscholastic Leaguer* 32, no. 2 (1948): 2.

———. "Editorial," *Interscholastic Leaguer* 30, no. 2 (1946): 2.

Bennett, R. "Sports Sponsorship, Spectator Recall, and False Consensus." *European Journal of Marketing* 33, nos. 3 and 4 (1999): 291–313.

Birch, J. "New Factors in Crisis Planning and Response." *Public Relations Quarterly* 39, no. 1 (1994): 31–4.

Boyd, Hugh. "Brahmas Tie." *Kingsville Record*, October 11, 1933, 2.

———. "Sideline Chatter." *Kingsville Record*, October 18, 1933, 2.

Boyle, R., W. Dinan, and S. Morrow. "Doing the Business: Reporting of the Business of Football." *Journalism* 3, no. 2 (2002): 161–81.

Braysmith, H. "Constructing Athletic Agents in the Chicano/Chicana Culture of Los Angeles." *International Journal of the History of Sport* 22, no. 2 (2005): 177–95.

Brown, S. "Can European Football Spur Interest in American Soccer? A Look at the Champions World Series and Major League Soccer." *Soccer and Society* 6, no. 1 (2005): 49–61.

Burgos, Adrian Jr. "Playing Ball in a Black and White 'Field of Dreams:' Afro-Caribbean Ballplayers in the Negro Leagues, 1910–1950." *The Journal of Negro History* 82, no. 1 (1997): 67–104.

Camarillo, Alberto M. "Research Note on Chicano Community Leaders: the G.I. Generation." *Aztlán* 2 (Fall 1971): 145–50.

Cinisomo, Vincent. "Los Yanquis: Latino Players Are at the Heart of America's Team." *Hispanic*, October 2000: 46.

Ciotola, Nicholas P. "Spignesi, Sinatra, and the Pittsburg Steelers: Franco's Italian Army as an Expression of Ethnic Identity, 1972–1977." *Journal of Sport History* 27, no. 2 (Summer 2000): 271–289.

Cohen, A. "Soccer Madness! The New Women's Professional Soccer League Has a TV Contract and the World's Best Players, But Time Will Tell Whether It Can Develop Facilities and A Following." *Athletic Business* (November 2000): 45–54.

Collins, S. "National Sports and Other Myths: The Failure of US Soccer." *Soccer and Society* 7, no. 2–3 (2006): 355–63.

Corpus Christi Caller, 17 March, 1980.

Crompton, J., and D. Howard. "The American Experience with Facility Naming Rights: Opportunities for English Professional Football Teams." *Managing Leisure* 8, no. 4 (2003): 212–26.

Delgado, F. "Major League Soccer: The Return of the Foreign Sport." *Sport and Social Issues* 21, no. 3 (1997): 285–97.

Delgado, F. ——. "Sport and Politics: Major League Soccer, Constitution, and Latino Audiences." *Sport and Society* 23, no. 3 (1999): 41–54.

DeVarona, D. " 'M's' in Football: Myths, Management, Marketing, Media, and Money: A Reprise." *Soccer and Society* 4, no. 2 (2003): 7–13.

Duval County Picture, 16 October, 1991.

Edinburg Daily Review, 9 October, 1991.

El Continental (El Paso, Texas).

El Paso Herald-Post.

El Paso Times.

Faflik, D. "Futbol America: Hemispheric Sport as Border Studies." *Americana* 5, no. 1 (2006): 1–12.

Farber, Michael. "Last Swing in Montreal." *Sports Illustrated*, 18 March, 2002.

Ferrand, M., and M. Pages. "Image Management in Sports Organizations: The Creation of Value." *European Journal of Marketing* 33, nos. 3/4 (1999): 387–401.

Flores Hernández, Benjamín. "Organización de corridas de toros en la Nueva España del siglo xviii y primeros años del xix." *Anuario de Estudios Americanos* vol. 61, no. 2 (2004): 491–515.

Foley, Douglas E., "The Great American Football Ritual: Reproducing Race, Class and Gender Inequality." *Sociology of Sport Journal* 7 (1990): 111–35.

Fridman, Daniel and David Sheinin. "Wild Bulls, Discarded Foreigners and Brash Champions: U.S. Empire and the Cultural Construction of Argentine Boxers." *Left History* 12 (2007): 52–77.

Gardner, A. "MLS puts heads together for new game plan." *USA Today*, August 1, 2002.

Gems, Gerald R. "The Construction, Negotiation, and Transformation of Racial Identity in American Football: A Study of Native Americans and African Americans." *American Indian Culture and Research Journal* 22 (1998): 131–44.

Giulianotti, R. "Supporters, Fans, and Flaneurs: A Taxonomy of Spectator Identities in Football." *Sport and Social Issues* 26, no. 1 (2002): 25–46.

Gomez, Pedro. "Latin Players Could Use More Support," *Sporting News*, June 3, 2002: 30.

Guttmann, Allen. "Sport, Politics and the Engaged Historian." *Journal of Contemporary History* 38, no. 3 (July 2003): 363–75.

Handman, Max. "San Antonio: The Old Capital City of Mexican Life and Influence." *The Survey* (1931): 163–66.

Harmon, Tom. "Champs of the Hardwood." *Spark, the Bi-Weekly News Magazine* 2:9 (April 23, 1951): 19–20.

Herbig, P., and R. Yelkur. "Differences between Hispanic and Anglo Consumer Expectations." *Journal of Management Decisions* 35, no. 2 (1997): 125–32.

Herbst, D. "Soccer Gets Some Passing Grades After a Promising First Year." *Soccer* (1997): 38–39.

Houston Chronicle, April 23, 1982.

Howell, Colin D. "Baseball and Borders: The Diffusion of Baseball into Mexican and Canadian-American Borderland Regions, 1885–1911." *NINE: A Journal of Baseball History and Culture* volume 11, number 2 (Spring 2003): 16–26.

Iber, Jorge. "Mexican Americans of South Texas Football: The Athletic and Coaching Careers of E.C. Lerma and Bobby Cavazos, 1932–1965." *Southwestern Historical Quarterly* 105, no. 4 (2002): 616–33.

———. "A Vaquero in the Backfield: The Career of Bobby Cavazos, Texas Tech's

First Hispanic All American." *College Football Historical Society* 14 (2001): 1–5.

Irwin, R., D. Zwick, and W. Sutton. "Assessing Organizational Attributes Contributing to Marketing Excellence in American Professional Sports Franchises." *European Journal of Marketing* 33, nos. 3/4 (1999): 314–27.

Jaimeson, Katherine M. "Reading Nancy Lopez: Decoding Representations of Race, Class, and Sexuality." *Sociology of Sport Journal* 15 (4) (1998): 343–59.

Jewell, T. and D. Molina. "An Evaluation of the Relationship between Hispanics and Major League Soccer." *Sports Economics* 6, no. 2 (2005): 160–77.

Kauffman, J. "Lost in Space: A Critique of NASA's Crisis Communications in the Columbia disaster." *Public Relations Review* 31 (2005): 263–75.

Kelley, S., K. Hoffman, and S. Carter. "Franchise Relocation and Sport Introduction: A Sports Marketing Case Study of the Carolina Hurricanes' Fan Adoption Plan." *Services Marketing* 13, no. 6 (1999): 469–80.

Kidd, Rodney. "Molding the Character of Youth: The Texas Interscholastic League and Friday Mountain Boys Camp." New York Times Oral History Program. University of Texas Regional History of Business in the Southwest, no. 5, ed. Meyer, I. Austin: University of Texas, 1971.

Kuper, S. "The World's Game is not Just a Game." *The New York Times*, May 26, 2002.

Laredo Times, March 14, 1982.

LeCompte, Mary Lou and William H. Beezley. "Any Sunday in April: The Rise of Sport in San Antonio and the Hispanic Borderlands." *Journal of Sport History* 13 (1986): 128–46.

LeCompte, Mary Lou. "The Hispanic Influence on the History of Rodeo, 1823–1922." *Journal of Sport History* 12(1) (1985): 21–38.

Lopez, J. "Welcome, MLS, to the Digital Age." *The Houston Chronicle*, January 26, 2006.

Lozano Armendares, Teresa. "Tablajeros coimes y tahures en la Nueva España ilustrada." *Estudios de Historia Novohispana* vol. 15 (1995): 67–86.

Lozano, Teresa. "Los juegos de azar. ¿Una pasión novohispana? Legislación sobre juegos de azar en Nueva España. Siglo xviii." *Estudios de Histora Novohispana* vol. 11 (1991): 155–81.

Lubbock Avalanche Journal, August 15, 1951.

Mahony, D. and D. Howard. "Sport Business in the Next Decade: A General Overview of Expected Trends." *Sport Management* 15, no. 4 (2001): 275–96.

Mariscal, J. "Chicanos and Latinos in the Jungle of Sports Talk Radio." *Journal of Sport and Social Issues* 23, no. 1 (1999): 111–17.

Markovits, A. and S. Hellerman. "The 'Olympianization' of Soccer in the United States." *American Behavioral Scientist* 46, no. 11 (2005): 1533–49.

Martin Alcoff, Linda. "Latino vs. Hispanic: The Politics of Ethnic Names." *Philosophy and Social Criticism* 31(4) (2005): 395–407.

Martin, Charles H. "Integrating New Year's Day: The Racial Politics of College Bowl Games in the American South." *Journal of Sport History* 24, no. 3 (Fall 1997): 358–77.

Mason, D. "What Is the Sports Product and Who Buys It? The Marketing of Professional Sports Leagues." *European Journal of Marketing* 33, nos. 3/4 (1999): 402–18.

May, Mark. "Legend by Example." *The Monitor* (McAllen, Texas), September 9, 1997, 1–3C.

Morgan, Thomas. "The Texas Giant Awakens." *Look* 27, no. 19 (1963), 71–75.

Mormino, Gary Ross. "The Playing Fields of St. Louis: Italian Immigrants and Sports, 1925–1941." *Journal of Sports History* 9, no. 2 (Summer 1982): 5–19.

Osborn, E. C. "Doc". "The History of Sports in the Rio Grande Valley." *Brownsville Herald*, December 6, 1942, 1.

Passwaters, M. "Houston 1836 Logo, Colors, Unveiled." In Major League Soccer press release, January 25, 2006.

Pescador, J. "¡Vamos Taximaroa! Mexican/Chicano Soccer Associations and Transnational/Translocal Communities, 1967–2002." *Latino Studies* 2, no. 3 (2004): 352–76.

Peters, Ken. "Southern California QB Sanchez to Enter NFL Draft." *Associated Press*, January 15, 2009, http://news.yahoo.com/s/ap/20090115/ap_on_sp_co_nc/fbc_usc_sanchez.

Ramos, R. "Kicking Around Houston 1836: Soccer Team Sends the Wrong Message to Latinos". *Houston Chronicle*, January 28, 2006.

Regalado, Samuel O. "Baseball in the Barrios: The Scene in East Los Angeles Since World War II." *Baseball History* 1 (1996): 47–59.

———. "Hey Chico! The Latin Identity in Major League Baseball," *NINE: A Journal of Baseball History and Culture* 11, no. 1 (Fall 2002): 18–19, 23.

Ressler, William Harris, Ian Rebhan, and Jesse Goldberg-Strassler. "Is This Heaven? It's the World Baseball Classic: Field of Dreams Moments in Global, Domestic, and Internal Marketing." *NINE: A Journal of Baseball History and Culture* 22(1) (2013): 78–102.

Ressler, William Harris, Sebastian Itman Bocchi, and Patricia Rodríguez María. "English- and Spanish-Speaking Minor League Baseball Players' Perspectives on Community Service and the Psychosocial Benefit of Helping Children."

NINE: A Journal of Baseball History and Culture 20(1) (2011): 92–116.

Riess, Steven A. 'Introduction: Sport and the American Jew'. *American Jewish History* 74 (1985): 211–22.

Roberts, Kenneth. "The Docile Mexican." *Saturday Evening Post* 200, no. 37 (1928): 41.

Romero, S. "What's in a Brand Name? Houston Just Found Out." *The New York Times*, January 27, 2006.

Rosales, Francisco Arturo, and Daniel T Simon. "Mexican Immigrant Experience in the Urban Midwest: East Chicago, Indiana, 1919–1945." *Indiana Magazine of History* 77, no. 4 (December 1981): 333–57.

"Rugby Football." *San Antonio Express*, December 23, 1893, 6.

Sammons, Jeffrey T. " 'Race' and Sport: A Critical, Historical Examination." *Journal of Sport History* 21, no. 3 (1994): 203–78.

San Miguel, Guadalupe. "The Struggle Against Separate and Unequal Schools: Middle Class Mexican Americans, and the Desegregation Campaign in Texas, 1929–1957." *History of Education Quarterly* (Fall 1983): 343–59.

Santillán, Richard. "Mexican Baseball Teams in the Midwest, 1916–1965: the Politics of Cultural Survival and Civil Rights." *Perspectives in Mexican American Studies* 7 (Spring 2001), 131–51.

Satterlee, T. "Making Soccer a 'Kick in the Grass.' " *International Review for the Sociology of Sport* 26, no. 3 (2001): 305–17.

Sheed, Wilfred. "Why Sports Matter." *Wilson Historical Quarterly* (Winter 1995): 10–25.

Sosa, Jason and Jacqueline McDowell. "Fan Perceptions of Latino Baseball Players and Their Influence on Overall Fan Satisfaction with Major League Baseball." *NINE: A Journal of Baseball History and Culture* 20(1) (2011): 81–91.

Teja, Jesús F. de la. "Discovering the Tejano Community in 'Early' Texas." *Journal of the Early Republic* vol. 18, no. 1 (Spring 1998): 73–98.

Thompson, Merrell E. and Claude C. Dove. "A Comparison of Physical Achievement of Anglo and Spanish American Boys in Junior High School." *Research Quarterly* 13 (1942): 341–46.

Trussell, Jake, weekly column, *Kingsville Record,* June 11, 1947.

———. "Brahmas Defeat Taft Quint Here Friday Night, 39–28." *Kingsville Record,* December 15, 1948.

———."Brahmas Win District Track and Field Meet." *Kingsville Record,* April 13, 1949.

———. "Brahmas Win Magic Valley Relays at Pharr." *Kingsville Record,* March 23, 1949.

———. "Cavazos Graduates at Tarleton College." *Kingsville Record,* January 25, 1950.

———. "Cavazos only Kingsville Athlete to Place in Border Olympics Held in Laredo." *Kingsville Record,* March 16, 1949.

———. "Former Brahma Gridders Make Good in College Play." *Kingsville Record,* October 19, 1949.

———. "Kingsville Record 1948 All South Texas Football Team." *Kingsville Record,* December 1, 1948.

———. "Browning's Brahmas Win 27–21 Thriller from Coyotes to Blast Alice Title Hopes." *Kingsville Record,* November 11, 1948.

———. "Brownsville Noses Brahmas 20–19 in Thrill-Packed Contest." *Kingsville Record,* October 13, 1948.

———. "Coaches Rate Brahma as 1948 Darkhorse." *Kingsville Record,* August 25, 1948.

———. "Hass Paces Hard-Fighting Brahma Herd to 18–13 Win Over Robstown Pickers." *Kingsville Record,* November 24, 1948.

———. "Laredo Tigers Get Breaks in 20–13 Win Over Brahmas." *Kingsville Record,* September 22, 1948.

———. "Marsters, Cavazos Chosen on All-District Cage Team." *Kingsville Record,* February 16, 1949.

———. "Thirty Brahmas Leave Camp Tuesday Morning." *Kingsville Record,* September 1, 1948.

———. Weekly column. *Kingsville Record,* August 19, 1953.

———. Weekly column. *Kingsville Record,* March 19, 1952.

———. Weekly column. *Kingsville Record,* December 2, 1953.

———. Weekly column. *Kingsville Record,* November 21, 1951.

———. Weekly column. *Kingsville Record,* November 28, 1951.

———. Weekly column. *Kingsville Record,* February 3, 1954.

———. "Thirty Brahmas Leave Camp Tuesday Morning." *Kingsville Record,* September 8, 1948.

Wallace Adams, David. "More Than A Game: The Carlisle Indians Take to the Gridiron, 1893–1917." *Western Historical Quarterly* 32 (2001): 25–53.

Wrigley, B., C. Salmon, and H. Park. "Crisis Management Planning and the Threat of Bioterrorism." *Public Relations Review* 29, no. 3 (2003): 281–90.

Yoseloff, Anthony A. "From Ethnic Hero to National Icon: The Americanization of Joe DiMaggio." *The International Journal of the History of Sport* 16 (1999): 1–20.

Interviews and Speeches

David Carrasco, Interview 154 (1973), Institute of Oral History, University of Texas at El Paso.

David Carrasco, Interview 250 (1976), Institute of Oral History, University of Texas at El Paso.

Hinojosa, Rene. interview by Joel Huerta, McAllen, Texas, 1999.

Lerma, Everardo C. interview by Joel Huerta. McAllen, Texas, 1995.

Lerma, Lydia Campbell. interview by Joel Huerta. McAllen, Texas, 1996.

Ramey, Dr. L.E., Speech given by this individual on April 4, 1989.

Theses and Dissertations

Baur, Edward Jackson. "Delinquency among Mexican Boys in South Chicago." Master's thesis, University of Chicago, 1938.

Folsom Cobb, Albert. "Comparative Study of the Athletic Ability of Latin American and Anglo American Boys on a Junior High School Level." Master's thesis, University of Texas, 1952.

Garcilazo, Jeffrey Marcos. "'Traqueros:' Mexican Railroad Workers in the United States, 1870–1930." PhD diss., University of California, Santa Barbara, 1995.

Gonzalez, Jovita. "Social Life in Cameron, Starr, and Zapata Counties." Master's thesis, University of Texas at Austin, 1930.

Guridy, Frank Andre. "Racial Knowledge in Cuba: The Production of a Social Fact, 1912–1944." PhD diss., University of Michigan, 2002.

Huerta, Joel. "Red, Brown, and Blue: A History and Cultural Poetics of High School Football in Mexican America". PhD diss., University of Texas at Austin, 2005.

Johnson, Roberta Muriel. "History of the Education of Spanish-Speaking Children in Texas." Master's thesis, University of Texas, 1932.

Kerr, Louise Año Nuevo. "The Chicano Experience in Chicago, 1920–1970." PhD diss., University of Illinois at Chicago Circle, 1976.

Kilbourne Harris, James. "A Sociological Study of a Mexican School in San Antonio, Texas." Master's thesis, University of Texas, 1927.

King, Genevieve. "The Psychology of a Mexican Community in San Antonio, Texas." Master's thesis, University of Texas, 1936.

McCarthy, Malachy R. "Which Christ Came to Chicago: Catholic and Protestant Programs to Evangelize, Socialize and Americanize the Mexican Immigrant, 1900–1940." PhD diss., Loyola University of Chicago, 2002.

Meyer, Francis Edward. "A Comparison of the Football Programs of Some AAA High Schools in the State of Texas." Master's thesis, University of Texas, 1958.

Pratt, J. "The Role of Non-Professional Soccer Clubs and Leagues on Latin American Immigrants in the United States." Master's thesis, Florida State University, 2005.

Walsh Shaw, Bruce. "Sociometric Status and Athletic Ability of Anglo American and Latin American Boys in a San Antonio Junior High School." Master's thesis, University of Texas, 1951.

Websites

Griffith, S. "Democrats Launch World Cup Ads to Troll for Latino Votes." http:// juantornce.blogs.com/hispanictrending/2006/07/democrats_launc.html.

Keeney, D. "Houston 1836: A Branding Blunder." http://www.keeneypr.com/en/ art/?140.

———. "Houston Dynamo Introduced as Team Hopes to End Houston 1836 Controversy." http:// www.keeneypr.com/en/art/?152.

Taylor, P., C. Funk, and P. Craighill. "Americans to the Rest of the World: Soccer Not Really Our Thing." The Pew Research Center, 2006. http://pewresearch. org/pubs/315/americans-to-rest-of-world-soccer-not-really-our-thing.

Trecker, J. "1836 is History in Houston; Dynamo It Is." http://msn.foxsports. com/soccer/story/5386256.

Veiga, A. "2006 World Cup Gives Univision Ratings a Boost." http://www.examiner.com/a-170364? World_Cup_Gives_Univision_Ratings_Boost.html.

Wagner, J. "A Living Case Study on Multi-Cultural Communications." http:// wagnercomm.blogspot. com/2006/02/living-case-study-on-multi-cultural. html.

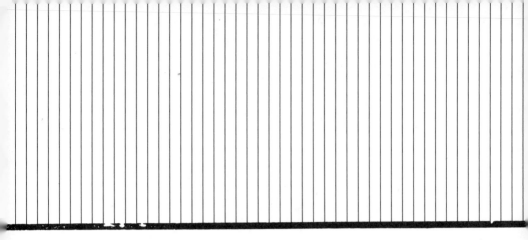

CONTRIBUTORS

José M. Alamillo is professor and coordinator of the Chicano/a Studies Program at California State University Channel Islands (Camarillo). He is the author of *Making Lemonade out of Lemons: Mexican American Labor and Leisure in a California Town, 1900–1960* (2006) and coauthor *of Latinos in U.S. Sport: A History of Isolation, Cultural Identity, and Acceptance* (2011). He teaches courses in Chicana/o studies, Latino/a studies, immigration and labor, sports, and community service-learning.

Enver M. Casimir is an instructor at The Brearley School. He is currently at work on a book-length project on the career of Kid Chocolate and the significance it held for Cubans. He has received fellowships from the American Council of Learned Societies, the Woodrow Wilson National Fellowship Foundation, and the National Research Council of the National Academies.

Jesús F. de la Teja is the Jerome H. and Catherine E. Supple Professor of Southwestern Studies and Director of the Center for the Study of the Southwest at Texas State University–San Marcos. He has published extensively on Spanish, Mexican, and Republic-era Texas, most recently an edited volume of biographies, *Tejano Leadership in Mexican and Revolutionary Texas*, and is book review editor for the

Southwestern Historical Quarterly. Currently he serves on the board of directors of Humanities Texas and the San Jacinto Museum of History.

Eduardo García is a native of the Juárez–El Paso borderland. His parents are migrants, and he currently resides in Albuquerque, New Mexico, where he is teaching courses on U.S. and European history. Eduardo received his B.A. in history at the University of Texas at El Paso in 2007, and a master of arts focusing on borderland history in 2010 from the same institution. As a lifetime resident of the U.S. Mexico border, he is a witness to the complexity of the border. Through history, he wishes to further understand and document the dynamics found there.

Joel Huerta is a visiting lecturer in the Latin American and Latino Studies Program at the University of Illinois at Chicago. He is working on a history and ethnography of high school football in South texas. He is also writing and photographing a book on street graphics and hand-crafted signage in the barrios of Texas. He lives in Evanston, Illinois.

Jorge Iber is a professor of history and associate dean of the College of Arts and Sciences at Texas Tech University. He has published widely over the last ten years on the topic of Latinos/as and sports in the United States. Among his many publications is a recent coauthored book titled *Latinos in U.S. Sport: A History of Isolation, Cultural Identity, and Acceptance.* He is currently working on a biography of former Major League Baseball pitcher Mike Torrez.

Michael Innis-Jiménez is assistant professor and director of graduate studies in the Department of American Studies at the University of Alabama. His research focuses on Mexican immigrant and Mexican American communities in the American Midwest and South. He is author of *Steel Barrio: The Great Mexican Migration to South Chicago* (NYU Press, 2013) and is working on a book on late-twentieth-century and early-twenty-first-century Mexican immigration to the Deep South.

Ricard Jensen is an Associate Professor in the Department of Marketing in the School of Business at Montclair State University, where he leads the Sports Marketing program. Jensen has published several academic articles about marketing sports to Hispanics and Latinos, including a book chapter describing why Hispanics are the future of Major League Soccer and a journal paper describing the controversy that ensued when the Phoenix Suns chose to wear "Los Suns" jerseys in the National Basketball Association playoffs to protest Arizona's laws against undocumented Hispanics and Latinos in the state.

Christine Marin, professor emeritus, served as the archivist and historian of the Chicano/a Research Collection and the Arizona Collection in the Department of Archives and Special Collections, Hayden Library, at Arizona State University for over thirty-five years. She also taught courses on the history of Mexican Americans and Latinos at ASU. She has published extensively on twentieth-century Mexican American history, including, most recently, "Community Organizing and Civil Liberties: Clinton Jencks, *Salt of the Earth,* and Arizona Copper in the 1950s," in the *Mining History Journal,* and "LULAC and Veterans Organize for Civil Rights in Tempe and Phoenix, 1940–1947."

William Harris Ressler has worked internationally as a strategic communication researcher and consultant and as a professor of communication, marketing, and psychology. His current research focuses on cultural identification and Minor League Baseball. He studies interactive and integrative approaches to internal and external communication, particularly as they relate to culture, community, and cause promotion.

Jason Sosa is a Senior Lecturer within the Department of Sport Management at Rice University. He earned his PhD at Texas A&M University within the Sport Management program. His research areas are Latin Studies in sport, and human resources organizational behavior. More specifically, he studies the influence of diversity within sport at the individual and group level.

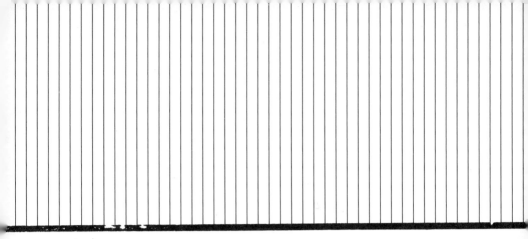

INDEX

and leisure activities in, 72; Gilbert
Martínez's journey to, 67–69;
growth of men's organizations in,
72–73; industrial landscape of, 69;
Mexican leadership in, 71–72; park
system in, 73–75; recreation and
community in, 70–71; recreation
opportunities for girls in, 79–80;
team sports in, 80–82
South Chicago Community Center,
76–77. *See also* Bird Memorial
South Chicago Neighborhood House,
76
Southern Arrows, 81–82
South Texas: confrontation of racism
in, 215–22; emergence of football
in, 208–9; Mexican Americans'
impact on high school football in,
226–27; racial views in, 230n27;
treatment and perception of Mexicans in, 214–15
sports: as economic opportunity,
103–4, 116–17; equality in, 65n85;
as outlet for energy, aggression,
and boredom, 212–13; as platform
to resist social control and cultural domination, 101–2; popular
coverage of Latino involvement
in, 284–87; in power struggles between nations, 131–34; as proving
ground for equality, 102; racial
bias in, 53–56, 58; scholarship on,
97–99; scholarship on Latinos in
American, 9–12, 184–85, 282–84;
scholarship on public relations
and, 260–61; scholarship on race
and, 151–53; social relations and,
100–101; stereotyping of Spanish-

surnamed athletes in, 185, 189; as
tool for cultural hegemony and
colonization, 101; as tool for imperialistic and hegemonic purposes,
99–101
Sports Illustrated, 284–85
sportsmanship, racial bias and, 53–56
Starr County, Texas, 224–25
stereotyping: of Mexican Americans
in Texas, 187–90; overcoming,
through sports, 186; of Spanish-
surnamed athletes as baseball
players, 185
Stowers, Carlton, 190–91
sugarcane alcohol, 30

Taylor, Gene, 169–70
tennis. *See* González, Richard "Pancho"
Texas: apportioning of school funds
in, 214; Bobby Cavazos and high
school football in, 196–202; E. C.
Lerma and high school football in,
192–96; football craze in, 208; Hispanic community in, 261–62; love
of high school football in, 190–92;
scholarship on Mexican American
athletic involvement in, 187; social
standing of Mexican Americans in,
187–88; stereotyping of Spanish-
surnamed students in, 188–90. *See
also* South Texas
Texas A&M University Javelinas,
192–94, 217
Texas Progressive Movement, 209–10
Texas Tech University, 200
third generation of Mexican Ameri-

cans, 151, 175
Thomas, Damion, 134
Thompson, Merrell E., 189–90
Torres, Eustebio, 85
Torres, Fred, 191–92
Tort, James F., 76–77
"Touch-down Extraordinario" (Ulica), 207–8
Trecker, Jamie, 265
treinta, 29
treinta y una, 29
Trujillo, Adolph "Fito," 166–69, 170, 174, 175
Trujillo, Alejandro, 156
Trussell, Jake, 199
trust, through cross-cultural communication, 241
Turner, Frederick Jackson, 212

Ulica, Jorge, 207–8
uniforms, of Miami Vandals, 160
University Interscholastic League (UIL), 210–14, 219–20
University of Alabama, 3–4
University of Mexico, 222
University of Southern California (USC) Trojans, 3–8, 281–82
Univision TV, 270, 272
Urrutia, Manuel de, 31
Uzcudun, Paulino, 48, 51, *53*

value in diversity, 240
Villaseñor, Santiago, 28
violence, of early football, 209
Viva Baseball! Latin Major Leaguers and Their Special Hunger (Regalado), 9

Wagner, John, 266, 273
Ward, Arch, 161
watermelon race, 21, *22*
Webb, Walter Prescott, 218
Weber, James T., 172
Wendel, Tim, 152
Whitlock, Chuck, 110–11
Wilson, Glen, 163, 166, 171, 172
women: intercultural friendships among, 163; marginalization of, in athletics projects, 213–14; obstacles faced by, in South Chicago, 78; protection of, from evils of society, 78; recreational opportunities for, in South Chicago, 83; republican motherhood and, 92n22; Richard "Pancho" González's relationship with, 140–42; separation between work and leisure for, 72; as targets for cultural assimilation, 78–79. *See also* girls
World Cup (2014), 257
World War II: impact of, on El Paso, 116; service during, 114–15

Yelkur, R., 271
YMCA, and basketball in Miami, Arizona, 155–56
Yoseloff, Anthony Y., 186
youth, scholarship on Mexican American, 227

Zaragoza, Socorro, 79
Zegers, R. V., 154
Zimmerman, Paul, 132, 136